D0224381

# The Seduction of Children

*of related interest*

**Counselling Adult Survivors of Child Sexual Abuse, second edition**
*Christiane Sanderson*
ISBN 1 85302 252 7

**Child Abuse and Child Abusers**
**Protection and Prevention**
*Edited by Lorraine Waterhouse*
ISBN 1 85302 408 2

**Creating a Safe Place**
**Helping Children and Families Recover from Child Sexual Abuse**
*NCH Children and Families Project*
ISBN 1 84310 009 6

**Creative Responses to Child Sexual Abuse, revised edition**
**Challenges and Dilemmas**
*Edited by Sue Richardson and Heather Bacon*
ISBN 1 84310 147 5

**Narrative Approaches to Working with Adult Male**
**Survivors of Child Sexual Abuse**
**The Clients', the Counsellor's and the Researcher's Story**
*Kim Etherington*
ISBN 1 85302 818 5

**Announcing**
**Coping with Survivors and Surviving**
*Julie Skinner*
ISBN 1 85302 822 3

**Sexual Abuse: The Child's Voice**
**Poppies on the Rubbish Heap**
*Madge Bray*
ISBN 1 85302 487 2

**Managing Child Sexual Abuse Cases**
*Brian Corby*
ISBN 1 85302 593 3

# The Seduction of Children

## Empowering Parents and Teachers to Protect Children from Child Sexual Abuse

*Christiane Sanderson*

Jessica Kingsley Publishers
London and New York

Figures 3.1 and 3.6 from Sullivan, J. and Beech, A. (2003) 'Are collectors of child abuse images a risk to children?' A. MacVean and P. Spindler in *Policing Paedophiles on the Internet* (pp.12 and 16). Reprinted with permission of the New Police Bookshop Publisher. Figures 3.3, 3.4 and 3.5 from 'Patterns of sex offenders and strategies for effective assessment and intervention' and Table 3.2 from Print, B. and Morrison, T. (2002) 'Treating adolescents who sexually abuse others', both in C. Itzin, *Home Truths about Child Sexual Abuse: Influencing Policy and Practice. A Reader.* Reprinted with permission of Thomson Publishing Services. Extract on pp.159-162 from O'Connell, R. (2003) *A Typology of Child Cyber Sexploitation and Online Grooming Practices* (pp.8-13). Reprinted by permission of R. O'Connell, Cyberspace Research Unit. Diagnostic criteria for posttraumatic stress (pp.209-210) reprinted with permission from the *Diagnostic and Statistical Manual of Mental Disorders*, Text Revision, © 2000 American Psychiatric Association. Table 6.1 from Finkelhor, D. and Browne, A, (1994) 'The traumatic impact of child sexual abuse: a conceptualization' *American Journal of Orthopsychiatry 55.* Reprinted with permission. Figure 6.1 from Bentovim, A. (2002) in V. Sinason, *Attachment, Trauma and Multiplicity: Working with Dissociative Identity Disorder* (p.28). Reprinted with permission of Thomson Publishing Services. Boxed text on p.224 from Stop it Now! UK and Ireland *Child's Play? Preventing Abuse Among Children and Young People.* Reprinted with permission of Stop it Now! UK and Ireland.

All rights reserved. No part of this publication may be reproduced in any material form (including photocopying or storing it in any medium by electronic means and whether or not transiently or incidentally to some other use of this publication) without the written permission of the copyright owner except in accordance with the provisions of the Copyright, Designs and Patents Act 1988 or under the terms of a licence issued by the Copyright Licensing Agency Ltd, 90 Tottenham Court Road, London, England W1P 9HE. Applications for the copyright owner's written permission to reproduce any part of this publication should be addressed to the publisher.
Warning: The doing of an unauthorised act in relation to a copyright work may result in both a civil claim for damages and criminal prosecution.

The right of Christiane Sanderson to be identified as author of this work has been asserted by her in accordance with the Copyright, Designs and Patents Act 1988.

First published in the United Kingdom in 2004
by Jessica Kingsley Publishers Ltd
116 Pentonville Road
London N1 9JB, England
and
29 West 35th Street, 10th fl.
New York, NY 10001-2299, USA

*www.jkp.com*

Copyright © Christiane Sanderson 2004

**Library of Congress Cataloging in Publication Data**
Sanderson, Christiane.
    The seduction of children : empowering parents and teachers to protect children from child sexual abuse / Christiane Sanderson.-- 1st American pbk. ed.
        p. cm.
    Includes bibliographical references and index.
    ISBN 1-84310-248-X (pbk.)
    1. Child sexual abuse--Great Britain. 2. Child sexual abuse--Prevention. I. Title.
    HV6570.4.G7S35 2004
    362.76'72--dc22

                                        2004003207

**British Library Cataloguing in Publication Data**
A CIP catalogue record for this book is available from the British Library

ISBN 1 84310 248 X

Printed and Bound in Great Britain by
Athenaeum Press, Gateshead, Tyne and Wear

*For Maxie*

# *Contents*

## List of tables

## List of Figures

# *Acknowledgements*

This book could not have been written without the help of a variety of people. They are too numerous to mention, although I would like to extend a special thank you to Didi Daftari, Caroline Gul, Angela Offord, Fuschia Peters, Andrew Smith, and Kathy Warriner for their support and inspiration, and Michael, James and Max for their patience.

# Introduction

[It is] adults' duty to keep children safe from harm, but this is only possible if they have sufficient information to assess when a child is at risk.

Tink Palmer, Barnardo's Policy and Practice Officer

The best way to keep your child safe is to educate yourself about child sexual abuse. If I had known more about the warning signs maybe I could have prevented my daughter from being sexually abused.

Mother of sexually abused five-year-old

Each day seems to bring new revelations about child sexual abuse (CSA), child pornography or the sexual grooming of children on the Internet. As a result many parents fear for the safety of their children and yet are not adequately equipped to recognise the early warning signs of CSA, or what action to take in how best to protect their children. This book aims to address parents' and teachers' fears around CSA by exploring the true nature of CSA and how best to protect children. To truly empower parents and teachers to protect children, parents and teachers need to have access to accurate knowledge and information about the real risks of CSA.

Adults and children often have misconceptions about CSA, fuelled by high profile cases in the media, which generate overwhelming fear and anxiety, yet do not serve to help protect children. It is crucial to separate fact from fiction and dispel myths and stereotypes around CSA. One way of achieving this is to increase awareness around CSA by providing access to accurate information and knowledge. This enables parents and teachers to challenge misconceptions and myths and reveals the reality of CSA.

Awareness of CSA means that real concerns are not swept under the carpet or ignored. It enables parents and teachers to talk to children about the dangers of CSA and how best to keep them safe. Talking about CSA removes the secrecy and silence that cloaks it, ensuring that it no longer remains hidden. Not talking about CSA plays into the hands of the child sexual abuser, who needs to silence the child in order to avoid exposure. Adults need to find a way of talking about CSA so that they can provide a language for children to talk about their experiences, without scaring them so much that they become afraid to go out into the community.

Parents and teachers also need to be equipped with knowledge about how to recognise early warning signs that can indicate the sexual abuse of a child. They need to know what motivates individuals to sexually abuse children and how these individuals befriend and manipulate adults and children to gain their trust. Parents need to know how to spot risky behaviours displayed by child sexual abusers and be aware of the warning signs in the child that indicate CSA. If adults are to teach children how to be safe, they need access to information that is of benefit to children, not information that is going to frighten them. But it is not just about equipping children, adults also need to be aware of the dangers in the community without becoming terrified and confining children to the home. All adults need to know in what ways children are at risk and how they can best protect them.

Children need to be protected from adults and older children who prey on them, or manipulate them into having sexual contact with them. This responsibility does not just lie with parents but with all adults in the community. The more aware we are about the dangers, without becoming overwhelmed by the emotional issues inherent in CSA, the more we can equip our children to protect themselves.

To really ensure the safety of all children it is essential to move from reaction to prevention. This can only happen with a public health and education campaign, such as a National Child Safety Watch, supported by changes in the criminal justice system and legislation. Local campaigns such as Stop It Now! UK and Ireland demonstrate the value of public education, but need to be taken up across the whole of the UK. The Government's proposed new Sexual Offences Bill, due to become law on 1 May 2004, addresses many of the concerns around CSA, especially the use of the Internet to distribute child pornography and the sexual grooming of children.

How society deals with child sexual abusers and their victims is also of crucial importance. Issues of treatment and rehabilitation need to be properly addressed and adequately resourced to ensure the safety of children. Protecting children is the responsibility of all adults and, as such, of the community in which they live. It is not until the whole community becomes involved in the protection of children that a clear and unified message is transmitted that our society will no longer tolerate the sexual abuse of children.

My aim throughout this book is to inform parents, teachers and adults about the reality of CSA in the hope that with such knowledge they will be more able to protect children and move towards preventing CSA. Each chapter will look in depth at issues such as the true nature of CSA, the development of children's sexuality, what motivates child sexual abusers, the use of the Internet as a medium for child pornography, and the sexual grooming of children. It will also consider the impact of CSA on children, the signs and symptoms that indicate CSA, and how to best understand the sexually abused child. Practical advice will be given on how to talk to children about sexuality and the dangers of CSA, along with proposals for preventing CSA in the future.

In order to provide a framework for this, it is essential to consider first the myths and the reality of CSA.

## The myths and the reality of child sexual abuse

While we seem to have weekly stories in the media about CSA, many aspects of what it entails are unknown to most people. We tend to hear about high profile cases, which often include abduction and murder as well as CSA, for example, the abduction and murder of Sarah Payne, Jessica Chapman and Holly Wells. These, however, represent only a small proportion of the CSA that occurs on a daily basis in our own neighbourhood and community.

Media coverage of high profile cases is not always representative of the danger children face. Nor does the media coverage necessarily reflect the full range of sexual abuse and sexual abusers. This can lead to limited knowledge and biased views about CSA, which, if inaccurate, actually fail to protect the majority of children. It can also lull parents and adults into a false sense of security that their own children are safe. Knowledge and beliefs about CSA vary enormously, often reflecting cultural attitudes, many of which are further reinforced by society and the media. In combination these can lead to the creation of myths. Such myths can be dangerous since they may lead to complacency and a failure to protect children.

It is useful to look at some of the most commonly held attitudes and beliefs about CSA, some of which have become deeply entrenched misconceptions, or myths. To separate fact from fiction, it is necessary to challenge misconceptions, dispel myths, and replace them with more accurate knowledge. Many of the myths belie the reality of CSA and create a false sense of security in adults and children, which can put children at further risk. This following section will identify some of the most commonly held misconceptions, challenge the beliefs behind them and replace them with up-to-date facts and data.

**MYTH:**     *The sexual abuse of children is not as common as people make out.*

**REALITY:**     CSA is undoubtedly more widespread than people realise. While estimates vary, depending on what type of research has been conducted, it is thought that CSA is commonly found in one in four girls, and one in six boys (see Chapter 1). Many researchers believe these figures represent only the tip of the iceberg as much CSA is hidden, with some children never disclosing their abuse or coming to the attention of the social services, the police or criminal justice system. The consequence of the belief that CSA is rare is that children's accounts of abuse are ignored or dismissed as fantasy. In addition, much CSA is not a one-off event for the child but is systematic and can sometimes last for many years.

**MYTH:**     *Girls are more at risk from child sexual abuse than boys.*

**REALITY:**     While the current data indicate that girls are more at risk from sexual abuse than boys, this may also be the tip of the iceberg. These figures may not accurately reflect the reality of the sexual abuse of children due to a reporting bias. It may be harder for boys to reveal their sexual abuse due to greater stigmatisation or because they feel more embarrassed to disclose. Cultural stereotypes of men being the active initiators of sexual contact make it harder for boys to talk about their experience as victims of abuse. In addition, CSA may lead boys to be more confused about their sexuality, making it even harder to disclose in a homophobic culture. Cultures that foster independence and insist on stoicism in males may further prevent boys from revealing their sexual abuse experiences in childhood. It is thought that girls are more at risk of sexual abuse in the home, whereas boys are thought to be more at risk from sexual abuse in the community (see Chapter 1).

**MYTH:**    *The sexual abuse of children occurs only in certain communities/ cultures/classes.*

**REALITY:**    Child sexual abuse occurs across all cultures, communities and classes. The danger of this belief is that by limiting our beliefs about abuse to certain types of environments, it ignores the reality of CSA in our own community and neighbourhood. This can lead to disbelieving that CSA can happen to any child and that all children are at risk. CSA does not just happen to other people, in other communities or cultures; it can happen to any child. That is to say that all children are vulnerable to a degree. If we really want to protect our children, we need to recognise the reality of CSA, even in our own community. Otherwise we are lulled into a false sense of security that our own children are safe (see Chapter 1).

**MYTH:**    *The sexual abuse of children is condoned in the Bible.*

**REALITY:**    The Bible is subject to all sorts of interpretations. Abusers may use such interpretations to provide an excuse to sexually abuse children. The Bible demands the protection of children and the banning of immoral sexual acts.

**MYTH:**    *Child sexual abuse occurs only in dysfunctional families.*

**REALITY:**    Families do not sexually abuse children, individuals do. The sexual abuse of children can occur in any family. Research has shown that CSA within the family can occur in all types of families, including those regarded as 'functional'. Similarly, child sexual abusers outside the family can win over parents from all sorts of families and not just the dysfunctional ones. The abusers are clever and highly manipulative in how they befriend parents and children, and they are able to deceive all types of families.

While most convicted paedophiles are male and white (NCIS 2002) and operate alone (NCIS 2002) they come from all ethnic backgrounds and sometimes are part of a paedophile club or ring. What they all have in common is that they all use children as a sexual object for their own sexual gratification. Therefore, the sexual abuse of children is inextricably linked with the exploitation, domination and degradation of children.

**MYTH:**     *My child is not at risk of child sexual abuse.*

**REALITY:**     All children are at risk of CSA. Child sexual abusers target all types of children, irrespective of class, race, colour, age or size. There are never 100 per cent guarantees of your child being safe. A child sexual abuser can dupe even highly aware parents. If they are really out to target your child they will do so. However, there are steps that parents can take to increase the child's safety level and reduce the risk of CSA.

**MYTH:**     *Child sexual abuse is on the increase.*

**REALITY:**     Child sexual abuse has existed over centuries (see Chapter 1). It is difficult to gain historical data due to the hidden nature of CSA and the secrecy surrounding it. Increased awareness of CSA, along with improved child protection services, enable more children and adult survivors to disclose their sexually abusive experiences. Also, as society addresses the unacceptable nature of CSA, and resources to combat it are made available, detection and reporting rates increase. While much CSA remains hidden, it is probably less hidden today than it was in the past.

**MYTH:**     *Strangers sexually abuse children.*

**REALITY:**     This is part of the mythology about 'stranger danger'. Current research shows that in approximately 87 per cent of cases the abuser is known to, and trusted by, the child. We can no longer protect our children from CSA by telling them to avoid strangers. The reality is that children are more at risk of being sexually abused by someone known to him or her in their neigh- bourhood and community than by a stranger. Most child abuse takes place in private domains, behind closed doors and out of public gaze (MacVean 2003).

**MYTH:**     *Child sexual abusers are monsters.*

**REALITY:**     The reality is quite the opposite. 'Monsters do not get close to children, nice men do…' (Ray Wyre, sex crime expert). The majority of child sexual abusers present themselves as extremely nice, kind, caring people. They need to present this mask of being nice, otherwise they would never gain access to their victims. Not only are they able to deceive children, they also deceive their parents. Many child sexual abusers ingratiate themselves into families, by first befriending the parents. Initially they show no obvious interest in the children until they have gained the parents' trust. Once this is achieved, they befriend the child by lavishing them with attention and becoming their 'special' friend too. If the parents trust them, the child is more easily won over, and it will be less likely to disclose the CSA. It is because they are so nice that adults and children like them.

Because child sexual abusers present themselves as being 'nice', children frequently develop what they believe to be a 'special' relationship. This means that often they do not hate the abuser, but rather 'love' them and want to protect them. This is even more likely to be the case in familial abuse. Often children do not want to lose the relationship or see the abuser punished; all they want is for the sexual abuse to stop. Child sexual abusers know this and capitalise on this by playing on the child's fears as a way of reducing the risk of disclosure.

**MYTH:**    *Child sexual abusers are easily identifiable.*

**REALITY:**    Gone are the days in which the child sexual abuser could be seen as the 'dirty old man in a grubby raincoat, hanging around outside the school or park gates'. Child sexual abusers come from all social classes, ethnic backgrounds and age groups. They appear as normal as anyone else. They need to appear normal to avoid exposure. They are members of the local community and come from all professions, from judges, lawyers, doctors, the clergy, policemen, teachers, and businessmen through to plumbers, lorry drivers, and those working with children. They are often regarded as pillars of the community and go about their daily business in their local neighbourhood without being detected. It is virtually impossible to pick child sexual abusers out in a crowd.

**MYTH:**    *Child sexual abusers are mad, bad or sad.*

**REALITY:**    This is a dangerous myth in terms of demonising the child sexual abuser and removing the responsibility for the abuse from the abuser. The majority of child sexual abusers are normal. Only a small percentage are thought to suffer from mental illness, and as such are not mad. A very small percentage appear to be sad and lonely due to a sense of inadequacy or poor social skills. The majority of sexual abusers appear absolutely normal. They are deemed 'bad' in terms of their sexual behaviour towards children, but they do not present themselves as bad people. If anything, they come across as being 'really nice, good people' who are well liked by both adults and children.

**MYTH:** *All child sexual abusers have been sexually abused in their own childhood.*

**REALITY:** While some paedophiles do have a history of abuse in their childhood, many do not. Current research has found that 66 per cent of paedophiles claim to have been abused in childhood. However, when interviewed using a lie detector, this figure falls to only 30 per cent. In addition, recent research shows that only one in eight children who has been sexually abused goes on to sexually abuse other children in adolescence (Skuse 2003). Thus, one needs to be cautious in embracing this belief entirely. Adult paedophiles may claim to have been abused in order to provide a rationale for their abuse of children, and also to elicit sympathy, or as an excuse.

The consequence of this misconception is a belief that only people who have been abused in childhood are capable of abusing children. It is also used to justify a cycle of abuse theory, which undermines the capacity for people to change and heal from their childhood experiences. It must be remembered that the majority of male and female survivors of child sexual abuse do not go on to sexually abuse children.

**MYTH:** *Only gay men sexually abuse boys.*

**REALITY:** Some men who are heterosexual, gay or bisexual do sexually abuse children. In reality, though, the majority of child sexual abusers are heterosexual.

**MYTH:** *Women do not sexually abuse children.*

**REALITY:** Research suggests that approximately 20 to 25 per cent of CSA is perpetrated by women. Cultural beliefs about women being the carers and nurturers make it difficult for people to accept that women can be violent or aggressive towards children. The under-fives are most at risk from female sexual abusers, usually in child-care settings, or when babysitting. This goes largely undetected due to the age of the child and the fact that some of the sexual activities are conducted around normal hygiene practices.

Adolescent boys are also at risk from being sexually abused by older females, though this is often not perceived to be abuse but rather an initiation into adult sexuality. In addition, beliefs about female sexuality, where women are the passive receivers rather than active initiators, make it hard for people to believe that women sexually abuse children. The reality is that women do abuse their power over children, and may do so sexually (see Chapter 3).

**MYTH:** *The Sex Offenders' Register is a good enough safety net.*

**REALITY:** This is a highly deceptive myth as 90 per cent of CSA is not reported and only 10 per cent of cases get to court. Currently there are are 21,413 sex offenders living in the community (Home Office 2003). What percentage of these have committed sexual offences against children is not clear as there is no national database analysis of sex offenders who have offended aginst children and those who have offended against adults. It is hoped that such analysis will become available when the new national database ViSOR comes online later in 2004 (Ford 2004). The Sex Offenders' Register does not include those child sexual offenders who are currently in prison or those who were convicted of sexual offences against children prior to the Sexual Offences Bill being enacted in September 1997. Thus, according to MacVean (2003) some 110,000 people, previously convicted of sexual offences against children before September 1997, are not included on the Sex Offenders' Register. It is clear that the Sex Offenders' Register does not reflect the actual number of child sexual abusers in the UK. In addition, the conviction rate is extremely low, probably no more than 5 per cent of cases (Wyre 2003). It is estimated that there are currently 250,000 child sexual abusers in the UK, with those on the register merely the tip of the iceberg. The majority of child sexual abuse goes undetected and is not disclosed or reported. Therefore it does not come to the attention of the police or criminal justice system. In a study by Abel *et al.* (1987) child sexual abusers committed an average of 229 sexual offences against children, involving an average of 75 children, prior to being caught, while another study found that 232 child sexual abusers had in total sexaully abused 17,585 children involving 38,727 acts (Wheaton 2003).

**MYTH:** *Naming and shaming child sexual abusers is the only way to protect our children.*

**REALITY:** This is a very dangerous belief as it can lull us into a false sense of security. Paedophiles on the Sex Offenders' Register represent less than half the estimated child sexual abusers in the UK. Focusing our attention on 'known' paedophiles stops us from remaining aware of those who are still 'unknown' and who are currently abusing children. It is the 'unknown' paedophile who presents the risk to children. 'Naming and shaming' forces paedophiles underground, or encourages them to seek out other paedophiles, which can further increase the risk to children. Being 'named and shamed' evokes high levels of stress, anxiety and tension in paedophiles, leading to further assaults as a release from such stress.

**MYTH:** *Child sexual abuse is always violent.*

**REALITY:** CSA can be violent, but the way it is inflicted does not necessarily involve physical violence at all. The majority of CSA involves deception, manipulation and subtle brainwashing of the child. Many paedophiles initially shower the child with extra special attention, affection and 'love' and then use bribery to ensure that they submit to the sexual abuse and keep silent. This is done either through the withdrawal of love and attention, or by rewarding the child with treats or gifts. Some paedophiles ensure the child's silence by threatening the child, their parents, siblings or pets.

**MYTH:** *Child sexual abuse never involves pleasure for the child.*

**REALITY:** Many children do experience sexual arousal and pleasure during CSA. This is natural and normal in terms of physiological arousal and does not mean that the child either wanted to be sexually abused or necessarily enjoyed it. Boys can have erections and girls can lubricate in the vaginal area, not just because of pleasure but also through fear. Children do not understand this and believe that the sexual abuse is their fault. Older children may experience orgasm as a result of CSA, which makes them feel even more ashamed. Child sexual abusers use such pleasure and arousal as a way of controlling the child and discouraging them from disclosing. They manipulate the child into believing that it is the child who wanted the sexual contact because they enjoyed it.

Pleasure derived from CSA results in the child feeling confused and betrayed – betrayed by the abuser, betrayed by their bodies in responding, and betrayed by themselves for complying with the sexual abuse. In reality the abuser is distorting the child's reality and preventing it from developing its own sexuality.

**MYTH:** *It is not child sexual abuse if the child consented.*

**REALITY:** A consenting person knows what they are doing, has an understanding of the consequences and is free from any manipulation or coercion. A child is not capable of knowing what they are getting into, or the consequences of that behaviour, and as such is not able to give consent. A child is not fully aware of its own sexuality or of sex and all its complexities. It is not yet a fully sexual being. Sexuality develops slowly over many years, and thus the child is still sexually naïve and not able to make informed choices. The child often has no choice but to comply with the sexual abuse. This is submission, not consent.

**MYTH:** *Child pornography is like adult pornography and is harmless.*

**REALITY:** A fundamental difference between adult and child pornography is that in most instances of adult pornography there is a degree of consent. This is not the case with child pornography. Child pornography is an act of child sexual abuse in that the child is not able to give consent. A further assumption is that pornography prevents actual attacks and offences against victims. There is currently insufficient evidence to support this notion, in that many paedophiles do progress from using child pornography to actual offending against children.

Many paedophiles use child pornography as a way of normalising the sexual abuse of the child. In encouraging the child to look at child pornography, the abuser provides the child with 'evidence' that it is normal for children to be sexual with adults. More crucially, in order to produce pornographic images a child is being sexually abused. While there are arguments suggesting that many of the images have been digitally enhanced, it is not clear what percentage are real and which are pseudo-images (see Chapter 4).

**MYTH:** *Pre-school children are not at risk of being sexually abused.*

**REALITY:** There is considerable evidence that adults sexually abuse even very young children. Much of this evidence comes from seized child pornographic images of infants being sexually abused by adults. It is estimated that around 33 per cent of child victims are below the age of six, 33 per cent are between the ages of six and twelve, and a further 33 per cent are between 12 and 18. Further evidence comes from medical records of babies with sexually transmitted diseases. The reality is that some paedophiles deliberately choose pre-verbal children to sexually abuse as the child cannot disclose their abuse. Furthermore, a young child who has been sexually abused from a very young age will believe that sexual activity between adults and children is normal and will not necessarily know that it is being abused. If anything the child normalises the sexual abuse by seeing it as a reflection of the 'specialness' of the relationship.

**MYTH:** *Children are sexual beings and provoke sexual attention.*

**REALITY:** While children are sexual, their understanding of sexual is entirely different from adults' understanding. The child does experience sensory pleasure from its body, including sexual areas. This does not mean, however, that the child seeks sexual activity with adults. For the child, sensory pleasure is about discovering its own body and feeling comfortable with it. Children learn about their bodies and those of others through observation and as a way of gaining knowledge about the world. While they might explore their own bodies, and the bodies of other children, this is quite different to the sexual abuse by an adult. These explorations are spontaneous, sporadic and consensual. Child sexual abuse, in contrast, is an exploitative, enforced and imposed activity conducted under threat and by manipulation (see Chapter 2).

No matter how provocatively a child behaves, the responsibility for sexual abuse always lies with the abuser and not the child, whatever the circumstances. Adults are responsible for interpreting the child's behaviour as 'sexual' or 'provocative'. It is the abuser's responsibility to protect the child from harm, not cause it. Most children do not behave in a sexually provocative way unless they have previously been sexually abused. The belief that children provoke sexual attention blames the child, making it feel even more guilty and confused.

Even if children are capable of sexual feeling, this does not mean that the abuser should exploit it. An apt analogy is that, although a young child might believe itself capable of driving its parents' car, this does not mean to say that the parents comply by giving the child the car keys and suggesting it should take the car for a drive. Adults are responsible for guiding the child's behaviour and should set appropriate boundaries.

**MYTH:** *Children have fertile imaginations and fantasise about many things, including child sexual abuse.*

**REALITY:** While children do have fertile imaginations and are able to fantasise about many things, this does not mean that they fantasise about being sexually abused. The majority of children do not have sufficient sexual knowledge or awareness to have what are, in essence, adult sexual fantasies.

This misconception results in the child not being believed, thereby ignoring the reality of their sexual abuse. Such beliefs also serve to move the responsibility of sexual abuse away from the abuser and on to the child.

**MYTH:**     *Children lie about sexual abuse.*

**REALITY:**     The reality is that children do not have sufficient awareness or sexual knowledge to lie about sexual abuse. In addition, it is not clear why young children would wish to lie about sexual abuse. Associated with this is the related belief that children make up stories about sexual abuse as a result of watching adult pornography. This is highly unlikely. While children may have knowledge about sexual acts from watching adult sexual activity, they cannot glean knowledge about the taste, texture and smell of semen without having some actual experience of it. The consequence of these beliefs is that the child is not believed and not taken notice of in its disclosure of CSA.

**MYTH:**     *Child sexual abuse does not cause any or much harm to the child.*

**REALITY:**     Researchers have found considerable evidence that CSA can cause significant harm to children and result in short and long-term consequences. The danger of this myth is that CSA is minimised in terms of harm and damage to the child. It can also lead to the argument that because it happened in the past, and the child was too young for it to matter, they should move on and forget it. This colludes with paedophiles' attitudes that the younger the child the less likely there will be any long-term harm, as the child will not remember it. In reality it serves to reduce the risk of detection and disclosure.

Child sexual abusers also claim that because children enjoy exploring their bodies they welcome adults engaging them in sexual activity. While CSA may not necessarily cause physical damage, especially if it does not include penetration, it nevertheless distorts the child's reality about the appropriateness of such experiences. Children rely on the guidance of adults about what is appropriate and inappropriate behaviour. Abusers telling them that CSA is normal and pleasurable leads the child to believe that it must want such sexual attention. This distorts the child perception of its bodily reactions and motivation. CSA frequently makes the child feel confused, dirty, guilty and ashamed.

Paedophiles often rationalise CSA by believing that because the child is not screaming or saying 'No', or because they may be smiling, that they must be enjoying it. In reality, the child is usually prevented from screaming, is unable to speak, or may smile as a response to fear, because it knows that that is what the abuser wants it to do. Children are trained by their abusers to behave in the way the abuser wants them to. As the child is powerless and helpless in the abuse, the child complies for fear of the consequences if it does not. Many children resign themselves to the sexual abuse, as they have no means of escape. Many survive the sexual assaults by complying and dissociating, hoping it will be over as soon as possible, so as to end the ordeal. Such beliefs also serve to fuel the child sexual abuser's romanticised notion of love rather than abuse.

**MYTH:**      *Children who are sexually abused know it is wrong and would tell.*

**REALITY:**      Children do not necessarily know that sexual activity between children and adults is wrong. This is especially so in the case of very young children. Pre-verbal children do not have the language to tell anyone about their experiences. In addition, young children are reliant on adults guiding their behaviour. If they are told that sexual activity with adults is acceptable, then they will believe this. Many believe this is a very 'special' relationship in which they are loved and cared for, not realising that they are being abused (see Chapter 5).

Most CSA does not start with an act of rape. Many paedophiles befriend children and develop a close friendship, called 'grooming', with the child over a long period of time before any sexual activity takes place. By the time sexual abuse occurs the child fears losing this 'special' friendship and does not want to get the paedophile into trouble, so they do not tell. Child sexual abusers also distort the child's reality by telling them that they want and enjoy the sexual activity and that, if they tell, they will not be believed or they will be blamed. Other paedophiles threaten children by telling them they will kill them or their parents. These are all-powerful reasons that stop children from disclosing CSA.

**MYTH:**      *Parents and adults should be able to tell if a child is being sexually abused.*

**REALITY:**      The impact of child sexual abuse varies from child to child, depending on the age of onset of the abuse, the relationship to the abuser, the duration and frequency of abuse, and the type of sexual activity. This means that children display a range of signs and symptoms. Because the children are often sworn to secrecy about the CSA they may try and communicate the sexual abuse in non-verbal ways. These can vary enormously, with some children becoming very withdrawn to those that re-enact their sexual abuse experiences with other, younger children.

This myth reflects the belief that mothers should know if a child is being sexually abused, and may well collude with the abuser. This belief again moves the responsibility away from the abuser by blaming the mother for behaviour that is beyond her control. It also places full responsibility for the care and nurturing of children entirely on the mother's shoulders. The responsibility for the protection of children from harm falls upon all adults irrespective of gender. Mothers cannot be expected to be all-knowing and ever watchful of their children. The consequence of this belief is that the mother is made to feel guilty in being blamed for the sexual abuse of her child.

Most parents and adults do not know what the range of symptoms of CSA is and what the symptoms represent. Awareness of the range of symptoms, in combination with other factors, may alert adults to what the sexually abused child is trying to communicate. If sensitively responded to it can be the first step in protecting the child from further sexual assaults (see Chapter 7).

There are cases in which parents do know about the sexual abuse of their children, either because they themselves are sexually abusing the child, or because they have links with other paedophiles in which they swap their children, or prostitute them. While such parents do exist, they remain in the minority. The majority of parents do not know their child is being sexually abused, due to the abuser's high level of manipulation of both adults and children.

**MYTH:**     *Paedophiles cannot be cured.*

**REALITY:**     There is as yet no known 'cure' for paedophilia. However, this does not mean that paedophiles do not respond to treatment. The belief that 'nothing works' is a very outdated view. In reality there are 'some things that do work'. Sexual offending in general is very difficult to treat because of the factors involved in sexual arousal and sexual behaviour. Treatment can and does help some child sexual abusers, in terms of recognising their offending behaviour and learning to manage their impulses and sexual arousal. Research indicates that between one-third and half can be taught to manage their sexual arousal to children and not act upon their desires. Salter (2003) argues that up to two-thirds of paedophiles do respond well to treatment, although he argues that one-third have no desire to change and will continue to re-offend. Given that a considerable proportion of paedophiles do respond to treatment, more resources should be made available to enable us to adequately protect our children (see Chapter 3).

**MYTH:** *Men have the right to get their sexual needs met, however they choose.*

**REALITY:** This myth comes from attitudes and beliefs that men are victims of their uncontrollable sex drives, and that they have a right to have these needs met in whatever way they choose. Men are perfectly capable of, and responsible for, controlling their sexual urges. This is not the responsibility of children. Believing that men cannot control their urges again shifts responsibility for the abuse onto the child. It must be remembered that many men do not sexually abuse children.

**MYTH:** *Child protection workers encourage children to make up stories about child sexual abuse.*

**REALITY:** Most child protection workers are acutely aware of, and conscious of, not directing children when disclosures of sexual abuse are being made. They know that if they lead or direct the child's disclosure, it will undermine and invalidate the child's case if it comes to court. Trained professionals allow the child to tell their story without prompting so as not to contaminate the child's disclosure. The consequence of this myth is that victims of CSA continue to be disbelieved, and those working to protect them are isolated, marginalised or discredited.

**MYTH:** *We should avoid telling children about CSA so as not to frighten them.*

**REALITY:** Not telling children about the danger of CSA results in the child not being protected. More importantly, by not talking to children about sexuality and CSA we allow other adults to control their knowledge, which puts the child at greater risk of being coerced into CSA. It is possible to guide children to be cautious about certain dangers without frightening them. In the same way we guide children in road safety, such as the 'green cross code', it is possible for parents and adults to communicate other dangers in the community without instilling fear. Parents can find age-appropriate ways to guide children as to how to conduct themselves in the community and what to watch out for (see Chapter 9). If parents are inhibited and frightened of CSA they will communicate their fear to the child non-verbally. It is this that will in turn frighten the child.

It is equally inappropriate for parents to restrict the child from going out into their neighbourhood. Keeping children locked up at home prevents the child from learning about its community and its dangers. Children need to learn to be streetwise. Ironically it is those children who are too terrified to go out, and who are not streetwise, who are more vulnerable to being sexually abused. Paedophiles have years of practice in identifying vulnerable children and can sense children who are fearful and lacking in confidence. For this reason, it is helpful for parents to know how to talk to their children about the dangers of CSA in order to protect them in the community (see Chapter 9).

**MYTH:**     *Children are sexualised by the media and fashion industry, and this is what makes them vulnerable to CSA.*

**REALITY:**     The majority of paedophiles like innocent and vulnerable-looking children who fit their notions of childhood. This is not usually a child who is provocatively dressed or wearing make-up. They are more likely to be interested in children who are stereotypically 'child-like' in how they look and dress. It is the child's innocence and vulnerability that make them attractive to the paedophile. What is emerging from child pornography is that paedophiles are finding increasingly younger children attractive. This may be due to the fact that many young girls from seven or eight upwards are dressing in more sexualised fashions, including wearing make-up. This prompts paedophiles to turn their attention to younger children who still dress in stereotypical child-like clothes.

### The aims of this book

The many beliefs highlighted above need to be challenged if we are to protect our children. The aim of this book is to explore some of these beliefs in more depth and replace them with more accurate knowledge about CSA, so that parents and teachers will have greater awareness. Such knowledge will enable them not only to identify children who are being sexually abused but also to protect them from CSA.

Chapter 1 considers precisely what is meant by CSA. It will explore the historical evidence of child abuse and child sexual abuse, and consider cultural factors in how CSA is conceptualised. Because child sexual abuse is socially constructed, it will look at the difficulties around defining CSA. The problems in defining CSA centre around which acts are considered to be sexually abusive and which are culturally acceptable behaviours between adults and children. The spectrum of sexually abusive behaviour is quite wide, and we need to be clear which acts are sexually abusive and which ones are not. The incidence of child sexual abuse in relation to definitions used will also be assessed.

In Chapter 2 consideration will be given to normal, or typical, sexual development in children. That children experience pleasure in their bodies is indisputable but whether their concept of sexual is the same as that of adults is challenged. Children's conceptualisation of sexual is significantly different from adults' concepts and adult interpretation. In having a better understanding of normal sexual development in children, parents and teachers are better able to assess whether the child's behaviour is age developmentally appropriate or not. Abnormal or atypical sexual behaviour will also be examined to distinguish it from natural, consensual sexual exploration and experimentation.

Chapter 3 will explore what is known about child sexual abusers. It will present profiles of different types of paedophiles and explore what motivates them to sexually abuse children. It will examine CSA both outside and within the family. Both male and female child sexual abusers will be considered, as well as children who sexually abuse other children. Consideration will also be given to the treatment of paedophiles and how they can be helped to prevent further offending.

In Chapter 4 attention will be directed at the use of the Internet in relation to CSA. The use of child pornography will be examined along with the dangers of Internet grooming. The scale of child pornography and range of images will be discussed, including how these images feature in the sexual abuse of children. It will also provide useful information to parents about the dangers of the Internet, what they need to be aware of, and how children are actually groomed on the Internet.

Chapter 5 will examine the sexual grooming of children offline. It will look at how child sexual abusers befriend parents in order to get access to their children. Once they have gained the parents' trust, the paedophile will turn his or her attention to the child to establish and develop a 'special' friendship. The process of grooming can take many months, even years, during which the paedophile slowly sexualises the child in order to commit the sexual assault. It is essential that parents, teachers and other adults are aware of how paedophiles groom children so that they can be alert to early warning signs and stop potential sexual assaults.

In Chapter 6 the impact of CSA on the child is assessed. The age of onset of child sexual abuse is significant in terms of the stage of development the child is at, and to what degree the child can understand its experience or make sense of it. Factors such as language and perception of abuse will be examined, along with the impact of CSA on the developing child. Effects on neurological functioning, memory and dissociation will also be assessed.

Given that some children are unable to verbalise their sexual abuse, either because they cannot name it, or are threatened into silence and secrecy, they often communicate their experience in a variety of non-verbal ways. Chapter 7 will consider the range of signs and symptoms that have been linked to CSA. While no one symptom indicates CSA, it is important to look at the constellation of symptoms before any intervention takes place. Emotional, interpersonal, behavioural, cognitive, physical and sexual signs and symptoms will be explored and how they might link to a history of CSA.

It is not sufficient to rely just on the signs and symptoms that the child might display; it is crucial that parents, teachers and adults come to understand the sexually abused child. Chapter 8 attempts to enhance adults' understanding of sexually abused children. Sexually abused children are often racked with shame and guilt, which can have a huge effect on how they relate to others. We need to fully understand the sexually abused child in order to respond to it sensitively. Children respond differently to CSA and we need to consider how best to help them come to terms with their experiences.

Chapter 9 will examine in detail how we can best protect children from CSA. It will look at how to talk to children about sex and sexuality and the dangers of sexual abuse. Throughout, age developmentally appropriate suggestions will be given to illustrate how to communicate such dangers to children without unduly alarming them and frightening them. Strategies and guidelines will be given to establish how we can equip children to be safer in the community.

In Chapter 10 consideration will be given on how to prevent CSA. It is only if all adults take responsibility for protecting children in the community that we can move from reaction towards prevention of CSA. To really protect children and prevent CSA necessitates national public health and education along with changes in legislation and the criminal justice system and in reporting in the media. Treatment and rehabilitation will also be addressed, along with community-based initiatives that involve all adults in the protection of children. The normalisation of CSA within cultures will be explored, and the impact of sociocultural factors, including the influence of the media, will be evaluated. While it may be impossible to totally eradicate CSA, it is only with increased awareness of the contributing factors, which underpin and sustain the sexual abuse of children, that we can prevent and no longer tolerate the sexual abuse of children.

This book will at times make for harrowing reading, reflecting the traumatic impact that CSA has on children. Throughout the book, case vignettes will be included to illustrate the points being made. These are based on real life examples in which the names and certain details have been changed in order to maintain confidentiality and ensure anonymity. In some instances the case vignettes are composites of actual cases. I would like to thank all my clients for sharing their experiences of sexual abuse. These have enabled me to gain a deeper understanding of the complexity of the impact and the effects of CSA. I hope that their accounts will enhance the reader's understanding of CSA and enable all readers to protect other children more effectively from being sexually abused.

## Chapter 1

# What is Child Sexual Abuse?

Child sexual abuse can be violent, but the manner in which it is inflicted doesn't have to involve violence at all. The majority of sexual abuse involves the subtle brainwashing of a child...rewarded with treats or extra love and attention, or bribed to keep silent.

Survivors Swindon

Child sexual abuse (CSA) is socially constructed in that it is heavily influenced by the culture and the historical time in which it occurs, which makes it hard to establish a universally agreed definition. In addition, cultures vary in terms of how they define abuse and what constitutes a child. This is particularly the case with regard to the age of consent, with some countries, such as South Korea, placing it at age 13, and other countries at 16. Such global variation impacts on child pornography and child sex tourism.

The lack of agreement in defining CSA makes it difficult to obtain meaningful statistics as to how widespread it is. The research data vary, depending on the definition used by the researchers. A major problem in generating a definition is to decide which sexual acts are sexually abusive. The spectrum of sexual acts employed in CSA is quite broad and includes both contact and non-contact behaviours.

This chapter will examine what precisely is meant by CSA by exploring the historical and social construction of CSA and how it is defined. It will consider the spectrum of sexual acts used in the abuse of children and report on incidence rates. Due to the hidden nature of CSA it is difficult to obtain accurate data on who the victims or perpetrators are. Current knowledge about victims and perpetrators will be examined, along with the nature of organised CSA and its relationship to child pornography, sexual trafficking of children and sex tourism.

CSA is one of a range of abuses that children may experience. The four main categories of child abuse are:

1. Physical abuse

2. Emotional abuse

3. Neglect

4. Sexual abuse.

## Historical patterns of child abuse

There are huge problems in defining childhood abuse because it is socially constructed and reflects cultural context and meaning, cultural relativity, race, ethnicity, class and the historical time in which it occurs. Lloyd deMause (1976,1991,1993,1998,2002) has written extensively on the historical evidence of childhood abuse, which is related to historical conceptualisations of children and childhood. The data show that attitudes, beliefs about children and patterns of parenting have changed dramatically throughout time.

DeMause shows how patterns of parenting in antiquity to the fourth century, which he calls the *infanticide mode*, were based on the idea that children exist to meet adult needs and convenience and that defective children were responsible for adults' misfortune. Unwanted children were commonly disposed of. Between the fourth and the thirteenth century, what deMause calls the *abandonment mode*, children were seen as being full of evil, so were beaten and kept at an emotional distance from parents or abandoned or sold into slavery. By the fourteenth to the seventeenth century parents were more emotionally attached to children yet still feared that children were on the brink of total evil. During this *ambivalence mode*, the parental task was to mould the child by restraining and beating it.

By the eighteenth century, what deMause calls the *intrusion mode*, children were seen as less threatening and less evil, with the parental duty being to conquer the child's mind. Commonly, parents sought to break the child's will in order to control their behaviour by the use of threats, guilt and punishment. The child was to be 'prayed with but not played with'. This was followed by the *socialisation mode* (nineteenth to mid-twentieth century) in which parents attempted to guide, train and teach manners, good habits, correct public behaviour and to conform to others' expectations. Beatings continued for misbehaviour, but children were no longer seen as intrinsically evil. According to deMause (1976,1991,1993,1998, 2002) this form of parenting is still the most common today.

Since the mid-twentieth century parenting patterns have been characterised by a *helping mode* in which children are seen as knowing what they need better than anyone else. The joint task of parents is to empathise with children and respond accurately to their needs at each stage of development. Punishment and discipline are de-emphasised due to the belief that if the child's potential is fulfilled at each stage, the child will grow up to be authentic, gentle, cheerful, resourceful, creative and unafraid of authority.

These changing parenting modes have had an impact on children and parents alike, with some parents unconsciously repeating their own childhood experiences and patterns of being parented. DeMause (1976, 1991,1993,1998, 2002) argues that, if parents were abused or traumatised in childhood, they may feel compelled to repeat this trauma when they become parents as 'trauma demands repetition'. While this may be the case for some parents it by no means implicates all, as many parents who have been abused do not go on to abuse their own children.

Cultural traditions also play a major role in parenting patterns. Some cultures, and subcultures, still advocate severe beatings to ensure compliance and adherence to cultural norms. This is not seen as abusive. On the other hand, some Western traditions, such as isolating infants in their own bed or room at night, rigid feeding schedules, or allowing them to cry without attending to them immediately, are seen as abusive.

In increasingly multicultural societies it is clearly important to ensure sensitivity to all cultural practices but at the same time to observe the needs of children within a child protection framework. What becomes crucial is to differentiate between culturally normative parenting and abusive, neglectful parenting. This can be very difficult but is critical in order to protect children.

A further issue in all child abuse is parental culpability. Inappropriate standards of care may be due to ignorance, religious beliefs, poverty, or the availability of and access to resources, and as such occur by default. This is clearly different to lack of parental concern. We must remember, however, that while adults can consider such issues, the child nevertheless may feel abused irrespective of whether this occurred by default or with deliberate intent.

## Definitions of child abuse

As child abuse is socially and culturally constructed, it stands to reason that there are many inconsistencies across cultures and subcultures in terms of defining precisely what constitutes abuse. However, in order to be clear what is meant by child abuse some definition needs to be employed. To reflect current thinking in the United Kingdom, the definition used in this book is taken from the Department of Health (2003) as follows.

### Physical abuse

Hitting, shaking, throwing, poisoning, burning or scalding, drowning, suffocating, or otherwise causing physical harm to a child. Physical harm may also be caused when a parent or carer feigns the symptoms of, or deliberately causes, ill health to a child. This situation is commonly described using terms such as 'fictitious illness by proxy' or 'Munchhausen syndrome by proxy'.

(Department of Health 2003)

### Emotional abuse

The persistent emotional ill-treatment of a child such as to cause severe and persistent adverse effects on the child's emotional development. It may involve conveying to the children that they are worthless, or unloved, inadequate, or valued only insofar that they meet the needs of another person. It may feature age or developmentally inappropriate expectations being placed on children. It may involve causing children frequently to feel frightened, or the exploitation or corruption of children. Some level of emotional abuse is involved in all types of ill-treatment of a child, though it may occur alone.

(Department of Health 2003)

### Neglect

The persistent failure to meet a child's physical and/or psychological needs, likely to result in the serious impairment of the child's health or development. It may involve a parent or carer failing to provide adequate food, shelter and clothing, failing to protect a child from physical harm or danger, or the failure to ensure access to appropriate medical care or treatment. It may include neglect of, or unresponsiveness to, a child's basic emotional needs.

(Department of Health 2003)

*Sexual abuse*

Forcing or enticing a child or young person to take part in sexual activities, whether or not the child is aware of what is happening. The activities may involve physical contact, including penetrative (e.g. rape or buggery) and non-penetrative acts. They may include non-contact activities, such as involving children in looking at, or in the production of, pornographic material, or watching sexual activities, or encouraging children to behave in sexually inappropriate ways.

(Department of Health 2003)

While the four types of abuse are considered to be quite distinct categories, arguably they may overlap and a child may suffer from any one, or some, or all of these abuses. It can also be argued that underlying physical abuse, neglect and sexual abuse is a degree of emotional abuse, especially in CSA, which combines both the sexual and emotional exploitation and violation of children.

## Historical perspectives of child sexual abuse

As in child abuse, Lloyd deMause (1976, 1991, 1993, 1998, 2002) has charted historical patterns of child sexual abuse and found evidence that it has always been widespread but not necessarily noted as sexual abuse due to the prevailing attitudes towards children at that time. DeMause argues that the evolution of childhood is characterised by moving from incest with children to loving children, from child abuse to child empathy.

Historical data indicate that in earliest times children were seen as *poison containers* for adults to put their bad feelings into. That is to say that, because children were seen as pure, they had the capacity to purify the bad in the adult. Such beliefs can still be seen today with notions of the virgin child, and some cultural beliefs that such children have the capacity to cure sexually transmitted diseases. This is particularly topical in many African countries where a virgin child is seen as an antidote to AIDS. Historically children were also often used in sacrifices, which is reflected today in the satanic ritual abuse of children such as 'Adam' whose torso was found floating in the River Thames in London.

Sexual encounters with sexually immature offspring are seen in primates who engage in incestuous mating. Although it is thought that there is a 'natural incest barrier', it is only really seen between the mother and the child. Sexually mature primates commonly do not mate with their own mother, yet mature males, who do not necessarily know which females are his offspring, may unwittingly mate with them. Studies of primates also show that mothers thrust their genitals against the genitals of both male and female offspring to teach them how to mate. This is crucial in that if they do not this, their offspring display impaired mating in adulthood.

According to deMause (1976, 1991, 1993, 1998, 2002), during the *infanticide mode* (antiquity to the fourth century) female children were frequently raped. Girls in Greek and Roman times were rarely in possession of an intact hymen. Male children were also invariably subjected to rape and sexual assault in being handed over to older men from the age of seven until puberty (which in those days was much later at around the age of 21) and not just in adolescence, as is commonly believed. Both Petronius and Tiberius report the sexual abuse of children sold into sexual slavery, child brothels, or male children who earned their living as rent boys.

A common practice during the *abandonment mode* (fourth to thirteenth century) was to sell children into monasteries and nunneries where young boys were subject to sexual assaults such as buggery. Children were also frequently beaten with such implements as the cat-o-nine tails, whips, shovels, canes, iron rods, bundles of sticks, the discipline (whip made of small chains), the goad (shaped like a cobbler's knife, used to prick a child's head/hands), and the flapper (pear shaped with a hole to raise blisters). Such beatings were often accompanied with some sexual arousal in the beater. There is also evidence of adolescent rape gangs preying on younger children, although such practices petered out by the end of the thirteenth century, which saw the beginning of the first disapproval of paedophilia.

This disapproval continued during the *ambivalent mode* (fourteenth to eighteenth century) in which church moralists protested against child molestation, although erotic whippings were still commonplace. Some historians believe that children were still sexually seduced by their care-takers, a prime example being Queen Elizabeth I, and Louis the XIII who is thought to have had his genitals and breasts licked and masturbated by members of the court (cited in deMause 1993). Despite such practices, children were nevertheless punished if caught masturbating themselves. These punishments went beyond verbal sanctions such as 'it makes you go blind' to include circumcision, clitoridectomy, infibulation, the cage, and genital restraints.

Changing attitudes towards the sexual abuse of children in essence preceded the humanistic, religious and political reforms associated with the Renaissance and Reformation, in which sexual abuse in general was brought under control. Mistresses and their male equivalents (catamites) were no longer tolerated in public.

During the *socialising mode* (nineteenth to mid-twentieth century) adults and parents generally became less sexually abusive and began to emphasise the education of children. This has continued into the *helping mode* seen today, in which most parents and adults attempt to help children reach their own goals with love and acceptance. Having said that, this does not mean that child sexual abuse no longer exists.

It is evident that it does, as seen in high profile cases of CSA and the abduction and sexually motivated murder of young children. DeMause argues that the current prevalence rate of child sexual abuse in the USA is as high as 60 per cent of all females and 45 per cent of all males, with half directly incestuous and half perpetrated by adults known to the child. Such sexual abuse is often prolonged over a number of years with 81 per cent abused before the age of puberty, and 42 per cent instigated below age seven.

As in child abuse generally, there are cultural influences in the sexual abuse of children. Differing cultures have different child rearing practices, which are normalised within that culture and seen as totally acceptable. In some cases abuse is considered to be a part of 'normal' child rearing practices and is not considered abusive by either adults or children. To see how widespread such practices are, we will look at the diverse range of sexual practices involving children.

## Cultural practices in child sexual abuse

According to deMause (1976, 1991, 1993, 1998, 2002) female children in many parts of India are frequently masturbated to 'make her sleep well', while boys are masturbated to 'make him manly'. Due to lack of space, many children sleep in the family bed where they may witness sexual intercourse between parents. In more rural parts, the child may be encouraged to participate in sexual activity with the parents, or they may be 'borrowed' to sleep with other members of the extended household.

Historically, in some parts of India incest was the rule rather than the exception, which is reflected in the old Indian proverb, 'For a girl to be a virgin at 10 years old, she must have neither brothers nor cousins nor fathers'. The Baiga, a group of people in India, still practise incestuous marriage between father/daughter, mother/sons, siblings, and grandparents/grandchildren. In some cases, five to six-year-old children move from incestuous family beds to sex dormitories where older youths or men use them sexually for up to three days at a time under threat of gang rape.

Child marriages are still considered by some as being perfectly acceptable. Often the child brides are sold to considerably older men and as such resemble a form of sexual slavery. Perhaps due to economic circumstances the selling of children into prostitution to satisfy the child sex tourism industry is not uncommon. In fact child prostitution represents up to 14 per cent of Asian countries' GDP. Girls may also be sold to become temple maidens and live in temples where they provide sexual services to worshippers (deMause 1976, 1991, 1993, 1998, 2002).

The use of children in sexual practices was also seen in China. Children were used as sexual slaves or servants, or sold into prostitution. Child concubinage was not uncommon, as was the pederasty of boys. Male children were castrated to become sexual eunuchs, while girls had their feet bound. Foot binding moulded the foot in such a way as to represent the lotus flower yet often resembled a substitute penis and was used in toe fetish during sexual congress.

Meanwhile in Japan, incestuous marriages were condoned in court circles. In more rural areas fathers were known to marry their daughters after the mother's death in accordance with feudal family traditions. Extended family incest was also tolerated between siblings, cousins, uncles and aunts. Family bed sharing and co-sleeping were not uncommon up to the age of 10 to 16 years of age, with girls sleeping with their fathers in the same bed (cited in deMause 1976, 1991, 1993, 1998, 2002).

According to deMause (1976, 1991, 1993, 1998, 2002), surveys show that there is a higher rate of CSA in Japan than America, with mother and son incest accounting for one-third of cases. This is often designed to make the son feel better and to relieve tension so they can study or work more effectively. Masturbation is also not uncommon by mothers in order to help their son to sleep.

In the Middle East, child marriages, including sibling marriages (in Egypt), child concubinage, sexual slavery and temple prostitution using both boys and girls were not uncommon. In many countries masturbation is decreed as necessary 'to increase the size' of the penis. Thus, older siblings play with the genitals of babies while older youths engage younger children in mutual masturbation, fellatio, and anal intercourse. According to deMause (1976, 1991, 1993, 1998, 2002) older brothers, cousins, uncles and teachers force 80 per cent of females into fellatio between the ages of three and six. Females tend to be sexually abused more so than males, which reflects the lack of value and status of females in such cultures. Nude public baths (hammam) are eroticised, and are well known rendezvous for sexual activity.

Most common in the Middle East is female genital mutilation, or more accurately *female genital excision* (FGE). This, however, is not seen as CSA but as an initiation rite, which has strong religious and cultural meaning. There are four types of FGE: Sunna, which involves the removal of the tip of the clitoris; clitoridectomy, which involves the removal of the entire clitoris; and pharaonic, where both the labia and clitoris are removed and the orifice sewn up. The opening is re-sewn after each delivery, on divorce and on the death of the woman's husband. The fourth, which is rarely practised, involves enlarging the vaginal opening by cutting the perineum (MacKay 2000).

While there are no comprehensive global records, the World Health Organisation (WHO) and UNICEF estimate that there are around 130 to 140 million females in the world today who have been subjected to FGE. In addition, based on current birth rates, it is estimated that two million females will undergo FGE each year (Hosken 1993; Toubia 1994, 1996; WHO 1996, 1999). It is thought that up to 80 per cent of females in Egypt, Sudan, Eritrea, Ethiopia, Somalia, Djibouti and Sierra Leone have been subjected to FGE, 50 to 79 per cent of females in Mali, Nigeria, Chad, Kenya and Senegal, 20 to 49 per cent of females in Yemen, Ghana, Cameroon and Niger, around 20 per cent of females in India (MacKay 2000). It is estimated that in Egypt, clitoridectomy occurs in 97 per cent of uneducated families and in 66 per cent of educated families.

Female genital excision is also practised in Europe and in America, albeit illegally. In the United Kingdom around 10,000 FGE type operations had been carried out by 1999, on females mainly from Eritrea, Ethiopia, Somalia and Yemen (Black and Debelle 1995; Horsken 1993; WHO 1999). However, the UK National Health Service now offers reversals of FGE, where these are possible. In France around 32,500 females, mainly from Mali and Senegal, had undergone FGE by 1999 (Hosken 1993; Toubia 1994, 1996; WHO 1999). Although FGE is seen in these cultures as being a fundamental part of cultural traditions and initiation rites, deMause (1976, 1991, 1993, 1998, 2002) argues that FGE is in essence an act of incest and a form of sadistic sexual pleasure. Further cause for concern is the increase in cosmetic surgery for both women and babies who undergo female genital reconstruction. It is estimated that to date over 168,000 girls have had cosmetic surgery on their genitalia at birth (deMause 1976, 1991, 1993, 1998, 2002).

While FGE is also practised in parts of Africa, there is a separate concern now at the increase in CSA as a result of the AIDS epidemic. Increasingly younger children who are still virgins are being subjected to unprotected child sex to reduce the risk of the perpetrators being infected with the AIDS virus.

That the use of children is a widespread phenomenon is reflected in worldwide child prostitution rates (Table 1.1; MacKay 2000).

As can be seen, child prostitution is global, as is the production and distribution of child pornography. While many child pornographic images consist of Western European children, a substantial proportion contain images of Asian and Oriental children. There is also evidence that there is a huge increase in the sexual use of children from Eastern Europe, especially Russia, both in child pornography and child sexual slavery.

This indicates that the sexual abuse of children is widespread and global. While individual countries may have different definitions of what constitutes a child, especially in terms of the legal age of sexual consent, and what constitutes child sexual abuse, some sort of definition needs to be arrived at to ensure a mutual understanding between author and reader. In the United Kingdom the Department of Health definition underpins most accepted definitions of CSA, although child protection agencies vary in their emphases. The National Society for the Prevention of Cruelty to Children (NSPCC) emphasises that it includes any child, depending upon the country's legal age, who is used for the sexual gratification of an adult. While this is representative

| Table 1.1 Child prostitution worldwide | |
|---|---|
| *Country* | *Prevalence rates in 2000* |
| Brazil | 600,000 |
| India | 450,000 |
| USA | 300,000 |
| Thailand | 200,000 |
| Philippines | 100,000 |
| Africa | 70,000 |
| Taiwan | 50,000 |
| Pakistan | 40,000 |
| Vietnam | 40,000 |
| Venezuela | 40,000 |
| Sri Lanka | 30,000 |
| Paraguay | 26,000 |
| Dominican Republic | 25,000 |
| Indonesia | 25,000 |
| Cambodia | 20,000 |
| Nepal | 20,000 |
| Colombia | 10,000 |
| France | 8000 |
| Britain | 5000 |
| Costa Rica | 3000 |
| Australia | 3000 |
| Romania | 2000 |
| Netherlands | 1000 |
| Estonia | 1000 |

*Data based on estimates from CSEC (2001), ECPAT (2004) and UNICEF (2004).*

of most sexual abuse, it fails to include older children or adolescents, such as older siblings who use children for sexual gratification.

## Definition of child sexual abuse

Any robust definition of CSA must be able to define the terms *child, sexual* and *abuse*. In this book a child will include children and young people up to their eighteenth birthday, when in law they are no longer seen as children. However, special consideration must be given to vulnerable young adults whose chronological age is above 18 but whose mental age is considerably younger. While in law these are not seen as children, they are arguably unable to give informed consent, making them more vulnerable to sexual abuse.

What is considered sexual is much harder to define, as this will vary from culture to culture and individual to individual. However, which acts are considered sexual, and which are not, are crucial when researching the incidence of child sexual abuse. Researchers have to define how they use the term 'sexual' in order to distinguish between sexual abuse and non-sexual abuse. Definitions of 'sexual' can be very narrow or very broad. Thus, if researchers have a very narrow definition, such as sexual intercourse, then the incidence of child sexual abuse may be found to be quite low. However, if researchers use a broader definition, such as showing or using a child in the production of pornography, which more accurately reflects children's experiences, then they are likely to find a higher incidence rate.

## The spectrum of child sexual abuse behaviours

The type of sexual activities engaged in with children covers an extremely wide spectrum and includes non-contact abuse, such as indecent exposure, exhibitionism, voyeurism and the use of children in the making or showing of pornographic images or films. Non-physical contact sexual abuse can also include the taking of photographs for pornographic purposes, the use of sexually inappropriate language towards the child, and insisting on forms of dress that may be sexually arousing to the abuser. It also includes nudity and watching the child disrobing or engaged in bathroom activities. Overt sexual behaviour in front of the child can also be considered sexually abusive.

## Non-contact behaviours

- Grooming the child
- Internet grooming
- Sexually inappropriate invasion of child's personal space
- Insisting on sexually seductive behaviour and dress
- Nudity
- Verbal comments of a sexual nature
- Disrobing in front of the child
- Forcing child to sleep in and share the same bed as adult beyond age-appropriate development
- Deliberate genital exposure
- Inappropriate watching of the child undressing or using the bathroom
- Encouraging the child to watch or listen to sexual acts
- Photographing the child for sexual gratification or later pornographic use
- Drugging the child in order to photograph it in sexually provocative poses, or as a prelude to sexual assault
- Engaging in overtly sexual behaviour in the presence of a child
- Exposing the child to pornography, often to desensitise the child, a potent part of the grooming process
- Filming child in sexually explicit poses
- Coercing child into paedophile ring
- Getting child to recruit other children for the child sexual abuser

## Contact behaviours

- Inappropriate, open-mouth sexual kissing
- Sexually arousing touch and fondling
- Touching a child's genitals or private parts for sexual pleasure
- Making the child touch someone else's genitals
- Playing sexual games
- Masturbation to the child, child to the abuser, or mutual masturbation
- Oral sex (fellatio or cunnilingus to the child, child to abuser, or mutual)

- Ejaculating over the child
- Placing objects, sweets, small toys into vaginal/rectal opening of child and then retrieving them
- Penetration of vagina or anus with large objects, including adult sex aids
- Digital penetration of the anus or rectal opening
- Penile penetration of the anus or rectal opening: sodomy
- Digital penetration of the vagina
- Penile penetration of the vagina
- Penile penetration of the anus or rectal opening
- 'Dry intercourse' – placing penis between upper thighs of child and simulating intercourse
- Forced sexual activity with other adults or children
- Coercing child into paedophile ring
- Filming sexual activity with adults or children
- Forced sexual activity with animal(s) – bestiality

Grooming the child for sexual purposes (see Chapter 5) is now acknowledged to be how child sexual abusers target and prepare children for future sexual encounters. The grooming of children is a well-known and long-established tactic employed by many paedophiles. It is a very subtle, painstaking yet powerfully seductive process that can take anything up to 18 months and is designed to prepare the child for sexual abuse. Many paedophiles who sexually abuse children in their local communities employ this technique. Because of its subtlety it often goes undetected, allowing large numbers of children to be sexually abused without being exposed.

Today the grooming of children is commonly associated with the Internet. Indeed, the new Sexual Offences Bill is to include the category of grooming on the Internet as an offence. In Internet grooming there may be no actual physical or sexual contact initially, but the abuser seduces the child with the intent of sexual contact at some point. Arguably what will be hard to establish is the issue of intent and at which point in the grooming process that becomes manifest. Grooming also occurs offline and will be considered in more depth in Chapter 5.

Child sexual abuse includes the full range of sexual activities involving physical contact. This includes inappropriate or open-mouth kissing, fondling the breasts or genitals, masturbation, oral sex, and digital and penile penetration. A summary of the full spectrum of behaviours associated with child sexual abuse, based on research of children's experiences, is given in the box above.

When considering what constitutes abuse, issues of consent emerge. It is argued that children are not able to give consent while under the age of legal consent. However, children develop at different rates with some seemingly much more physically mature at an earlier age than others, yet remaining emotionally and mentally quite immature and thus vulnerable. In addition, a child may be assumed to give 'consent' in the absence of saying 'No'. This hardly constitutes consent, as the child is unable to resist due to the imbalance of power, status and authority, or degree of manipulation and coercion.

Children seek out adult role models that are invested with authority or some kind of status. This gives the adult power over children, which can be exploited in a sexual way. Some celebrities seem to have exploited children's and young adolescents' idolisation of them by sexualising their encounters. The child may believe him or herself to have assented but this is not the same as 'informed consent', which includes a full understanding of the power dynamics involved in such relationships. More importantly, such abusers appear not to consider the power and status invested in them by children and adolescents and how this is abused when they engage them in sexual activities.

The working definition of child sexual abuse employed in this book is broadly based in that it incorporates the full range of sexual acts committed against children, including non-contact and contact behaviours involving family members as well as those outside the family. Child sexual abuse is defined in the box on the following page.

## The incidence of child sexual abuse

It is unclear precisely how widespread child sexual abuse actually is. This is primarily because CSA is by its very nature hidden. It is thought that only 10 per cent of cases are actually reported or come to the attention of the criminal justice system. This means our knowledge is extremely limited and only based on those cases that are reported. This impacts on the collection of data for research purposes and statistical analysis.

### Definition of child sexual abuse

The involvement of dependent children and adolescents in sexual activities with an adult, or any person older or bigger, where there is a difference in age, size or power, in which the child is used as a sexual object for the gratification of the older person's needs or desires, to which the child is unable to give informed consent due to the imbalance of power, or any mental or physical disability. This definition excludes consensual sexual activity between peers.

Incorporated into this definition are all types of sexual encounters and behaviours ranging from grooming, sexually suggestive language or gestures, the use of pornography, voyeurism, exhibitionism, fondling, masturbation, through to digital and penile penetration. It includes any sexual acts imposed upon a child or adolescent by any person within the family constellation, or outside of it, who abuses their position of power and trust.

It includes any older children and adults who have power over, and investment of trust from, the child. Within the family it includes fathers, mothers, stepfathers, stepmothers, resident male/female friends of the family, uncles, aunts, brothers, sisters, stepsiblings, grandparents, cousins and all other permutations of male and female relatives in the extended family. Individuals outside the family include male and female adults, or older peers, who are 'in loco parentis' and as such have authority and power over the child, such as babysitters, nursery workers, teachers, sports coaches, youth workers, youth club workers, community workers, carers, representatives of religious institutions and pastoral carers, and those who care for children in institutional, residential, or foster care. Also included are other persons in the community who may or may not be known to the child, such as neighbours, shop keepers, or those who live or work in the local community.

Research data on the incidence of CSA vary enormously depending on the definition of sexual abuse employed, whether it includes non-contact or only contact behaviours, and on the methodology used to obtain data, such as clinical samples versus population estimates, retrospective or current. It is commonly thought that up to one in four girls and one in six boys experience some form of sexual abuse in childhood. Girls are more likely to be sexually abused by someone in the family, while boys are more likely to be sexually assaulted by someone outside the family, although one must guard against generalising this trend.

## Who are the victims of child sexual abuse?

Clearly, children of both sexes are victims with estimates that the most vulnerable are girls. It is estimated that 73 per cent of all victims of child sexual abuse are females, while 27 per cent are males (ChildLine 2003). One must be careful when interpreting these data as they may reflect reporting bias, rather than number of victims. Males are generally more reluctant to disclose such experiences in cultures that are homophobic and have strong stereotypes about masculinity and sexuality. In such cultures, where males are expected to be able to protect themselves from assault and are supposed to be the sexual initiators, boys may experience huge shame and guilt if they are victimised.

Gender differences in the socialisation of children may play an important role in how boys interpret and come to terms with CSA. Boys are generally discouraged from talking about their feelings and taught to be stoical and to 'take it like a man'. These messages may generate shame and embarrassment in sexually abused boys, preventing them from talking about their experience. The gender difference in reporting CSA means that the sexual abuse of male children remains 'hidden'.

The sexual abuse of children can begin at any age, from a few weeks old (there are babies with sexually transmitted disease) to the age of 18. While studies do vary in their estimates it is thought that the age group most at risk is the five to twelve-year-olds, although increasingly younger children are being used in the production of child pornographic images.

Although approximately five to ten children are abducted and murdered each year, it is unclear how many children are sexually assaulted per year or per day. These figures represent only those cases that have come to the attention of the police or media and are merely the 'tip of the iceberg'. Most offences are committed by people known to the child (87%), many of which are never disclosed. In addition, CSA is often systematic and repeated over a period of years, with an average duration of more than one year. During this time the frequency of the sexual assaults can increase, with progressively more severe sexual acts being committed.

To the year ending March 2002, the UK organisation ChildLine received and counselled 8402 children experiencing child sexual abuse (ChildLine 2003). Of these 6122 were girls (73%) and 2280 (27%) were boys. In evaluating these figures we must be clear that these are children who are old enough to phone the helpline and who have been able to identify that they are being sexually abused. Many children who are being sexually abused may be too young to phone or are unable to get access to the phone. They may not identify that what is happening to them is CSA, because they are told that such behaviour is normal and part of a special relationship. In addition, many children may be too terrified to make a disclosure for fear of the consequences. This is especially the case if they have been threatened by their abuser into keeping silent or are made to feel ashamed and guilty.

The majority of children calling ChildLine were aged between 12 and 15 years (61%), with five to eleven-year-olds representing 22 per cent, and 16 to 18-year-olds representing 17 per cent. The general finding that most sexual abusers are known to the victims can be seen in the ChildLine figures in which 57 per cent of the reported sexual abuse was perpetrated by someone in the caller's family, and 30 per cent were known to the child but not a family member. Only 13 per cent were reported as being strangers (ChildLine 2003).

Such data are crucial in understanding the sexual abuse of children today. No longer can we protect our children by warning them about 'stranger danger'. We need to acknowledge that in the majority of cases (87%) the child knows their sexual abuser. These children are often sexually abused on a daily basis, behind closed doors and intimidated or manipulated into silence.

Focusing only on high profile cases of abductions and killings by strangers is highly deceptive, and may lull parents and children into a false sense of security that people known to them do not sexually abuse. It is imperative that parents and teachers find ways of talking to children about the dangers of child sexual abuse in the family and community and not just to beware of strangers. Notions of child sex predators who are strangers no longer reflect the reality of child sexual abuse and are in fact a myth.

## Who are the perpetrators of child sexual abuse?

Paedophiles can be anyone – male or female, adult or older child. They can be a parent, a relative, a neighbour, family friend, teacher or doctor. In many respects, child sexual abusers are ordinary people who children encounter in their everyday lives. They can come from any social, racial or religious background and are often well-respected members of society and the community. They hold down jobs, play sports, have friends and are seen as 'nice' people. While some paedophiles may fall outside these parameters, the majority do not (see Chapter 3).

Research data on perpetrators of child sexual abuse vary enormously as the majority (90%) remain undetected. Early studies showed that between 91 and 97 per cent of perpetrators were male. However, more recent research has found that between 20 and 25 per cent of child sexual abusers are female. There is some controversy around this in that many feminists believe that most female abusers do so as a result of being forced or coerced into such acts by their male partners. Current research does not bear this out (Saradjian 1996). While their male partners may have initially forced some females, many go on to sexually abuse independently or actively initiate the assault.

The difference in offending between male and female child sexual abusers may be as a result of differences in gender socialisation. Traditionally males have been encouraged to *act out* or *externalise* any aggressions perpetrated against them, while females have been encouraged to *act in* or *internalise* any acts of aggression. While this is less gender-specific nowadays, one can still see examples of this. If another child hits a little boy he may be instructed to 'go and hit him back'. In contrast, little girls are encouraged to sit down next to the parent and instructed 'to keep away from such "nasty" children'.

Such behaviour, if reinforced, may go some way to explain gender differences in adults in which childhood abuse and trauma is transformed into *acting out* in males, or *acting in* in females. Thus, abused males may go on to perpetrate violence and sexual abuse, whereas females report more mental health problems such as depression and self-mutilation. A recent study carried out by the Institute of Child Health at Great Ormond Street Hospital in London (Salter *et al.* 2003; Skuse 2003) found that one in eight boys sexually abused in childhood goes on to sexually abuse in adolescence, with an average age of onset of 14.

This study bears out other findings that there seems to be an increase in reports of sexual abuse of children by older children, especially young adolescents. This includes older children within the family, such as older siblings, stepsiblings and cousins, and children outside the family such as older friends, older pupils at school, babysitters and older children in the neighbourhood. Indications are that one-third of sexual offences against children are committed by adolescents below the age of 17 years, many of them victims of CSA themselves (NSPCC 2003).

We can no longer afford to deny, or deceive ourselves about, the hidden nature of child sexual abuse. Although Home Office statistics (2003) show that there are currently 21,413 sex offenders on the Sex Offenders' Register living in the community, this is not a true indication of the number of convicted paedophiles. While McVean (2003) argues that there are around 110,000 convicted paedophiles not on the register, the more accurate and true figure may be as high as 250,000. The sobering truth is that we do not know who most child sexual offenders are as sexual abuse occurs in private. Given that the majority of paedophiles are not exposed, convicted and placed on the Sex Register, one must question how useful such a register is. While it may provide some comfort to parents and those involved in child protection, it is evidently not inclusive of all paedophiles.

For this reason equal attention should be given to those as yet *unknown* paedophiles whose sexual offending is as yet undiscovered if we are really to protect our children. Arguably, the danger of the unknown paedophile is much greater than those paedophiles already on the Sex Offenders' Register. Relying and focusing attention only on those paedophiles already known to the police ignores the reality of the everyday sexual abuse of children. Parents, teachers and responsible adults must be aware of the as yet unknown paedophile in the community if they are really to protect all children from sexual abuse.

While Chapter 3 gives a more detailed account of what is currently known about perpetrators of child sexual abuse, it is helpful to give a brief overview here of their common characteristics. Equipped with such knowledge parents and teachers may be more acutely aware of those who sexually assault children.

Although paedophiles vary enormously, they do share many commonalties. The majority of paedophiles are highly skilled at identifying vulnerable victims, whom they target. This skill is to some degree intuitive, but also comes through practice and experience. They are easily able to identify with children, often more so than most adults, which enables them to be 'master seducers of children'. They have an excessive interest in children although this is not always overtly manifested. They may actively seek employment in which they have frequent and regular contact with children. Chosen professions can include teachers, nursery or child care workers, babysitters, children's camps, or school bus drivers. They can be involved in specialist jobs in which they have access to children such as doctors, dentists, church leaders, social workers, police officers, sports coaches, scout or youth club leaders, clowns or magicians, or photographers specialising in child photography.

Child sexual abusers often congregate in places that children frequent such as toy or children's wear shops, parks, adventure playgrounds, public sports or playing fields, swimming pools, shopping centres, theme parks, or fun fairs. They are often seen as being 'nice' to children and enjoy entertaining them, organising children's parties, taking children out on day trips, or away for the weekend. They have an enormous capacity to attract children, and in many respects are like 'pied pipers'. They favour activities with children in which they can exclude other adults, often suggesting that others go off and enjoy themselves while they happily stay behind to look after the children.

Most paedophiles are skilled at manipulating children and use powerful seduction techniques, including child and group psychology involving peer competition, peer pressure and motivational techniques as well as threats and blackmail. A common technique with which to seduce the child is to give them 'special' or extra attention. They seduce the child by befriending it, paying the child special attention by talking and listening about any worries or concerns it may have. They enjoy spending time and are caring and affectionate. They may show the child preferential treatment, buying it gifts, or by satisfying the individual child's need. These behaviours are all designed to isolate the child from its peers and thereby make it easier to sexually assault it.

Paedophiles share hobbies and interests that appeal to children. They may collect toys or dolls, build toys, model planes or boats, all of which are designed to attract children to them. They often know the latest computer games, music, videos and films that children are interested in. They also know the current language and jargon that children use, appear to like the same food, drink, interior decoration and clothes. They present themselves as being 'child-friendly' so that the child begins to see them as an older friend, with whom she or he can talk and spend quality time.

---

### Behaviours that may be cause for concern

- The way they play with the child that might make other adults uncomfortable
- Always favouring the child
- Creating reasons to be alone with the child
- Refuse to allow a child sufficient privacy to make their own decisions on personal matters
- Insist on physical affection such as kissing, hugging or wrestling, even when the child clearly does not want it
- Are overly interested in the sexual development of a child or teenager
- Insist on time alone with the child with no interruptions
- Spend most of their spare time with children and have little interest in spending time with people their own age
- Regularly offer to babysit children for free or take children on overnight outings alone
- Buy children expensive gifts or give them money for no apparent reason
- Frequently walk in on children/teenagers in the bathroom
- Treat a particular child as a favourite, making them feel 'special' compared with others in the family
- Pick on a particular child

---

Paedophiles who target older children or teenagers will demonstrate this age group's interest by sharing alcohol, drugs or pornographic material with them. These are all designed to lower the child's or teenager's inhibitions, by engaging them in activities that by their nature they will have to keep secret from their parents, thus setting them up to keep the sexual assault secret.

All in all, the signs that someone has a sexual interest in children are extremely subtle and not necessarily obvious. However, there are some types of behaviour frequently associated with child sexual abusers that parents and teachers need to be aware of. Stop It Now! UK and Ireland (2002a) include the warning signs listed in the box above.

## Organised sexual abuse of children

While many paedophiles act alone, some do seek out other people who have a sexual interest in children. This is to offset stigmatisation and feelings of being marginalised by society. Such affiliations range from informal friend-ships to highly organised sex rings. Often these contacts are made in cyberspace through the Internet. While some merely communicate through the Internet, some actively seek out other paedophiles and socialise with them. In some cases paedophiles become involved in groups such as child sex rings in which they trade children among themselves. Sex rings commonly consist of groups or networks of unrelated adults, in which they trade related, or unrelated, children. However, it is known that parents also establish paedophile rings in which they 'swap' their own children with those of others, or unrelated children.

Child sex rings not only trade children for sexual purposes, they also engage in the filming, production, and distribution of child pornography. Because of the addictive nature of paedophilia, there is a constant demand for new children. Local and national child sex rings may also have links with child sex rings in other countries, and become involved in the global manufac-ture and distribution of child pornography. It is clear that child pornography is linked to global activities in procuring children to satisfy the increasing demands of paedophiles, which can lead to child sexual trafficking.

The global sexual trade of children and child sex trafficking of children is primarily focused on the buying and selling of children into sexual slavery. Such children are commonly bought from families in economically deprived countries, often unbeknown to the parents, to be sold for sexual purposes. Such children are frequently used in the manufacture of more sadistic types of child pornography in which the child is tortured and sexually mutilated, or ritualistically murdered.

Alternatively such children may be sold into child prostitution, especially in countries where sexual offending laws against children are less restrictive and more 'liberal', with lower ages of consent, in order to satisfy the increas-ing demands of 'sexual tourists'. It has been known for sexual tourists to engage in sexual activity with a child in one country, who then goes on to sexually assault a child in his or her own country. This has led to welcome implementation of measures to prosecute such sexual tourists in their own country of origin for sexual assaults against children instigated while abroad.

While these activities might seem extreme, or take place in other countries, it has to be remembered that each time a pornographic image of a child is created, a child is being sexually abused. Those involved in the production of child pornography, and the consumers of such material, are therefore implicated and culpable in the sexual abuse of the child even if they have had no actual sexual contact with it. If we are to protect children from such abuses we need to be aware of the links between paedophiles in our own community and the global sexual abuse of children.

## Chapter 2

# The Development
# of Children's Sexuality

Repressing children's sexual knowledge keeps children naïve and innocent... Denying information leaves control of children's sexuality in the hands of adults.

Martinson (1995)

Children's sexual thinking is not confined to thinking about sexual intercourse but broader universe experience.

Goldman and Goldman (1982)

Parents are partly to blame if they don't tell their children about [sexual matters] – I used it to my advantage by teaching the child myself.

A convicted paedophile

Children's sexuality is still a difficult topic for many parents and adults to feel comfortable talking about. This may reflect parents' own fears, anxieties and inhibitions around sexuality. Sex and sexuality may be associated with negative beliefs such as it being dirty, forbidden, degrading or representative of domination and submission. Accompanying such beliefs may also be a sense of embarrassment about their body and nudity, which may be subtly transmitted to the child, making it self-conscious and uneasy.

Parents and adults play a major role in the development of the child's understanding of the world. They act as powerful role models which children invariably imitate and copy. Therefore if parents and adults have negative attitudes towards sex, the child will acquire these. In turn, parents who have a more comfortable, easy and relaxed attitude towards the body and sexuality will make children more comfortable and relaxed in relation to their own body and sexuality.

It is interesting to note that, while parents are happy to answer fully many of their children's questions, the one area that many feel uncomfortable with is sex. They may blush, feel embarrassed, squirm or behave in a flustered manner. Many parents try to evade and avoid answering such questions by distracting the child's attention onto safer territory. Children pick up both the non-verbal behaviour and the evasion and learn to associate talking about sex with embarrassment and anxiety.

In order to protect children from sexual abuse they need to know and understand sexuality at a developmentally appropriate level. This involves using age-appropriate language and providing sufficient information for the child's level of understanding. When parents answer children's questions at an age-appropriate level the child, having received the required information, moves on to the next big question about its world, such as 'why is there a moon?'.

In enabling children to have a healthy understanding of the world and their part in it, it is necessary to provide appropriate information. Adults need to avoid projecting their own fears, anxieties and inhibitions around sexuality on to their children, so that they can extract meanings that will give them confidence in, and acceptance of, their bodies and sexuality. This confidence is what will protect them from being exploited and sexually abused by others.

Adult fears and anxieties around sexuality, especially when in relation to children, are demonstrated in how little is known, and indeed written, about the sexual development of children other than in the context of biological, anatomical and hormonal changes. Children's sexuality is one of the most under-researched areas of child development. Apart from psychodynamic formulations of children's sexuality, the majority of child development books largely ignore children's sexuality, especially before puberty.

This became apparent while researching this book in that there was very little information available to parents on the sexual development of children. This represents a real problem. If parents and professionals are ill informed about normal sexual development how can they determine when a child is behaving in a way that fits outside of this, or which indicates CSA. It also means that parents find it hard to interpret, understand and accept their child's sexual development. If parents do not understand or accept their child's sexuality, what chance do children have to develop healthy, confident attitudes to this aspect of their development.

The development of sexuality in children is a normal part of their general development. Parents read books to find information on how children develop physically, emotionally and cognitively. These are frequently plotted on developmental charts to ensure that the child is developing normally. Behaviour is similarly assessed to see if it fits into the normal range. If there are worries or concerns, professionals are consulted. One area that is not monitored or compared, though, is children's sexual development. While overt anatomical differences may be investigated, the emotional and behavioural components of sexuality are not.

Yet, if parents do not have access to information on normal sexual development, or are embarrassed to discuss it, they are unable to judge what constitutes typical sexual development in children, and what does not. Unless parents have access to such knowledge they will not be able to distinguish between normal and abnormal sexual behaviour. This reduces their chances of protecting children from sexual abuse. Similarly, other adults, especially teachers and nursery workers, also need to have a good solid understanding of typical sexual development to which they can compare atypical sexual behaviour that may be a cause for concern. It is only with such knowledge that we can adequately and effectively protect children.

The few psychological texts that are available on children's sexuality are based largely on retrospective studies such as Kinsey *et al.* (1948, 1953). What seems clear is that there is very little *direct* investigation by psychologists or child development experts. In contrast, there is substantially more information on the atypical sexual behaviour of children who have been sexually abused (see Chapter 7).

This chapter will examine what is known about normative, or typical, sexual development in children and the factors that influence sexual behaviour of children. It will then go on to discuss consensual and experimental sexual development and try to identify how this differs from the sexual behaviour of children who have been sexually abused or who are sexually abusing other children.

**Possible reasons for the direct lack of investigation of children's sexuality**

- Socially sensitive subject – sexual research with children may generate discomfort and be viewed with suspicion by both children and adults.

- Ethical issues – children cannot give informed consent to participate in such research; consent must be sought from the parent or guardian.

- Such research may be viewed as unnecessarily intrusive.

- Respect for children's rights to privacy imposes a justifiable limit on research into children's sexuality.

- Respect for sociocultural and religious attitudes and beliefs of the parents of the children.

- Interpretation of the research findings may be biased and open to misinterpretation, which could fuel distorted views of children's sexuality.

- Children's interpretations of sexuality may be totally different from adult interpretations – sensual rather than sexual.

- Children may feel inhibited in talking about sexuality with a stranger.

- Children might find it difficult to verbalise or discuss their experience of sexuality due to limited vocabulary or embarrassment.

- Natural or direct observation of sexual games are hampered as these are usually not conducted in public.

- Sexual behaviour in young children is often infrequent and unpredictable in that natural play may not include overt sexual behaviour.

## Typical sexual development in children

One of the difficulties in any research is one of definition. Sexuality is biologically and socially constructed and reflects cultural and religious beliefs. It is also lodged in the historical time in which individuals live and is dependent on family attitudes and beliefs around sexuality. Parents' attitudes around sexuality were originally acquired in their own childhoods and reflect the attitudes and beliefs transmitted by their own parents. Thus the way we express our sexuality is learned from childhood and shaped by our experiences, both in childhood and as adults.

Sexuality therefore includes biological and physiological factors, as well as sociocultural beliefs. Such beliefs include the interpretation and meaning of sex and sexuality, and its purpose. Given that sexuality is learned and shaped by experience, it is crucial that parents and adults understand that there are real differences between adults' and children's understanding and conceptualisation of sex and sexuality.

Definitions of sex and sexuality may therefore vary from culture to culture, within subcultures and in the historical time in which they occur. The *Shorter Oxford English Dictionary* (OUP 1993) focuses its definition of sex on biological and anatomical differences in relation to gender and procreation. Sexuality is defined as the quality of being sexual and having sex, possession of sexual powers, or capability of sexual feelings and recognition of, or preoccupation with, what is sexual.

While these definitions establish a framework for understanding sex and sexuality they do not clarify what sexuality actually is. Many adults may be no clearer on the basis of these definitions. They are quite specific and clinical and based on adult conceptualisation. Children will not have such a knowledge base and so will find these definitions hard to understand. To enable further understanding, especially in terms of children's experience, it might be useful to look at sensuality.

Like adults, children are capable of experiencing a full range of sensory experiences and are thus sensual from birth. The *Shorter Oxford English Dictionary* focuses on the senses, sensory and physical sensation, as opposed to reason and appetites and pleasures connected with the gratification of the senses. Sensuality is further defined as chiefly animal instincts and appetites of a lower nature, as distinct from reason. It is associated with a source of evil, the lusts of the flesh, and excessive indulgence in the pleasure of the senses. In the latter part of this definition we can see the influence of cultural and societal judgements derived from religious and philosophical ideologies.

Children are born with the full range of sensory experiences. These consist of taste, smell, touch, sound, vision and kinaesthetic experiences such as close proximity and ambience. Child psychologists such as Piaget (1952) believed that the newborn infant relies on these sensory capacities to learn about the world. It is their primary source of gathering information about themselves and their experience of the world. These senses become associated with certain people, behaviours and experiences. Through these associations the child develops understanding and meanings, which influence how they interpret their experiences and how they think about them.

Even very young children are capable of describing their sensory experiences. They are able to differentiate between something that tastes nice and something that tastes unpleasant. If they are unable to verbalise this, their physiological reaction will demonstrate how they feel about the experience. This demonstrates that children are fully sensing individuals who relate to their bodies in a sensory way and can distinguish between sensory stimuli.

Parents and adults teach children how to interpret sensory stimulation and which words to use to describe their experiences. The child who gurgles and laughs with delight when having its toes or tummy tickled will equally gurgle and laugh when it touches its genitalia. The young child has not learned that this body part is a sexual zone, as it does not have an adult conceptualisation of sex. To the child it is just another part of the body that is capable of pleasurable reactions. How the parent reacts and identifies these reactions plays a crucial part in how the child learns to feel about its body.

Thus, for children sexuality is very different to that in adults in that it is not specifically directed at genital pleasure but pleasure experienced throughout the whole body, and consists of:

- how we think and feel about our bodies
- everything that has to do with being male and female
- our relationships with one another
- how we grow and change
- how we reproduce.

As the emphasis is on sensory stimulation, children learn about sexuality from the sensory experiences their body is exposed to and the guidance the parents give them.

If the child is told that touching sexual areas of the body is dirty or disgusting, the child will interpret this as dirty and disgusting. Children rely on parents for what psychologists call 'social referencing', which means that they look to their caretaker's verbal and emotional reaction as a way of regulating and moderating their behaviour. A parent who looks embarrassed, anxious and fearful when the child explores these areas of the body will transmit to the child that exploration of these areas is a source of embarrassment or anxiety. This can cause a child to feel ashamed of its body and sensual experiences. In contrast, the parent who smiles at the child who is touching its genitals and says 'I know that feels good' conveys respect for the child's feelings and experience.

---

### How young children learn about sexuality

- The way they are touched, held, comforted, caressed, cuddled and cared for
- Through self exploration and learning how their bodies feel to themselves
- Parental guidance – by learning what is OK and not OK to do
- From words family members say, and do not say, to refer to body parts
- By observing how family members express affection and caring for one another
- Reactions to the expression of sexual feelings – smiling, frowning

---

Adults and parents can influence children's experiences in a powerful way. Parents guide children's understanding and interpretation, and invest certain body parts with erotic and sexual qualities and meanings. This is not driven by the child, but reflects adult conceptualisations, attitudes and beliefs. Parents guide the child to distinguish between good and bad touch, and set boundaries around what is appropriate sexual behaviour. The parent who equips the child with accurate information is protecting the child from being manipulated by child sexual abusers who usually provide false and distorted messages about sexuality.

Guidance should be given to children, without shaming them, that genital self-exploration is generally not something to be indulged in publicly. While the genitals are a source of pleasure, others, especially much older children or adults, should not instigate touching these areas. This gives the child permission to claim its body as its own with the right to say 'No' when it is touched by someone else.

An example of this is the three-year-old boy who asked his mother to kiss his penis, just like she kisses his big toe. The mother clearly boundaried such activity by stating that this is not something that adults do to, or with, children. She explained that his penis is a more private part of his body, which feels nice when stroked by him, but that it is not appropriate to be stroked, or indeed kissed, by others. The message transmitted here is that it is natural to feel nice feelings when he strokes his penis and that such self-exploration is OK. It is however not appropriate for others, especially those older than he, to engage in such activity.

Children need therefore to learn about sex and sexuality in a non-shaming way. Young children do this intuitively as a response to sensory stimulation. As they develop and grow, greater cognitive understanding is acquired about what is sexual and what is not. Older children begin to know with *whom* they can have sex, at what *age*, and *when* and *where* it is appropriate to have sex. They also need to know *why* people have sex, not just in terms of reproduction, but also as a form of emotional expression. It is imperative that parents are aware of their own beliefs and attitudes to ensure that children are guided appropriately and are able to develop healthy and confident attitudes to their bodies and sexuality.

Children are naturally curious. In evolutionary terms, this curiosity is essential in order to find out about the world, to learn about boundaries, to find out what is safe and what is dangerous. The child demonstrates the same curiosity about itself and its body. In order to find out about its world and its place in it, the child needs to explore. This exploration promotes understanding and helps the child to acquire knowledge and meaning. Included in this is the exploration of its own body, and that of others. Very young children naturally explore their own bodies, including those parts of the body deemed 'sexual' by adults. Having engaged in such self-exploration they become curious about exploring the bodies of others. This usually includes mummy and daddy's body and those of other children.

Mutual exploration in children merely represents a natural curiosity about anatomical similarities and differences between gender, which is incorporated in play as the developing child attempts to discover self and other. Such exploratory interactions may have little or no erotic intent and as such are developmentally appropriate. This differs from deliberate sexual interactions, which incorporate erotic intent and may be viewed as developmentally inappropriate. Physiological and sensual arousal may be the same in both but the purpose differs.

To gain a better understanding of the development of children's sexuality it is helpful to review what researchers have found to date.

## The development of sexual excitation in children

Many researchers (Kanner 1939; Langfeldt 1981a, 1981b) believe that the capacity for sexual arousal is present at birth. Indeed, there is some evidence of sexual reactions in utero. Using ultrasound scans, Masters and Johnson (1986) found that male babies in the womb are capable of reflex erections. Such erections are also seen in newborn babies. Conn and Kanner (1940) found that male babies aged between three and twenty weeks had erections between five and forty times a day. Such erections are associated with thumb sucking, restless behaviour, fretting and crying. Such reflex erections may represent a physiological response which can be prompted by feeding, sucking, a full bladder and defecation. Kanner (1969) also found that erections during sleep were more frequent in children than in adults. In the case of female babies, Langfeldt (1981a) found evidence for sexual arousal based on amount of vaginal lubrication.

These primarily reflexive responses may become associated with sensual responses to closeness. Thus they are not erotically neutral (such as the knee jerk reflex) but can be viewed as some expression of pleasure that accompanies them. Martinson (1981) observed this in three to four-month-old babies in which stimulation of the genitals elicited smiling and cooing. This suggests that erections and vaginal lubrication start as reflexive reactions to genital stimulation (such as having a nappy changed) but become associated or endowed with pleasurable feelings and as such are eroticised.

This arousal represents a more generalised state of emotional excitement than erotic or sexual arousal. It is experienced as sensory pleasure rather than sexual. Such sensory arousal, which is non-sexual, can be elicited through physical sources such as friction with clothing, being cleaned at nappy change, or rhythmic stroking. This is akin to the sensual stroking of the fur of an animal or blanket, which offers a soothing sensual experience.

Emotional excitement and its accompanying arousal can also be elicited when watching exciting situations such as play-fighting, fires, accidents or violence (Kinsey et al. 1948). It is thought that initially erotic and arousing reactions are indiscriminate but gradually give way to more selective responses. This is seen in late teenagers whose sexual responses become more focused on specific erotic cues or direct stimulation of the breasts or genitals.

Although some of these early reflexive responses result in orgasm, this is not the primary goal. Kinsey *et al.* (1953) reported that while orgasms among infant boys and girls do occur, what is unclear is how frequently they occur and what proportion of infants experience these. He suggested that, although these probably do not occur every day, they are more frequent than adults realise.

## Sexual development in children

The progressive nature and development of sexual behaviour in children is dependent on a number of factors. These consist of sociocultural norms and expectations as reflected in the family. These family interactions and values are intertwined with interpersonal experiences and intrapsychic influences. These in turn become integrated into the development of the child's cognitive abilities with regard to thinking, interpreting and extracting meaning.

Each stage of development is associated with certain characteristics in children's sexual development. Because parental responses are crucial it is useful to know how best to respond to children's emerging sexuality (see Table 2.4). Such responses allow children to feel comfortable with their bodies and sexuality, which ultimately can protect them from CSA.

### Sexual behaviour in pre-school children (0–4)

The development of sexual behaviour, like other childhood behaviour, takes the form of play. Play is a spontaneous, light-hearted information-gathering process that represents a continuum of curiosity about the world, self-discovery, and delight in the body and exploring differences and similarities. It is way of gaining an understanding and constructing meaning about the world and the child's experience of it.

Solitary play that is most evident in the first two years of life is often considered to be autoerotic in being self-pleasurable not sexual. Later it becomes increasingly more social, and as such socio-sexual. In the autoerotic phase, between birth and two years of age, the child's play is solitary as peer interaction is limited. Natural curiosity and observation drives this play. The most common form of sexual play focuses on self-exploration and self-manipulation. It is most frequently seen between six and twelve months with over one-third of infants playing with their genitals. The baby discovers that when certain parts of the body are touched, poked, rubbed, exposed to the air, or otherwise stimulated pleasant sensations occur. This is usually discovered by accident.

If the sensory experience is pleasurable, it is more likely to be repeated. This can be seen during nappy changing when the baby touches or strokes its genitals. This stimulation is thought to represent soothing and comfort behaviour, a form of tension reduction or distraction that is accompanied by physical and sensual pleasure. To what extent such touching is repeated is dependent on how the parent reacts to such self-exploration. If the baby's hand is hit or pushed away the touching is less likely to recur. Parents negatively or positively reinforce such accidental touching of the genitals by their responses.

Between the ages of two and four there is an increased interest in bathroom activities (initially through potty training) in which the child follows and watches the adult with apparent fascination. This is accompanied by a delight in the use of lavatorial language such as 'pooh pooh' and 'wee wee'. These words are often endlessly repeated while monitoring adult responses and testing their reactions to its use. Slang words for body parts, especially the genitals, are also constantly repeated to monitor adult responses.

The infant may poke and squeeze the breasts of adult females, which is often accompanied by laughter or running away in delight. This represents curiosity and exploration of observed differences between adult males and females. The child may also indulge in showing the genitals to others. This is dependent on the guidance and limits set by parents. An overly punished child might resort to occasional streaking.

Prior to age one the infant is not capable of volitional behaviour necessary for manual masturbation due to lack of muscle control. As the baby gets older and has more dexterity and muscle control (around the age of two and a half to three) the toddler may simulate masturbation either by using their own hands, or by rubbing the genitals. This often involves using stuffed toys, blankets, dolls, arms of chairs or by rhythmically thrusting the genitals against objects. The function of this behaviour is to obtain soothing and pleasurable stimulation.

Genital touching, exploration and sexual play occur earlier in boys at around six to seven months, compared to girls, where it occurs around 10 to 11 months. Autoerotic activity is twice as common in the first year of life in boys as it is in girls. This may in part be due to the penis being more overtly displayed and accessible, and thus more observable in terms of masturbation. While the most common activity in boys is fondling the penis, in girls the autoerotic activity is focused on the manual stimulation of the clitoris rather than exploration of the vaginal opening. Two out of three female children learn to masturbate through accidental discovery during this phase. Those that do not may not learn to masturbate until adulthood.

Infantile masturbation is thus a normal activity with erotic potential derived from manual stimulation, thigh friction, rubbing genitals against toys, dolls, furniture and adults. Such masturbation is seen as a healthy process of self-discovery. In fact, Spitz (1949) found that masturbation was more frequently observed (61–91%) in healthy home environments than in residential treatment centres. Although autoerotic self-exploration and masturbation is normal practice, it is by no means universal and as such is dependent on culturally influenced practices and family acceptance.

Masturbation during this phase is initially discovered accidentally as the infant explores the body randomly. When in contact with the genitals it is experienced as a source of pleasure, which is then repeated. This can awaken an erotic component in which the genitals are associated with desire and pleasure. As the child develops, the self-exploration becomes more focused and the sexual intent more obvious (Kleeman 1975). This early autoerotic play may not be remembered during this phase but re-emerges and is relearned during later stages of development. One study of four to fourteen-year-old boys found that 38 per cent reported masturbation between the ages of three and seven.

From two onwards, more peer interactions and socio-sexual play replace solitary play. This is characterised by showing off the genitals, especially erections, to others. This is accompanied by embarrassment, covering up and peeking. Here the emphasis is on discovering and learning about gender differences and similarities in terms of genitals. Sexual activities increasingly involve interactions with others which include kissing, hugging, touching, using rude words and telling rude jokes, although these may not always be experienced as erotic. In cultures and families where free expression is tolerated there may be less inhibition in touching genitals.

While most children investigate and exhibit their own and their peers' genitals, the interest is fairly cursory and superficial. The most popular games are 'playing house', 'mummies and daddies', and 'doctors and nurses'. When playing 'mummies and daddies' the children may hug, kiss, lay in bed together, side by side, and pretend to make babies. Usually these occur fully dressed, or partially unclothed, very rarely naked. This is primarily imitative play based on observation of parental behaviour.

Children may also undress dolls and put the male on top of the female, rub them together and make sounds that essentially reflect what they know about adult sexuality, including looking flirtatious and seductive. When playing 'doctors and nurses' the child may include their own experiences of having ears or throat checked. Occasionally this may extend to other body parts such as inserting a thermometer into other orifices. They may also experiment with sticking fingers or other small objects inside other openings such as mouth, nostrils, ears, belly button, or genitals. If such behaviour causes pain or discomfort the child will stop. If the child persists with such behaviours, especially in genital orifices, this may indicate that the child has been sexually abused.

Even when unclothed, the activity does not normally proceed beyond a showing off of the genitals. Less frequent is actual fondling of each other's genitalia, or sticking fingers or objects into the vagina, or anal cavity. It is also unusual for children to engage in mutual masturbation, oral–genital sexual activity, or actual intercourse at this stage (see Table 2.1).

Thus, this socio-sexual exploration is primarily exhibitionistic and voyeuristic. It is innocent and discovery-based, and does not consist of more adult type of sexual activity, which is associated with much older children or those who have experienced or been exposed to adult-type sexual activity.

### Sexual behaviour in school age children (5–12)

According to Kinsey et al. (1948, 1953), by age five, 10 per cent of children will have had their first socio-sexual experience. This reaches a peak for boys by age 12 (39%) and girls by age 9 (14%). While the erotic intent may increase as the child gets older, sexual play nevertheless remains a sporadic activity and does not necessarily increase with the approach of puberty. Masturbation

**Table 2.1 Summary of sexual development and sexual behaviour in pre-school age children, 0–4 years of age**

| Characteristics | Typical sexual behaviour | Atypical sexual behaviour |
|---|---|---|
| Limited peer contact | Self-exploration | Discusses sexual acts |
| Curiosity about their bodies | Self-stimulation | Uses sexually explicit language |
| All babies and toddlers touch their genitals | Touches, rubs own genitals (random) | Has physical sexual contact with other children |
| All experience genital pleasure | Watches others' bodies | Shows adult-like sexual behaviour or knowledge |
| Genital touching increases, especially when tired or going to sleep | Pokes female breasts | Relates to other adults and children in a sexual manner |
| Increasing awareness of gender | Looks at genitals | Rubs themself sexually against others |
| Increasing interest in anatomical differences | Shows off genitals | Compulsive genital touching |
| Increasing interest in differences between children's/adults' bodies | Interested in bathroom functions | Forces sexual contact on other children |
| Curiosity about how babies are made and where they come from | Uses childish/'dirty' language to talk about body parts | Does not stop masturbation or sexual play when asked to |
| Associate genitals with elimination (urination, bowel movements) | Lavatorial language | Inserts objects into openings even if painful |
| Towards end of stage, sense of modesty develops – private/public | Imitative pretend play – 'mummies and daddies', 'doctors and nurses' | Preoccupied with sexual behaviour and activities |
| | Inserts objects into openings but stops if painful | Acts out adult-type sexual behaviour with toys or objects |
| | | Knowledge of taste, texture and smell of semen |

becomes less random and more specific and with intent. Children discover creative ways of masturbating, and it is intentionally repeated. Girls discover that if they lift the vagina toward a waterspout or showerhead in the bath the water stimulation feels good. Boys find that climbing and shimmying down poles feels good on their penis. This information may then subsequently be shared with peers and friends.

This stage is also accompanied by an increase in questions such as, 'Where do I come from?' and 'How are babies made?'. Children seem to be both drawn to and repulsed by overt affectionate or sexual behaviour. They may express a desire to look at pictures of the human body yet be embarrassed and start giggling if they see kissing on television or film. Thus the child might be privately fascinated by affectionate behaviour yet publicly 'grossed out' by it. This may represent the emergence of feelings of privacy and an understanding of the need to cover up, or knock, before entering a bedroom.

There is a continued fascination with dirty jokes, which are repeated endlessly even though the child may not really understand the punch line. The child will also continue to mimic and practise behaviour that has either been observed or experienced. Depending on the sociocultural environment, children may start to have 'boyfriends' and 'girlfriends', albeit very innocently, consisting of no more than holding hands and kissing. The game of 'kiss chase' epitomises this period in which traditionally the girls chase after the boys, wishing to kiss them, while the boys appear to be repulsed by this, making strenuous efforts to avoid capture and the ignominy of being kissed by a girl.

The end of this stage is characterised by a wider range of sexual interests. As there is more peer contact there is more opportunity for experimentation. Nevertheless, there are still periods of inhibition and dis-inhibition. There is huge variation during this stage due to levels of sexual suppression and inhibition toward the end of childhood. Socio-sexual activity and games now consist of mooning, spin the bottle or strip poker (see Table 2.2).

### Sexual behaviour in adolescents/teenagers (13–16)

When coming into puberty, children become increasingly more reticent about public sexual activity and become aware of more social restraints. Thus sexual behaviour begins to merge with more adult behaviour. This is linked to puberty in which hormonal changes activate the development of secondary

**Table 2.2 Summary of sexual development and sexual behaviour in school age children, 5–12 years old**

| Characteristics | Typical sexual behaviour | Atypical sexual behaviour |
|---|---|---|
| Increased peer contact | Increase in consensual experimental interactions | Masturbates in public |
| Other children may bring up new ideas about sex | Touches self – more specifically genitals | Compulsively masturbates |
| Increased need for privacy while bathing and undressing | Masturbates in private – sporadic | Forces sexual activity on other children |
| More inhibited | Increase in pretend play – 'mummies and daddies' | Non-consensual experimentation |
| More modesty about body | Kissing, touching, showing, holding hands | Shows adult-like sexual behaviour |
| More self-conscious about body | Repulsed by/drawn to opposite sex | Shows adult-like sexual knowledge |
|  | Asks questions about menstruation, pregnancy, sexual behaviour | Knows texture, taste and smell of semen |
|  | Talks about sex more | Preoccupation with sexual behaviour and activity |
|  | Increased sexual or obscene language | Relates to adults and children in sexual manner |
|  | Tells dirty jokes | Does not stop sexual behaviour when asked |
|  | Mooning |  |
|  | Exhibitionistic |  |
|  | Dating |  |
|  | Petting |  |
|  | 'Dry humping' (simulating sexual intercourse) |  |
|  | Digital or vaginal intercourse in pre-adolescents |  |
|  | Vaginal intercourse in pre-adolescents |  |

sex characteristics. Hormones influence not only these physical changes but also emotional sensations and reactions.

During puberty there may be an increase in masturbation, which may or not be more exhibitionistic. There is an increase in 'locker room' behaviour in which children may appear nude in front of each other, slap each other's bottoms and retell dirty jokes. Boys may engage in masturbation competitions or ejaculation contests to see who can ejaculate the first, furthest, or the most. Girls begin to compare breast size, bodies and their figures in the nude.

This is accompanied by an increased interest in romance. Teenagers may develop crushes on their peers, both same sex and opposite sex, or adult role models ranging from pop-stars, sporting heroes or teachers. Some adolescents begin dating, which now involves kissing, including open mouth kissing, petting (under and over clothes), touching each other's genitals, 'dry humping' (simulating intercourse), digital vaginal stimulation, or mutual masturbation. Much of this is conducted privately, although kissing and petting competitions in groups do take place. These experiences may subsequently be recounted to other peers to impress.

Self-discovery and observation still primarily determines many of these activities, although children towards the end of this stage do take this sexual activity further. Depending on cultural, moral, religious, or health restrictions, penile/genital contact may be avoided although oral sex may be indulged in. Increases in such activity, including full sexual intercourse, will become more predominant as the child goes through puberty and adolescence (see Table 2.3).

## Parental reactions to children's sexual expression

As can be seen, normative sexual development in children is primarily a learning experience based on information gathered about their own bodies and those of others. Auto-stimulation, self-exploration, kissing, hugging, peeking, touching and exposing genitals to other children is a normal part of child development. In order to compare similarities and differences, children need to explore their own bodies, and those of others, both visually and tactilely. In addition they try out gender roles and behaviours through such games as 'mummies and daddies'. In many respects it represents children exploring the capabilities of their bodies, and is no different to running, jumping, reading or learning. Just as part of all these other activities is

**Table 2.3 Summary of sexual development and sexual behaviour in adolescents/teenagers, 13–16 years old**

| Characteristics | Typical sexual behaviour | Atypical sexual behaviour |
|---|---|---|
| Hormonal changes | Asks questions about relationships and sexual behaviour | Masturbates in public |
| Menstruation in females | Uses sexual language | Has sexual contact with much younger children |
| Development of secondary sex characteristics | Talks about sexual acts between each other | Seeks out the company of younger children and spends an unusual amount of time in their company |
| More self-conscious about body and body changes | Masturbates in private | Takes younger children to 'secret' places or hideaways |
| Increased need for privacy around the body | Experiments sexually with other teenagers of same age | Plays 'special' games with younger children (removing clothes, 'doctors and nurses'), which are unusual for their age |
| Mood swings | Consensual experimentation | Insists on hugging or kissing a child when the child does not want to |
| Confusion about body changes | Digital vaginal intercourse | Frequently uses aggressive language about adults or children |
| Confusion about self-identity | Oral sex | Shows sexual material to younger children |
| Fears about relationships | Petting | Makes sexually abusive phone calls |
| Doubts around sexuality | Sometimes consensual sexual intercourse | Views child pornography on the Internet or elsewhere |
| Fears of getting pregnant | | Exposes his or her genitals to younger children |
| Fears about being attractive and finding partners | | Forces sex on another adolescent or child |
| | | Threatening or bullying children to keep the 'secret' |
| | | Offering bribes such as money or gifts to children to ensure their silence |

imitated, learned and rehearsed for later adult skills, sexual play is a form of sexual rehearsal for later adult sexuality.

What is significant is that natural sexual exploration is continuously balanced by curiosity about other parts of the child's universe. The child is fascinated by how babies are made *and* why there is a moon; by what the physical differences are between males and females *as well as* how to finish homework quickly so they have a longer time to play.

Most importantly, these explorations are usually conducted within similar age groups: similar size, generally mixed gender groups, and friends rather than siblings. Children participate on a voluntary basis ('I'll show you mine if you show me yours') rather than being forced or coerced into such activity. The relationship between the child and its peers when not engaging in sexual activity is amicable and friendly, not hostile or aggressive.

Furthermore, sexual play is driven by curiosity, which is spontaneous, light-hearted, and fun. Much humour and healthy mischievousness, such as who can urinate the furthest, accompany it. Sexual play and exploration is exciting, sometimes feels funny, and has the capacity to make the child giggle. Although it may sometimes feel confusing or guilty, generally it is not accompanied by a deep sense of shame, fear or anxiety. Most children, if discovered in sexual play and instructed to stop, will happily do so and move on to some other equally interesting play activity.

## Parental reactions to children's sexual behaviour

As sexual development is a normal part of all child development, parental reacions need to be appropriate to the developmental age of the child. Parents need to balance the child's sexual interest along with other interests. Parents also need to set boundaries and guidelines about the appropriateness of personal space, closeness, proximity, nudity and self-touching. They need to regulate language, dress, gender role behaviour, appropriate TV, videos and music that the child is exposed to. And while parents may be alarmed or perplexed by observing sexual play in children, they need to be aware of their responses to the child's activity. The response of the parent can have a greater impact on the child than the actual sexual behaviour itself (see Table 2.4).

**Table 2.4 Summary of parental reactions to children's sexual expression and sexual behaviour**

| Pre-school, 0–4 | School age, 5–12 | Adolescents/teenagers, 13–16 |
|---|---|---|
| Holding, touching, cuddling | Be available to talk | Encourage discussion about sex |
| Babies need to like all their body parts including their genitals | Remember sex is a natural part of life | Talk and ask questions |
| Allow child to enjoy and take pleasure in body | Provide age-appropriate information | Maintain calm and non-critical atmosphere |
| Convey respect for the child's feelings and experience | Repeat information if necessary | Be relaxed and comfortable talking about sex – otherwise the teenager will go elsewhere for their information |
| Do not shame the child for touching its genitals | Check out what the child already knows | Use language that feels comfortable and is understandable |
| Remember genital play and masturbation are normal and universal | Ask what the child thinks | Keep a sense of perspective |
| Accept child's genital exploration | Keep answers simple and age-appropriate | Keep a sense of humour |
| Be positive in responses by smiling and acknowledging that 'it feels good' | Do not frighten the child | Be honest about own discomfort in talking about sex |
| Do not punish child for their sexual experimentation | Do not evade questions about sex | Relate sex to love, intimacy, caring, respect for oneself and partners |
| Use correct words for sexual body parts | Teach child that sexuality is a valuable part of human experience | Share your own values and beliefs |
| Model affectionate, caring relationships | Review reproduction facts | Discuss importance of responsibility for choices and decisions |
| Guide child to distinguish between 'good' and 'bad' touch | If shy talking about sex, practise with an adult friend first to get used to talking about sex without feeling embarrassed | Help teenagers to consider pros and cons of sexual behaviour |
| | Read books about sex with the child | |
| | Set rules around sex such as What, When, Where, with Whom, and Why | |

*continued on next page*

| Pre-school, 0–4 | School age, 5–12 | Adolescents/teenagers, 13–16 |
|---|---|---|
| Guide child's genital exploration by explaining about privacy – private vs. public | Think like a child – look at it from the child's point of view | Provide open, honest communication |
| Allow child to say 'No' if it feels uncomfortable around certain touch or physical contact | Set sex into context of other knowledge about the child's world | Talk about healthy and unhealthy relationships – disrespect, emotional blackmail, roller-coaster emotions, clinging, neediness, smothering, emotional, physical, and sexual abuse |
| Talk with the child | | Encourage the teenager to be streetwise and aware of risky situations such as date rape, alcohol and drugs |
| Answer child's questions about sex | | |
| Talk about how people reproduce | | Role-play/rehearse how they might deal with unwanted sexual advances/pressure |
| Provide age-appropriate information | | |
| Set sex into context in relation to other things in the child's world | | Do not lecture |
| Set appropriate rules and boundaries | | Do not nag |
| Listen to the child | | Brief discussions are better than lengthy, drawn-out ones |
| Do not judge the child | | |
| Try to relax and feel more comfortable around child's sexual behaviour | | |
| Try to feel more comfortable talking about sex with the child | | |
| Be calm and relaxed when talking to child as you would when talking about other things that interest the child | | |

While it is important for parents to prevent unnecessary, inappropriate and unwelcome sexual stimulation, care must be taken not to make the child feel guilty for normal sexual curiosity, sexual exploration and socio-sexual play. Parents need to discourage coercion and exploitative sexual behaviour without stifling all sexual expression. They need to demonstrate good judgement about personal boundaries, nudity, bath-time (avoid too great a disparity in ages), sleeping arrangements and a sense of privacy. In the same way that parents socialise children in terms of learning appropriate behaviour and knowledge about themselves and the world, they need to socialise children's sexual behaviour within the behavioural norms of society.

Thus much of sexual behaviour in children is role-play, based on imitative behaviour in order for the child to learn about adult roles. Parents must be aware that children may have a very different understanding and interpretation of sexual behaviour and they need to guide the child appropriately, using language that will foster understanding rather than make the child feel ashamed or guilty. Such guidance can be reinforced with appropriate sex education at school.

## Differences in age-appropriate sexual play and sexual abuse

There are numerous differences between age-appropriate sexual play and sexual abuse that need to be clarified. These are given in the box on the following page.

## Atypical sexual behaviour in children

The sexual behaviour displayed by children who have been sexually abused, or who sexually molest other children, is significantly different to what we see in typical sexual development of children. Children who have been sexually abused tend to engage in persistent, inappropriate sexual behaviour. They display many more sexual behaviours, often much more sophisticated in terms of knowledge and sexual acts compared to their peers. Such children may act out the full spectrum of adult sexual behaviour, including oral sex, forcible penetration of objects into the vagina and anus, and vaginal and anal sexual intercourse. The focus and interest in sex is thus out of balance with their peers, in terms of the intensity and frequency with which they engage in sexual activity. This is characterised by a distinct obsessive/compulsive quality to it rather than the sporadic interest seen in typical sexual development.

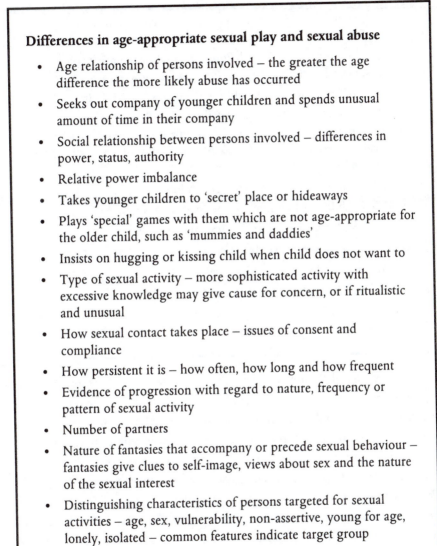

**Differences in age-appropriate sexual play and sexual abuse**

- Age relationship of persons involved – the greater the age difference the more likely abuse has occurred
- Seeks out company of younger children and spends unusual amount of time in their company
- Social relationship between persons involved – differences in power, status, authority
- Relative power imbalance
- Takes younger children to 'secret' place or hideaways
- Plays 'special' games with them which are not age-appropriate for the older child, such as 'mummies and daddies'
- Insists on hugging or kissing child when child does not want to
- Type of sexual activity – more sophisticated activity with excessive knowledge may give cause for concern, or if ritualistic and unusual
- How sexual contact takes place – issues of consent and compliance
- How persistent it is – how often, how long and how frequent
- Evidence of progression with regard to nature, frequency or pattern of sexual activity
- Number of partners
- Nature of fantasies that accompany or precede sexual behaviour – fantasies give clues to self-image, views about sex and the nature of the sexual interest
- Distinguishing characteristics of persons targeted for sexual activities – age, sex, vulnerability, non-assertive, young for age, lonely, isolated – common features indicate target group
- Use of fear, intimidation, aggression, coercion, exploitation would indicate sexual abuse
- Ritualistic or sadistic behaviours are not associated with consensual exploration

- Secrecy – if attempts to secure secrecy are present there is a need to explore the reasons for this as they differ from the secretive nature of consensual sexual activity
- Deliberate sexual/erotic intent – as opposed to mutual experimentation or exploration
- Lack of spontaneity, fun, delight – mutual experimentation includes a lot of giggling and fun, not fear and terror
- Lack of mutuality – if the child feels as though it is being abused, or blames him or herself for what has happened
- How the activity was revealed – did disclosure result from an inadvertent comment or following a period of distress or changed behaviour, also if the victim disclosed
- Shows sexual material to younger children
- Views child pornography on the Internet or elsewhere
- Exposes his or her genitals to younger children
- Forces sex on to other children
- Makes sexually abusive phone calls
- Frequently uses aggressive sexual language about adults or children
- Shares alcohol or other drugs with younger children

For sexually abused children the genitals may function as the 'central organising principle' in their development, which can result in sexually preoccupied behaviour and compulsive masturbation. If the child has been exposed to too much sexual stimulation, either through sexual abuse, boundary violations or exposure to pornography, it cannot integrate its experiences in a meaningful way. In seeking to integrate such experiences and make sense of them, the child becomes preoccupied with sex. This results in acting out their premature sexual experiences in the form of developmentally advanced and frequent sexual behaviour. This preoccupation with sex is also seen in sexual themes in their art work or in more general play activities.

Acting out may also be an unconscious attempt to alert the adult to the sexual abuse and the child's confusion. In many respects it reflects their deep shame, intense guilt and pervasive anxiety about sexuality. The sexual behaviour and activity may also be an attempt at making a human connection in a world that is chaotic, dangerous and unfriendly. The child may already see itself as a sexual object and use it as a commodity to make friends or gain an adult's attention. This may be the only way the child knows how to relate to others. Often the child finds it hard to make friends within their own peer group so chooses younger, more vulnerable children to engage in sexual activities.

All sexually abused children are emotionally very vulnerable and for many of them sex becomes a coping mechanism to deal with their distress, especially their pain, their feelings of hurt, their fears and anxieties, and their intense loneliness and sense of abandonment. Thus sex becomes a type of comfort behaviour. These children take no delight in their bodies and do not see the sexual activity as fun.

The confusion around sex may lead to rage, anger, anxiety and fear which are then paired with aggression. This aggression is then acted out in the sexual activity with other children. The sexual behaviour in sexually abused children is never spontaneous or light-hearted. Rather it consists of aggression, the use of force, violence or threats, coercion and a lack of mutual consent. They often swear the other child into secrecy under threat of violence or getting into trouble.

When the sexual activity is discovered the child does not stop the activity, as we would see in more typical sexual development. The sexually abused child will often present a blasé, matter of fact attitude about the sexual behaviour, showing little or no emotion. It will frequently deny all responsibility and have no empathy for its victim.

Other associated behaviours that may indicate that the child has been sexually abused relate to shame and embarrassment about their bodies. They may show an enormous reluctance to change their underwear for weeks on end. They may also feel compelled to sniff soiled underwear. These can be related to fears and anxieties about their bodies, or a form of protection. Unconsciously the child may see dirty and soiled underwear as a protection from being sexually assaulted or as a symbolic representation of how they feel about themselves as dirty and smelly.

Fears and anxieties may be reflected in bathroom activities such toileting with the child urinating or defecating outside the toilet, on the floor, on beds, or outdoors. The sexually abused child may also stuff the lavatory with loo paper until it overflows. Others may use excessive amounts of loo paper because they relate wiping and cleaning themselves to masturbation. While these behaviours may indicate sexual abuse they cannot be seen in isolation. It is crucial that adults put them into context with other behaviours displayed by the child, which may indicate a history of sexual abuse. For a more detailed discussion of the range of indicators of child sexual abuse, and the signs and symptoms that are associated with such abuse, see Chapter 7.

Suffice it to say that there are considerable differences in sexual development in children. Normal sexual development is characterised by curiosity and exploration, which is spontaneous, fun and consensual. Such sexual interest is directed at the self and in relation to children around the same age. It is sporadic and generally embedded with other interests in the child world.

In contrast, the sexual development of children who have been sexually abused is characterised by compulsive sexual behaviours, which are more aggressive, out of balance with their peer group and include more adult-type sexual acts. Sexual activities are most frequently directed at younger, more vulnerable children, and as such are not consensual but based on coercion or force. They lack mutuality and exploration, which are based on curiosity, but represent an acting out of sexual acts perpetrated on them.

It is crucial that parents and teachers can distinguish between typical sexual development and sexual behaviour in a child, on the one hand, and what is considered atypical, on the other. Such knowledge enables adults to be aware of a child who may be experiencing sexual abuse, or who may be sexually abusing other children. Given that currently about 30 per cent of CSA is committed by adolescents it is necessary to be able to identify those who are at risk of sexually abusing other children, before they embark on a lifelong path of CSA. We will return to adolescents at risk of sexually abusing children in the next chapter, which examines the different types of child sexual abuser

## Chapter 3

# Child Sexual Abusers

No single 'profile' accurately describes or accounts for all child molesters.

Prentky *et al.* (1997)

I was disabled and spent months grooming the parents, so they could tell their children to take me out and help me. No-one thought that disabled people could be abusers.

Convicted paedophile

In order to protect children it is essential to be aware what type of person sexually abuses children. If we can get into the mind of a paedophile we may find out what motivates them and what type of child is at risk. It also enables us to identify how paedophiles target and groom the child and what strategies they use to stop the child from disclosing. Armed with accurate information, it becomes possible to protect children from being abused.

Our knowledge about paedophiles and child sexual abusers is nevertheless limited to the 10 per cent who come to the attention of the criminal justice system. We know virtually nothing about the 90 per cent of child sexual abusers who have not been detected. This means that researchers and clinicians have to infer from their limited knowledge base what motivates child sexual abusers, and the significance of patterns of sexual offending against children. Although the knowledge base is still in its infancy, increased awareness and reporting of CSA does provide considerable information, which can be used effectively in the protection of children.

In previous decades, parents, teachers and children were warned about 'stranger danger' and instructed to be aware of strangers lurking near playgrounds and parks. These were often thought to be easily identifiable as 'dirty old men in raincoats'. Nowadays, we need to warn children not just about 'stranger danger' but also about adults who may be known to them in their community or neighbourhood. This is not to instil fear and suspicion in the child so that it is too afraid to go out in its local environment, but to allow it to be more aware of potential dangers.

High profile cases of child abductions, and sexually motivated murders of children such as Sarah Payne, Holly Wells and Jessica Chapman, have understandably generated enormous fears and anxieties in both parents and children. However, it is important to note that these are not a representative example of the range of child sexual abuse (CSA). The abduction and sexual killing of children does happen but is rare in comparison with the level of CSA that occurs on a daily basis in many communities. Around five to eight children a year are abducted and murdered in the UK, a figure that has remained stable for the last 30 years.

The biggest risk of CSA is in the local community, with 87 per cent of sexual assaults committed by someone who is known to the child, such as a family member, neighbour or family friend (ChildLine 2003). Such abuse is much more systematic, often continues over a number of years, and includes a large number of children in the same area. The abuse is often not detected, leaving the abusers free to sexually abuse increasingly more children.

It is crucial that parents, teachers and other professionals who are concerned with the welfare of children are aware that CSA does not always start with abduction or rape or end in murder. To believe that all paedophiles are the same and commit such extreme offences can lull us into a false sense of security. CSA has many permutations, consists of many different types of abusive acts, and includes very different types of abusers.

The majority of those who are paedophiles are people who are known to us, yet we may not be aware that they sexually abuse children. Invariably they are trusted, not demonised, and as a result they represent a much more sinister danger to our children by remaining undetected. There is a fine balance between demonising paedophiles, which instils fear in children, and equipping them with sufficient knowledge to feel safe and protected in their community. Parents, teachers and other professionals can facilitate this balance. The better informed adults are about paedophiles the more effectively they can equip children to keep safe.

It is not my intention in this chapter to demonise paedophiles. While I understand that they invoke fear and terror in both adults and children, and have the capacity to destroy their victims and families, my aim is to provide accurate knowledge about what motivates such individuals to sexually abuse a child. Demonising them does not achieve anything and only makes paedophiles reluctant to talk about their motivations and experiences. Ultimately, this impedes our understanding of the mind of the paedophile, which in turn may deprive us of relevant information that may enable us to protect children more effectively.

There is some evidence to suggest that some sexual abusers were themselves victims of CSA. A recent clinical study found that 35 per cent of male child sexual abusers had a history of CSA, with the majority abused by a female relative (Glasser *et al.* 2001). However, a relationship between CSA and later sexual offending against children was not supported in female sexual abusers. This suggests that there are other factors that may lead to sexual offending against children. Ray Wyre (1996) has suggested that to understand why some victims go on to abuse, one needs to look at the type of abuser, the relationship formed with the child and the child's experience of the abuse.

This is particularly evident when looking at the child and adolescent child sexual abuser. Reports of CSA by children and teenagers have increased dramatically over the last ten years. This reflects what researchers have discovered in working with adult paedophiles, namely that many paedophiles start sexually offending against children while teenagers. If health professionals and clinicians can detect such early abuse and provide appropriate intervention, a long career of CSA may be diverted, thereby protecting hundreds and thousands of children.

Demonising paedophiles as a special category of people, who all share the same characteristics, creates a 'them and us' mentality, with paedophiles being evil, mad or bad, and those who do not sexually abuse children as being 'normal', sane and good. This fails to take into consideration the fact that people who behave as good, upstanding citizens, and appear to be normal and sane, can and do sexually abuse children.

Paedophiles possess a wide range of characteristics, including the range of 'normal' behaviour. Indeed, the fact that they look and behave normally creates a sense of trust in adults and safety in children. The fact that they do not look odd, different or strange, or behave in abnormal or suspicious ways, makes them harder to identify. It also makes it easier for them to target and groom both parents and children.

Child sexual abusers need to have access to children. They need to instil a sense of security and trust in both parents, teachers and children in order to target their victims and groom the desired child. If they look strange or suspicious it is harder to find a victim. Paedophiles make deliberate attempts to appear as normal as possible to allay any fears or suspicions that adults and children might have.

Paedophiles, however, are not uniform and have different patterns of sexual offending against children. Researchers have identified a number of different types of paedophiles with different characteristics, motivations and a range of different strategies to sexually abuse children. This chapter will look at these different types of paedophile with the aim of increasing awareness and understanding of the range of child sexual abusers.

The chapter will look first at the development of the sexual arousal cycle of paedophiles, followed by an examination of some of the factors that need to be overcome before CSA can take place. It will then look at the various types of adult male paedophiles, including those that sexually abuse within the family. This is followed by an exploration of the different types of female child sexual abusers, their characteristics, motivations and behaviours. Consideration is also given to current knowledge about children and adolescents who sexually abuse children.

## Typical arousal cycle of paedophiles

Research demonstrates that fantasy-masturbation-orgasm to deviant sexual fantasies increases the possibility of moving on to contact sexual offending (Sullivan and Beech 2003, 2004; Sandberg and Marlatt 1989), how this overcomes internal inhibitors (Marshall *et al.*, 1999) and contributes to rehearsal and motivation for further offending (Ward and Hudson 2000). Sexual preferences once conditioned are notoriously difficult to change (Conrad and Wincze 1976; Laws and Marshall 1990, 1991; McConaghy 1975). All sexual behaviours are learned and acquired through observation or direct experience. They are heavily influenced by cultural values and beliefs, socialisation of males and females, as well as attitudes within the family. Early childhood experiences, including issues of power and status, can also influence the development of sexual behaviour. Aggressive sexual behaviours are further influenced by exposure to pornography and early childhood sexual trauma.

Paedophilia and CSA can be understood as learned behaviour in which the pairing of fantasies and images of children is combined with masturbation, which both establishes and maintains the sexual behaviour towards children. Prior to any actual assault on a child a paedophile might typically begin his arousal by fantasising and masturbating to children. Initially this could be to innocuous, non-sexual images of child(ren) from magazines or children's clothing catalogues. At this stage the image may be a headshot in which the child is fully clothed. If the paedophile has had previous encounters with children, he may fantasise and masturbate to these.

Like much learned behaviour in humans, it is the association between two separate and distinct stimuli that creates a new, or habitual, behavioural response. A good example is a smoker who associates smoking with drinking alcohol and cannot engage in one without the other. The paedophile associates fantasies or images of children with sexual arousal, and thus whenever he sees or thinks about children he becomes sexually aroused. This sexual arousal and pleasure in relation to children leads to masturbation in which the cycle of fantasy, arousal and masturbation is repeated, leading to learned behaviour. This becomes what psychologists call classical, or Pavlovian, conditioning.

Orgasm and ejaculation as a result of masturbation to the fantasies or images of the child has a rewarding component. Psychologists believe that behaviours that have a pleasant and satisfying outcome are more likely to be repeated than those that are unpleasant. Thus the paedophile is rewarded, or positively reinforced, in the arousal cycle through orgasm, a process called operant conditioning. Sullivan and Beech (2004) show how sexual arousal occurs and develops (see Figure 3.1). The reward of orgasm may stimulate the abuser to repeat the arousal cycle to obtain maximum pleasure and relief.

Thus the pairing of fantasy and masturbation, plus the positive reinforcement of the orgasm, conditions the sexual arousal to, and sexual behaviour with, children. This becomes learned behaviour, which is maintained by repeated masturbation to images and fantasies of children. Over time, this repeated cycle may result in the paedophile habituating to the initial images and fantasies. That is to say, with repeated exposure the abuser may find the images or fantasies become less stimulating and arousing, especially if they are fairly innocuous or non-sexual. One can liken this to watching one's first horror film. Although initially arousing and terrifying, repeated exposure reduces the terror, prompting the individual to seek out increasingly more scary films in order to recapture the feeling of arousal and terror.

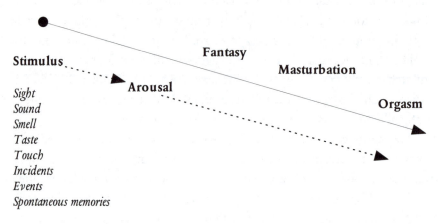

*Figure 3.1 Sexual arousal cycle (adpated from Sullivan and Beech 2003, p.12)*

Similarly, the paedophile needs increasingly more sexualised or erotic imagery of children, which may only be achieved by looking at more erotic images of children such as child pornography. Repeated exposure to such erotic images results in further habituation with the paedophile no longer finding them as satisfying or by taking longer to masturbate to them. Over time this cycle may prove increasingly less satisfying, prompting the abuser to act out the fantasy. In looking at child pornography, the abuser rationalises that because other children are being sexually abused in the pornography he can also find a child to sexually assault. This can lead to an escalation of the offending by the paedophile actually targeting and grooming a child in reality, instead of relying on erotic images.

## Typical child sexual abuse cycle

Wolf's (1984) cycle of sexual offending clearly illustrates the stages of sexual offending leading up to and immediately after abuse contact (see Figure 3.2).

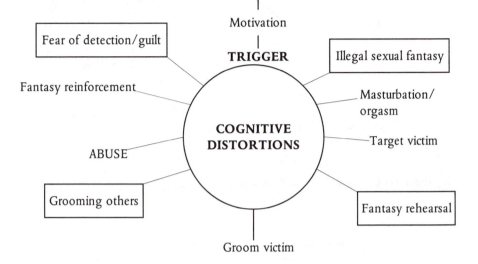

*Figure 3.2 Cycle of sexual offending (Wolf 1984)*

Expanding on Wolf's cycle of sexual offending, Eldridge (1990) proposes three further cycles to understand how sexual offenders react after committing the sexual offending and how this impacts future offences. Eldridge (1998) identifies three cycles – the 'continuous cycle', the 'inhibited cycle', and the 'short circuit cycle' – each of which are associated with different offending patterns.

In the continuous cycle (Figure 3.3) the sexual abuser will activate the cycle continuously and consistently but with a new victim each time. In the inhibited cycle the sexual offender may become blocked, or inhibited, after committing a sexual offence and avoid further sexual offending for a period of time. Despite abstaining from committing a sexual contact offence they nevertheless retreat into the sexual fantasy-masturbation-orgasm cycle to child pornographic images fuelling their sexual interest in children and attempt to overcome their inhibitions. Once these inhibitors have been overcome they may reoffend with a new victim (see Figure 3.4).

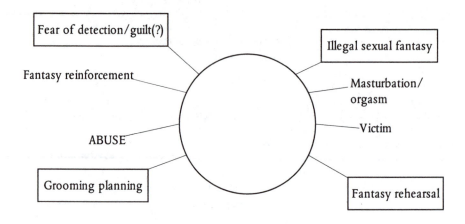

*Figure 3.3 The continuous cycle (Eldridge 2000)*

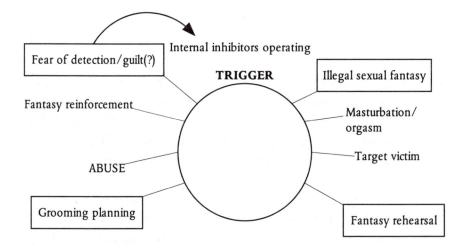

*Figure 3.4 The inhibited cycle (Eldridge 2000)*

The short circuit cycle is commonly associated with sexual offenders who repeatedly abuse the same child, with whom they have regular contact such as within the family, or a child that has already been groomed by them (see Figure 3.5). Here the abuser, having already groomed the child and overcome any inhibitions, moves straight from fantasy rehearsal to sexual abuse (Eldridge 1998).

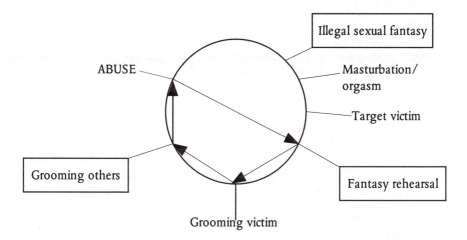

*Figure 3.5 The short circuit cycle (Eldridge 2000)*

To assist a better understanding of the conceptualisations proposed by Wolf (1984) and Finkelhor (1986), Sullivan has developed the concept of 'the spiral of sexual abuse'. The spiral of abuse expands upon the work of Wolf and Finkelhor by 'illustrating the developing and escalating nature of abuse' (Sullivan 2002). As can be seen from Figure 3.6, the spiral of abuse clearly depicts the development of sexual abuse from motivation to actual contact offence, incorporating the role of illegal sexual arousal, guilt and fear of consequences, cognitive distortions, fantasy and masturbation, refining cognitive distortions and preparation to offend. This framework provides greater flexibility to understand the variety of sexual offending patterns from opportunistic stranger attacks to carefully planned sexual abuse within families, and can be applied to both male and female sexual abusers. Sullivan also incorporates the development of strategies such as the targeting, grooming and re-grooming of victims, including the grooming of others, especially parents or those who are responsible for the care and protection of children such as teachers and carers.

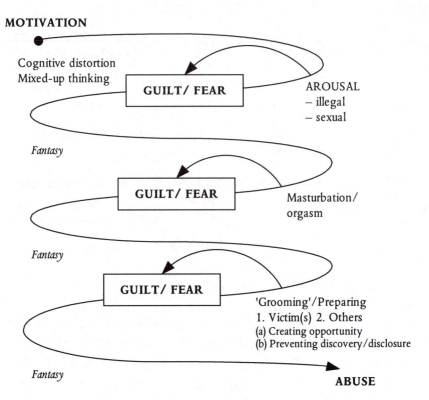

*Figure 3.6 The spiral of abuse (Sullivan and Beech 2003, p.16)*

The typical child sexual abuse cycle involves an interlocking series of thoughts, feelings and behaviours, which culminate in sexual assault. This incorporates highly addictive and compulsive behaviour patterns, which are focused on short-term gratification. This cycle is as follows:

- predisposition to sexually abuse children
- fantasy and masturbatory arousal – rage, anxiety, boredom, depression, stress
- distorted thinking
- high risk behaviours – child pornography
- high risk situations – parks, schools, bathtime
- target selection – choosing victim for age, appearance
- planning
- grooming the victim

- overcoming victim's hesitancy
- initiating offence
- maintaining secrecy
- remorse or fear of detection
- distorted thinking – re-interpreting the child's experience and responsibility
- normalising behaviour
- maintaining behaviour
- trapped
- escalation of offences to maintain same level of high.

Once the paedophile has overcome any internal and external inhibitors s(he) will start the grooming process (see Chapter 5). Throughout the grooming process, the paedophile will repeat the cycle of fantasy, masturbation and ejaculation in anticipation of the actual assault. In many ways the abuser is practising the sexual abuse in his/her head with opportunities to elaborate and refine his/her strategies for abusing. Fantasy allows the abuser to re-live past sexual assaults, which can be embellished.

When the abuser finally breaks down the child's resistance, the sexual assault can commence. This may necessitate the abuser reinterpreting the victim's behaviour as 'she wanted it' or 'he made me do it', which serves to justify the assault. This leads to further distorted thinking in which the abuser re-interprets the victim's behaviour, and minimises the level of harm. The abuser uses this kind of distorted thinking to distort the child's reality, thus allowing him to rationalise and normalise his behaviour.

Murphy (1990) has identified a number of cognitive distortions that child sexual abusers engage in, especially justification – by denying the moral and psychological impact of CSA, distorting the victim's experience, and devaluing or dehumanising the victim. Justification has also been found by Durkin and Bryant (1999) in which abusers deny the victim's experience and level of harm, denying the abuser's responsibility by blaming the victim, all of which facilitates further sexual offending.

Other researchers have found evidence for faulty cognitive processing (Ward *et al.* 1998, 2000), including a lack of empathy and issues around intimacy. It is thought that paedophiles lack awareness of other people's beliefs, desires and needs and that they are unable to infer or interpret the mental states of others. Deficits in cognitive processing are thought to cluster around describing, explaining, interpreting, evaluating, denying, and minimising others' experiences. However, these may not be actual deficits but represent deeply embedded and habitual distortions, which allow paedophiles to sexually abuse children.

This goes some way to describing how paedophiles establish their sexual arousal to children, and how it is maintained, yet it does not explain all the factors that are seen in CSA. While sexual arousal to children is essential, abusers may have other motivations that are not sexually driven. Groth *et al.* (1982) argue that CSA is in essence a pseudo-sexual act which serves to satisfy non-sexual needs such as the need for power and control. Phelen (1995) suggests that child sexual abusers distort and confuse sex and love with power and control issues and rationalise these by misinterpreting the child's responses.

Many child sexual abusers re-interpret negative feelings in order to justify the assault. Such distorted thinking allows the abuser to 'normalise' the sexual behaviour, which then serves to maintain the sexual abuse. Paedophiles often retreat into sexual fantasies about children during times of stress or when in an emotionally vulnerable state, which reactivates the cycle to abuse, in which they become trapped.

It can be seen that in order to commit CSA certain factors must be present, not least sexual arousal to children, the ability to overcome both internal and external inhibitors, as well as the child's resistance.

## Preconditions for child sexual abuse

Finkelhor (1984) proposes a multi-factor model based on a variety of causal factors that researchers and workers in the field have identified as contributing to CSA. This hierarchical model includes individual factors related to the abuser, the victim, and the family, as well as social and cultural factors. The model provides an adaptable and flexible framework, which can accommodate new developments and research data to aid our understanding of child sexual abuse, both outside and inside the family.

Central to the model is the issue of responsibility, which is firmly lodged with the abuser. The model clearly emphasises that sexual abuse can only take place if the abuser already has sexual feelings towards children. Although

Finkelhor includes aspects of the child's and non-abusing parent(s)' behaviour, it is made abundantly clear that these are only considered relevant in response to the abuser's sexual interest (Sanderson 1995).

The strength of the model is that it incorporates both psychological factors, such as the motivation of the abuser, the existence of internal inhibitors and the vulnerability of the child, and sociological factors, such as socialisation, the use of pornography, social tolerance of eroticising children, unequal power relationships between adults and children, and power relationships between males and females (Sanderson 1995). Consideration is given to the fact that children do not necessarily have to be passive victims, although they often are. If children are made aware of the dangers of sexual abuse, are given permission to resist, and provided with information about how to resist, they may be able to protect themselves.

Finkelhor (1984) argues that all the known factors contributing to CSA can be grouped into four preconditions, which need to be met prior to abuse taking place. The presence of only one condition, such as the opportunity to sexually abuse the child, is not sufficient to explain CSA. It can only be achieved if all four preconditions are met in the following order:

1. *Motivation:* The potential abuser needs to have some motivation to sexually abuse a child. Thus, he/she will need to find children erotically and sexually desirable.

2. *Internal inhibitions:* The potential abuser must overcome internal inhibitions that may act against his/her motivation to sexually abuse.

3. *External inhibitions:* The potential abuser has to overcome external obstacles and inhibitions prior to sexually abusing the child.

4. *Resistance:* The potential abuser has to overcome the child's possible resistance to being sexually abused.

Each of the four preconditions contain a number of factors and components that need to be present (see Table 3.1). These are now described.

*Precondition I: Motivation*

This is the thinking stage, which is characterised by the motivation or desire to abuse a child sexually. This motivation may come from any one, or a mixture of two or all three, of the following.

| Table 3.1 Preconditions for sexual abuse | | |
|---|---|---|
| | *Psychological* | *Sociological* |
| **Precondition 1: Factors related to motivation to sexually abuse** | | |
| Emotional congruence | Arrested emotional development<br><br>Need to feel powerful and controlling<br><br>Re-enactment of childhood trauma to undo the hurt | Masculine requirement to be dominant and powerful in sexual relationship |
| Sexual arousal | Childhood sexual experience that was traumatic or wrongly conditioned<br><br>Modelling of sexual interest in children by someone else<br><br>Misattribution of arousal cues<br><br>Biologic abnormality | Child pornography<br><br>Erotic portrayal of children in advertising<br><br>Male tendency to sexualise all emotional needs |
| Blockage | Oedipal conflict<br><br>Castration anxiety<br><br>Fear of adult females<br><br>Traumatic sexual experience with adult<br><br>Inadequate social skills<br><br>Marital problems | Repressive norms about masturbation and extramarital sex |
| **Precondition II: Factors predisposing to overcoming internal inhibitors** | | |
| | Alcohol<br><br>Psychosis<br><br>Impulse disorder<br><br>Senility<br><br>Failure of incest inhibition mechanism in family dynamics | Social toleration of sexual interest in children<br><br>Weak criminal sanctions against offenders<br><br>Ideology of patriarchal prerogatives for fathers<br><br>Social toleration for deviance committed while intoxicated<br><br>Child pornography<br><br>Male inability to identify with needs of children |

*Adapted from Finkelhor (1984)*

| Precondition III: Factors predisposing to overcoming external inhibitors | | |
|---|---|---|
| | Mother who is absent or ill | Lack of social support |
| | Mother who is not close to or protective of child | Barriers to women's equality |
| | | Erosion of social networks |
| | Mother who is dominated or abused by father | Ideology of family sanctity |
| | Social isolation of family | |
| | Unusual opportunities to be alone with child | |
| | Lack of supervision of child | |
| | Unusual sleeping patterns of child | |
| **Precondition IV: Factors predisposing to overcoming child's resistance** | | |
| | Child is emotionally insecure or deprived | Unavailability of sex education for children |
| | Child who lacks knowledge of sexual abuse | Social powerlessness of children |
| | Situation of unusual trust between child and offender | |

EMOTIONAL CONGRUENCE

The abuser wants to satisfy an *emotional need*. Initially this may not be overtly sexual but may be represented by power or anger. There is a 'fit' between the adult's emotional needs and the characteristics of the child, which may have arisen because the adult is arrested (or stuck) at the same psychosexual level of development as the child. It could also be due to the abuser's low self-esteem and belief that the child will make him or her feel *powerful*. In some cases the abuser may be playing out the role of abuser in reversing an earlier traumatic experience. Alternatively, the abuser's own socialisation experiences as a child encourage a belief that a child is an appropriate object of sexual interest.

SEXUAL AROUSAL

The abuser is sexually aroused by children and/or non-consensual sex. Early childhood experiences may have *conditioned* the abuser to find children sexually arousing through fantasy. If this is combined with exposure to child pornography, the child becomes an object of sexual arousal.

BLOCKAGE

The adult abuser is in some way *blocked* in his/her ability to form relationships with adults. The child thus becomes the object in forming a relationship. In addition, there may be no other source of sexual gratification that is as satisfying as the child. This may be due to fears around adult men or women. Some, but by no means all, child sexual abusers may be poorly socially skilled or have unsatisfying adult relationships.

Although these three components are relevant, not all three need to be present for CSA to occur. They are nevertheless important in explaining the variety of motivation abusers have for sexually abusing children. The three components explain examples of abusers who are not primarily sexually motivated but enjoy degrading victims by wielding power. It also describes the paedophile who, while sexually motivated towards children, may crave a variety of sexual experiences despite access to other sources of sexual gratification. In some cases, all three elements are present and account for whether the motivation is strong and persistent, weak and episodic, or whether the focus is primarily on girls or boys, or both.

### Precondition II: Overcoming internal inhibitors

This precondition is characterised by the abuser giving him or herself permission to sexually abuse a child. Once Precondition I is met, the abuser has to overcome internal inhibitions against acting on the motivation described above. No matter how strong the sexual interest in children might be, if the abuser is inhibited by taboos against sexual activity with children, s(he) will not abuse. While most people do have some inhibitions towards sexually abusing children, the majority of child sexual abusers do not, or are able to overcome them. This disinhibition is a fundamental aspect of child sexual abuse.

Permission to abuse can be obtained by the abusers persuading themselves that what they want to do is not harmful to the child, or that it is justified. Often this is accompanied by thoughts such as it is not the abuser's fault but the child's fault in wanting to be sexually abused, or that the child is precocious, or seductive. The use of alcohol or drugs can also act as disinhibiting factors.

This permission stage is *not* a motivation to abuse, but a procedure for unleashing the already existing motivation. Individuals who have inhibitions about sexual activity with children, who are not motivated or sexually aroused by children, generally do not sexually abuse them. It must be emphasised that such distorted thought processes or the use of alcohol or drugs do not *cause* CSA but merely act as *disinhibitors* to enable the assault to happen. Both are commonly used by abusers as excuses when the sexual abuse is found out.

### Precondition III: Overcoming external inhibitors

This precondition considers the external environment, which can create the opportunity to sexually abuse, or prevent it from taking place. The child sexual abuser has to overcome external factors that may control or prevent the sexual assault. These include the family, neighbours, peers, and society's prohibitions as well as the level of supervision of the child. Although a child cannot be supervised constantly, lack of supervision can be a contributing risk factor in vulnerability to sexual assault. In cases where the child not only lacks supervision but is also emotionally or psychologically isolated from family and peers, there is an increased risk of sexual assault.

Other external restraints include physical proximity to children and level of opportunity to be alone with a child. The abuser has to *set up* the situation in which to carry out the abuse, and create the opportunity to be alone with the child. This necessitates a degree of forward planning, clever timing and manipulative skills to ensure the optimal external environment in which to sexually assault the child without any unforeseen interruptions. If abusers are unable to overcome external barriers to sexually abusing then the offence may still not happen.

### Precondition IV: Overcoming the child's resistance

In this precondition the abuser must be able to overcome a child's possible resistance to the sexual assault. Many paedophiles target specific children, whom they intuitively sense are vulnerable, who are not assertive, but are timid, appear lonely and unhappy. Such children lessen the chance of drawing attention to the abuser when approached. Children who lack close physical affection, who are emotionally and psychologically needy or insecure, who lack friends and support from the family are also deemed to be more vulnerable and less likely to disclose. In addition, children who are young for their age, are naïve and lack knowledge of such dangers, or have physical or mental disabilities, may also be at an increased risk.

Knowing which factors make children vulnerable is essential in formulating prevention programmes. Identifying behaviours that constitute a risk, while emphasising those that foster resistance or avoidance, can empower children to protect themselves. It important to emphasise that children who are not vulnerable are also sexually abused. Many children may be forced or coerced despite displaying resistance and avoidance behaviour. In such cases the capacity to overcome a child's resistance has nothing to do with the child, or the child's relationship with the abuser, but is as a result of force, threat or violence.

Types of resistance that the child can offer include overt resistance such as shouting to attract attention to the potential abuser, saying an extremely loud 'NO' or by running away. Alternatively, a child with a confident, assertive demeanour can convey strong messages to the abuser not to attempt a sexual assault for fear of detection or exposure. However the child resists, there is always the potential that they can be overcome through coercion and manipulation, or be forced to submit by the use of violence.

Acknowledging that children can resist or protect themselves from CSA enables appropriate skills and behaviours to be incorporated into prevention programmes that aim to teach children how to be safe in the community. This allows them to move about freely in their community rather than be confined to their home. It allows them to develop appropriate skills in exploring their external world, free of extreme fears and suspicion, in a way that is essential for their sense of autonomy and independence. These are skills that prepare them for adulthood when they will have to negotiate the external world.

While Finkelhor's preconditions underlie all CSA, there is enormous variation between child sexual abusers and paedophiles. In order to establish the different patterns of sexual offending, motivation and the sexual activities in relation to children, it is helpful to look at how paedophiles have been categorised and how this can aid our understanding.

## Types of paedophiles

Researchers differentiate between two broad categories of paedophiles: *predatory paedophiles* and *non-predatory paedophiles*.

*Characteristics of predatory paedophiles*

Predatory paedophiles are less common than their non-predatory counterpart and are primarily the paedophiles who come to the attention of the media in high-profile cases of abduction and sexual murder. Such cases are in the minority, involving an average of five to six children a year. While this category of paedophile is deeply disturbing, it must be remembered that they do not represent the majority of paedophiles active in CSA.

---

**Main characteristics of predatory paedophiles**

- Sexual abuse occurs within the context of abduction
- Expression of anger and hostility in a sexual way, such as raping a child
- Does not even attempt to seek consent
- Abuser expresses other needs in a sexual way
- Abduction in order to sexually abuse children
- Threatens the child
- Ignores the child's distress
- Abuser justifies his behaviour
- Sexual abuse is often aggressive and sadistic

---

*Characteristics of non-predatory paedophiles*

Non-predatory paedophiles represent by the far the largest proportion of child sexual abusers. Many of these (87%) are known to the children they abuse and adults in their community.

Non-predatory paedophiles are further categorised into *regressed paedophiles* and *fixated paedophiles* (sometimes referred to as *preferential child molesters*). Regressed paedophiles (see Table 3.2) are primarily sexually attracted to adults, and are often in a stable relationship with a woman, but under stress regress to sexually abusing children. The regressed paedophile often has feelings of sexual inadequacy and sexually assaults children impulsively, or as an expression of anger or hostility.

**Main characteristics of non-predatory paedophiles**

- Believe that children can give consent to sexual acts, including babies
- Believe that children are sexual
- Believe that children enjoy sex
- Presence of distorted thinking and beliefs
- While actions are predatory, they do not accept this
- Children are given no choice in the sexual abuse
- Use influence, power and control to form relationships
- Entrap the child
- Distort child's inability to say no; silence or accommodating behaviour as evidence that child wanted it

By far the largest category of paedophile, and the main focus of this chapter, is the fixated paedophile. Their pattern of offending suggests we relinquish the myth of the strange man in a dirty raincoat who lingers in parks, near school playgrounds or public lavatories preying on young children. In addition to the two categories already stated, Ray Wyre (1987, 1996) has provided detailed descriptions of three other types of paedophiles: the *parapaedophile,* the *inadequate paedophile* and the *inadequate fixated paedophile.*

## Characteristics of the fixated paedophile

As the fixated paedophile is perhaps the most common type of paedophile, and certainly the one that is most likely to engage in the 'grooming' of children, this chapter will focus primarily on this category. The main sexual orientation of the fixated paedophile is towards children, although we do not know how many men are sexually aroused to children yet control their behaviour. Some men get adult women to play the role of children.

The main characteristic of the 'fixated paedophile' is that they engage in highly predictable behaviour in relation to children, following clear patterns of behaviour to make contact with children. They may have poor relationships with peers and only feel really comfortable around children. The fixated paedophile goes to great length to portray their behaviour as 'normal'. They tend to adopt a pseudo-parental role and take an enormous time to foster relationships with children. They can be highly seductive (not necessarily sexually seductive) in drawing the child into a 'special friendship'. This type of paedophile often molests large numbers of children in their lifetime career of CSA, sometimes as many as 150 to 200 children (Abel *et al.* 1987).

The fixated paedophile uses child erotic material and child pornography to fantasise and masturbate to. He may also use adult pornography to lower the inhibitions of children. Any friends are likely to consist of other paedophiles with whom he shares information, and trades photographs and in some cases children. He often lives alone, or with his parents or mother. He is usually over 25 but appears to have little or no experience of adult relationships or dating with either sex. If married, it tends to be a marriage of convenience primarily driven to get access to children. The fixated paedophile is often quite precise and ordered in his manner and considers status to be very important.

The fixated paedophile has strong cognitive distortions and will claim any offence is out of character, a one-off occurrence. The sexual interest in children often begins in adolescence. The fixated paedophile often presents himself as a 'new man' who really enjoys the company of children and knows how to make them feel special. He is particularly adept at giving them the sort of attention they need and knows how to talk and listen to them.

This type of paedophile often deliberately sets out to gain the trust of the parents to gain access to the child. Alternatively he may belong to a children's organisation in order to be around children. He intuitively tends to select vulnerable children, who may be physically and emotionally neglected. He usually has a preference for children of a particular age range. The older the child he targets, the more likely he is to stick to that gender. The fixated paedophile often gives clues to his behaviour in his use of language about children, for example, 'clean, pure, innocent rosebuds', and commonly wants to exclude other adults when with children.

The fixated paedophile may have an interest in photographing children and commonly prefers limited sexual involvement with children. The focus may be on touching, exploring the child's genitalia, mutual masturbation, or oral genital contact. Full sexual intercourse or buggery is less common.

The majority of fixated paedophiles go undetected in the community because they appear so 'normal'. They are rarely regarded suspiciously but are seen as remarkably child-friendly. It is in the interest of this paedophile to maintain this façade in order to gain trust from family, friends, and neighbours, get access to children and have them entrusted to his care. This type of paedophile can remain undetected for years, during which he may abuse hundreds of children.

The fixated paedophile is frequently accepted by members of the community and is highly regarded by adults without any knowledge of his sexual abuses against children. If exposed, members of the community often react with shock and disbelief. Refusing to believe the child re-inforces the power such a paedophile wields in the local community, enabling him to avoid exposure and detection. Such paedophiles may never be caught, and consequently do not feature on the Sex Offenders' Register.

The fixated paedophile sexually abuses children both outside and within the family. To aid our understanding of sexual abuse in the family, researchers have identified different types of incestuous child sexual abusers.

---

### Table 3.2 Summary of typology of paedophiles

#### *Regressed paedophile*

'Although this is a widely accepted working category, I am not convinced that it is a valid one as I am aware it can easily be used to excuse behaviour. When writing reports for the court it is too easy to accept that this "type" exists, whereas further questioning of the offender may reveal that arousal to children has been a problem for many years. He may have controlled such desires but we cannot assume that he has not previously offended.' (Wyre 1996, p.6)

- Primarily sexual arousal to adults
- Interest in children emerges in adulthood
- Stress usually a precipitating factor
- Arousal initially impulsive
- Arousal may wax and wane with stress
- Victim seen as pseudo-adult
- Offender abandons parental role
- Usually targets female victims
- Usually married or in common law relationship
- Problem could be alcohol-related
- Poor quality of lifestyle, little sense of direction, feelings of hopelessness
- Undeveloped poor relationships

---

*Adapted from Wyre (1987)*

### *Fixated paedophile*

- His main sexual orientation is towards children. We do not know how many men, sexually aroused to children, control their behaviour. Some men get adult women to play the role of children.
- Engages in highly predictable behaviour
- Has poor relationships with peers
- Molests large numbers of children
- Adopts pseudo-parental role
- Is seductive in his approach
- Follows clear patterns of behaviour to make contact with children
- Takes time to foster relationships with children
- Uses child erotic material
- Uses child pornography
- Uses adult pornography to lower inhibitions of children
- Seeks to portray his behaviour as normal
- If he has friends they are probably paedophiles
- Share information with other paedophiles
- Has strong cognitive distortions
- Will claim any offence is out of character, a one-off occurrence
- Used to live alone or with parents or mother
- Is over 25 years of age, yet has no dating pattern with men or women
- Enjoys the company of children
- May have pictures and decor at home that will appeal to children in adolescence
- Knows how to give attention to children and make them feel special
- Knows how to talk to children, and more especially knows how to listen
- Presents himself as a 'new man'
- May deliberately set out to gain the trust of the parents
- May be precise, well ordered
- Considers status important, and uses authority to seduce
- By intuition, selects vulnerable children, physically and emotionally neglected
- Does not usually marry, but may be in a marriage of convenience
- May attach himself to a family to get access to children
- May belong to children's organisations

- Will have preference for children of a particular age range
- The older the child he targets, the more likely he is to stick to that gender
- Gives clues in his use of language about children, for example, 'clean, pure, innocent rosebuds'
- Often wants to exclude other adults when with children
- May prefer limited sexual involvement (no buggery)
- Enjoys photographing children
- May create or participate in networks of paedophiles and child sex rings
- Interest begins in adolescence

### Parapaedophile

- Not primarily interested in children sexually
- Offence may be a one in a lifetime act or persistent
- Fewer child victims involved
- Other vulnerable individuals at risk – elderly, handicapped
- General abuse of others; men abuse their wife, friends, and workers
- Primary victim criteria are vulnerability and opportunity
- Amoral or morally indiscriminate
- Uses force, manipulation or lures victims
- Victims may be strangers or acquaintances
- An incestuous father may be this type, morally indiscriminate
- Sexually an experimenter, motivated by boredom and the need for new experiences
- More and more stimuli sought to obtain satisfaction

### Inadequate paedophile

- Has the problem of dealing with sexuality when unable to form relationships
- May be suffering from a mental handicap, senility, mental illness
- Behaviour may be age-appropriate, i.e. paedophile may have a mental age of 12
- May be seen as a social misfit, withdrawn
- Is insecure, sexual behaviour motivated by curiosity?
- Sees children as non-threatening
- Is unable to deal with anger; frustration builds up

| *Inadequate fixated paedophile* |
| --- |

- Lacks the interpersonal skills to form social relationships with children
- Usually molests strangers or molests very young children
- Is an older person
- Hangs around schools, public lavatories, etc.
- May expose hilmself to children
- May make obscene phone calls to children
- Uses child prosstitutes
- Is lonely and isolated

| *Seductive incest cycle* |
| --- |

The following is an outline of the cycle and may apply to natural fathers and stepfathers. Sex abuse as an offence ranges from non-contact sexual abuse through to sadistic rape. The majority of sexual abuse on children will not be penile penetration into the vagina or anus. The most common forms are mutual masturbation and oral sex.

- He tickles child
- He baths child
- He begins to be aroused sexually, fantasises
- Child comes into his bed
- He knows the child enjoys being tickled
- He may use 'sex education' as a pretext to introduce next stage
- Tickling becomes increasingly intimate
- He masturbates the child
- He attempts to trap the child with threats, keeping secrets
- He rationalises that the child enjoys the sexual contact
- He increases sexual contact
- He thinks in a distorted way
- He finds it difficult to stop sexual contact having started it
- He reinforces his behaviour through masturbation

## Sexual abuse in the family

Sexual abuse within the family can include either the biological father or step-fathers and any other male figures who are invested with trust by the children, and who have some power or authority over the child. This could include the mother's boyfriends, uncles, grandfathers, close male family friends as well as older brothers. Females also sexually abuse children within the family, and this will be considered later in this chapter.

Many child sexual abusers within the family use similar seduction techniques as seen in the fixated paedophile's seductive incest cycle described in Table 3.2. Others have different motivations and patterns of offending. Williams and Finkelhor (1990) have identified five types of incestuous fathers: *sexually preoccupied, adolescent regressives, instrumental self-gratifiers, emotionally dependent* and *angry retaliators.*

In their study of 118 incestuous fathers who sexually abused their daughters, Williams and Finkelhor (1990) found that there were distinct differences between these five types. These differences included the age of the child at onset of CSA, anything from four weeks old to 15 years, and the range of behaviours that led to the sexual abuse. They found that typically fathers started to sexually abuse their daughters either between the ages of four and six, or between ten and twelve, although around 63 per cent of the fathers in this study reported that they had been sexually attracted to their daughters for a period of years before initiating the sexual abuse. Although the sample size is small, the study nevertheless goes some way in identifying different types of incestuous fathers.

## 1. Sexually preoccupied

Twenty-six per cent of the fathers fell into the category of sexually pre-occupied. One feature of this group is that they described an obsessive sexual interest in their daughters, sometimes from birth. These were often 'early sexualisers' with one father reporting that 'he had been stimulated by the sight of his daughter nursing and that he could never remember a time when he did not have sexual feelings for her'. According to Williams and Finkelhor (1990) he began sexually abusing her when she was four weeks old. Many of the abusers in this group reported being sexually abused in childhood.

## 2. Adolescent regressives

Thirty-three per cent of the abusers in the study were categorised as adolescent regressives who only became sexually interested in their daughters when they entered puberty. The focus for these incestuous fathers centred on the changing body of the child as she entered puberty and became more 'grown up'. In some cases, the fathers had built up a sexual attraction over the years and reported 'masturbating to fantasies of the daughter before they acted' (Williams and Finkelhor 1990). Many of these men appeared to have regressed to being young adolescents themselves. As one abuser said, 'The father–adult in me shut down and I was like a kid again' (Williams and Finkelhor 1990).

### 3. Instrumental self-gratifiers

This category of fathers was represented by 20 per cent of the sample, most of whom reported that they were not sexually or erotically attracted to their daughters. Many reported that when they were sexually abusing their daughters, they were thinking about someone else, such as their wife. The motivation of these fathers seemed to be the need for self-gratification and their daughters were merely a vehicle, or receptacle, to achieve this. Williams and Finkelhor (1990) found that these men abused their daughters sporadically, frequently felt guilty about what they were doing, and were concerned about any harm they might be causing. To dispel the guilt they rationalised that their daughter was sexually aroused.

### 4. Emotionally dependent

The fathers in this category, represented by slightly more than 10 per cent of the men studied, were often inadequate, saw themselves as failures, and were lonely, emotionally needy and depressed. Given their sense of inadequacy, they turned to their daughters for 'close, exclusive, emotionally dependent relationships', which they connected not to their daughters' sexuality but to a need for an intimate relationship. The motivation here was primarily closeness, companionship and friendship which became sexualised. Although these men described their daughters in terms of an adult lover, the average age of onset of the sexual abuse was six to seven years.

### 5. Angry retaliators

The final category, consisting of 10 per cent of the sample, appeared to sexually abuse their daughters more out of anger than sexual desire. This included anger at the daughter for making demands on the mother's time and attention, or anger at the mother for neglecting the abuser. This is clearly reflected in the case of the father of a three-year-old who stated that, 'My daughter has no sex appeal for me at all. What I did was just an opportunity to get back at my daughter for being the centre of my wife's life. There was no room for me' (Williams and Finkelhor 1990). In some cases the father sexually abused his daughter because she physically resembled the mother. These abusers were more likely to engage in sadistic abuse such as beating, tying them up or gagging them. Some of the men enjoyed raping their daughters and becoming sexually aroused by the amount of violence used. Typically, these abusers had histories of criminal assault and rape outside the family.

Williams and Finkelhor's study also found other factors associated with the sexual abuse. Thirty-three per cent reported abusing alcohol or drugs, while 43 per cent described marital discord as a significant reason for the sexual abuse (Williams and Finkelhor 1990). One has to be careful in interpreting these findings as they may represent excuses and justifications for the sexual abuse of their daughters.

A history of childhood abuse was reported by a significant number of these men, with 70 per cent believed to have been sexually abused, 50 per cent to have been physically abused by their fathers and 44 per cent to have been physically abused by their mothers. While this would indicate the 'intergenerational transmission of sexual abuse', commonly referred to as the cycle of abuse, it is important to remember that many people who have been sexually or physically abused do not go on to sexually abuse children. It does, however, demonstrate the importance of research in discovering which factors are implicated in those who go on to abuse and those who do not.

As can be seen, adult male paedophiles are not uniform and consist of a range of types, all with different patterns of offending behaviours and motivations to sexually abuse children. Traditionally it was thought that males perpetrated most child sexual abuse. This has resulted in most research studies concentrating on gaining a greater understanding of what motivates these men and how they gain access to children. As a result of increased reporting of CSA perpetrated by females, researchers have turned their attention to developing profiles of female abusers.

## Female child sexual abusers

Over the last few years there has been an increased awareness of the sexual abuse of children by females. Early literature suggested that CSA by women was extremely rare, and not found in more than 2 per cent of cases of sexual assault against children. Evidence that women sexually abuse children has been available over the last 30 years, but has remained largely hidden. This is often due to stereotypes about female sexuality and the idealisation of women as caring and nurturing.

Stereotypes of females as not being sexual aggressors make it hard for people to believe that women can sexually abuse. Traditionally females have been seen as the passive receivers in sexual encounters, not as sexual aggressors. In addition, some people find it hard to comprehend precisely how females could sexually abuse. Research shows that females who sexually abuse children commit a range of sexual acts including touching of the genitals, forcing the child to suck the woman's breast or genitalia, forced mutual masturbation, penetration of the child's vagina or anus with objects, and actual intercourse. Sometimes the sexual abuse is accompanied by physical beatings of the child (Elliott 1993).

Stereotypes of women as carers and nurturers make it incomprehensible to many adults that women can and do behave in a sexually abusive or exploitative way. When women are implicated in the sexual abuse of children people recoil with horror and disbelief. A common response is to question the child to see if the sexual abusive act was misinterpreted. Much of the sexual abuse occurs in private and may be an extension of normal caring for the child, such as rituals around personal hygiene. Normal care-taking practices may become highly eroticised for both the female abuser and the child. Any sexual arousal in the abuser promotes further sexualised exploration and behaviour.

Finkelhor and Russell (1984) found that 20 per cent of sexually abused boys and 5 per cent of sexually abused girls were abused by female perpetrators. In Britain ChildLine found that 9 per cent of children who called their helpline and identified their abuser were sexually abused by a woman (ChildLine 2003). Michelle Elliott (1993) found that of 127 victims sexually abused by females who contacted her 33 per cent were males and 67 per cent were females.

As with male paedophiles, the majority (85%) of female victims knew their abuser. In 75 per cent of cases the female abusers acted alone with 62 per cent being mothers, 7 per cent grandmothers, 7 per cent stepmothers, 13 per cent babysitters and the remaining 11 per cent were aunts, teachers and nuns. In the case of male victims, 50 per cent reported being sexually abused by their mothers. The age at which abuse started ranged from before the age of five in 83 per cent of cases, between the ages of five and ten in 16 per cent of cases, and between age 10 and 15 in 1 per cent of cases (Elliott 1993).

In the case of male victims, 91 per cent reported that the abuser was related to them. Of these 96 per cent were mothers and 4 per cent were step-mothers. When there was more than one perpetrator, 45 per cent were mothers and 22 per cent were stepmothers along with sisters, grandfathers and other males. Thirty three per cent were abused by babysitters or family friends. Fifty-five per cent of men reported that the sexual abuse started before age five, 35 per cent between the ages of five and ten, and 10 per cent between age 10 and 15 (Elliott 1993).

Elliott (1993) also found that many victims of female sexual abuse were reluctant to disclose their experiences for fear of not being believed, with some pretending that their abuser was male to ensure that they would be believed. More recent research, based on increased reporting by children and adult survivors, indicates that females perpetrate 20 to 25 per cent of CSA. Thus, although still considerably less than CSA by males, the number is signif-icant enough to warrant investigation. Initially female abusers were seen as one single category of perpetrator who had been forced or coerced into sexually abusive acts by dominant male partners. Research no longer supports this as it has been established that female abusers also have a variety of offend-ing patterns and motivations when sexually abusing children. Saradjian (1996) in reviewing the research literature has identified the following char-acteristics of female child sexual abusers.

One early study by Faller in 1987 identified five separate categories of female child sexual abuser: *the polyincestuous abuser, the single parent abuser, the psychotic abuser, the adolescent abuser* and *the non-custodial abuser.* Half this clinical sample of 40 women suffered from psychological problems, including mental retardation and psychosis. In addition more than half had problems with alcohol or drug dependency, while three-quarters abused their children in other ways alongside the sexual abuse.

## 1. Polyincestuous abuser

This was by far the largest category, represented by 72.5 per cent of the sample. The main feature of the polyincestuous abuser was that the woman was coerced or forced into the sexual assault by a dominant male partner. The

**Main characteristics of female child sexual abusers**

- Low self-esteem, feelings of inadequacy and vulnerability
- Troubled childhoods
- Lack of nurturing in childhood
- Need for nurture and control
- Early marriage
- Child and woman close in age
- Experience of aloneness, isolation and separation from others
- Woman alone or partner frequently absent
- Need for substitute gratification with the child
- Negative and abusive relationships with male peers
- History of indiscriminate or compulsive sexual activity
- Severe psychological disturbance or mental illness
- Alcohol or drug addiction
- Treating children as extensions of themselves
- Unsatisfactory and parasitic relationship with children
- The child being unwanted or the wrong sex
- The woman may be 'stuck' in her relationship with her own mother

female rarely instigated the sexual abuse, and she rarely acted alone of her own volition. In the case of multiple victims both partners perpetrated the abuse.

## 2. Single parent abuser

Only 15 per cent of the sample were single parents who were not in an ongoing relationship. Often the mother developed a strong relationship with the oldest child who took on adult responsibilities and was seen as a surrogate partner.

## 3. Psychotic abuser

Only 7.5 per cent of the females were diagnosed as suffering from some psychotic illness at the time of the sexual abuse. This would indicate that only a small proportion of female child sexual abusers suffers from severe mental health problems.

### 4. Adolescent abuser

Faller (1987) found that adolescent females represented 7.5 per cent of the sample. These young teenage girls were found to have problems in peer relationships and friendships, and had no sexual outlets other than the children they were abusing.

### 5. Non-custodial abuser

There was only one female in the sample in this category. She did not live with the child but would sexually abuse it during access visits, perhaps to satisfy her emotional needs due to having separated from her partner.

A later study conducted by Matthews *et al.* in 1991, which consisted of 16 female child sexual abusers, found that all but one had had a history of childhood sexual abuse. Further common features in these women were childhood experiences of isolation, alienation and few opportunities to develop interpersonal skills, leaving them feeling socially inadequate. Despite this small sample, the researchers identified four categories of female child sexual abuser.

### 1. The teacher/lover

The category of teacher/lover principally involves an older adult woman engaged in a sexual relationship with a pre-pubescent or adolescent boy, whom she regards as her peer. This type of female sexual abuser is often seen as relatively harmless as the sexual relationship is seen as primarily initiating young boys into sexuality. Such experiences of initiation are often reflected in literature and films such as 'The Graduate'. This theme of young boys being initiated into their first sexual experience is seen as innocuous and representative of all young boys' fantasies.

While this may be true anecdotally, the clinical literature tells a very different story, with many adult male victims feeling disturbed by CSA. This type of sexual relationship is generally non-consensual due to the imbalance of power, which the female abuser is exploiting. Rather than the motive being initiation into sex, the female may be acting out intense, unexpressed anger at adult males. Because such anger cannot be expressed safely at adult men, the female chooses a younger, adolescent male as a safer target. Thus, deeply suppressed hostility and aggression against adult males may underlie this apparently 'innocuous', culturally 'acceptable' form of child sexual abuse.

## 2. The intergenerationally predisposed offender

This category was by far the largest in this sample. The females in this category all initiated the sexual abuse of the child, often their own children. Commonly, predisposed offenders had a long history of early, severe and persistent CSA within the family. Although the apparent motive for sexually abusing their own children might be the gratification of emotional needs for non-threatening intimacy, it might unconsciously represent a way to discharge their own sexual abuse onto their children. These female abusers were found generally to target very young children.

## 3. The male coerced

The females in this category are initially coerced into sexually assaulting children by a dominant male partner, with a history of sexual offending against children. Such females are commonly extremely dependent and are unable to assert themselves in relation to the male partner, who may be sexually abusing her too. Children targeted by this type of abuser included those both within and outside the family. Although these women were initially coerced into such sexual activities with children, Matthews (1993) found that 44 per cent went on to initiate the sexual abuse independently of their male partner.

## 4. The experimenter–exploiter

This category was mostly associated with adolescent girls who were relatively naïve about sex and sought to experiment sexually with younger children. These girls would often sexually assault children who they were babysitting or looking after. Their sexual assault was seen to be as a result of wishing to experiment sexually with young children in the absence of peer relationships.

A similar typology has been developed by Saradjian (1996) who isolated five categories of female child sexual abusers in her analysis of 50 female sexual abusers: *women who target pre-pubescent children, women who target adoles-*

*cent children, women who are coerced by men to offend, women who co-offend (with women or men)* and *women who are involved with ritual abuse groups.*

What becomes clear from these studies is that there are different motivations and reasons why females sexually abuse children. Common to all three studies are females who are coerced or forced into sexually abusing their children, those females who target primarily adolescent children and those who sexually abuse as a result of their own sexual abuse histories.

While these characteristics have been found in the research literature, more research needs to be conducted to validate the reliability of these differing typologies. This will be crucial to enhancing understanding and finding ways of preventing such abuse. In particular it might dispel myths around female sexual abusers and increase awareness of how common CSA by females actually is. What will also be useful to explore is how children are accessed, targeted and groomed by female perpetrators, especially in female-dominated professions such as child care.

Along with increased awareness of CSA by female perpetrators, researchers have found that older children and adolescents account for 30 per cent of CSA. While this is due to higher levels of reporting and disclosure, it also reflects knowledge about paedophiles, many of whom start sexually abusing children during their teenage years. Consideration will now be given to what is known about child and adolescent abusers.

## The child/adolescent abuser

Increased reporting of CSA has highlighted the number of sexual offences against children perpetrated by other children and adolescents. It is thought that approximately 30 per cent of all CSA is committed by adolescents, with 500 teenagers convicted each year for sexual offences against children (Vizard 2000; Vizard *et al.* 1995). It is vital to identify potential child sexual abusers and paedophiles before they get locked into a lifelong cycle of sexual offending against children.

It is also crucial that they have access to therapy and treatment to prevent future sexual assaults on children. Once children enter puberty there is an increase in sexual fantasy which heralds the laying down of the sexual arousal cycle. If teenagers begin to fantasise about sexually sadistic acts and the abduction of younger children for the purposes of sexual abuse, a life-long sexual offending cycle may become established. The influence of pornography at this age also has huge implications for future sexual arousal.

A number of police operations such as Operation Appal in 2001 have found a number of young adolescents downloading child pornography on the Internet. These adolescents have subsequently been placed on the Sex Offenders' Register. Whether this constitutes CSA is somewhat complex. Some researchers argue that providing the images downloaded are of children who are of the same age as the teenager this does not constitute CSA and as such the adolescent should not be treated as a paedophile in the making (Taylor 1999). However, if the images downloaded are of considerably younger children, then this would give cause for concern.

Some police officers believe that it is very rare for young adolescents to download sexual images of same age peers. If anything they download adult pornography. Often the potential adolescent child sexual abuser downloads a wide range of material, not just images of peers but also babies being abused. An example of this is a 13-year-old boy placed on the Sex Offenders' Register in 2001, having downloaded 326 images of CSA, including the sadistic sexual abuse of babies.

To date we do not know the impact of early exposure to child pornography to later sexual development, although it is thought that there is an association between sexual arousal and the use of pornography. Researchers have yet to establish to what extent exposure to and the use of pornography acts as a catalyst for later sexually inappropriate behaviour. Many adolescent child sexual abusers are victims of CSA themselves and may have been shown child pornography while a victim to normalise and facilitate the CSA. Such exposure may be incorporated by the child and later adolescent into their fantasy and sexual arousal cycle.

Adolescents may be ensnared into using the Internet to view child pornography by an adult child sexual abuser. Rachel O'Connell, who has investigated the use of cybersex and its relationship to CSA, argues that 'young people can quickly become integrated into [virtual] communities, sometimes lured with images of girls of their own age but then expand to even more hardcore material' (O'Connell 2003a). Clearly this blurs the boundary between the adolescent as victim or offender.

Given that the majority of adolescent child sexual abusers are victims of CSA themselves, it is crucial that a national strategy be developed for dealing with such young offenders in terms of intervention and treatment. Such therapeutic intervention would provide a safe environment for the adolescent to explore their own trauma and experience of CSA, but also enable them to stop their sexualised behaviour and prevent their sexual offending against children in the future. To date there are only limited resources and therapeutic measures available, which is why many adolescent child sexual abusers are seen as offenders rather than victims who need to be protected.

Putting such children on the Sex Offenders' Register may be counterproductive in the long term in promoting prolonged sexual offending against children. An example of this is the case of an 18-year-old youth who savagely murdered an 11-year-old boy in 1998 shortly after release from secure accommodation to which he had been sentenced after committing a string of sexual attacks on young boys since the age of 14. Child protection and treatment may well have prevented further sexual offending against children.

Thus the issues surrounding the adolescent child sexual abusers are extremely complex in blurring the boundaries between victim and abuser. What is clear is that the earlier such children are identified and given therapeutic input, the more likely it is that they will not go on to offend. We know that a percentage of victims of CSA do go on to sexually abuse other children, with recent research suggesting that one in eight victims become offenders (Salter *et al.* 2003; Skuse 2003). To avoid this, early identification of both victims and potential offenders becomes paramount.

Stop It Now! UK and Ireland (2002a) have produced the list shown on the following page of behaviours seen in children and young adolescents that may give cause for concern.

Researchers have found that the high risk age group for adolescent CSA is around age 15 to 16 (Araji 1997; Elliot 1994) although children as young as 11 have been known to sexually assault younger children. The child victims are often younger than those abused by adults, which is why toddlers and babies are more at risk. Despite the younger victim age group, the sexually abusive acts incorporate the same spectrum as CSA by adults and include forcible penetration of vagina and anus with fingers and objects, as well as oral, anal and vaginal intercourse (Shaw *et al.* 2000).

**Warning signs of sexually harmful or abusive behaviour in children or adolescents**

- Seeks out the company of younger children and spends an unusual amount of time in their company, having little interest in spending time with people their own age
- Insists on time alone with child with no interruptions
- Regularly offers to babysit children for free or take children on overnight outings
- Takes younger children to 'secret' places or hideaways
- Plays 'special' games with them ('doctor and patient') unusual for their age
- Insists on physical affection such as hugging, kissing or wrestling with child even when the child clearly does not want to
- Overly interested in the sexual development of child or teenager
- Refusal to allow a child sufficient privacy or make their own decisions
- Frequently walking in on children/teenagers in the bathroom
- Picks on a particular child – can include younger sibling
- Treats a particular child as a favourite, making them feel 'special' compared with others, can include younger sibling
- Buys children expensive gifts or gives them money for no apparent reason
- Tells you they do not want to be alone with child
- Becomes anxious when a particular child or young person comes to visit
- Frequently uses aggressive sexual language about adults and children
- Shows sexual material to children
- Makes sexually abusive telephone calls
- Shares alcohol or other drugs with younger children or teens
- Views child pornography on the Internet or elsewhere
- Exposes his or her genitals to younger children
- Forces sex on another adolescent or child

Adolescent child sexual abusers are more likely to be female, acting as babysitters, who engage in such activity under the auspices of sexual curiosity and experimentation with younger children. The sexual acts are usually less serious assaults and consist of fondling, stimulation of the genitals and vaginal and anal penetration with objects. Occasionally it can include full rape (Lightfoot and Evans 2002). They may also be re-enacting their own sexually abusive experiences. Male adolescent child sexual abusers tend to have a gender preference in the children they abuse and to engage in a higher level of invasive behaviour, which sometimes has sadistic components such as anal penetration (Aylwin *et al.* 2000).

The child or adolescent abuser can abuse children within the family, such as siblings, stepsiblings, cousins and the children of family friends. Research shows that older children often sexually abuse younger children within the family. The older child may dominate the younger child by bullying and using threatening behaviour to ensure compliance and secrecy. While they may treat the younger child with normal sibling rivalry and disdain in the presence of the parents, they will sexually seduce them when the parents are not present. The fear inculcated in the younger child may be so great that they are unable to disclose the CSA to the parents and frequently continue to suffer for years.

Alternatively they may sexually abuse children outside the family such as younger children at school or in youth clubs. Such children use their age, power or status to seduce, coerce or force the younger child into sexual activity and ensure their silence. As in adult paedophiles the adolescent abuser may target and groom a specific child. To understand this process Wyre (2000) has identified the typical cycle of grooming among adolescent abusers.

The adolescent child abuser initially starts by touching the child outside his/her clothing. If the child resists, he stops and tries again later. If he is reported, there is nothing that could easily lead to a conviction. Having touched the child sexually outside his/her clothing, he waits and then moves on to greater intimacy. This leads to mutual masturbation, which may continue for a considerable period of time until ejaculation occurs. During these encounters not much talking takes place. The abuser finds out if the child or any friends have done it before. The child is warned not to tell and keeps this secret. The sexual activity may evolve into mutual oral sex. This frequently leads on to intercourse, or anal sex, initially to the child, and later to the abuser.

If the CSA is discovered or disclosed, the child/adolescent abuser may rationalise his or her behaviour as merely consensual sexual exploration and experimentation to minimise the abusive nature of the activity. This is a way of defusing the seriousness of the sexual activity and to deflect and dilute responsibility away from the abuser on to the victim. It is thus crucial to be able to distinguish between abuse and consensual exploration. According to Itzin (2002), in order to distinguish CSA from normal sexual experimentation between children the following need to be considered.

## 1. Age differential

Most consensual sexual experimentation occurs between peers of roughly the same age. The greater the age difference the more likely it is to be non-consensual and therefore CSA. This is especially the case when the abusing child is post-puberty and the victim is pre-pubertal.

## 2. Power differential

The power relationship between the abuser and the victim is crucial and may outweigh the age differential. This is especially the case of an older sibling who has some authority and status over younger siblings. Often the older child may be left in charge of younger siblings, which can present an opportunity to sexually abuse. As they are in loco parentis, the abuser is invested with power which is then sexually exploited. In the case of CSA outside the family, the child/adolescent abuser may have status, in terms of a reputation, or authority over the child such as a group leader.

## 3. Sophistication of the activity

The type of sexual activity engaged in may not be age-appropriate, especially if it involves an excessive knowledge of sexual behaviour and range of sexual acts. Sometimes the sexual activity is highly ritualistic or unusual within teenagers.

## 4. Consenting or compliant

A crucial factor in distinguishing sexual abuse from experimentation is the issue of consent. It is important to establish to what extent, if at all, both parties consented or whether one party complied or co-operated because of the power imbalance. Dynamics of coercion and threat must also be considered. In order to assess CSA it is necessary to establish how the activity came about and in what circumstances.

## 5. Persistence of activity

The persistence and repetition of the sexual activity must also be established. Normal consensual experimentation is often sporadic and relatively brief. If the sexual activity is frequent, obsessive, or prolonged over time, this can indicate CSA.

## 6. Changes of activity

A further consideration is the pattern of sexual activity, and whether it changes over time. This is especially so if it is systematic, repetitive, increases in frequency and consists of regular patterns with several partners.

## 7. Overt aggression

If the sexual activity includes the presence of overt aggression, violence or threats of violence, it is more likely to suggest CSA than mutual experimentation.

## 8. Experience of the receiving person

Consideration must also be given to how the victim feels about the sexual activity. If the abused child experiences the sexual encounter as abusive then it is highly likely that it is non-consensual. In these instances, the victim may blame himself or herself for the sexual encounter, which would further indicate abuse as in consensual sexual experimentation the child rarely blames itself.

## 9. Attempts to secure secrecy

The issue of secrecy is crucial in distinguishing between consensual sexual experimentation and abuse. Attempts to secure secrecy and the reasons for this need to be clarified, as secrecy does suggest abuse, although young people may be secretive about mutual and consenting behaviour for other reasons.

## 10. How was the activity revealed

Disclosure of the sexual activity is a further factor. The circumstances around the disclosure may be highly significant especially if it is associated with the abused child being upset or changes in behaviour. Sometimes disclosure may follow an inadvertent comment in which the child is attempting to expose the 'secret'. Who discloses may also be pivotal, as the abuser rarely discloses unless forced to.

## 11. Any 'target' victim

Consideration must also be given to the type of victim that is being engaged in sexual activity. If there are common characteristics of age, sex or vulnerability in victims this may indicate a target group, which is likely to mean CSA.

## 12. Nature of fantasies

The nature of the fantasies that the child abuser engages in may also be significant as these give clues to self-image, views about sex, and the nature of sexual interest. Those with a number of abusive-style fantasies are more likely to express these in abusive situations.

Print and Morrison (2002) have collated a wealth of information about child and adolescent sexual abusers which examines risk factors and experiences that predispose these youngsters to sexually abuse younger children. The potential risk factors cluster around a history of childhood abuse, leading to unmet needs, which they seek to satisfy through CSA. Table 3.2 summarises the predisposing factors in adolescents who sexually abuse children.

Commonly found risk factors in child and adolescent sexual abuse cluster around early family dynamics, early sexual experiences, general cognitive distortions, inappropriate sexual interest and opportunity. Eileen Vizard, director of the NSPCC Young Abusers Project in North London, argues that 'without exception these children are victims of appalling childhoods, most often sexual abuse and physical and emotional abuse too, and nobody has been there to help or protect them' (Vizard 2000; Vizard et al. 1995). This clearly indicates that many young adolescent child sexual abusers need to be seen as victims of childhood abuses, and not just as sexual offenders. This has huge implications for therapeutic intervention and treatment as opposed to custodial sentencing.

**Table 3.2 Predisposing factors in adolescents who sexually abuse children**

| Predisposing factors | Early sexual experiences | General cognitive distortions (attitudes / values / beliefs) | Inappropriate sexual interest | Opportunities |
|---|---|---|---|---|
| Cold parenting | Pornography | Sexism | Inappropriate sexual behaviour is learned | Victim availability (babysitting) |
| Lack of empathy | Sexual abuse | Patriarchal views | Self-reinforcement | Peer group influences |
| Disrupted attachments | Lack of protection | Adult men can do what they like to women and children and get away with it | Early intervention crucial | Family context |
| Inconsistent care | No resolution of abuse experience | Media influence | Reinforced by pornography | Family arrangements |
| Physical abuse | No negative consequences for their abuser | Pornography | Sexual fantasy | Absence of adult supervision |
| Emotional abuse | Lack of appropriate sexual information | Society messages about masculinity/sexuality | Masturbation and sexual activity | Minimum threat of detection |
| Domestic violence | Sex seen as dirty | Sexual activity fused with aggression | Strength and physical/psychological maturity | |
| Attention deficit | | Sexual activity divorced from close relationships | Increases in response to number of abusive acts committed | |
| Conduct disorder | | Sexual ignorance | Sexual activity used as compensation for non-sexual problems/anxieties, powerlessness, failure/loss of relationship | |
| Severe learning difficulty | | Sexual myths | Sexual preoccupation/rumination especially when alone, bored, hurt | |
| Lack of close friendships | | Females as sex objects | | |
| Poor socialisation | | Attributions: | | |
| Delinquent peer group | | 'I am not responsible' | | |
| Poor social/coping skills | | 'I am the victim' | | |
| Poor anger management | | 'I can't win' | | |
| Affective disorders | | | | |
| Low self-esteem | | | | |
| Inability to trust | | | | |
| Over-controlled family | | | | |
| Enmeshed family | | | | |
| Chaotic/disengaged family | | | | |

*Adapted from Print and Morrison 2002, p. 299*

## Treatment of child sexual abusers

Treatment needs to be made available both to victims of child sexual abuse and to perpetrators. This is especially the case in those victims of CSA who go on to sexually offend against children. A prime example of this is the adolescent child sexual abuser. Early treatment and intervention may well divert a lifelong pattern of sexual offending against children.

While there is still no known cure for child sexual abusers, research indicates that many do respond to treatment. It is only in the last decade that beliefs around the treatment of paedophiles have changed. It is thought that between one-third and half of child sexual abusers respond to treatment in learning to manage their arousal and implement strategies to avoid offending (Salter 2003). One-third, however, do not respond to treatment at all and remain a risk when returned to the community.

Currently most treatment for sexual offending against children is offered while the offender is in prison. Given that less than 5 per cent of child sexual abusers who go to court are convicted it is hard to draw any real conclusions about the effectiveness of treatment. We can only know how effective treatment is for those offenders who come to the attention of the criminal justice system and are given a custodial sentence. It is impossible to know how effective treatment is with those child sexual abusers who remain undetected.

Effectiveness of treatment is primarily based on whether the child sexual abuser reoffends and comes into the criminal justice system again. This may be a distorted figure as many may reoffend but not get caught. Further consideration needs to be given to access to treatment. Most treatment programmes are offered while the child sexual abuser is imprisoned. Treatment is not sustained upon release back into the community. It may be that sustained access to treatment outside of custodial sentencing could increase the effectiveness of treatment and reduce reoffending rates.

Access to treatment programmes *prior* to offending may be a powerful way of preventing CSA. With this in mind the Home Office and Department of Health, along with a number of charities, have funded pilot schemes that aim to provide help to those who are concerned about their sexual arousal to children prior to committing an offence. Stop It Now! UK and Ireland provides a helpline for those who have concerns about their sexual arousal to children. In their first year they have received over 700 calls from members of the community seeking advice and help to manage their arousal and prevent any future sexual offending (see Chapter 10). Future evaluation of and research on individuals who seek treatment prior to sexual offending may provide invaluable knowledge about patterns of CSA and child sexual abusers that to date has eluded us.

Locking child sexual abusers up in prison does very little, if anything, to encourage reform or rehabilitation. While it may temporarily protect children while they are in prison, there is no guarantee that they will be safe once released. If anything, the pent-up stress of being in prison may easily be unleashed upon release to commit an offence that the paedophile has been merely fantasising about and masturbating to while in prison.

Paedophiles are just as isolated in prison as they are in the community, often segregated from the rest of the prisoners for their own safety. This isolates and marginalises them and, by being thrown together with other child sex offenders, may well fuel fantasies and increase knowledge about how to sexually offend against children and avoid getting caught. It also serves to fuel paedophiles' distorted beliefs about sexual offending against children when among their peers, seeing themselves as misunderstood and victims of society's ignorance. This makes it more likely that they will reoffend.

Beliefs about treatment of child sexual abusers have changed dramatically over the last 30 years, moving from 'nothing works' to looking at 'what works' and those interventions that 'do work'. It is now known that chemical castration on the whole does not work. This is primarily due to the fact that while it may reduce libido and minimise frequency of sexual arousal, it nevertheless does not stop the sexual desire and fantasies about children. In addition, it has virtually no impact on the cognitive aspects associated with sexual offending against children. To some degree chemical castration can fuel the child sexual abuser's frustration in that the desire and impulse to sexually abuse children remains but physiologically their sexual arousal is inhibited in terms of erection. Such frustration may prompt the sexual abuse of a child upon release from prison, rather than reduce offending. There are also ethical considerations associated with chemical castration in terms of side-effects and the invasiveness of this form of treatment.

Given the limitations of chemical castration, the primary form of treatment in prison is the Sex Offenders' Treatment Programme (SOTP) first introduced in 1991 as a reaction to the 'nothing works' philosophy historically held (Martinson 1974) and the awareness that 'some things do work' proposed by later researchers such as McGuire and Priestley (1985). The things that are most frequently believed to work are changes in beliefs around sexual offending against children and the management of fantasies and impulses to sexually abuse. It is thought that such management can reduce reoffending by between 10 and 30 per cent.

Currently, SOTP is offered in 27 prisons and is thought to account for the reduction in re-conviction rates. However, SOTP is not compulsory for all child sex offenders but is based on the prisoner 'volunteering' to take part. Such volunteers may be looking for potential pay-offs such as extra privileges or early release. This suggests that SOTP is a mixture of threat and offer, or 'throffer' as Wilson (1999) refers to it. The offer is treatment and promise of release, while the threat is potential failure to secure release.

The core programme of SOTP is available to all males in prison who have enough sentence time left to complete the programme fully. Although all sex offenders are eligible, the majority do not access the treatment available. For instance, there are currently 5600 sex offenders in prison of whom only 839 completed treatment in 2002, well below the Government target of 950 (Silverman and Wilson 2002). This is the fourth year running that the target has not been achieved despite being reduced from 1160 in 2001. This indicates that just over one-sixth of sex offenders actually receive treatment in prison. This seriously undermines the adequate provision of treatment to all sex offenders, which increases the danger of reoffending. Most sex offenders return to the community, where there is no follow-up or sustained treatment and insufficient supervision by the hard-pressed probation service.

It is thought that SOTP is most effective with high-risk or medium-risk sex offenders and as such these are given priority. Other exclusions include those who cannot speak English, those whose IQ is less than 80, those who are mentally ill, those who are appealing against their conviction, those who represent a real suicide risk, and those who persistently act out and engage in self-injury.

The Sex Offenders' Treatment Programme is based on cognitive behavioural therapy which works on the principle of the dynamic relationship between thoughts, feelings and behaviour (McGuire 2000). The focus is on decision-making processes, self-esteem, self-statements and cognitive skills. Its aims are to acknowledge that many sex offenders are damaged individuals who have a right to a human response. It is designed to help such individuals get rid of anger, resentment and self-loathing. To reduce their deep sense of loneliness, SOTP enables them to develop normal relationships, in some cases for the first time ever. It also encourages sex offenders to examine what they have done and to show genuine remorse and empathy towards their victim(s) through role-plays. Finally it focuses on the development of strategies to manage their sexual arousal and impulses and to avoid getting into situations where opportunities arise to sexually abuse. All in all the aim is to enable the sex offender to live a normal life once released back into society.

There are two components to SOTP, consisting of a core programme and an extended programme. The *core programme* consists of 20 blocks across 85 sessions, which address distorted thinking, empathy for victims, risk management and relapse prevention planning. In essence it addresses the following:

- Distorted beliefs about relationships
- Awareness of effects of sexual offending on victims
- Responsibility and consequences of sexual offending
- Relapse prevention strategies
- Identifying the nature of the offender's cycle of abuse
- Strategies to avoid high-risk situations.

The *extended programme* is used with those sex offenders who have difficulty with anger control, who are unable to express their feelings, who have problems managing stress, have deviant sexual arousal and who may have drug or alcohol problems. More specialist residential or custodial treatment centres tend to offer this extended programme, which includes the development of extra skills around:

- Deviant arousal
- Interpersonal relationships
- Communication skills
- Anger and stress management
- Substance abuse.

While denial of sexual offences does not result in exclusion from SOTP, such issues may be addressed separately or attended to by special denial programmes. While many clinicians believe that SOTP is effective in reducing reoffending by up to 30 per cent in some cases, there has been relatively little evaluation in relation to reoffending. Treatment seems to be most effective with those who demonstrate low deviancy and low denial, such as familial sexual abusers, but seems largely unsuccessful for those sex offenders who abuse children outside the family.

In addition it is thought that SOTP is quite effective in the short term, but less so in the long term. This may in part be due to the fact that very few treatment programmes are available once the sex offender is released back into the community. Given the vilification of paedophiles, there is virtually no support other than supervision by the probation service upon release. The stress of being demonised, the isolation and lack of adequate and sustained support may all contribute to reoffending after a period of time. This indicates that any treatment implemented in prison needs to be maintained and sustained to some degree to allow the sex offender to stop reoffending while in the community. This calls for increased attention to and resourcing of treatment programmes after release to fully rehabilitate the paedophile and integrate them back into the community (see Chapter 10).

It is clear that our knowledge about child sexual abusers and paedophiles is extremely limited as it is primarily based on the 10 per cent of individuals who come to the attention of the criminal justice system. We know virtually nothing about the 90 per cent who as yet remain undetected. Future research may illuminate our knowledge about the variety of sexual offending patterns against children by all types of child sexual abusers. It is not until we have accurate knowledge about what motivates child sexual abusers and how they sexually offend that we can fully protect children. Treatment of victims of CSA, as well as child sexual abusers, is also essential in terms of preventing CSA in the future.

Increased awareness and reporting of CSA, along with higher detection rates, may provide crucial information about child sexual abusers and their patterns of behaviour in relation to children. One area where there seems to be an increase in detection rates is the use of the Internet for child pornography and the grooming of children. The relationship between CSA and the Internet is a complex yet potent one and will be addressed in the following chapter.

## Chapter 4

# Child Sexual Abuse and the Internet

The Internet has opened up a new world for children which is educational, informative and most of all fun. But we are aware of the potential for paedophiles to misuse modern technology to abuse the trust that children place in them by attempting to 'groom' them through chat rooms.

Hilary Benn, Home Office Minister (2003)

The Internet brings massive benefits, opening up a world of opportunities for young people, but sadly it also brings new risks from paedophiles who try to abuse their trust. The Sexual Offences Bill…brings in a new offence of grooming, which will protect children from the insidious use of the Internet by paedophiles.

David Blunkett, Home Secretary (2002)

The Internet plays a significant role in the lives of children today by opening up a whole new world. It provides excellent educational opportunities, access to a huge range of information and can be fun. However, it also plays a central role in the sexual abuse of children in a variety of ways. First, it is an easy anonymous medium for accessing and distributing child pornography. Second, it is a way for paedophiles to share images of children and to exchange and trade child pornography. This can extend to the sharing, buying and selling of children over the Internet. Third, it also allows paedophiles to feel part of a community, albeit in cyberspace. Being part of a 'virtual' community engenders a sense of belongingness, in which paedophiles feel less stigmatised and marginalised. Sharing their interest in children with others legitimises paedophiles' predilections and feeds their rationalisation that it is acceptable to sexually abuse children.

The explosion of child pornography has been phenomenal. US Customs estimate that there are currently more than 1,000,000 websites specifically for child pornography generating a $2–3 billion industry per year. In 2003 the NSPCC estimated that there were over 20,000 child pornographic images posted on websites every week (Pedowatch 2004; Protectkids 2004).

In the UK recent research by the NCH (formerly the National Children's Homes) charity shows that there has been a 1,500 per cent increase in child pornography since 1988 (NCH 2004). As a result of this increase and major police investigations such as Operation Ore, 549 people were charged in 2001 compared to 35 in 1988. Given such a huge rise in child pornography, leading children's charities including the NCH are urging the Government to increase funding for police to investigate such crimes.

The amount of images collected can be vast. In 2003 a man in Lincolnshire was found to have over 500,000 images, while a man in New York had collected over 1,000,000 images.

Many of these child pornography images are often hidden or disguised in stealth sites such as Disney, Barbie, Pokémon, My Little Pony and Action Man which link to hard core child pornography sites (Protectkids 2004) which children can unintentionally access while searching for popular characters or when searching for information and pictures to help with their homework.

The area of biggest concern for most parents and adults is the use of the Internet to groom children in order to sexually abuse them. Child pornography facilitates the sexual seduction of children on- and offline and can lead to committing an actual contact offence. This is of such concern that the new Sexual Offences Bill will make 'sexual grooming' of children on- and offline an offence with a maximum penalty of 10 years imprisonment. This new criminal offence of 'sexual grooming' is '…designed to catch those aged 18 or over who undertake a course of conduct with a child under the age of 16 leading to a meeting where the adult intends to engage in sexual activity with a child. It will enable action to be taken before any sexual activity takes place where it is clear that this is what the offender intends (Blunkett 2002).

If we are to protect our children, it is crucial that we know how the Internet is being used and how paedophiles groom children for sexual purposes. This chapter will explore in depth how paedophiles use the Internet for the purposes of child pornography and to access actual children. There is much controversy surrounding the issue of child pornography on the Internet, not least because of how widespread it seems to be and how this relates to CSA. Increased awareness of how child pornography impacts on paedophiles in terms of the fantasy arousal cycle will help us to understand why, and how, some paedophiles actually go on to sexually abuse a child.

The chapter will also examine the use of the Internet by paedophiles to 'groom' children for sexual purposes. By looking in detail at patterns of behaviour it will enable parents to understand the mind of the paedophile, how they select and target children through chat rooms in order to befriend them, and then groom them for sexual purposes. Throughout, consideration will be given to ever evolving technology and how law enforcement, child protection agencies, parents and teachers can protect children.

## The use of Internet child pornography by paedophiles

Child pornography exists primarily for consumption by paedophiles. If there were no paedophiles, there would be no child pornography.

Metropolitan Police Service Pornography Information Line

Technology does not abuse children...people do.

Jones (2003)

It is thought that child pornography is intrinsically related to the sexual abuse of children, and that paedophiles are the primary producers, distributors and users of this insidious material. The main reasons that paedophiles use and collect child pornography are given in the box on the next page.

As can be seen there are a number of reasons why paedophiles use child pornography on the Internet, ranging from simply collecting a wide variety of photographs of children through to behaving sexually inappropriately with children. Child pornography also provides an underground support structure of paedophile networks, which give easy access to masturbatory material. These virtual communities provide increased empowerment and control to paedophiles by validating and normalising their sexual interest in children.

In the words of one paedophile, 'Over the years leading up to the incident [the sexual assault of an 11-year-old girl], I had collected a lot of child pornography from the Net...I saw websites detailing how to abuse children. It said things like "be authoritative, make her feel silly for saying no". The worst stuff on the Net is posted by people who want to share their experiences. It made me feel it was OK.'

### Function of child pornography on the Internet

- Building up a collection of child pornography
- For sexual arousal and gratification – influential in the fantasy, arousal, masturbation cycle
- Contact with other paedophiles – facilitating social relationships in virtual communities and real life
- Medium through which to exchange and trade images with other paedophiles to enlarge or complete child pornography collections
- To gain access to children by exchanging, buying or selling children
- Using child pornography in the grooming process with the child to lower their inhibitions
- As 'blackmail' to silence the child and ensure that it keeps the 'secret'
- To preserve the child's youth by maintaining a pictorial record of the child's appearance at the 'desirable' age even after it has grown up and matured
- Catalyst for behaving in sexually inappropriate way with children
- Child pornography as therapy – to control their sexual interest in children by providing sexual relief without being in contact with actual child
- Remaining in a fantasy world – a way of avoiding real life

A further problem is the use of child pornography on the Internet to promote increased fantasy and sexual arousal towards children. The Internet thus creates a facilitating environment for the expression of paedophiles' sexual interest, which can lead to the sexual grooming of children and the committing of actual contact offences.

## Collecting child pornography

Sullivan and Beech (2004) suggest that there are three potential motivation typologies:

1. collecting as a part of a larger pattern of sexual offending, potentially including contact sex offending

2. collecting to feed a developing sexual interest in children

3. accessing indecent images of children out of curiosity.

Individuals who are in the early stages of developing a sexual interest in children may benefit the most with initiatives such as Stop It Now! and the NSPCC paedophile helpline to access help and therapeutic input to interrupt the development of a lifelong pattern of sexual offending against children. A common characteristic among child sexual abusers and paedophiles is the collecting of child pornography. Many paedophiles obsessively collect images of children, establishing vast collections of thousands and thousands of images. Such collections are characterised by an addictive quality in completing collections by swapping and exchanging images. These are often carefully catalogued, indexed and ordered by number and series, in a narrative form. A series of pictures may have a narrative in showing the child undressing across a series of poses, which often reflect the content of the paedophile's fantasy. In many ways it resembles a 'collector syndrome' (Taylor 1999) that is equivalent to the stamp or football card collections that many adolescents indulge in, but with more sinister and tragic consequences.

---

**Typology of child pornography**

1. Indecent images – accessing, downloading, uploading, collection, distribution

2. Stories – written child pornography (currently not against the law but may be influential in the fantasy-arousal-orgasm cycle)

3. Research – knowledge base, feeds cognitive distortion

4. Role-play – with other paedophiles in chat rooms

5. Webcams

6. Networking – reinforcement of deviant attitudes

7. Grooming

(Adapted from Sullivan and Beech 2004)

Although paedophiles should by no means be underestimated in terms of their power to manipulate and abuse children, much of their behaviour signifies arrested adolescent development. This is manifest in the addictive nature of collecting child pornography images reminiscent of collecting stamps or football cards and the desire to belong to clubs reminiscent of gangs to which entry needs to be earned.

However, paedophiles who access the Internet and deem themselves to be merely curious or 'hobbyists' or collectors of images fail to realise that every image of a child being sexually abused is a permanent record of the fact that a child has been violated. Detective Superintendent Peter Spindler of the Metropolitan Police Service, London, argued that 'child pornography' or 'kiddie porn' have become acceptable, passive descriptions which fail to accurately describe the reality of the sexual acts forced upon children and suggests that 'child abuse images' is a much more appropriate phrase (Spindler 2003). Similarly the use of the term 'Internet paedophile' conjures up the perception that they are not really paedophiles but merely voyeurs, hobbyists, collectors or traders and as such pose no serious threat to actual children. Such perceptions fail to recognise the link between fantasy-arousal and actual sexual abuse (see Chapter 3)

Some paedophiles keep photographic images of children that they have already sexually abused as 'trophies' or reminders of the sexual encounter(s). These images capture the child's appearance at the age most desirable to the paedophile. Many paedophiles keep these images as personal memorabilia that they may fantasise and masturbate to, or they may be shared with others and appear in child pornography collections (Taylor *et al.* 2001a).

There is considerable evidence that some of the images of children are not necessarily explicitly pornographic. Many paedophiles enjoy looking at pictures of children who are in natural settings, fully clothed without any sexual connotations. Any erotic content is in the paedophile's mind. Rachel O'Connell's extensive research on the content of pictures depicting children used by paedophiles on-line found that these images can be placed on a continuum, from erotic material in which children are partially dressed, to nudity, to sexually explicit and sadistic sexual acts (O'Connell 1998). On the basis of this research, Taylor *et al.* (2001a) analysed a database of 80,000 images of children used paedophiles to establish a typology of paedophiles' picture collections, consisting of the categories in Table 4.1.

## Table 4.1 A typology of paedophile picture collections

| Level | Category | Description of image |
|---|---|---|
| 1 | Indicative | Non-erotic and non-sexual, no nudity. Children are dressed or in swimming costumes, or underwear. Often these are from clothing catalogues or advertisements. Others resemble family snap shots with children playing in natural settings and behaving in non-sexual ways. These images are *not illegal*; they merely show sexual interest in children. It is the paedophile's fantasy that sexualises the image. |
| 2 | Nudist | Images of naked, semi-naked children in legitimate, nudist settings. These are *not illegal* but show sexual interest in children. |
| 3 | Erotica | Covert photographs of partially clothed and varying degrees of nakedness of children, taken surreptitiously in natural settings such as paddling pools, swimming baths, beach, or innocent play. Taken in safe areas with high powered tele-photo lenses with parents and children unaware of being photographed. These are *not illegal* but are sexualised by the paedophile. |
| 4 | Posing | Deliberately posed images of children fully or partially clothed or naked. Often high quality, well produced, possibly professionally photographed with some degree of 'artistic' merit. *Not necessarily illegal* but sexualised by paedophile. |
| 5 | Erotic posing | Deliberately posed images of fully, partially clothed or naked children in sexualised or provocative poses. To some degree the equivalent of adult soft porn. Well produced, high quality taken outdoors, hotel rooms or opulent settings, in Western European locations. Implicitly sexual, stylised provocative poses, not explicitly sexual behaviour. Children often pretty, well fed, clean. These pictures may be associated with grooming. Often images are reproduced from magazines and scanned for distribution on the Internet. May have some artistic merit. *Not necessarily illegal.* |
| 6 | Explicit erotic posing | Images are sexually explicit, focus on genital/anal areas in which child is either naked, or partially clothed. Production and perusing are *illegal.* |

| 7 | Explicit sexual activity | These images involve touching, mutual and self-masturbation, oral sex and intercourse by child but not involving an adult. Production and perusing are *illegal*. |
| 8 | Assault | Images of children subjected to a sexual assault, involving digital touching by adults. Production and perusing are *illegal*. |
| 9 | Gross assault | Grossly obscene pictures of sexual assault, involving penetrative sex, masturbation or oral sex involving an adult. Production and perusing are *illegal*. |
| 10 | Sadistic/ bestiality | Images showing child being tied, bound, beaten, whipped or otherwise subjected to something that implies pain. Images where an animal is involved in some form of sexual behaviour with a child. Production and perusing are *illegal*. |

*Adapted from Taylor et al. 2001 and O'Connell 1998.*

It is clear from this continuum of images that not all images used by paedophiles are necessarily pornographic in nature or illegal. Some of them may be innocent snaps of children to which the paedophile becomes sexually aroused and fantasises and masturbates over. Such snaps cannot be controlled, which raises concerns about how paedophiles use photographic images of children. In this instance, the sexual arousal to children is not always dependent on graphic, erotic or pornographic images, but is 'in the eye of the beholder'. Many paedophiles collect photographs of children that are innocent. Their collections often include children's clothing catalogues or 'parent and child' magazines.

What becomes complex in these images of children is that many of them (levels 1–3) are not necessarily pornographic or illegal. They are just images of children in natural settings. Because of this, paedophiles do not believe that they are doing any harm as none of the children are being violated or sexually abused. The eroticisation and sexualisation is created by the paedophile in how he/she uses the images. In their mind they are just building up a collection and there is nothing illegal in that. In addition, some of the more sexualised images (levels 4–7), in which children are being exploited, do not necessarily involve adults and as such the child is not technically being sexually abused. It is only those images in levels 8–10 where actual sexual abuse by adults is taking place.

Child pornography images typically consist of smiling children who appear to be compliant and actively participating in their own sexual abuse. Often they appear to lovingly embrace the adult who is sexually assaulting them, giving the impression that they are enjoying the sexual assault. These images portray, and feed into, the paedophile's fantasy that children enjoy sexual activity with adults. This fantasy obscures the reality of CSA in which children may be in excruciating pain and distress, to the point of screaming, which is edited out. In some cases the children are drugged to ensure compliance, minimise resistance and give the impression of enjoyment.

These fantasy pictures also serve to legitimise the sexual abuse of children by normalising and sanitising it. This further fuels paedophiles' fantasies, enabling them to act out their individual fantasy in committing an actual offence. They frequently justify such sexual assaults by believing that the child is enjoying the experience because it did not resist, say 'No', complied, smiled or responded to the sexual approach. This serves to deny the reality of CSA and to 'romanticise' it as a mutually consensual, satisfying and enjoyable experience, which does no harm to the child whatsoever.

Paedophiles commonly misinterpret the child's reaction and response to sexual abuse with distorted thoughts such as, 'you know a baby likes sexual activity because it will thrust its genitals towards you', or 'if you throw a baby up in the air and it shouts blue murder, you know it does not like it. If however it gurgles and laughs, you know it does'.

Over half of child pornography on the Internet involves the sexual abuse of girls. It is estimated that 85–90 per cent of these are still images taken in the last 10 to 15 years that have been scanned into a computer from photographs or videos. Moving images from video formats are less common due to the poor quality of reproduction, something that will undoubtedly change with advances in digital photography. New images increasingly feature younger and younger children, especially girls.

More recent images produced in the last two years show an increase in child pornography using boys in the nine to twelve-year-old age group and more girls in the younger age group. There were more new images of level 7 and above for boys (26%) compared to girls with only 7 per cent. In the nine to twelve-year age group boys featured in 56 per cent of the images, and girls in 41 per cent of images. This was reversed in the nine-year-old and below age group, with 59 per cent of images featuring girls and 44 per cent boys.

While the typical age group featured in child pornography seems to be in the seven to eight, and ten to eleven-year-old age group, more recent images suggest that the age of children is reducing, especially for girls, with many appearing to be under five years of age. This may be due to the fact that many paedophiles prefer images of young and innocent looking children, who are not dressed in a sexually provocative way or wearing make-up. Increasingly, eight or nine-year-old girls wear adult-type clothing, including adult-like make-up. Such children may not fit paedophiles' fantasies, so they choose increasingly younger girls who do not dress or behave in adult ways, and thus look more childlike and innocent.

Another worrying feature of more recent images is an increase in level 10 images featuring explicit sadistic sexual activity. Most of the children used in level 7 and above in child pornography consist of white Caucasian children, with typically Nordic features who are slim and fair. The emphasis is on clearly visible genitalia with no secondary sex characteristics such as pubic hair. Asiatic children are more frequently seen in level 5 and 6 images, while black children are extremely rare. As yet it has not been possible to account fully for the marked absence of black children in child pornographic images.

It is thought that most children who are used in pornographic images at level 7 and above are from primarily Western Europe, America, Australia and South America, with a dramatic increase in Eastern European children. Level 5 and 6 images are more likely to consist of Asiatic children from Japan and Thailand. Many of the settings and locations of the images feature domestic background scenes such as bedrooms, living rooms, kitchens and other living areas.

Despite the poor quality of moving images on the Internet, there have been a number of cases, most notably the Orchid Club in 1997, in which children are sexually abused online. This involves a digital camera recording the sexual abuse of a child in real-time images tailored to club members' requests and specifications. Club members request a particular type of child, of a specific age, being subjected to specific sexual acts. A requisite child is then found and sexually abused for club members to watch via live transmission. Many of the members of the Orchid Club who availed themselves of this service came from America, Europe and Australia.

A further complexity of child pornographic images is that not all the pictures are photographs of actual children being sexually abused. To satisfy the huge demand for new images of new children many of the images are pseudo-images, which have been computer-generated, photoshopped, superimposed or doctored. Because no child is actually being abused, many paedophiles believe that they are not offending against children in any way. This justifies their belief that they are not doing any harm in looking at pseudo-images of child pornography, and that such activity should be seen as an acceptable form of sexual interest and not be criminalised. These pseudo-images can consist of the following (Taylor 1999).

### 1. DIGITALLY ALTERED

These are originally innocent photographs of children which are digitally altered to sexualise the child. An example would be a child in a swimming costume, which is digitally removed to show the child naked. Alternatively, another child's head or body part may be superimposed onto an image. This satisfies the paedophile's need to add new children to their ever expanding collection.

### 2. COMBINATION OF SEPARATE IMAGES

Several separate images are combined into one photograph. A common example may be a baby's or child's hand superimposed onto an adult's penis.

### 3. MONTAGE OF VARIOUS PICTURES

In these photographs various images, some of them sexual, will be put together to form a sexualised scenario involving sexual abuse.

As these pseudo-images technically do not represent a child actually being abused, and as such are merely technological wizardry, they allow the paedophile to justify his or her use of child pornography and deny the reality of CSA. It counteracts the argument that many child protection workers put forward that every time a pornographic image of a child is downloaded, a child is being sexually abused. The use of pseudo-images is not a legitimate excuse in that, even if there is no victim, these pseudo-images fuel paedophiles' fantasies which can become a catalyst for CSA.

It is currently not known how many child pornographic images involve the actual sexual abuse of a child and how many are pseudo-images. What is clear is that the technology exists to produce child pornography without the use of a child at all (Healy 1997). Whether this justifies the use of pseudo-images of children being sexually abused by paedophiles is hotly debated. Superimposing innocent pictures, such as school photos, onto the bodies of children being sexually abused is unjustifiable. Arguably, no parent would want a paedophile to use photoshopped images of their child in their fantasy-arousal cycle.

It is unknown what percentage of child pornography images are digitally generated. It is possible that some paedophiles claim that the images downloaded are computer-generated and therefore not harmful. Spotting genuine images would greatly help authorities to convict paedophiles. Advances in computer science will enable the development of systems that detect digital tampering and discriminate between real images and fake ones. One such system has been developed by Hany Farid at Dartmouth College, New Hampshire. It is able to discard computer-generated images as fake and thereby narrow down those likely to be genuine. In a database of 10,000 natural images and 5000 computer-generated images of child pornography, Farid was able to discard just over half of the supposedly computer-generated ones as fakes.

Some people argue that the use of pseudo-images, in which no child is actually being abused, can be therapeutic to those who have a sexual interest in children. It is similar to the argument proposed for the use of adult pornography in reducing rape, i.e. if child pornography is used purely for fantasy and arousal purposes, allowing the discharge of unacceptable urges, it serves to reduce the incidence of CSA. Others argue that fantasy and the use of child pornography fuels the paedophile's desire to sexually abuse and is linked to the cycle of offending.

Perhaps the biggest concern is that the issue of what percentage of child pornographic images are pseudo-images is a red herring that distracts from the majority of images of child pornography, which are real. This is aptly summed up by Rachel O'Connell, director of the Cyberspace Research Unit, who argues that, 'Why bother confecting images when so much of the real thing is available. Frankly, those paedophiles with advanced computer skills – and there are a significant number – use them to avoid detection. And this is what we should be worried about. The people who get identified by their credit card details are the naïve ones. There are plenty of adult paedophiles who have learnt how to cover their tracks and they are operating without any monitoring by police' (O'Connell 2003d).

It is still unknown to what extent child pornography acts as a catalyst for the expression of inappropriate sexual urges, and what percentage of paedophiles are 'lookers, or doers' (Reynolds 2002). American research quoted by Findlater (2002) indicates that around one-third of child pornography users concurrently sexually abuse children. As yet we have no accurate knowledge as to how many of those child pornography users investigated in high profile operations such as Operation Ore are also involved in CSA. Although 70 per cent of those questioned have no previous convictions for sexual offences against children, this does not guarantee that they might not sexually offend in the future, or that there is a history of previous assaults that have remained undetected.

There may be a number of motivations as to why adults look at, or download, child pornographic images. Max Taylor, director of the COPINE Project (Combating Paedophile Information Networks in Europe), which conducts research on the risks posed to children by child pornography on the Internet, has identified six types of involvement in child pornography on the Internet.

### 1. Confirmed collector

These are essentially individuals who collect large quantities of images, which are carefully catalogued and indexed by age, sex, or sexual activity. Such collectors can amass thousands of images.

### 2. Confirmed producer

These individuals engage in the sexual assault of children and take photographs of them, which they trade and exchange with other paedophiles.

### 3. Sexually omnivorous

This collector may have a wide range of odd and unusual sexual activities, which happen to include children.

### 4. Sexually curious

Curiosity is what drives this user, who may have only a small number of images to see what CSA is all about. In some cases this can be a step to growing involvement.

### 5. The libertarian

These users of child pornographic images download images as a matter of principle in exercising their right to freedom of access – some may consider themselves as 'political paedophiles' and use this as a way of rationalising their sexual interest in children.

### 6. The entrepreneur

These individuals develop websites and sell CD-ROMs of child pornographic images. They may be marginally involved in the wider sex industry.

As can be seen, there are number of reasons and motivations why people access child pornographic images from the Internet and they may be used for different purposes. Child pornography users are not uniform and have a variety of different motivations in wanting to look at and download images of children. Some may just look and download images, but not engage in any actual sexual assault, while others download as a prelude to sexual assault. Some are producers and/or distributors of child pornography and may or may not be involved in actual sexual assaults.

It is worth noting that while not all paedophiles who download child pornography necessarily follow on to sexually abuse children, there are many paedophiles who do sexually assault but make no use of child pornography at all. Thus the relationship between child pornography and CSA is still unclear. Research conducted by US Customs indicates that over one-third (36%) of those who buy child pornography on the Internet are not just viewers but actually sexually abuse children too (Wheaton 2003). What, however, is clear is that '...once a picture is in the public domain, it remains in circulation regardless of the fate of the producer' (Taylor 1999). One could argue that whether the photograph is a real image, or a pseudo-image, it will be stored and collected by paedophiles for years to come, and used for fantasy and arousal purposes long after the child has become an adult.

While the majority of child pornography consists of visual images of children, in some cases it can also be accompanied by text material in the form of stories involving sexual activities with children. While these are not illegal, they nevertheless play a crucial role in the sexual fantasy-arousal-masturbation cycle and can lead to actual sexual offences being committed on children. Whether there are accompanying visual images or not, the text primarily consists of erotic stories, some of which can be obscene and sadistic in nature, involving the sexual abuse of children. These are also highly collectable and are traded with other paedophiles.

While much of the focus has been on the use of child pornography on the Internet, recent concerns focus on new technology and how this may be exploited by paedophiles. Rachel O'Connell, director of the Cyberspace Research Unit at the University of Lancaster, and member of the Home Office Task Force on Child Protection on the Internet, has highlighted the dangers of the new generation of mobile phones that have Internet access and picture messaging services. These are open to exploitation by paedophiles in trading child pornography and the sexual grooming of children (see Chapter 5).

## Fantasy and child pornography

A common feature seen in most paedophiles is repetitive and highly predictable behaviour. The use of fantasy, combined with images of children and masturbation, serve to maintain the sexual arousal cycle. In masturbating to the fantasy, and images of children, the paedophile reinforces the arousal and satisfaction gained from the fantasy. This cycle of fantasy, sexual arousal, masturbation and ejaculation sets and sustains the paedophile's sexual desire, and has the potential to drive the urge to commit CSA.

Child sexual abusers report a diverse range of sexual fantasies, which are used for different purposes. Sullivan and Beech (2003) have categorised these into the following typology:

1. imagined non-contact

2. imagined consenting contact

3. imagined consenting contact becoming non-consenting contact

4. imagined non-consenting contact becoming consenting contact

5. imagined non-consenting contact throughout.

Each of these fantasy categories may contain appropriate and inappropriate (illegal) fantasies along with a variety of 'fantasy themes' to support the offender's fantasy life. Child pornography available on the Internet caters for these diverse fantasies ranging from innocent, legal images of children to extreme violence and sadistic images.

Even in the absence of child pornography the paedophile uses fantasy to establish and maintain sexual arousal to children by anticipating and rehearsing how he or she may target, groom and sexually abuse a child. In many ways the abuser is practising CSA in his/her head with opportunities to elaborate and refine his/her strategies for abusing. Fantasy also allows the abuser to re-live past sexual assaults, which can be embellished.

Initially the paedophile will masturbate to a particular fantasy. The combination of fantasy, sexual arousal, masturbation and ejaculation contributes to the conditioning of sexual abuse of children. The pleasure associated with masturbation and the release of ejaculation reinforces the abuser's fantasies. Over time this cycle may prove increasingly less satisfying, prompting the abuser to enact the fantasy. One way of doing this is to move on to child pornography.

It has been argued that looking at child pornography allows for the controlled release of sexual impulses towards children, which prevents actual CSA taking place. While this argument may have some value in relation to adult pornography, it may be less plausible in the case of CSA. The addictive nature of child pornography and the disinhibiting effect it has on the paedophile in terms of their thinking may actually promote the sexual abuse of a child in reality.

Although we do not know how many users of child pornography move on from 'just looking' to 'actually doing', many paedophiles report that over time just looking at child pornography becomes less satisfying to them in terms of their arousal. It is thought that the paedophile finds it harder to become aroused by the images and that masturbation and ejaculation are less satisfying. This is a result of habituation whereby repeated exposure to stimuli that were once novel, exciting and arousing loses the intensity of arousal. A good example is horror movies, which initially are very scary, but become less so with repeated watching. This prompts people to seek increasingly scary or arousing stimuli to satisfy the arousal.

Such habituation prompts some paedophiles to move along the continuum from innocent non-erotic images of children to more erotic and sexualised images, to sexually explicit level 9 and 10 images in which the sexual assault of the child is explicit. When the child pornography at this level ceases to be as satisfying, some paedophiles progress to actual sexual assault.

Some classic examples of the disinhibiting effect come from the following child pornography users (cited in Silverman and Wilson 2002).

> '[Viewing pornography on the Internet] made me want to do the things I wanted to do. It gave me more courage to do them…knowing that I've seen it on there…they were doing it…I can do it.'

> 'I would say it fulfilled my interest that I had anyway, that was in me…but it seemed to reinforce it…made me want to act it out.'

> 'It wasn't on the first night that I abused, but probably looking at the images on the Internet then…I seemed to notice her more.'

A study conducted by the Federal Bureau of Investigations in the USA in 1998 found that less than half of child pornography users sexually abuse children in reality. Current estimates are that approximately 30 per cent actually abuse, while 70 per cent do not. One has to be careful with such estimates, however, as just because they have not had any previous convictions does not mean that they do not have a history of sexual offending against children.

It is thought that the majority of child pornography users use pornographic images as a substitute for sexual offending. Another crucial factor in child pornography is that it affects paedophiles' thinking in providing a powerful justification for sexual activity with children. Child pornographic images legitimise sexual activity between adults and children and validate the paedophile's sexual interest. This can lead to cognitive distortions in which the paedophile rationalises that because other children are being sexually abused in the pornography, he or she can also find a child to sexually assault. This can lead to an escalation of sexual offending by actually targeting and grooming a child in reality. Thus child pornography can lend support to the paedophile's fantasies and can empower them to abuse. In the words of one paedophile, 'I was finding more explicit stuff on the computer and I was looking at the computer and thinking, oh…they're doing it…it can't be that bad'.

Once the paedophile has overcome any internal and external inhibitors he or she may start the grooming process (see Chapter 5). Throughout the grooming process, the paedophile will repeat the cycle of fantasy, masturbation and ejaculation in anticipation of the actual assault. When the abuser finally breaks down the child's resistance, the sexual assault can commence. This may necessitate the abuser reinterpreting the victim's behaviour as 'she wanted it' or 'he made me do it', which serves to justify the assault. This leads to further distorted thinking, in which the abuser rationalises his or her behaviour by reinterpreting the child's experience.

If the abuser experiences negative feelings, these also have to be re-interpreted in order to justify the assault. Such distorted thinking allows the abuser to 'normalise' the sexual behaviour, which serves to maintain the sexual abuse. Many paedophiles retreat into sexual fantasies about children during times of stress or when in an emotionally vulnerable state, which reactivates the cycle to abuse.

Thus, child pornography is used as a way of modifying the paedophile's moods, and to manage tolerance and withdrawal effects. Any conflicts such as society's attitudes, the nature of relationships and negative feelings about the self are further rationalised away, allowing the paedophile to relapse into sexual offending against children. The paedophile now becomes trapped in an addictive cycle of sexually offending against children in which child pornography plays a central role.

It is clear that child pornography does not cause sexual offending but that '...individuals who are already pre-disposed to sexually offend are the most likely to show an effect of pornography exposure and are most likely to show the strongest effects' (Seto et al. 2001). While some paedophiles may use child pornography as a substitute to offending, for some it acts as a blueprint and stimulus for future contact offences against children.

## Contact with other paedophiles

The use of child pornography on the Internet allows for contact with other paedophiles in cyberspace. This allows the paedophile to retain a certain anonymity yet feel part of a 'virtual community', giving them a sense of belongingness. Given that paedophiles are commonly vilified and stigmatised by isolating and alienating themselves from the community, the sense of belongingness they feel in being in contact with other paedophiles can provide a breeding ground for justifying their sexual interest in children. In effect, it empowers the marginalised paedophile. In being in contact with other paedophiles, the paedophile feels less alone in their interest and feel less like a pervert. This allows them to normalise CSA and blame society for its lack of understanding and draconian laws, which are designed to make the paedophile feel bad.

Contact with other paedophiles is also a way to expand a collection of child pornography. Paedophiles will trade images of children to complete their collections. They may also learn tactics and strategies from other paedophiles in how to groom children, how to manipulate them and prepare them for sexual contact. Thus it can act as a breeding ground to acquire new knowledge and information, not just about how to access child pornography and how to expand their collection but how to sexually abuse a child.

Research has shown that the exchange of information between paedophiles online centres around the following (O'Connell 2003a):

- exchange and trading of child pornography
- information about online grooming
- information on the selection and targeting of children
- information on how best to target and groom a child
- information on ways to avoid detection
- how to procure or buy a child over the Internet
- where to buy sexual accessories that might be used in the sexual abuse of a child.

Information about how to train children to be sexually responsive can be accessed, including graphic details about how to manipulate, seduce and prepare a child for sexual intercourse. Details about the sexual abuse of younger rather than older children in reducing the chances of exposure or disclosure can also be accessed. These are all designed to improve the paedophile's strategies to entice and ensnare children for the purpose of sexual grooming and the commission of sexual assaults.

## Buying, selling or exchanging children on the Internet

A further use of the Internet for paedophiles is to provide access to information on how to procure a child for sexual purposes. Contacts can be made through the Internet with people who provide a child for sexual purposes at a fee to the paedophile. The paedophile provides details of their requirements such as age, gender and look of child, and the kind of sexual activity they wish to engage in. Once a price has been agreed, the paedophile then has the opportunity to meet and sexually abuse the child. The most recent example is the case of the 19-year-old trainee teacher, Luke Sadowski, who tried to procure a nine-year-old girl for sex at a cost of £250.

As a response to the buying and selling of children over the Internet, websites have been set up that are designed to detect such trading in children. While there are clear rules and regulations around blatant 'entrapment' or officers acting as agents provocateurs, current legislation allows some level of undercover operations. Police officers from the High Tech Crime Unit of Scotland Yard's Child Protection Command trawl Internet websites and chat rooms, masquerading as either children, or paedophiles, in order to flush out and make contact with paedophiles. Such contact not only enables them to understand the minds of paedophiles but also allows them to access information about the variety of ways paedophiles sexually offend against children.

While the number of undercover online officers is limited in the UK due to lack of funding, this is not the case in America where there are currently some 50,000 online officers. This is presumably why most of the major UK investigations into child pornography have been as a result of information passed to the police by American agencies. The US Immigration and Customs Enforcement Agency has a number of websites designed to attract paedophiles without falling into the category of 'entrapment'. This is done by not explicitly advertising sex with children but by offering 'fantasy tours' in which the paedophiles give details of their own fantasies.

It was precisely such a 'fantasy tour' website that led to the arrest of Luke Sadowski. The US customs site bartered with Sadowski over a period of months over the price of the child, amount of time he could spend with the child, whether she was a virgin or not, and the sexual acts to be committed. As Sadowski was unable to afford travel to the US he was directed to a contact in the UK who would assist him in his fantasy tour. Unbeknown to him, the US investigator had passed on the information to undercover detectives in London. After several e-mails and telephone conversations with this London contact, a meeting was finally set up, resulting in Sadowski's arrest by the Metropolitan Police as he arrived at the hotel where he was to meet the nine-year-old Lithuanian girl.

Sadowski was found to be carrying an imitation Glock handgun, a condom and a teddy bear ostensibly for the little girl he was about to sexually abuse. After the arrest the police found further weapons, leg shackles, three sets of handcuffs, a police baton, a knife and roll of tape at his student accommodation, most of which were bought over the Internet. They also found a number of newspaper articles about paedophiles and child murders, some covered in semen stains showing that Sadowski had masturbated over the stories.

The judge was only able to sentence Sadowski to 18 months imprisonment for using the Internet to try to buy sex with a nine-year-old girl. It is not until the new Sexual Offences Bill comes into effect in spring 2004 that the law will be toughened up, making the procurement and sexual trafficking of children over the Internet a criminal offence carrying a maximum penalty of 14 years imprisonment.

Some paedophiles use the Internet to swap children who are already being sexually abused. In some cases these are paedophiles' own children, which are exchanged for sexual purposes. Alternatively the paedophile trades children that he or she has 'broken in' and wants to trade for another child. This ensures the constant rotation of children between paedophiles. Some paedophiles use the Internet to pass on or trade children that they have 'broken in' but who have outgrown the age group that most interests them to swap them for a younger child.

## Using child pornography in the grooming of children to reduce inhibition

Child pornography not only enables the paedophile to overcome any inhibitions but can also be used in the sexual grooming of children. Some paedophiles use child pornographic images to desensitise the child to sexual activity and acts. In showing the child adult and/or child pornography, the abuser aims to overcome any resistance the child may have to sexual activity. In viewing adult/child pornography children are shown directly that sexual activity between adults and children is normal and that it is OK to engage in such activities.

This is frequently accompanied by verbal statements, such as, 'Look, if it wasn't OK these children and adults would not be allowed to do this. As they are, it must be OK. Would you like to try it and see?' as a way of normalising such activity. Older children may be shown adult pornography, which is potentially arousing and sexually exciting, making it easier to engage the child in sexual behaviour with the paedophile.

## The extent of child pornography on the Internet

It is clear that child pornography has a huge audience worldwide, which suggests that sexual interest in children is much more widespread than was once thought. Even though not all child pornography users actively sexually offend against children they are nevertheless feeding the increasing and growing demand for the global sexual exploitation of children. Irrespective of its relationship to actual sexual offences, there is a powerful argument that the possession of child pornography should be subject to severe sanctions.

The use of pornography thus becomes a powerful tool in the sexual abuse of children. The use of the Internet for child pornography is a huge multi-million pound industry worldwide. It is thought that there are currently 260,000 international subscribers to child pornography sites on the Internet. Recent examples such as the Wonderland Club, Operation Candyman, Operation Orchid, Operation Avalanche in America, and Operation Ore have shown on what scale child pornography exists and provided insight into the extent, breadth and diversity of offenders and behavioural types.

Operation Cathedral took four years to investigate the Wonderland Club in the late 1990s, involving 13 countries, and found what was effectively a global swap shop. The entry requirement to qualify as a member of the Wonderland Club was 10,000 fresh child pornography images. In total the police seized 750,000 individual images and 180,000 digitalised video clips of pre-pubescent children, some only a few months old.

Operation Avalanche, a massive undercover sting operation in the US in 2002, resulted in the Federal Bureau of Investigations passing on the names and credit card details of 7272 individuals resident in the UK who had used their credit cards to access images of children, some as young as a few months old. This launched the UK's biggest paedophile investigation, Operation Ore. To date some 1700 people have been questioned and arrested. It is believed that the FBI have a further 10,000 UK names and addresses that they are due to pass on to the National Crime Squad and National Criminal Intelligence Service.

These figures are highly disturbing, not only in terms of the quantity of names but also the cost and time to fully investigate all those on the list. It has taken over a year to investigate 1700 names, which barely represents a quarter of the names on the original list. It is questionable whether the police will be able to investigate all the names on that list, let alone cope with any new lists.

In addition, it is highly unlikely that the criminal justice system, especially the courts, can cope with the processing and sentencing of so many individuals. Custodial sentences will put enormous pressure on already overstretched prison facilities, while community sentences and being placed on the Sex Offenders' Register will create huge demands on an already overstretched police and probation service. This presents serious dilemmas in how to deal with those individuals who are investigated.

It is also phenomenally costly and time-consuming to amass electronic evidence from individual computers, and there are not enough experts to analyse the material. Some UK police forces have waited months for a computer expert to become available. It can take up to 15 hours to gather evidence from a computer hard disk and cost on average £2500 to analyse each computer fully and retrieve forensic evidence and records. Given that each name investigated so far through Operation Ore necessitated the forensic examination of on average two to three computers demonstrates the huge cost involved. To cope with the scale of investigation the Association of Chief Police Officers has requested an extra £100,000 million of funding from the Government for a national strategy to co-ordinate the investigations and any further necessary action. They were allocated a mere £500,000. When this money is distributed among the 43 police forces, it allows the analysis of approximately two and a half computers per regional police force, which translates to one paedophile per region.

This scandalous lack of funding and manpower seriously undermines Operation Ore's investigations. Not surprisingly the police are concerned how long it will take to complete the investigation of the remaining names on the list, with estimates of up to two years. All they are able to do at present is to prioritise names on the list in terms of frequency of access and number of images downloaded. This means that to date only 10 per cent of the names have been investigated Although the Government has promised the allocation of £25 million over the next three years, what is not clear is how this will be allocated.

The majority of names provided to Operation Ore are male (99.9%) ranging from 25 to 65 years of age. They are predominantly middle class pro-fessional people, comprising teachers, magistrates, solicitors, civil servants, local and county councillors, a crown prosecutor, a judge, two former members of parliament, 390 police officers, top business people and celebrities in the entertainment industry. Although 95 per cent had no previous convictions for sexual offending against children, claiming that they had only ever initiated one visit to a child pornography website, out of curiosity rather than developing a future interest, 46 were actively abusing children when investigated. As a result of Operation Ore, 60 children have been placed in care.

Many of the individuals investigated during these operations claim that they are merely exercising their right to access such pornography, are not actually sexually abusing a child, and that such viewing is therefore harmless. This is patently absurd in the case of real images, which have not been digitally enhanced or artificially doctored, as each image represents a child being sexually assaulted. Although the viewer may not actually be in sexual contact with the child, by accessing such images he or she is supporting the sexual abuse of children by creating a demand for child pornography and providing the financial resources to sustain the industry.

The police are acutely aware of this and have set up initiatives to identify the children who are being abused through picture-tracking, attempting to find them in order to stop any further abuse. Sadly many such initiatives and operations are critically under-resourced with too few officers and not enough financial support to follow through appropriate investigations. Such lack of resourcing results in the failure to protect children. Given the limited amount of resources, in already over-stretched criminal investigations, individual police forces need to prioritise where resources are allocated. Often there are differences between what individuals expect from their police force, with some preferring resources to be diverted into fighting street crime at the expense of protecting children.

A good example is the Metropolitan Police who have consistently made child protection their key priority. According to Detective Superintendent Spindler the role of the police is to provide strategic aims 'to protect children from sexual abuse' and to 'help make the UK cyberspace the safest place in the world for Internet users' (Spindler 2003). To this effect four primary objectives have been identified:

1.  victim identification – identify past and present victims, locate them and develop a comprehensive database of victims

2.  suspect location – identify and arrest suspects and Internet users who have a sexual predilection for children

3. industry co-operation – work with Internet industry to remove child sexual abuse images and reduce opportunities for access to children for paedophiles

4. crime reduction and public safety – through the media reassure public of police commitment to adequately police the Internet to ensure that the fear of crime is placed firmly on the offender.

However, the London Boroughs do not always support this, with less than 50 per cent citing child protection as a priority within their local community. This impacts on the allocation of their resources and budgets, which are diverted into fighting other crimes. This would indicate the need for a nationally set budget for child protection, which has to be allocated specifically for this purpose and not be used at the discretion of the local authorities and regional police forces.

What is needed is a national increase in resources to ensure effective law enforcement along with a national campaign emphasising the need for child protection. A public health and education programme such as a national child safety watch, which raises public awareness of the dangers of CSA and the use of the Internet, is also needed to ensure that children are appropriately protected. It is only with such initiatives that we can effectively protect children and prevent CSA (see Chapter 10).

The responsibility of Internet Service Providers (ISP) is also called into question in allowing the pornographic images to be transmitted. There is much controversy as to what extent ISPs can, or should, monitor or censor child pornography, given that child pornography is a global activity. Difficulties arise in unifying all countries to refrain from transmitting such images. The sexual abuse of children is of global concern and should demand universal restriction of child pornography on the Internet.

The major credit card companies such as Visa, MasterCard and American Express have also become involved in monitoring and investigating the volume of child pornography users. To date they have identified 260,000 incidents of credit card use to view child pornography in the UK alone, with Visa identifying 100,000 transactions. Visa has implemented a system in which they identify purveyors of child pornography which they then report to global police forces. To date they have withdrawn Visa privileges to 80 per cent of 400 child pornography sites and been influential in having them shut down.

It is only the combined action of all parties involved, including governments, criminal investigation agencies, ISPs, designers and manufacturers of electronic technology, the credit card companies and all those involved in child protection, that will facilitate the reduction of child pornography on the Internet. This in turn will ensure the protection of children and the prevention of CSA by transmitting a unified global message, which refuses to tolerate the sexual abuse of children.

## Sexual grooming of children on the Internet

Sexual grooming on the Internet primarily consists of paedophiles using personal websites to target children who meet the paedophile's specific predilection for age, gender and looks. In particular paedophiles target websites that provide public information about the child's profile. The aim is to befriend a child online to sexually abuse offline at a later date. Many paedophiles systematically trawl and search sites that are hosted by ISPs and search engines that request that children provide a personal profile about themselves, their looks, hobbies and interests, including a photograph.

The sexual grooming of children on the Internet is a huge concern for parents and children. It has also been addressed by the Government who funded a £1.5 million advertising campaign in 2002 to warn children and parents of the dangers of chat room paedophiles 'without demonising the Internet'. This campaign was successful in increasing awareness in 11 per cent of children about the dangers of Internet chatrooms and how not to give out personal details. The campaign also generated increased awareness in 12 per cent of parents with regard to Internet safety. The Government is to follow up this campaign with a further £1 million advertising campaign to reinforce the danger of the Internet.

In addition, the Government is introducing new legislation in 2004 in the new Sexual Offences Bill, which will make the sexual grooming of children on and offline a criminal offence with a maximum penalty of 10 years imprisonment. In order for parents, teachers and children to enjoy fully the use of the Internet without worrying about being selected or targeted by a paedophile, it is essential to be aware of how paedophiles use the Internet to sexually groom children. Having such information can offer some level of protection.

However, detecting and prosecuting paedophiles who sexually groom children on the Internet is difficult and complex. This is primarily due to the lack of reporting by children, but also due to the absence of good forensic evidence. Most chat rooms do not have a facility to save transcripts of online conversations, so unless the child saves conversations onto a hard disk, or downloads such transcripts, it may be difficult to obtain evidential records of sexual grooming to construct a solid court case. Peer-to-peer file sharing software such as KaZaA, Morpheus and Grokster has dwarfed any previous paedophile network activity. Peer-to-peer file sharing allows images to be accessed free of charge and anonymously, making it impossible to trace.

More and more child sexual abusers are thought to be abandoning the use of fixed Internet contact with children by accessing children through mobile phones. Currently in the UK 60 per cent of secondary school children own a mobile phone, and 20 per cent of primary school children. Increasingly paedophiles are exploiting the new technology in the new generation of 3G mobile phones, which have Internet access and camera attachments, to target and groom children. According to O'Connell (2003c), in Japan, where such phones are more readily available, there has been a 260 per cent increase in child sexual abuse and child pornography offences using mobile phones. In addition, in 90 per cent of child sexual abuse cases investigated, the initial contact was instigated via mobile phone.

High profile Internet safety campaigns which have encouraged parents to monitor and supervise their children's use of the computer and Internet access will need to be revised with the availability of new generation G3 mobile phones with features such as Internet access and cameras. Such G3 mobile phones can allow children access to Internet sites in which they can be groomed, view child pornographic images, and be encouraged to take pictures of themselves in sexual poses and send them to the paedophiles. Such production and trading in images implicates the child in illegal activities of being both the producer and distributor of child pornography.

As pre-paid phones cannot be traced, in the absence of records of who owns the handset it will be very difficult to obtain concrete evidence of such activities. A further concern is that current technology is not available to retrieve messages on mobile phones, or track the content of any pictures sent.

This makes it almost impossible to prove or retrieve forensic evidence to prosecute.

A number of UK mobile phone companies are developing technology to bar any inappropriate web content from mobile phones owned by children, while O2 have launched a safety and awareness campaign for children and parents to minimise such risks (O2 2004).

To facilitate the responsible use of these new mobile phones, and allay parental fears, the UK mobile phone operators have devised a joint code of practice to safeguard children from unsuitable content on their mobiles (O2 2004). The code covers content such as visual images, Internet access, chat rooms, online gambling and mobile gaming. The main points of the code are:

- barring unsuitable material to under 18 year olds, through a process of age verification

- moderating chat rooms made available to under 18 year olds

- provision of filters that parents and carers can apply to the mobile operator's Internet access service so that Internet content can be restricted

- that mobile operators will work with law enforcement agencies to deal with the reporting of content that may break the criminal law

- that they will provide advice to customers on the nature and use of the new mobile devices.

It is hoped that such a code will ensure that safeguards are in place to protect children. While it is a joint code of practice, each operator will provide a copy of the code which can be accessed from their individual websites. This needs to be considered by the criminal justice system in implementing the new 'anti-grooming' legislation. Without hard evidence it may also be difficult to establish 'intention' to sexually groom a child. Thus, although the new legislation is largely welcomed by child protection agencies there is considerable doubt about how it can be effectively implemented.

Further concern centres around the limited capacity to save copies of communications on mobile devices such as the new 3G mobile phones. It may be impossible to retrieve information from mobile facilities such as SMS, MMS, and video messaging and voice mail. Researchers such as Rachel O'Connell are very concerned about such new technology and strongly urge mobile phone product developers and software engineers to take such factors into account by incorporating facilities to save copies of conversations, which can be used as evidence in court. Many paedophiles are highly computer literate, are already aware of the loopholes and limitations of mobile technology, and may already have moved from fixed Internet use to mobile Internet use in their quest to avoid detection.

In addition it is not uncommon for paedophiles to target children from other countries in the hope of avoiding detection and/or prosecution due to different legislation in other countries. An example of this was the former US marine Toby Studabaker, who befriended Shevaun Pennington, a 12-year-old girl from the UK, over a period of a year, culminating with their meeting up in Manchester en route to Frankfurt in July 2003.

Paedophiles are highly ingenious in attemping to avoid detection. According to Protectkids (2004) many paedophiles use computers in public libraries to engage in online sexual activities and view child pornography as a way of minimising the monitoring and detection of their activities.

According to O'Connell (2003a) there are two different types of paedophiles who surf the Internet to entice and ensnare children for sexual purposes. One is overtly predatory in his intention – what O'Connell calls the cyber-rapist – while the other is equally predatory but operates in a much more covert manner by befriending and grooming children for sexual activity. To what extent these two types of paedophile are distinct is still unclear and needs further investigation and research.

### Cyber-rapist

The primary aim of the cyber-rapist is to engage a child in online sexual activity, though overt coercion, control and aggression. The cyber-rapist operates on the principle of 'hit and run' whereby he spends very little time getting to know the child but uses an opportunity to engage in sexual exchange as quickly as possible. In addition, he rarely targets the same child twice and does not arrange to meet the child. The 'hit and run' tactic employed by the cyber-rapist makes him much harder to detect than the paedophile who grooms the child over a period of time. O'Connell (2003a) has identified the following characteristics associated with the cyber-rapist:

- Use of control and direct aggression
- Uses aggressive demands when coercing child into rape fantasies
- Aim is to achieve sexual release online

- Rarely interested in arranging meetings with child offline
- Rarely schedules another encounter with the same child online
- Spends considerably less time cultivating trust of the child
- Employs a 'hit and run' mentality
- Does not consider damage limitation
- Goes straight into rape fantasy by asking child what it feels about the specific sexual act being done to it
- Looking for a negative reaction from the child as this fuels his sexual excitement
- Non-contact sexual abuse
- Rationalises behaviour as not serious as it is not real but online, in cyberspace and therefore not physically abusing the child
- Sees the cyber-rape as cathartic – cannot engage adults to enact in rape fantasies therefore targets children whom he thinks are more malleable
- Psychological profile similar to other types of rapists
- Driven by power rather than sex.

Given the difficulty in detecting the cyber-rapist, more research is needed to understand fully his motivations and sexual offending pattern against children. O'Connell recommends that this category of Internet paedophile may require specific new legislation to deal with the fact that although sexual rape is carried out in cyberspace, no actual contact is made with the child. Furthermore, because of the 'one-off' nature of the cyber assaults it may be much harder to obtain forensic evidence of the assault, making it much harder to keep track of his offending behaviour, and achieve detection or prosecution. Researchers also need to assess the psychological impact of cyber-rape on the child in terms of short and long-term effects.

## Covert sexual grooming by paedophiles

The majority of paedophiles who enter chat rooms to target children for the purposes of sexual grooming behave in a much more covert and subtle manner than the cyber-rapist in that they counterbalance overt coercion with intimacy. They spend a considerably longer period of time in the selection, targeting and befriending of a child. In building up a friendship the paedophile gains the child's trust and gives the illusion of mutuality in his relationship with the child. This makes it much easier to manipulate and seduce the child into sexual contact. There are a number of stages that the paedophile has to negotiate in order to complete the sexual grooming. Prior to this, the paedophile needs to select a victim.

## Victim selection

The majority of paedophiles will hover in chat rooms on the Internet frequented by children. They will frequently choose chat rooms in which the chat service provider requests the child's 'personal profile' online. This consist of the child's real name, age, location, hobbies and interests, including a photograph of the child. These profiles are publicly available to all those who use the chat room facility. The public profile usually provides sufficient information to satisfy the paedophile's curiosity that the selected child will fit his preferences for age, gender, appearance and proximity.

The paedophile also provides a description of himself to the members of the chat room, albeit heavily disguised. The majority of paedophiles masquerade as a particular kind of child with regard to age, gender and hobbies and interests in the hope of attracting an equivalent child. This necessitates constructing a profile that is plausible and representative of an actual child. The paedophile then waits for a response from the selected child. Once this is obtained, the paedophile will activate a vetting procedure in which he will check to see how malleable the child is and how likely he will be able to proceed in grooming the child.

Paedophiles have to be quite skilled in this so as not to blow their cover. This means that they have to spell and misspell like a child, use child-like syntax and grammar, and age-appropriate language and slang. To verify his target and ensure that he is not a victim of a 'sting operation' designed to entrap him, he may hack into the child's computer to ensure that everything on the hard disks fits the profile of a child that age. He will check music files, e-mails to and from friends, and other information related to problems at school or at home.

Some paedophiles spend as much time verifying their target as they do grooming the child. This also provides the paedophile with background information about the child. Needless to say this verification process is equally implemented by undercover police officers who pose as children and ensure that their hard disks are compatible with a child of the chosen age. Once he has verified the child and chooses to pursue the conversation, they will start to chat online. After a period of getting to know the child, the paedophile might send the child a private message, or suggest that they move from a public to a private chat room in which they can have an exclusive one-to-one conversation.

Alternatively, some paedophiles lurk in chat rooms, listening to the conversations of the children to assess whether one fits his specific preferences for age, gender and malleability. After a period of time he might introduce himself to the particular child he has been observing and strike up a conversation. While most paedophiles pretend to be children, a proportion pose as adults, albeit younger than they actually are, and present themselves as mentors to the child.

In her five-year study of child cybersexploitation and online grooming practices, O'Connell (2003a) identified a consistent pattern in the way paedophiles approached children in chat rooms. She was able to identify five distinct stages although these were not always sequentially activated. Some paedophiles skipped some stages, while others stayed longer in some stages. The order and number of stages varied among paedophiles, as did the goals associated with each stage. A clear pattern emerged, which served a specific purpose, whether this was the psychological manipulation and seduction of the child, or the risk assessment of exposure. The five stages identified by O'Connell (2003a) are: the friendship forming stage, relationship forming stage, risk assessment stage, exclusivity stage – mutual love and trust, and the sexual stage. Each is now described.

## 1. THE FRIENDSHIP FORMING STAGE

The amount of time taken by a paedophile in this stage can vary enormously and is dependent upon the level of contact. The paedophile will flatter the child and encourage it to chat in a private chat room, to isolate it. According to O'Connell this stage is characterised by:

- getting to know the child
- establishing a level of contact during which the paedophile monitors the child's responses

- requesting a non-sexual photograph of the child in order to verify that the child matches his predilections and as a way of identifying the child in the real world.

## 2. RELATIONSHIP FORMING STAGE

This is an extension of stage 1 but the paedophile now begins to form a relationship with the child. This is achieved by getting the child to reveal more about itself:

- engaging the child in talking about school and home life
- creating the illusion of being the child's 'best friend'
- interspersing the online contact with questions related to risk assessment.

## 3. RISK ASSESSMENT STAGE

During this stage the paedophile gathers information which enables him to assess the level of risk in terms of detection. This stage is characterised by asking the child specific questions such as:

- location of the computer
- number of users who access the computer
- relationships with parent(s), guardian, siblings and friends to assess likelihood of detection or exposure.

## 4. EXCLUSIVITY STAGE – MUTUAL LOVE AND TRUST

There is a change of tempo as the paedophile builds up a sense of mutual love and trust with the child, by suggesting it can discuss 'anything' it wants. This is achieved by:

- reminding the child that they are 'best friends', that he understands the child and that the child can tell him anything
- building up a strong sense of mutuality – mutual respect, a mutual agreement to keep their activities 'secret'
- introducing the notion of trust
- focusing on intimacy
- setting up the next stage.

## 5. THE SEXUAL STAGE

The emphasis is now on increasing intimacy and the introduction of sexual material to facilitate the paedophile's fantasy enactment. This achieved by describing particular sexual scenarios, which aim to produce sexual gratification. Underlying these sexual enactments is the paedophile's perception of mutuality, in which the child feels loved and the paedophile desires that the child fall in love with him. This illusion of love is sustained by fluctuating between inviting the child to participate and emotionally blackmailing it if it resists. The emotional blackmail is fundamentally based on the potential withdrawal of the friendship. This mutuality is enacted through online mutual masturbation, oral sex or virtual penetrative sex. Examples include the following:

- Begins to ask direct questions such as 'Have you ever been kissed?' or 'Do you ever touch yourself?'

- Initially these are fairly innocuous.

- Very intense conversations which are difficult for the child to navigate as they are unusual and unfamiliar.

- Paedophile starts to use leverage, such as 'You can talk to me about anything.'

- Reinforcement of trust and love, which is a vital part of the paedophile's fantasy life.

- Presents himself as a sexual mentor guiding the child to greater understanding of his/her sexuality or future lover.

- If child is uncomfortable or the paedophile senses a potential break in the relationship, he will relinquish the pressure and express regret, to which the child responds with forgiveness, which establishes even deeper mutuality.

- Begins to outline rationale for relationships such as a loving, lasting friendship/relationship.

- Gently begins to intimate his intentions such as 'Maybe we could meet one day and I could show you how much I love you' or 'Maybe you could take photographs of you touching yourself.'

- Sends pornography to the child to encourage child to engage in the fantasy sexual activity, or to lower inhibition.

- Gets the child to take child pornographic image of itself by using a webcam or digital camera to send to the paedophile. These can approximate what the paedophile has sent, or what matches a particularly set of suggestions outlined by him that fit his fantasy – effectively making the child both producer and distributor of child pornography.

- Gets child to record pornographic video stream images in real time which are transmitted to the paedophile.

- Blurs boundaries of child's involvement – creator and distributor of child pornography.

- Sexual content initially mild but becomes more explicit, such as descriptions of oral sex.

- Focus is primarily on the child, such as child touching itself, or describing what it feels like.

- Assures the child that by engaging in such activities the child will grow into a wonderful lover.

- Teaches the child how to self-masturbate.

- Discusses techniques for how to bring the adult to orgasm if they meet.

- May progress to face-to-face meeting and actual sexual contact.

In order to step up the level of communication, the paedophile may send the child a mobile phone so that they can speak to each other more frequently and easily but asks the child to keep this a secret and to only use it to communicate with each other. Following on from this the paedophile may seek to establish physical contact by arranging to meet, perhaps to go to a concert or football match. If the child does meet the paedophile the sexual seduction will be activated as in the grooming process. Again, because the child has built up this 'special' friendship in which it has emotionally invested it becomes difficult to withdraw, rendering the grooming process complete and paving the way for sexual abuse to occur.

Throughout these stages the paedophile will implement damage limitation tactics in providing positive encouragement and high praise to the child to reduce the risk of being caught. The aim is to ensure that the child is not frightened into disclosing the 'secret'. Such damage limitation exercises have an almost ritualistic type quality in the paedophile consistently reminding the child how much he loves it. The ultimate goal for most paedophiles is to seduce and groom the child online in order to enact the sexual fantasy offline by arranging to meet the child. This process can take many months, sometimes years. Evidence for this comes from cases such as Michael Wheeler, aged 36 from Cambridge, who sexually groomed two 13-year-old girls on the Internet for 18 months before finally luring them into an actual sexual relationship.

Once that actual sexual contact takes place the paedophile may continue sexual contact for some time or conclude the grooming process. This is most likely if he fears exposure and detection, or if the child outgrows the paedophile's preferred age. The paedophile might then trade the child, callously sever all contact or request the child to recruit friends that he can also involve in sexual activity.

It is evident that the online sexual grooming of children is a slow, gentle yet deliberate process that can take place over a considerable period of time before any actual sexual contact is made with the child. It is therefore crucial that parents and teachers are aware of this process so that they can intervene before the child is actually sexually assaulted and effectively protect children. Parents need to familiarise themselves with computers and the Internet in order to monitor Internet access, and a website contact, especially if the computer is the child's own, or is in the child's room rather than accessible for all the family. Clearly it is not just fixed Internet technology that puts children at risk, but the increase in new mobile technology such as the 3G mobile phones that also poses enormous risks to children. In the same way that parents discuss other dangers with their child, it is important to discuss the dangers of the Internet and mobile phones. To facilitate this, Chapter 9 gives a detailed account of how parents and teachers can best protect children from Internet grooming.

However, it is not just the responsibility of parents, teachers or children. It is crucial that accurate knowledge about such dangers is disseminated to all who come into contact with children. Prevention needs to be supported by a national child protection strategy and public health education campaign, which give a clear message of zero tolerance of sexual offences against children, including the use of child pornography on the Internet. This needs to be supported by global co-ordination between governments, ISPs, credit card companies, product developers and child Internet safety groups.

While the new anti-grooming legislation is a welcome step in protecting children from online grooming, there are a number of problems, not least access to evidential records that need to be addressed to ensure these measures are effective enough. Otherwise it will create an illusion of protecting children, which is not supported in the criminal justice system. All these initiatives need to be supported, properly resourced and funded to protect children. In the absence of this paedophiles will continue to avoid detection.

Having explored the nature and scale of child pornography on the Internet and the sexual grooming of children online, the next chapter examines how children are sexually groomed offline. It is noticeable that both online and offline sexual grooming share similar dynamics, and combined knowledge of the two will further empower parents and teachers to be aware of the seductive nature of paedophiles in their sexual offending against children.

## Chapter 5

# The Grooming of Children

Monsters don't get close to children, nice men do...

Ray Wyre

The establishment (and eventual betrayal) of affection and trust occupies a central role in the child molester's interactions with children... The grooming process often seems similar from offender to offender, largely because it takes little to discover that emotional seduction is the most effective way to manipulate children.

Anna C. Salter

Basically we are wolves in sheep's clothing that is why parents and children trust us, and that is how we avoid detection...you'd be amazed at how easy it is to fool parents, adults and children...they just have no idea.

A paedophile, age 30

Most cases of child sexual abuse rarely start with a direct act of sexual assault or rape. Commonly, paedophiles spend considerable time targeting, enticing and ensnaring a child for sexual purposes. This process is called grooming. Many professionals working in the area of child protection have known about the sexual grooming of children by paedophiles for some considerable period of time. With the implementation of so-called 'anti-grooming' legislation contained in the new Sexual Offences Bill, it will finally be recognised as an actual criminal offence with a maximum penalty of five years imprisonment. This is in part due to the fact that increasingly paedophiles are targeting children and sexually grooming them via the Internet.

The new criminal offence of 'sexual grooming' of children on and offline is '...designed to catch those aged 18 or over who undertake a course of conduct with a child under the age of 16 leading to a meeting where the adult intends to engage in sexual activity with a child. It will enable action to be taken before any sexual activity takes place where it is clear that this is what the offender intends' (Sexual Offences Bill 2004).

To complement the new criminal offence of 'sexual grooming', the Government are introducing a new civil order to strengthen the protection of children, covering a much wider spectrum of behaviour such as explicit communication with children via e-mail or in chat rooms, or hanging around schools or playgrounds. This new order can be made by the courts, on application of the police '…in respect of an adult who is deemed to be acting in such a way as to present a risk of sexual harm to children, irrespective of whether such a person has been previously convicted of a sex offence or not. The order will contain such prohibitions as are necessary to protect a particular child, or children in general from him… The penalty for breach of the order will be a maximum of five years imprisonment' (Sexual Offences Bill 2004).

Essentially grooming is the process paedophiles and child sexual abusers engage in to get access to a child and to prepare it for sexual abuse. It is based on emotional seduction with the ultimate goal being sexual contact. Grooming takes place either through targeting the child's family, to get access to the child, or by approaching and befriending a child directly. Gaining the trust of the child occurs either through face-to-face encounters with the child, or increasingly via the Internet, in which the paedophile may pose as someone of the child's age.

The grooming process is extremely subtle for both the parents and the child being groomed, with neither necessarily being aware of the hidden motives behind this process. It is crucial that parents are aware of how they can get drawn into the sexual grooming of their child in order to protect their child. In essence grooming increases access to children and decreases detection. If parents are unaware of this process they may unwittingly get caught up in the sexual abuse of their child.

This chapter will explore the sexual grooming of children by examining the grooming process and how paedophiles groom and seduce parents and families, as well as children. Having identified the factors involved in grooming children, guidance will be provided in terms of what to be aware of and look out for. Acquiring this knowledge empowers parents, and children, to circumvent the grooming process, and thereby prevent any further seduction or sexual assault. The only sure way to protect children is to make ourselves, and our children, aware of how they are being enticed or manipulated for sexual purposes. A number of case vignettes are included in this chapter to illustrate the complex factors associated with grooming.

## The grooming process

When grooming a child and its family, paedophiles can go to extraordinary lengths, and display tremendous patience over many weeks, months, even years. The grooming process is a subtle form of manipulation, or emotional seduction, which relies on forming bonds of friendship and intimacy with the child and its parents. Paedophiles devote a considerable amount of energy and time to developing their manipulative skills because the better they are at grooming, the greater the access to children and the less chance of detection. They are highly skilled in their deception of others, honing their skills through practice and exchanging knowledge with other paedophiles.

Remember paedophiles are sexual predators dressed up as nice men, or wolves in sheep's clothing. They have a huge vested interest in being seen as normal and nice, so that they can blend into the background and avoid suspicion. As Ray Wyre reminds us 'Monsters don't get close to children, nice men do...' Paedophiles need to cover up who and what they really are: predatory, devious, deceptive, manipulative, methodical and controlling. To cover up they need to have a range of skills to successfully groom children and parents, and avoid detection. To groom children paedophiles pretend to be:

- charming
- sympathetic
- understanding
- helpful
- generous with time, money, gifts, treats
- attentive
- affectionate
- emotionally available
- child oriented and child friendly.

With these skills the paedophile can embark on the grooming process in which he uses emotional seduction to achieve sexual conquest. The grooming process consists of several stages that build upon each other to achieve the ultimate goal of sexually assaulting the child. These stages are listed below.

### Stages in the grooming process

- Victim selection – identify target area, identify victim, whether a parent(s) or child
- Recruitment of victim – engage victim – parent(s) or child
- Befriend victim – parent(s) or child
- Gain trust
- Build up a relationship
- Engage child in innocuous forbidden activities – food, drink, entertainment, bed times
- Test child in keeping innocuous secrets
- Isolate and alienate child from family or friends – paedophile is the child's 'best friend'
- Illusion of love and trust – best friend, confidante
- Test out non-sexual physical contact – accidental touching
- Break down defences
- Lower inhibitions – adult or child pornography
- Manipulate child to perform some of desired sexual acts
- Emotional blackmail – withdrawal of love, friendship
- Repeated sexual assault(s)
- Reinforce silence and 'secret' – coercion, threats, play on child's fear, guilt, embarrassment
- Termination of relationship – child no longer innocent and no longer desirable, child no longer preferred age

## Victim selection

In order to select a victim paedophiles need first to choose a target area in which children live or congregate. Many paedophiles choose to live in communities which are heavily populated by children to increase their choice. They tend to choose areas where there is a high degree of anonymity in which they are unlikely to be detected. To further reduce the likelihood of detection, many paedophiles use false names and adopt a false identity. Paedophiles are commonly found in large urban areas with cheap housing, and in areas where there is some level of social deprivation. They often choose housing estates, including those that are usually thought of as unpopular, and those which have a high concentration of single mothers with children.

The motive behind choosing such communities is that children in these environments are often considered to be more vulnerable and thus easier to manipulate. This by no means suggests that paedophiles do not operate in less socially deprived areas. They clearly do but they find different ways of selecting victims. They do this by frequenting areas in which children congregate such as schools, shopping centres, game arcades, play grounds, parks or by becoming involved with children. This can be professionally, such as teachers, child care workers, sports and extracurricular coaches, pastoral care workers, children's entertainers or in a voluntary capacity such as youth and community workers or club leaders.

The paedophile may target a specific child who fulfils certain desired characteristics. These can be a specific age, certain physical characteristics, personality and degree of vulnerability. In terms of age, some paedophiles prefer a specific age group, which can consist of quite a narrow band. Common examples could be young infants who are still in nappies, three to five-year-olds, six to eight-year-olds, pre-puberty and those who are post-puberty. Most paedophiles tend to target those children who will fit their desired age group and demonstrate little or no interest in those who fall outside that range.

The grooming process can be quite slow and methodical and paedophiles have been known to target a child for up to 18 months to two years before any sexual activity takes place. This means that they may start to look for a child who is not yet in the preferred age group but will enter this age during the grooming process. In addition the paedophile may have several children who are being groomed, varying in ages and at different points in the grooming cycle, ensuring a constant supply of sexual contacts.

The paedophile may also have a preference for children of a specific physical type. This preference will include ethnicity, hair, eye and skin colour, and body build. Children who fit these ideal physical characteristics will be most as risk of being targeted. The personality of the child will also be a factor. Paedophiles generally tend to prefer children who are 'children' and appear quite child-like. This often includes children who appear to be quite innocent, not very worldly wise, and who seem quite immature for their age. They are often compliant, timid, non-assertive in relation to adults and peers, and appear to lack confidence.

This represents the paedophile's own fantasies about what children should be like and therefore fits their fantasy about childhood innocence, which is a strong component in wanting to sexually abuse them. This is reflected in the language paedophiles use about children in referring to them as 'innocent', 'pure' and being like 'rosebuds'. In reality, such children are easier to target as they lack knowledge, are more likely to invest their trust in an adult, and less likely to defend themselves in terms of repelling advances, or telling anyone.

In addition, paedophiles tend to target children who display a degree of vulnerability. Vulnerable children most at risk are those who feel unloved and unwanted, or who are unpopular, lonely, and friendless or being bullied. Such children may have family problems and lack adequate parental supervision, or are excluded from being part of a peer group and so do not have the luxury of safety in numbers. Due to their loneliness and isolation, lack of confidence or low self-esteem, these children crave attention and affection, and a feeling of 'specialness'. The paedophile will play on this by filling whatever void these children have.

In this respect paedophiles are quite chameleon-like in becoming whatever the child needs, be it friend, older brother/sister, buddy, confidante, mentor, or counsellor. Vulnerable children will soak up any attention paid to them and become especially vulnerable to anyone who wishes to befriend them, let alone someone who promises friendship, love, trust and respect. Paedophiles are extremely intuitive in sensing the unmet needs in children and will go to great lengths to satisfy the child's needs for affection and attention while minimising the chances of disclosure.

A high-risk group are those children who have learning disabilities or suffer from some form of mental disorder. These children are particularly vulnerable to CSA because they either do not understand what is happening to them or are unable to articulate their experience. Historically it has been difficult to get sufficient evidence from these vulnerable children, which has meant that many paedophiles who select such victims have gone largely undetected.

New legislation aims to redress this by introducing two new offences to protect these most vulnerable of children. Given that these children often do not have the capacity to give consent, and are more susceptible to inducement, threat or deception, sexual activity with children with learning disability, or mental disorder, will carry a maximum penalty of life imprisonment. Exploitation of children in care, who may 'consent' to sexual activity because of their dependency on the carer, will come under the offence of 'breach of a relationship of care' and carry a maximum penalty of seven years imprisonment.

Very young children are also especially vulnerable to being groomed and sexually abused. They are more easily manipulated because of their naïvety and lack of knowledge and understanding. The emotional and sexual seduction by the paedophile appears perfectly normal to a young child, as they have no other frame of reference. This makes the grooming process easier, and because the child normalises the sexual activity and does not necessarily see it as abusive, it is much less likely to disclose. Pre-verbal children further reduce the risk of detection, as they have no way of articulating or communicating their abuse – a fact that a lot of paedophiles capitalise on when selecting their victim.

### Recruitment of the victim – grooming the parent(s)

> Parents are so naïve – they're worried about strangers and should be worried about their brother-in-law. They just don't realise how devious we can be. I used to abuse children in the same room with their parents and they couldn't see it or didn't seem to know it was happening.
>
> A convicted child molester

Many paedophiles start by targeting the family of the child to gain their trust and ensure access to the child with the parents' permission. The paedophile quickly establishes what the unmet needs of the parent(s) are and how he can best fulfil them. These may include isolation, loneliness, and lack of companionship, financial pressures, child care difficulties, lack of confidence or general unhappiness. His chameleon-like character will enable him to adopt whatever persona or identity necessary to fulfil the parent(s)' need and thereby ingratiate him to the family. The paedophile's charming, sympathetic and understanding demeanour lends potency to emotional seduction of the parent(s) who very quickly becomes dependent on this friendship and help.

This makes it easier to deflect suspicion and to invalidate any disclosure the child might make.

In the case of single parent families, paedophiles have been known to place advertisements in personal or lonely-hearts columns emphasising that they are not averse to children. This can be very seductive to single parents who may have anxieties and fears that any potential future partner may not welcome existing children from a previous relationship. Another good potential source is advertising babysitting services in local shops or newsagents' windows. This again can seem attractive to a single parent who may have difficulty finding a babysitter, or who may feel that a male babysitter can contribute to their child's welfare, especially in the absence of any other male role models in the family.

In some cases paedophiles pursue the mother of a specific child, to start a romantic relationship with her in order to gain access to the child. Even though the relationship with the mother includes a full sexual relationship, the hidden agenda is the grooming and sexual abuse of the child. In the case of those paedophiles whose sole interest is in sexual contact with children, they will fantasise about the child that is being groomed during adult sexual intercourse in order to perform adequately.

Paedophiles who target vulnerable mothers are hypervigilant to being exposed. As soon as there is any danger of being found out they move on to another relationship, another community or another part of the country to avoid any disclosures being made. The use of false names and identity reduces the risk of detection and prosecution. This means that such paedophiles may never appear on the Sex Offenders' Register, thus further avoiding detection. Such paedophiles are able to sexually abuse a large number of children without ever being found out. One American study found that on average child molesters offend against 150 boys and/or 20 females before being caught (Abel et al. 1987).

While single parent families are perhaps most at risk from such paedophiles, it by no means suggests that these are the only families or children who are at risk. Paedophiles equally target families in which both parents care for the child. In such cases the paedophile will exude charm to ingratiate themselves to both parents, gaining their trust, in order to get access to the targeted child. This is usually through community connections, recreational activities or entertainment. It could be in the park, at the swimming pool or sports events. First and foremost the paedophile looks at the child in the family to check that it fits the preferred criteria. Once this is established the paedophile will concentrate on the parents. This is achieved very subtly in the paedophile appearing to show very little or no interest in the child at all. By paying little or no attention to the child they deflect suspicion by not being physically too close or overly affectionate. This is crucial to allay any doubts in the parents' minds that they have an interest in the child.

As the paedophile befriends the parents and gains their trust, he may gradually offer to babysit or look after the child. He may offer to take the child out to the park, to the cinema, zoo, theme parks, funfair, concerts, swimming pool or to play sport with the pretext to give the parents a break. This can be very seductive to the parents who may not have the time or energy to participate in such activities, need a break, or who financially cannot always afford such treats. It is fundamental to gain the parents' trust because the child will take its lead from his or her parents in trusting someone who has now become a family friend.

## Befriending the child

Once the parent(s)' trust has been gained the paedophile directs attention towards the child. As with the parent(s) the paedophile intuitively identifies the child's unmet needs and attempts to fulfil them, by spending time with the child and paying it special attention. Paedophiles are often extremely knowledgeable about children's interests, more so than many parents. They know what current musical trends are and show knowledge about the latest CDs and who is in the pop charts. They take an interest in children's TV programmes, movies, and videos. Paedophiles may also show a great interest in playing computer games and are often happy to play these with the child for hours on end. Many parents may not show such an interest and have neither the time nor inclination to play endlessly the latest computer games with their children. The paedophile will also show knowledge of popular terminology, slang, the latest fashion, books, popular activities, drinks and food. Thus, the paedophile speaks the child's 'language' more so than parents and shows a real interest in the child's world. This is all designed to gain the child's trust in being treated as an equal or 'special' friend.

When looking after the child the paedophile is initially still reserved about any kind of physical contact but will focus all his or her attention on the child's needs and interests. This ensures that the child feels safe and that they can trust the paedophile, as well making the child feel 'special'. In attending to the child's needs, the paedophile will allow the child to do things that they are normally not allowed to do. They may allow the child to drink or eat forbidden food e.g. fizzy drinks or junk food. The paedophile may also allow the child to watch forbidden TV programmes or videos, to swear, or stay up later than their usual bedtime.

The paedophile will allow the child to partake in these forbidden things and request that the child should not tell the parents so that they will not get into trouble. This ensures the beginning of keeping secrets, albeit benign ones. The dynamic of 'I won't tell if you don't tell' seduces the child into a sense of mutuality in believing this to be a 'special friendship' based on mutual trust, respect and love. Many paedophiles thrive on this *illusion of love*. They certainly play on convincing the child that they love them, but appear to need the child to love them back. To some extent this feeds into the false belief that the relationship is built on genuine love and not covert predatory sexual behaviour. This allows the paedophile to relinquish responsibility for the sexual activity by saying that the child was complicit in it.

This sense of complicity manipulates the child into keeping any secrets. It is also a way of testing the child. If the child betrays this little 'secret' then the paedophile may have reservations of continuing the grooming process for fear that the child will disclose details of the time spent together and activities engaged in. Some paedophiles will then either continue to gain the child's trust, redouble their efforts, or more commonly ruthlessly drop the child, abort the grooming process, and move onto a more malleable child. In those circumstances the child will feel deeply hurt, betrayed and abandoned by the person they saw as their friend.

### Alienation of child from parents and friends

If the secret is not revealed, the paedophile may start to alienate and isolate the child from its parent(s) and friends. Common phrases used to ensure isolation include:

- 'Your parent(s) don't really care that much for you. I care about you more than anyone else.'
- 'Your parent(s) don't love you the way I love you.'

- 'Your parents don't understand you. I understand you more than anyone else.'
- 'Your parents don't trust or respect you. I really trust and respect you.'
- 'Parents never really want you to grow up. I want you to.'
- 'Other children make fun of you. I know what that feels like and I really understand and want to help you. I am here for you.'
- 'Don't tell your friends about us. They will be jealous.'

Paedophiles play on the 'specialness' of their friendship by telling the child that their parents do not understand them by placing restrictions on them in terms of forbidden foods and activities. The paedophile may also argue that the parents are not interested in the child in the way in which the paedophile is, as the child's 'best friend'. Once this 'special' relationship is established for a period of time the paedophile may begin to engage in more physical contact. This is not seen as inappropriate because of the 'special' bond that now exists. Physical contact is seen as a sign of intimacy and friendship and so seems benign. Such physical contact may initially be accidental, brushing the shoulder, breast or genital area or through play-fighting or tickling games. The paedophile may also begin to hug the child upon greeting and saying goodbye.

Such physical non-sexual contact increases the child's acceptance of touch and is a way of identifying limits. It also desensitises the child and gradually breaks down any inhibitions the child might have. Over time the physical contact gradually becomes more sexualised, leading to sexual touching. The paedophile is still continuing to test the child in terms of the child telling its parents. Providing the child does not reveal the physical aspects of the relationship the paedophile will continue to sexualise the child. This can be achieved by watching age-inappropriate TV programmes or videos in which there are increasingly more explicit sexual scenes between adults. These can be sexually exciting and arousing for the child. If the child shows an interest in these the paedophile may suggest acting them out. It may also pave the way to start looking at pornography, again initially between adults but gradually adult/child pornography may be introduced. Such pornography functions to desensitise the child to sexual activities and lower its inhibitions and provides a guide to what the paedophile expects from the child sexually.

The purpose of this is to normalise such sexual activity by showing the child that because other children engage in such activities with adults it is OK to be sexual with 'special' friends. The paedophile may also suggest taking photographs of the child. These may start off being fully clothed and non-sexual but become increasingly more sexually posed and explicit. As the child has already seen nude and sexual photographs of children the child becomes less inhibited and more willing to engage in such activity. Children who dream of becoming models may be particularly susceptible to the taking of photographs.

The paedophile may coerce the child by promising the child incentives such as rewards, money or gifts. Alternatively he may use emotional blackmail by playing on the importance of the relationship, saying 'If you really cared for me the way I care for you, and value the specialness of our friendship, then you would do this for me'. If the child resists, the paedophile will lift the pressure, apologise and seem contrite. The child in turn will feel guilty for upsetting the paedophile and forgive him. To prove that the child is really sorry, the child may well give in to performing the sexual act that was initially resisted. The grooming process has been so subtle and gradual that the child has become dependent on this 'special' friend and craves the continuation of this friendship. The child may now be so invested in the friendship and thus so afraid of losing it that the threat of terminating this 'special' relationship will ensure the child's sexual compliance.

Often the child will continue to spend time with the abuser *not* for the sexual components of the friendship but because the child is afraid of the consequences if it fails to comply with the sexual demands. This is especially the case when the child is lonely and friendless and has a huge emotional investment in being made to feel special.

### Reinforcing silence and secrecy

If the child is resistant, or threatens to disclose, the paedophile may remind the child that they have a number of other secrets that may have to be revealed if the child were to tell their parents. In many respects secrecy joins hands with threats. The paedophile will remind the child that they have already engaged in keeping other secrets from their parents. They will emphasise that the child will get into trouble for not having told the parents of all the other 'forbidden' things that they have already kept secret. A further coercion is that the paedophile may get into trouble and that would result in the ending of their 'special' relationship. As the child is now so invested in this 'special' relationship it will fear losing it, and is obliged to comply in order to keep the relationship. Common threats that ensure secrecy are:

- 'If you tell your mother what happened she'll hate you.'
- 'If you tell your parent(s) what happened they won't believe you.'
- 'If you tell your parent(s) they will punish you.'
- 'If you tell your mother it will kill her.'
- 'If you tell your mother I will kill her.'
- 'If you tell I will kill you.'

In some cases the child may become aroused when in sexual contact, especially if this is done slowly and 'gently'. Due to this arousal the child may believe that it really desired and wanted the sexual contact, and thus it is to blame. The paedophile may use this to confuse the child further by telling the child how much they seem to enjoy it and must want it. This is compounded if the child has an orgasm. Not only does the child feel confused and betrayed by its own body, but also ashamed and guilty due to the secrecy and furtiveness of the behaviour. In reality the child is merely experiencing normal physiological responses to being sexually touched. This does not mean that they wanted it, or are to blame. Depending on the developmental age of the child and its ability to extract meaning from this experience it may believe that 'I was sexually aroused and had an orgasm, therefore I must have wanted it'. Such shame and guilt will make it harder for the child to reveal the secret. The abuser blaming the child by saying 'Look what you made me do' may reinforce this.

Sexual contact with the child can include sexual kissing, fondling, being masturbated by the child, or masturbating the child. It may consist of mutual masturbation, mutual oral/genital sex and digital penetration. It does not always necessarily consist of full genital or anal intercourse, although this may be the case. The fact that no intercourse takes place makes the detection of sexual assault more difficult as there is no visible evidence of bruising, lacerations or penetration. Despite this the child still feels violated and confused by the activity.

The myriad of components in the grooming process is reflected in this example of a typical fixated paedophile. Initially, the paedophile fantasises and masturbates to previous sexual contacts, or over anticipated contacts. He often targets vulnerable or neglected children. He may get to know a child informally, either at a club or in the street. Often he will get to know the parents first to develop trust, while continuing to get to know the child socially. He may take the child to the cinema, or a funfair. He deliberately accompanies the child home to further develop trust with parents, which in turn promotes the child's trust.

During these encounters with the child, or in the car on the way to and from trips, he finds out what is troubling the child at home or at school. In a sense he becomes a 'counsellor' to the child in order to develop the friendship needed to gain trust. The paedophile may start to invite the child to his home while encouraging the child to tell its parents where they are going, ensuring a sense of safety. When the child leaves or arrives, some form of physical contact takes place, for example play-fighting. He may teach the child to play games, for example chess or monopoly. They may just watch television together, during which the paedophile may put his arm around the child. If the paedophile encounters any resistance, he withdraws, but tries physical contact again a couple of meetings later.

If physical contact is accepted, there is a dramatic increase in fantasy and expectation, reinforced by masturbation as he looks forward to the child becoming a sexual partner.

## The grooming of younger children

With a very young child the abuser may gain the child's trust by playing innocent games that become increasingly sexualised. By introducing sexual components the abuser hijacks the game, which was originally instigated by the child. Because the child was the original initiator it may blame itself for having suggested the game in the first place, and believe that it set up the final version because it secretly wanted the sexualised components. A good example of this is the following case vignette with the child initiating and playing the age-appropriate game of 'doctors and nurses'.

## Petra

Petra, aged three and a half, loved to play doctors and nurses. Her abuser would willingly play this game endlessly, allowing the child to initiate the game as frequently as she wanted to. Initially Petra would be the nurse and examine the abuser's ears and mouth with the appropriate implements. Sometimes the abuser would examine her. Over time the examination would include listening to her chest without her vest on, thus encouraging her to get undressed. The abuser then went on to check out her other orifices, particularly the vagina to make sure that everything was 'alright down there'. He would then recommend that she needed medicine to make her better, but rather than put the medicine in her mouth he suggested he should put these into her vagina.

A variety of sweets would then be inserted into her vagina, which he would then retrieve orally, digitally or by using tweezers. He would then consume these. To Petra this was just an extension of the game 'doctors and nurses' and she thought nothing of it. In fact she loved to play the game of doctors and nurses and felt special that her abuser was so happy to play with her. She felt this symbolised the 'special relationship' she had with her abuser, which was aided by the abuser consistently referring to her as 'special' and his 'little princess'. Although Petra did not feel abused by her abuser, the sexual components of this game were recurrent themes in her drawings.

In some instances, if the child is resistant or the abuser fears detection, he or she may drug the child. This may be through the use of date-rape drugs such as rohypnol, tranquillisers or sleeping tablets. As these drugs induce drowsiness and loss of memory the child is not aware of being sexually abused and thus cannot disclose the abuse. However, it may come to light as the example on the following page demonstrates.

Once the child has been sexually abused the abuser may begin to lose interest in the child, because part of the purpose of grooming is now satisfied. In addition, many paedophiles relish the build-up and anticipation of 'breaking the child'. Throughout the grooming process the abuser may have fantasised and masturbated about breaking down the child and overcoming any resistance. The abuser may also have consistently masturbated to these fantasies. More crucially, when sexual contact has taken place the child is no longer 'innocent' which was once the predominant attraction.

## Cleo

An extended family member whom she trusted frequently looked after Cleo. He often babysat her and her sister and would be responsible for getting them ready for bed. Cleo felt uncomfortable around him but could not pinpoint why this might be so. One day while she was at a relative's house she spotted some tablets and told the female relative that these were exactly the same tablets that the family member gave to her when he looked after her. What she did not know was that these were in fact sleeping tablets that she was being given prior to being sexually abused. The female relative was immediately concerned and confronted the family member, during which the sexual abuse was discovered.

Given that the grooming process can require up to 18 months to two years before sexual contact takes place, the child may well have reached the desired age range. If the child goes beyond the preferred age, the paedophile will reject the child and become involved with another child who he is already grooming. In some cases, if the abuser belongs to a paedophile ring, the child may be passed on to another member in the sex ring who is interested in children of that age. The child may be passed from paedophile to paedophile over a number of years.

Some children who are terrified of being abandoned and rejected by their abuser may offer to 'recruit' new children for the paedophile. Such a child will compromise itself to ensure a continuing friendship with the abuser by providing the abuser with a constant supply of new children. This can increase feelings of guilt and shame in feeling responsible not only for their own abuse, but the abuse of those children he or she recruited. This can haunt the child and remain on their conscience throughout their lives. An apt example of this comes from Saul.

### The grooming of older children

The grooming of older children involves other strategies and components. Often these children are recruited without the parent(s) being groomed, although the paedophile may offer to meet the parents as a way to allay the child's fear or suspicion. The paedophile may capitalise on the older child's burgeoning sexuality by providing non-contact ways of sexually arousing the child. A common example of this is looking at adult soft pornography or

## Saul

Saul had been groomed and sexually abused by a professional man for a number of years. He had valued this friendship enormously as he felt misunderstood at home and extremely lonely. He lacked confidence and felt that his peers did not like him. When his abuser started to take an interest in him he felt 'special' in a way that he had never done before. He spent many hours with his abuser, which was unwittingly encouraged by his parents because they felt this would be in Saul's interest in developing his confidence.

Over the years the abuser increasingly introduced pornographic material into their activities and eventually initiated regular sexual assaults. When Saul reached the beginning of puberty, his abuser started to lose interest in him and to reject him. Saul was devastated and could not comprehend his 'special' friend. Initially he tried to keep the relationship going by deliberately putting himself at risk of injury, culminating in him having an accident. As a result of his injury the abuser visited him at his home and Saul felt that he had managed to regain his interest. When he recovered from his injury, the abuser again rejected him. Saul felt he only had one option to retain this friendship, which was to become his abuser's 'pimp' by recruiting younger children, bringing them to the abuser's home to be sexually abused. As an adult, Saul felt both ashamed and guilty for the compromises he felt he had to make to ensure his abuser's friendship.

watching adult movies which contain explicit sex scenes. As the child becomes sexually excited the abuser may suggest trying out some of the images or scenes that caused the child to become sexually aroused. Due to this arousal the child might become willing to comply, without fully realising what is happening.

More significantly, the very fact that the child was aroused will makes the child feel guilty for the sexual activity. This is compounded if the child had an orgasm during the sexual encounter, a fact the paedophile will play on. If the child becomes resistant about future sexual activity the paedophile will remind the child of how aroused he or she was the last time, how much they wanted and enjoyed it, even to the point of orgasm. As the child still has very little, if any, sexual knowledge, he or she has little choice but to believe that the paedophile is telling the truth. Thus the child takes full responsibility for the sexual abuse, and blames itself. The sense of guilt and embarrassment further prevents the child from exposing the 'secret' for fear of being blamed by its parent(s).

Paedophiles may also ply older children with alcohol or drugs in order to aid the grooming process and sexual abuse. Teenagers frequently experiment with alcohol and drugs and often keep this secret from their parents. The paedophile manipulates this by offering the teenager illegal substances, knowing that this is a way of seducing the child into keeping secrets. Alcohol and drugs also lower the older child's inhibitions, making it easier to move into physical and sexual touching. Having been complicit in indulging in alcohol or drugs, which it has kept secret from its parents, the child has no option but to keep the sexual activity secret too. To disclose the sexual assault would mean that the child would also have to reveal other secrets, such as its use of alcohol or drugs. Without realising it, the teenager has been seduced into sexual abuse in which he or she feels trapped, with no escape.

The following is a real-life example of a professional fixated paedophile, an active member of the Paedophile Information Exchange, targeting and grooming an older child without the family's involvement (cited by Wyre 2000). This paedophile was employed to make 'straight' kids 'bent' and paid for photographs he took of children. The paedophile has intuitive feelings about a boy in the street as a likely victim. He identifies the boy's school and finds out where the boy lives and his preferred leisure activities and hobbies, for example where he plays football. He then goes on to find out where the boy usually goes to play and how late the boy can stay out. The paedophile then attempts to establish which sweet shop the boy frequents and whether he hangs around outside alone. He also tries to find out how much of a loner the boy is.

After careful consideration, the paedophile decides when to make an approach. It could be at the sweet shop. He approaches the boy asking whether he 'needs a little more money' and offers to pay. The paedophile may engage the boy in a casual chat. If the boy accepts payment, he leaves the shop on his own. This is designed to appear to be seen as a 'nice man' and not as a stranger. This allays the boy's fear, seducing him into thinking that he is not at any risk. The whole scene and pursuit gives a feeling of power and encouragement to the paedophile in which the final outcome is abuse, while the monetary gain is secondary.

The paedophile manipulates meeting the boy again and starts a very informal conversation during which he finds out how much pocket money the boy gets. In doing so he may undermine the boy's parents in not giving their son enough money, attention, or time. The paedophile might then ask what the boy's interests are. Even though he may already know these, he pretends he does not. The paedophile then tries to find out what the boy's mother and father do, and do not let him do, and who has the power base in the home. The paedophile may even be willing to be introduced to the mother and father and appear more than happy about this.

Such a paedophile may well use a number of false names. He may offer to take the boy out to such places as the funfair, during which he offers the boy free rides. The assumption is that 'children will do anything to get free rides at a fairground'. The paedophile may then let the boy know that he is a photographer and asks the boy whether he can take some innocuous photographs. He may invite the boy home, where magazines such as *Health and Efficiency* may be lying around. The paedophile may then ask the boy whether he would like to have his photograph taken in his underpants.

The paedophile pays for the picture, and they go to a place where the money can be spent. He may offer more money for more photographs, thereby entrapping the boy. The paedophile may then introduce another boy, encouraging them to engage in mutual masturbation. If the boy is resistant the paedophile is willing to stop at this point as the photographs already obtained can easily be distributed through various sources, especially on the Internet.

Once the boy accepts mutual masturbation the breaking-in process has begun. The paedophile might then introduce anal intercourse (buggery) or he may introduce a girl and encourage them to engage in sexual activity, which is then photographed or filmed. The paedophile may then pass the boy's name and address around on computer lists and get the boy involved in prostitution. Some 'paedophiles' have 'safe houses' which they use for 'sex with children'.

## Grooming within the family

While the focus of the sexual grooming of children has primarily focused on paedophiles targeting children outside the family, it must be remembered that sexual abuse also occurs within the family. As in CSA outside the family, most sexual abuse within the family does not start with an act of sexual penetration or rape. The sexual grooming of the child reflects very similar dynamics, although they may be amplified. The abuser needs to target the child within the family and may pick the child that appears most vulnerable, or the one that has a conflictual relationship with the non-abusing parent. Children who resemble the non-abusing parent may also be more at risk, as is the child who is not the abuser's biological child.

The abuser may initially pay the child a lot of attention and affection in order to gain the child's trust. This attention may mask hostility towards the child, or be a way in which the abuser fills the child's unmet needs. If there are other children in the family, the abuser may alienate the child from his or her siblings by favouring the child, giving it extra privileges, or spoiling it in terms of gifts and treats. This creates jealousy among the siblings which only serves to isolate the victim. The abuser may also alienate the child from the non-abusing parent by suggesting that the child is unloved or unwanted by that parent.

This alienation serves to exclude the child from the rest of the family. This makes the grooming process much easier and ensures that the child will not reveal the secret. In essence the abuser activates the 'divide and conquer' principle, knowing that if there is any unity among family members it will undermine his or her power base. Such divisiveness makes it easier to groom the child because its sense of isolation makes it even more dependent on the love and affection of the abuser.

Once the attentive relationship has been established the abuser may start what has been called 'the seductive incest cycle' (Wyre 1987), which applies to any close family member who has some power or authority over the child. The abuser follows this extra attention given to the child by tickling the child. Such close contact may cause the abuser to become sexually aroused. This can lead to sexual fantasies about the child which may be masturbated to. The abuser may move on to bathing the child, during which further sexual arousal and fantasy occurs.

The child may then be encouraged to come into the abuser's bed. As the abuser already knows that the child enjoys being tickled, tickling starts again. The abuser may use 'sex education' as a pretext to introduce the next stage. Tickling becomes increasingly intimate, and starts to include more sexualised behaviour. The abuser may start to masturbate the child, which if done 'gently' may be experienced as arousing for the child. In order to ensure not being found out, the abuser attempts to trap the child with rewards, privileges, or threats to keep the secret.

## Saskia

Saskia had recently returned home to her mother, having been in care for three years. Her return was prompted by her mother no longer being a single parent and about to marry for the first time. Saskia was delighted to be returned to her mother as her experience of being in care had made her very needy and vulnerable. The relationship between Saskia and her mother was conflictual in that her mother found it difficult to show her any love or affection. In contrast, her new 'father' appeared very loving, and paid Saskia a lot of attention. He would hug and cuddle her while sitting on his lap, and willingly play endless games.

One such game involved role-playing different animals and play-fighting. One such animal that Saskia's 'father' particularly liked to play was being a snake. Saskia, never having seen a snake, was fascinated as her 'father' writhed along the floor. One day her 'father' asked Saskia if she would like to see a more lifelike snake. Prompted by her interest, he revealed his penis. He encouraged her to touch 'this snake' to see if she could make the snake grow bigger. As his penis became erect, Saskia became increasingly more fascinated. This game was regularly repeated until one day Saskia was invited to see if she could make the snake 'spit' by rhythmically stroking it. Saskia duly stroked the snake until her 'father' ejaculated.

Over time the 'snake game' would become more elaborate to see if the 'snake' would also spit if it was licked, thus setting up oral sex. Finally, the game developed into exploring whether the 'snake' would 'spit' in other environments including inside its little 'hole', namely Saskia's vagina. Although Saskia initially enjoyed the 'snake game' she became increasingly more uncomfortable with the sexual components. She wanted her 'father' to stop playing this game by telling her mother but felt guilty about having let it get this far. Her 'father', however, played on her guilt by telling Saskia what a clever little girl she was for initiating this game and making the 'snake' spit. He also reminded her that if she stopped or told her mother that she would be taken back into care. Saskia's fear of being rejected again and taken into care was so great that she continued this game for another six years, pretending to enjoy it so she would not lose the affection shown to her by her 'father'.

As in the grooming cycle the abuser will prepare the child slowly and gradually for more sexualised activity. Initially it may be rubbing the penis or vagina, which can be sexually arousing. Ritualistic games may be played involving the genitalia, as a prelude to penetration or sexual intercourse. An illustration of this grooming process can be seen in the case vignette above.

Throughout the grooming process the abuser thinks in a distorted way, interpreting and rationalising the child's responses by believing that the child enjoys the sexual contact, especially if the child experiences arousal or orgasm. The abuser increases sexual contact, which he finds difficult to stop. Fantasy, anticipation, actual sexual contact and masturbation re- inforce the sexual abuse. The distorted thinking is reinforced when the child behaves in an affectionate manner towards the abuser. The abuser rationalises that, as the child seeks close physical contact, it must mean that the child enjoys the sexual activity. The illusion of love also plays a significant part. Many abusers believe that the relationship is based on mutual love and the sexual activity is the ultimate expression of that love. Some abusers even go as far as to imply that they wish to marry the child if the mother dies, or if they were to divorce her.

The abuser may also use a variety of other excuses for his/her behaviour, suggesting that the child is very seductive and that the abuser is the victim. Another common excuse is that the child touched the abuser in a sexually pro-vocative way and that he or she could not help him or herself, or that he was drunk or on drugs and did not know what he was doing. If discovered engaging in sexual activity the abuser may claim that the child had an infec-tion and that he was only checking. If the child makes a disclosure, the abuser may claim that the child is lying or misinterpreted whatever game was being played.

Another way the abuser may begin grooming the child is through elicit-ing protective behaviours from the child by claiming to be unhappy or sad and needing comfort from the child. In this instance the abuser is emotionally seducing the child by making the child his or her confidante and reminding it of how needy, desperate, sad or lonely they are and how little the non-abusing parent understands them. The child who does not wish to see a close family member suffer may comfort the abuser by giving lots of love and affection which the abuser begins to sexualise. A statement such as 'If you really loved me and wanted to make me happy you would do this for me' becomes a potent message for the child to comply with that behaviour so as not to further upset, or cause distress to, the abuser. This dynamic was prevalent in the example on the following page.

As can be seen the grooming process is a powerful way of gaining the child's trust through innocent or innocuous activities, which draw the child in. The child initially may enjoy the games or activities prior to becoming

## Kim

Kim's mother was frequently upset and unwell which meant she would often take to her bed. Kim was constantly worried for her mother and would try to make her happy. Initially this would be by bringing her cups of tea while she was in bed. Sometimes her mother would say that she needed a hug or cuddle and ask Kim to embrace her. Kim would happily do this, but it never seemed to be enough. One day her mother asked her to come into her bed so Kim could rub her back and give her a really big hug.

This became a daily ritual, which was increasingly sexualised. Kim's mother would ask Kim not only to stroke her back but also to 'massage' her chest and breasts. This ultimately extended to stroking her genitals to make her happy. Over several months Kim's mother also stroked Kim to thank her for being so nice to her, culminating in mutual masturbation. Although Kim was confused and unhappy about this ritual, she did not want to upset mummy and appear ungrateful, and as such could never refuse this comfort.

sexualised. Because the child desires the closeness, affection or 'special' attention, it may find it extremely hard to say no when the behaviour does become sexualised. This is exacerbated in those cases where the child has been encouraged to keep secrets or when the child is threatened by the withdrawal of attention and affection. The child becomes hooked into a cycle in which it feels trapped and cannot escape.

The abuser may also coerce or threaten the child with punishment, or tell the child that if he or she does not comply, then they will start sexually abusing a younger sibling. The child, who feels protective of its siblings, will do anything to avoid this and feels it has no choice but to allow the sexual abuse to continue in order to protect a younger brother or sister. Trusting the abuser to stick to this 'bargain', many adult survivors are often devastated to discover years later that the bargain was not upheld and that the abuser also sexually assaulted the very siblings they thought they were protecting.

### Protecting children from being groomed

When parent(s) find out that their children have been sexually groomed and sexually abused they often react with disbelief and horror. This is in part because they have been seduced themselves in the grooming process, and feel hurt, angry, betrayed and guilty for the part they may have played in the process. A human response to such strong feelings is to deny what has happened, and how they have been used.

Stop It Now! UK and Ireland (2002b) have collated a number of common responses from parents to illustrate this:

- 'My child would have told me if they were being abused and they haven't – so it can't be happening.'
- 'He was the perfect father; he was involved with the children, he played with them and when our daughter was ill he looked after her so well.'
- 'I thought they were just fooling around. He couldn't be abusing anyone at 14.'
- 'My brother would never do that to a child. He has a wife and children.'
- 'My friend has had a longstanding relationship with a woman. So how can he be interested in boys?'
- 'She was their mother: how could she be abusing them?'
- 'He told me about his past right from the start. He wouldn't have done that if he hadn't changed and I'd know if he'd done it again.'

While these are all understandable human responses to the horror of CSA, parents and teachers can no longer afford to deny the reality of how paedophiles entice and ensnare children in the sexual grooming process. It is crucial that parents and teachers are aware of the dangers of grooming both on and offline to protect their children adequately (see Chapter 9). To help recognise the sexual grooming of children, parents and teachers need to be aware of the behaviour of adults or older children given in the box opposite.

### How to prevent grooming

The best way to protect children, or to divert the grooming process before sexual assault takes place, is to prevent the sexual grooming of children. In the same way that parents discuss other dangers with their child, it is important to discuss the dangers of grooming. In the words of a convicted paedophile, 'Parents shouldn't be embarrassed to talk about things like this – it's harder to abuse or trick a child who knows what you are up to'. In order to remain aware of sexual grooming of children, parents and teachers need to be vigilant, question and talk to the child.

---

### How to recognise grooming

- Those who get too close to a child
- Those who aim to exclude the child from other adults or children
- Spend most of their time with children and have little or no interest in spending time with people of their own age
- Regularly offer to babysit children for free or take children on overnight outings alone
- Buy children expensive gifts or give them money for no apparent reason
- Treat a particular child as a favourite, making them feel 'special' compared with other children
- Pick on a particular child
- Take children to their home or 'secret' places or hideaways
- Play 'special' games with children that are not age-appropriate for the abuser
- Those who refuse to allow a child sufficient privacy or make their own decision on personal issues
- Insist on physical affection such as kissing, hugging or wrestling even when the child clearly does not want it
- Are overly interested in the sexual development of a child
- Insist on time alone with the child with no interruption
- Enjoy taking lots of pictures of children
- Show sexual material to children on the Internet, via mobile phones
- Share alcohol or drugs with younger children or teens
- Expose their genitals to children
- Force sex on a child or adolescent

---

Children clearly require the protection of adults. In their naïvety and lack of knowledge, children tend to trust other adults. Their fear of people is not yet developed, their intuition not yet fully loaded with sufficient information and experience to keep them from harm. This is what makes them vulnerable to paedophiles' emotional seduction and manipulation. Arguably, parents who do not have accurate information about how paedophiles operate are no different to their children in investing their trust naïvely. To prevent being groomed, and the sexual grooming of children, parents need to have access to accurate information to empower them to make appropriate decisions in the protection of their child(ren). This is the only way to prevent the devastating impact of CSA, which will be explored in the following chapter.

---

### Prevention of grooming

- Pay attention to the child
- Pay attention to people in the child's life
- Do not surrender responsibility for the child to others
- Know the child's teacher, coach, day care worker, youth group leader, babysitter, parents of friends, and significant others in the child's life
- Ask questions, stay involved, make unannounced visits
- Talk to child
- Teach them to recognise grooming behaviour
- Teach child to be wary of any physical contact initiated by an adult or older child
- Teach them to trust you with their problems and pain
- The safest child is the one who knows he or she can bring his/her problems and concerns to parents and caregivers without reproach and retaliation
- Give child permission to say 'no' to other adults or older children if they feel uncomfortable

## Chapter 6

# The Impact of Child Sexual Abuse on the Child

[In child sexual abuse] the person is perceived as other then they are. The person's actual identity is being assaulted…the power is that of defining the other… You will be as I decide you are and as I define you, regardless of what you may have thought you are.

Mollon (2000)

Child sexual abuse has a huge impact both in the short and long term. They don't just f\*\*k your body they also f\*\*k your mind. That's what *really* screws you up.

25-year-old survivor

The impact of child sexual abuse (CSA) can vary enormously. That it has an impact on the child is clear, but whether the impact is harmful is in dispute by a small number of researchers. While most of the literature indicates that CSA is always harmful to the child, a handful of studies claim the contrary, that it can be a positive experience for the child. Such studies argue that more harm is done by the reaction of adults and professionals to disclosure, and that this accounts for the traumatisation seen in children.

Whether CSA is viewed as harmful to the child depends upon one's definition of harmful, and which dimensions of harm are measured. Many paedophiles claim that because children are sexual beings, and show an interest in sexuality, adult/child sexual activity is not harmful, especially if it is loving and gentle. However, only if violence and threats and physical pain accompany CSA can it be considered harmful to the child.

A further problem is who decides that CSA is harmful to children. Is it what the child experiences and the meaning it extracts from it, what adults or professionals believe, what abusers believe, or society's attitude to CSA? When studying the impact of CSA, researchers face a myriad of problems in assessing which factors impact the most. A further consideration is the type of sample group studied. If it is a clinical sample, that is to say those who have come to the attention of mental health professionals, child psychologists, and other child protection workers, including teachers, then the data may be skewed in the direction of a harmful impact as witnessed in the child's behaviour.

In non-clinical samples, difficulties arise in identifying which children have experienced CSA and those who have not. This can be due to the child not defining its experiences as sexual abuse, being reluctant to talk about it due to fear of exposure, or threatened into silence, or not being able to remember the sexual assaults. That is to say some children, despite not showing any of the behaviours associated with CSA, may nevertheless have been sexually abused. Thus one has to be careful when interpreting data that has been collected in a variety of different ways, and the methodology employed, to study the impact of child's sexual abuse.

That CSA has an impact on children is unquestionable, what is in dispute is in which direction the impact goes – positive or negative. What is also clear is that the impact is not just sexual but emotional and psychological. This is particularly the case when sexual grooming has taken place or where there is sexual abuse within the family. When affection and sexual abuse, love and pain are entwined reality becomes distorted, creating illusions and misperceptions. Many children feel they are unable to trust their own perceptions about what is appropriate and what is not. They can no longer trust themselves, never mind anyone else. They become confused about how to feel, whether to listen to the inner hurt and pain or whether to 'enjoy' the abuse because that is what the abuser wants.

This confusion can have huge damaging effects on the child both short and long term. Doubt and uncertainty, fear and embarrassment, guilt and shame all prevent the child from seeking help from those who could protect them. To cover up their shame and guilt they hide away, shunning peers and intimacy with other adults for fear that the 'secret' will slip out. Their loneliness and isolation reinforce their fear, making them more dependent on the abuser. The child feels trapped with no escape, sentenced to endure the CSA until they are old enough to escape.

As the impact of CSA varies from child to child, this chapter will examine the factors that are associated with the severity of impact on the child. It will also explore the impact of CSA on the neurological development of young children and how this affects dissociation and memory deficits. It will also evaluate to what extent the impact of CSA can be understood within a post traumatic stress disorder model and consider some alternative traumagenic models. What will become clear is that CSA impacts at many different levels of functioning, which explains the range of symptoms seen in children and adult survivors.

## Factors associated with the impact of child sexual abuse

Most studies indicate that CSA impacts on the child in numerous ways, many of which are harmful. The differential effects of the impact of child CSA can be accounted for by the following factors:

- The age of the child at onset.
- The duration and frequency of the sexual abuse.
- The type of sexual act(s).
- The use of force or violence.
- The relationship of the child to the abuser.
- The age and gender of the abuser.
- The effects of disclosure.

Researchers have found that the greatest trauma occurs if the child is closely related to the abuser, if the abuse is prolonged and frequent, if the sexual activity includes penetration, and if accompanied by violence and aggression (Groth and Birnbaum 1978). Other factors include the degree of participation of the child in the sexual activity, negative parental attitudes to disclosure, and most crucially the child's age at onset of the abuse, with older children seemingly more traumatised due to increased cognitive development and awareness of cultural attitudes towards child sexual abuse.

## Child's age at onset of the abuse

One of the most crucial factors in the impact of child sexual abuse is the age of onset. However, there is much controversy between professionals and researchers about the link between severity of impact and age of onset. Some researchers have found that the younger the child, the more vulnerable it is to trauma due to its impressionability while others argue that the naïvety of the younger child in some way protects it from harm and stigmatisation.

Neurobiological research shows that trauma encountered by very young children, before the age of three, when the brain is not fully developed, has the capacity to resculpt the brain when subjected to traumatic experiences (see below and Table 6.1). Until recently psychologists thought CSA led either to the development of intrapsychic defence mechanisms or arrested psychosocial development, which were thought to account for later difficulties. More recent research (Teicher 2002), using brain imaging techniques, indicates that early childhood stress, a factor in CSA, may create permanent damage to the neural structure and function of the developing brain, which leaves an indelible imprint.

If the abuse occurs during critical formative periods when the brain is being physically sculpted, it induces a cascade of molecular and neurobiological effects that inevitably alter neural development (Teicher 2002). 'Maltreatment at an early age can have enduring negative effects on a child's brain development and function... Stress sculpts the brain to exhibit various antisocial, though adaptive, behaviours' (Teicher 2002).

Research on dissociative identity disorder (DID) combined with clinical data suggests that the younger the age of onset, the more likely the child is to *dissociate* and develop *psychogenic amnesia* (Putnam 1985). *Dissociation* is defined as '...a disturbance or alteration in the normally integrative functions of identity, memory or consciousness' (DSM IV, APA 1994). In essence dissociation is an instinctive, creative defence against psychic trauma, which is highly adaptive as an initial defence against sexual abuse to minimise the perception and experience of trauma (Gil 1988). While initially adaptive, it can become non-adaptive and counterproductive as a defence strategy as the child develops (Fraser 1997; Gil 1988; Sanderson 1995) in that it interferes with the child's ability to cope effectively with reality (Kluft 1984).

Children are most likely to dissociate when '...an individual is exposed to an overwhelming event resulting in helplessness in the face of intolerable danger, anxiety and instinctual arousal' (Eth and Pynoos 1984). Kluft (1986) argues that dissociation is most likely to occur in the presence of chronic and inconsistent abuse wherein both love and abuse are present. Dissociation is a form of 'blanking' or 'spacing out' in which the child no longer feels present. Children commonly report sensations of leaving their body, observing it from a distance, usually from the ceiling, during dissociation. In a sense it is a way for the body to anaesthetise itself from the experience of painful arousal. If the abuse is chronic, ritualistic, or contains multiple abuses and abusers, the young child is unable to integrate such experiences at a cognitive level.

Abusers may use this lack of cognitive understanding, limited memory capacity and verbal ability as a rationale for sexually abusing children under the age of three (Sanderson 1995). There are a number of advantages for paedophiles to abuse such young children, which include:

- they are too young to understand

- they are too young to remember

- they are less likely to tell

- they are too young and naïve and so do not recognise that this is inappropriate behaviour

- because they are so young and will not be able to remember they will not be affected by it

- they can be manipulated to believe that this is a very 'special' relationship and that the sexual activity is normal.

This is clearly demonstrated in the following example of Anoushka.

Arguably, in many ways Anoushka did not display any harmful effects from the sexual abuse, as she did not see it as abusive. Abusers play on this with younger children in distorting their perception and understanding of what is appropriate behaviour within a loving, adult/child relationship. In fact Anoushka was confused that other adults who supposedly loved her did not play these special games, and she felt rejected when they did not.

Although the young child may not experience the sexual activity as abusive, this does not mean that it does not have an impact, if not in the short term, then potentially in the long term. Meiselman (1978) noted that the younger the age of the child, the more seriously disturbed as an adult they seem. She found that 37 per cent of adult survivors, whose sexual abuse started in early childhood, were seriously impaired on a number of dimensions, compared to 17 per cent of those who were subjected to post-puberty sexual abuse. Finkelhor (1979) and Russell (1986) also showed that the younger the age of onset, the more severe the effects. An interesting finding by Tufts (1984) proposes that chronological age of onset of abuse is less important than the number of stages of development that the CSA spans.

## Anoushka

Anoushka had been sexually abused from the age of three to five by a close family relative. The abuser presented himself as especially loving, caring and affectionate. He made Anoushka feel 'special' and he frequently called her 'my little princess'. He consistently undermined Anoushka's mother by saying that she, her mother, did not really care for Anoushka very much at all and that he was the only one in the world who did. Because he was so attentive and appeared to enjoy playing with her for hours on end (which mummy could not always do), Anoushka had no choice but to believe him. The 'specialness' of the relationship, he suggested, meant that only they could play the 'special' games her mother would not, namely, the sexual activity.

When the sexual abuse was discovered at age five, Anoushka could not understand why all the adults were telling her that this was abuse and that her abuser was bad. As far as Anoushka was concerned he never hurt her, he was always nice and gentle with her, and he loved her. Anoushka also could not understand why she was no longer allowed to see this relative, who had always been so nice to her, and became angry with her mother whom she saw as depriving her of this 'special' relationship.

This case vignette demonstrates the difference in impact across a number of cognitive developmental stages, and level of knowledge and understanding. Initially Tania believed the sexual activity to be normal, which led to a normalisation in which she believed that all fathers do this to their daughters. When recognising that this was not the case, she realised that what was happening to her was not the norm. Yet she did not want to lose her stepfather and so was unable to disclose, even when she had the opportunity. In addition, the fact that she was being sexually aroused to orgasm made her feel ashamed and guilty, further ensuring her silence. Thus, older children experience a different impact and extract a different meaning from the sexual abuse experience. An older child may know that sexual activity between adults and children is inappropriate and feel more ashamed in being implicated in such experiences. They may blame themselves for not saying 'no' or disclosing the sexual abuse and come to believe that because they did nothing about it they must have wanted it.

This is compounded when the child experiences sexual pleasure and orgasm. The impact of this is that the child feels betrayed by its body in becoming sexually aroused. The sense of guilt is reinforced if the child has an orgasm, leading them to conclude that they must have wanted the sexual activity. In combination, this adds to the child's confusion and engenders a sense of betrayal, not only by the abuser, but also by its own body.

## Tania

Tania was abused by her stepfather from the age of 7 until 16 when she left home. Tania had never known her biological father and was delighted finally to have a 'daddy' like all the other children. Her stepfather was much more loving, caring and attentive than her mother, who always seemed to be unhappy or preoccupied. Tania loved spending time with her stepfather because he listened to her, taught her about all sorts of things in the world, and took an interest in her schoolwork.

Within a year of becoming part of the family, Tania's stepfather started to stroke her breasts and genitals, kissed her clitoris and inserted his little finger inside her vagina. Tania initially was not sure if this was OK but her stepfather told her that this is what daddies did to all little girls to show them how much they loved them, and that if she loved him she would touch him 'down there' too.

Tania stopped questioning whether this was OK or not because she believed her stepfather. After all, he had taught her so much about the world, and he was very knowledgeable, so he must be right. Anyway he never hurt her; in fact sometimes when he kissed her 'down there' it felt really nice. When Tania was 12 she was allowed to have a sleepover at her friend's house. She had never had a sleepover before and was very excited. However, she became very confused when her friend's father did not come into the bedroom that night to kiss her and her friend 'down there'.

In her confusion, Tania asked her stepfather about this. He said that she must not talk to other people about this special kissing because he would get into trouble and be sent away and she would be taken into care. Tania did not want to lose her stepfather and so kept silent. However, Tania increasingly realised that what he was doing was wrong.

But she could not tell her mother because she did not want to be taken into care, nor did she want to tell because actually she liked the feeling of being kissed 'down there'.

From this point on Tania's stepfather started to increase the sexual activity and began to have actual sexual intercourse with her. Tania did not really like this but wanted to make her stepfather happy. She also worried about falling pregnant, so her father arranged for her to go onto the pill. Tania was only 13. When other children spread rumours about her and her stepfather, she strongly denied them because she did not want her stepfather to get into trouble and be sent away. She endured another three years of daily sexual intercourse until she was finally able to leave home. A final condition for doing this was to go away for a week with her stepfather and live as 'man and wife' in the marital bed. Although Tania cried each night, she felt it was a price worth paying to be able to leave home and put an end to what she now identified as sexual abuse.

However, her stepfather continued to visit her in secret and demanded that she have sexual intercourse with him. This continued for another two years until Tania finally left the country to live abroad, as far away as possible from him and his sexual advances.

## The duration and frequency of sexual abuse

The research on the relationships between duration and frequency and the impact of CSA is contradictory. Some studies have found that the more frequent and the more prolonged the CSA, the greater the impact and the more likely the child is to be traumatised. Russell (1986) found that 73 per cent of adult survivors who were sexually abused for more than five years reported considerable to extreme traumatisation compared to 62 per cent who were molested for between one week and five years, and 46 per cent who were abused only once. Tsai and Wagner (1978), Bagley and Ramsay (1986) and Urquiza and Beilke (1988) all noted that the longer the duration and the more frequent the abuse, the greater the impact and the more predictive of increased traumatisation.

Other studies (Finkelhor 1979; Langmade 1988; Tufts 1984) however found no difference in terms of the severity of impact. Courtois (1988) found the complete opposite in that the longer the abuse lasted the less the traumatisation. This may reflect a normalisation process in which the child believes its experience to be normal and thus accepts it without questioning. To some degree the child 'accommodates' its experience to that which is expected of him or her. It may also represent a form of *learned helplessness* in which the child is resigned to its experience, a phenomenon seen in victims of domestic violence. Such children may grow into adults who normalise CSA to such a degree that to be abused is all they expect. They may enter abusive relationships in which they are further sexually abused, or in which their children may be at risk of being abused.

Repeated CSA is thought to activate dissociation and to impact on memory functioning. Research by Lenore Terr (1991, 1994) distinguishes between Type I and Type II trauma, and the impact this has on the child. Type I trauma is a single traumatic event which, due to novelty, surprise and accompanying stress, is more likely to be remembered by the child. This is especially the case if the child is able to talk about it and thereby process it. While the impact may be traumatising, it is easier for the child to integrate this experience without disrupting memory too greatly.

In contrast, Type II is a multiple event in which the child may be repeatedly traumatised. The impact of Type II trauma is that the child needs to protect itself from these repeated events by galvanising massive defences against the multiple traumas experienced. The child will need to prepare, or make itself forget, these experiences in order to get through a frightening childhood. One way of doing this is by dissociating the emotions from memory. Thus, the memories of the sexual abuse become fuzzy and unclear and divorced from emotion. This enables the child to cope and survive such frightening experiences.

Each time the child experiences such a traumatic event, it teaches itself to become walled off from terrifying feelings. Repeated practice allows the child to remain removed from the experience, with increasing holes in the memory of the event. Children are naturally able to dissociate, as is seen in their capacity for creative, 'pretend' play. To a degree, dissociation is a form of 'pretending' that this frightening experience is not happening to them. The more frequently the trauma is experienced, the more practice the child has at dissociation and forgetting. This can then become a habitual response in the presence of overwhelming feelings and experiences. Forgetting is even more likely because children are rarely able to talk about CSA, which prevents the processing and integrating of the experiences within the self and the memory system.

Despite the lack of consensus among researchers on the relationship between duration and frequency and the impact of CSA it is likely that they are two of a number of factors implicated, and it is the combination of factors that influences the severity of the impact.

## Type of sexual activity

Research into the relationship between type of sexual activity and the severity of impact is also inconclusive. Some studies have found a link (Bagley and Ramsay 1986; Landis 1956; Peters 1984; Russell 1986; Tufts 1984) while others have not (Anderson and Phelps 2000; Finkelhor 1979; Fromuth 1985). Russell (1986) found that 59 per cent of survivors who experienced actual or attempted intercourse, fellatio, cunnilingus, analingus and anal intercourse reported severe traumatisation, compared to 36 per cent who experienced digital exploration of the genitals and unclothed parts of the body, and 22 per cent who were subjected to unwanted kissing and touching while clothed. Bagley and Ramsay (1986) support this finding, indicating that penile penetration is a powerful factor in terms of the impact of the sexual abuse.

The contradictory findings may be accounted for in that the type of sexual activity is not predictive on its own but must be seen in combination with other factors, especially the age of the child. In addition, the child's reaction to CSA and the meaning it extracts from its experience may be more important than the actual sexual act committed.

## Physical force and violence

The use of physical force and violence to accompany CSA can have a considerable impact on the child. Several studies have found that the more physical force and violence used by the abuser, the more negative the impact of the sexual abuse (Finkelhor 1979; Friedrich 1987; Fromuth 1985; Russell 1986; Tufts 1984). Physical force and violence accompanying the CSA seem to be associated with an increased degree of behavioural disturbance in children (Tufts 1984) and the internalising and externalising of symptoms (Friedrich 1987).

While some studies do not show an association between severity of impact and physical force/violence (Anderson and Phelps 2000; Bagley and Ramsay 1986) this may be due to a reduction of trauma in that the child can more easily attribute blame to the abuser (MacFarlane et al. 1986). The overt use of physical violence makes it easier for the child to recognise that the CSA was unwanted and forced upon the child. This makes it easier for the child to blame the abuser rather than itself because the subtle mixture of love/affection and sexual activity are not present. If physical violence is present outside the sexual assault(s), it will serve to keep the CSA hidden in that the child focuses primarily on surviving the physical violence while obliterating the sexual abuse.

Recent research indicates that if the abuse is ritualistic and/or sadistic it is likely to have a greater impact on the child as the child has to incorporate the cruelty and sadistic components with the sexual abuse. This is further compounded if some of these acts also include bestiality.

## Relationship of the child to the abuser

The impact of the relationship between the child and abuser is also unclear, with some studies indicating that the closer the blood relationships the greater the impact (Anderson *et al.* 1981; Friedrich *et al.* 1986; Landis 1956). It may be that the relationship of the child to the abuser is hard to measure and should not be evaluated on blood ties, but needs to consider the closeness and quality of the relationship. Arguably the closer the relationship between the child and the abuser, the more the child will feel betrayed. Such close relationships do not need to include blood ties but may be based on the amount of trust the child has invested in the abuser. This could be a family friend, a teacher or someone who has befriended and groomed the child over a number of years. It is the betrayal of trust in that person that may represent significant difference in the severity of impact of the sexual abuse.

This may also account for differences in findings between natural parents and step-parents. Some research suggests that the impact is greater if the abuser is a natural parent rather than a step-parent (Bagley and Ramsay 1986; Finkelhor 1979; Russell 1984) while Tufts (1984) found the impact was greater if it was a step-parent. To fully understand the impact on the child, more research needs to be conducted looking at the quality and closeness of the relationship, the meaning the relationship has for the child, the level of trust invested in the abuser and the level of betrayal of trust experienced by the child.

> ## Sarah
>
> Sarah's father had always been physically violent towards her, her brother and her mother. That is all she remembers about her father whose daily physical assaults frequently ended in her mother being hospitalised. When Sarah was five her mother was hospitalised with a fractured pelvis and leg after a particularly severe beating. From that night onwards Sarah's father came into her bedroom and started to sexually assault her. Sarah was so terrified, knowing how violent he could be. She froze and had no option but to submit under the threat of more violence. This was the beginning of several years of nightly sexual assaults. The persistent CSA continued until her mother was finally able to leave her violent husband when Sarah was 11. Sarah always remembered the physical violence but had no recollection of the sexual assaults until she was in her late twenties.

## Age and gender of the abuser

Increasingly reports of children sexually abusing other children are emerging. Early studies suggested that the older the abuser, the more traumatic the impact (Finkelhor 1979; Fromuth 1985). Russell (1986) found that lower levels of trauma were experienced if the abuser was under 26 or older than 50. It may be that when the abuser is younger, or even a child or adolescent themselves, it may be harder for the child to distinguish between consensual sexual experimentation and CSA. The child may feel more implicated because the perpetrator is a child rather than an adult, making it appear more acceptable.

This is particularly the case with children who have a crush on a slightly older teenager or young adult. Crushes on older, more experienced children are a relatively normal part of development. A glance around the average teenager's bedroom will confirm this in terms of posters of their favourite pop or sports stars blue-tacked to the wall. However, these are merely crushes on which the children project their fantasies and desires and highly unlikely to become reality. When children have a crush on an older person, which then becomes sexualised, the child might believe itself to have wanted the sexual attention because of their crush. Some stars and celebrities have played on this in terms of manipulating children into sexual activity.

In terms of the gender of the abuser, it is probable that when the sexual abuser is female the impact of CSA is increased. This may reflect cultural values and beliefs about gender stereotypes whereby females, who are seen as carers and who are nurturing, are incompatible with CSA. This is certainly the case in younger children who are generally socialised to seek out females, especially their mothers, for comfort and nurturing. If she is also the sexual abuser, the child is unable to seek such comfort, thereby making the child feel even more betrayed and abandoned. The child is unable to get its basic needs for affection, love and care met by the sexually abusive female and thus feels entirely alone and bereft.

When the sexual abuser is a trusted female such as a teacher, godparent or a close family friend, who at times plays the role of a surrogate mother figure, the impact may also increase in severity. Cultural stereotypes of females being caring and nurturing, and not capable of CSA, have been a long-held myth. We see parents instructing their children to seek out a 'mummy' or adult female when they feel themselves to be in danger. Given the increased reporting of CSA by females, this is perhaps no longer appropriate advice to a child.

## The effects of disclosure

Many children find it extremely difficult to disclose CSA. The child may be too young to express their experience verbally or they may not be able to name it as CSA. They may fear not being believed, that they are to blame, or that they will be punished. Many children may wish to protect the abuser, especially if he or she is a trusted person whom they like and do not want to see punished. Other children may feel embarrassed, guilty or so ashamed about the abuse, they do not want to reveal their secret. When the abuser threatens the child with punishment, being sent away, being killed or killing their parent(s), the child will feel even more terrified about disclosing for fear of the consequences.

Thus many children do not disclose, and some never disclose CSA, even in adulthood. Children may, however, try to communicate their experiences in more subtle ways, such as through their behaviour or in their art work. This necessitates a sensitivity towards and understanding of what it is the child may be endeavouring to communicate non-verbally. Understanding the behavioural symptoms of CSA can alert adults to such communications, which symbolise the child's experience (see Chapter 7).

Children often fear parental reactions to disclosure of CSA. If the parental response is negative this can aggravate the trauma and impact of CSA (Anderson and Alexander 1996; Tufts 1984), while positive responses to dis-

## Laura

Laura, aged five, felt rejected and abandoned by her mother when her younger sister was born. She felt excluded from her mother's love, affection and attention, which she felt was all poured into her younger sibling. Laura craved her mother's love and did everything she could to gain her approval and affection, such as helping her to look after her sister and being the model, compliant child. Yet, none of this seemed to work. One day Laura's mother asked Laura to come into bed for a cuddle, which thrilled Laura as she so rarely received such a degree of affection. This became a daily ritual, which became more and more sexualised over the years, involving stroking the breasts, nipples and genital area. Although Laura was uncertain about whether this was allowed, her need for affection outweighed any doubts. This daily ritual continued for many years until Laura was well into adulthood.

closure of CSA can minimise the impact of the sexual abuse, although this is not necessarily always so. Other factors, such as the insensitive treatment by other adults like child protection workers, the police, and the criminal justice system, can all have a further impact, which can exacerbate the trauma. Indeed, such experiences can have the effect of re-traumatising the child, especially if it is repeatedly questioned about the details and specifics of CSA.

Clinical evidence suggests that disclosure to a trustworthy family friend or peer has a positive effect on children in dealing with their experiences. It seems that by being able to name their experience, and talk about it, the child is able to process what has happened and to integrate the experience. This suggests that the keeping of the 'secret' and having to be silent compounds the impact of the sexual abuse. Arguably, the taboo around child sexual abuse is not the sexual activity itself, but the talking about it.

It can be seen that the impact of CSA can vary enormously from child to child, depending upon the factors discussed above. While some children may not experience CSA as abusive or indeed traumatic at the time, many do. Evidence of childhood abuse occurring before the neural structures and pathways of the brain are fully developed can have a huge impact in physically resculpting the brain.

## Mary

Mary had been sexually abused by a close family friend for a number of years prior to accidentally disclosing to her mother. While her mother was horrified and constantly watched over Mary whenever the family friend was present, her father could not, and would not, believe that this close friend, whom he had known since his childhood, would do something like this. His refusal to believe it meant that the friend continued to visit on a regular basis, and although the sexual abuse stopped, Mary felt that her relationship with her father broke down. He seemed no longer able to look at her, touch or hug her. Mary felt that her father was angry with her and blamed her for the sexual abuse. Mary already blamed herself for causing so much upset in the family and felt sure that the sexual abuse must also have been her fault.

### Neurobiology and child sexual abuse

Researchers such as Glaser (2000), Nemeroff (1999), Perry (2000, 2002) and Schore (2002), using neuroimaging techniques and psychophysiological studies measuring autonomic function, startle reactivity and brain electrical activity, which highlight brain structures and functioning, have demonstrated how early life stress can activate significant changes in brain development. This research mirrors similar findings in animals subjected to early life stress. The specific area implicated is the neuroendocrine system, consisting of the hypothalamic–pituitary–adrenal axis (HPA) and other neuroendocrine axes and neurochemical functioning, especially catecholamines, serotonin and other neurotransmitters.

The main area of damage appears to be in the development of the *limbic system*. The limbic system is a collection of interconnected brain nuclei (neural centres) that play a pivotal role in the regulation of emotion and memory, in particular the *hippocampus* and the *amygdala*, both of which lie below the cortex in the temporal lobe. The hippocampus is important in the formation and retrieval of both verbal and emotional memories, which are critical for *declarative memory*. As the hippocampus does not mature until the age of three or four, trauma experienced by small children will be remembered quite differently to trauma experienced as an adult. This accounts for the common finding that young children, and indeed a considerable proportion of adult survivors (33%), have either no memories, or only partial memories, of the sexual abuse (Williams 1992).

The hippocampus evaluates and sorts incoming events, comparing them to previously stored information, or *schemas*. A young child who is still in the process of developing schemas is unable to find a match for its experience and is unable to store the event, especially when such an event is confusing in being loving yet hurtful. Language is also important for declarative memory because the system requires words to function effectively. If a child is unable to 'name', that is to say denote it as CSA, it makes it difficult to store the information. In addition, if the child is unable to talk about its experience, as it is still pre-verbal, then the experience and event cannot be fully processed.

Some level of physiological and emotional arousal accompanies CSA at the very least. This emotional arousal also stimulates other parts of the brain, especially the *thalamus* and amygdala. Excessive emotion creates levels of stimulation that interfere with hippocampal functioning and inhibit the cognitive and sorting capacities required to put information into appropriate schema and words.

The amygdala is central in creating the emotional content of memory, such as feelings relating to fear, fear conditioning and aggressive responses. It is thought that early childhood abuse, including CSA, may disrupt the healthy maturation of the brain, and in particular the limbic system, due to levels of stress associated with premature sexualisation. Stress leads to the secretion of *adrenal steroid hormones*, including human *glucocorticoids* needed for the *fight, flight or freeze* response. Research shows that sustained or excessive exposure to glucocorticoids appears to lead to damage or atrophy of the hippocampus (Bremner 1999, 2002; Sapolsky 1996). This can lead to memories not being stored in declarative memory but stored as *somatic sensations* and *visual images* and as such becoming part of the *non-declarative* system (van der Kolk 1994). This represents a software problem, which may necessitate new approaches to therapy such as re-programming.

In addition, repeated activation of the *hypothalamic–pituitary–adrenal axis* (HPA) can put stress on other bodily and organ functions, which can manifest in stress-related illnesses. The impact of stress responses creates problems in the regulation and modulation of emotion, which can affect the child's interaction with others. In addition to the cognitive effects, in term of the formation, storage, consolidation and retrieval of memory, the child's psychological development can also be affected. The child undoubtedly experiences a great deal of internal anxiety, which may be re-enacted. When internal anxieties are combined with interruptions in cognitive functioning the child is prevented from developing an organised sense of self. This 'failure of mentalisation' (Fonagy 2002) inhibits unified self-representations and creates discontinuity in developing the child's self.

Many of these phenomena are implicated in a variety of psychiatric disorders, in particular post traumatic stress disorder (PTSD), attention deficit hyper-activity disorder (ADHD), and conduct disorders as well as antisocial personality disorder. While some of these may manifest in childhood, other may not emerge until adulthood as depression, substance abuse, self-mutilation, borderline personality disorder (BPD), dissociative disorders and body dysmorphic disorder (BDD).

Andersen and Phelps (2000), Burgess *et al.* (1995), LeDoux (1994, 1998), Pollack and Sinha (2002) and Teicher (2002; Teicher *et al.* 2002) have argued that severe stress activates the adrenal and cortisol system, in particular the HPA as well as the noradrenergic system, such as the hippocampus, which is crucial in learning and memory. Krystal (1988; Krystal *et al.* 1995, 1998) proposes that neuropeptides and neurotransmitters released during stress affect neuromodulators in memory function in the hippocampus and amygdala, and this may interfere with laying down memory traces. Such responses to stress activate primitive flight/fight responses to enhance survival. Severe stress results in a cascade of events that have the potential to alter brain development irrevocably, especially during critical/sensitive periods such as very early childhood.

Stress-induced programming of the glucocorticoid, noradrenergic, vasopressin–oxytocin stress response system augments responses that have an impact on neurogenesis in synaptic overproduction and priming myelination during sensitive periods. The consequences associated with this include the reduction in size of the midportions of the corpus callosum, attenuated development of the left neo-cortex, hippocampus and amygdala, abnormal frontotemporal electrical activity, and reduced functional activity of the cerebellum vernis. This provides a neurobiological framework through which early abuse increases the risk of PTSD, depression, symptoms of ADHD, BPD, DID and substance abuse.

Historically it has been argued that the developing brain evolved to be moulded by experience and through adaptation (Teicher 2002). However, as the developing brain is not sufficiently evolved to cope with severe stress and abuse, the resulting damage incurred is non-adaptive. Exposure to early stress generates molecular and neurobiological effects which act on altered neural development in an adaptive way, preparing the adult brain to survive and reproduce in a dangerous world. What is beneficial to survival is mobilisation of the flight/fight responses, to react aggressively to challenges without due hesitation. This creates a heightened warning system for danger, which produces robust stress responses that facilitate recovery from injury. Such responses are seen as adaptations to an adverse environment and ensure that the child will survive to adulthood, to reproduce and ultimately ensure evolutionary success.

Thus, adequate nurturing enhances less aggressive, more stable, social, empathic and hemispherically integrated development, which enhances the ability for social animals to build more complex, interpersonal structures to enable humans to better realise their creative potential. The dilemma is between short-term survival versus long-term cultural systems (Teicher 2002).

Nemerhof (1999) proposes that early stress results in persistent sensitisation of central nervous system (CNS) circuits integrally involved in the regulation of stress and emotion. Underlying substrates increase vulnerability to subsequent stress, depression and anxiety. This induces long-lived hyper (re) activity of corticotropin releasing factor systems and alterations in neurotransmitters. The increase in stress responsiveness results in the emotional regulatory system being affected. This could account for observed long-term effects in children and adults, including violence, that to some degree accounts for the 'intergenerational transmission of abuse'.

Child sexual abuse also impacts on the regulation of emotion. Forrest (2001) suggests that early stress affects interaction between infant and caregiver and may result in lateral inhibitions between conflicting subsets of self-representation, which are normally integrated into a unified set. Thus stress associated with severe early CSA creates discontinuity in the organisation of the self. This failure of integration of the self into an organised, unified whole results in catastrophic internal anxieties in the child, which may unconsciously be re-enacted.

From the above it can be seen that the developmental experiences of CSA in early childhood have a significant impact on neurobiological development, which affects not only the unified organisation of the self and the regulation of emotion, but creates a complex internal world full of anxieties for the child. The combination of neurobiological alterations in the developing brain may result in the increased risk of post traumatic stress disorder.

## Post traumatic stress disorder (PTSD)

The impact and effects of CSA are increasingly incorporated within a post traumatic stress disorder model. The current Diagnostic and Statistical Manual of Mental Disorders (DSM IV), used by clinicians to diagnose mental distress, includes CSA within its framework (APA 1994). This has been an important step in recognising, clarifying and describing the impact of CSA, thereby validating the experience of children. In categorising CSA as a major psychological stressor and including it in DSM IV it acknowledges the impact CSA has, rather than minimising the effect of such experiences.

Although PTSD was originally formulated to account for the trauma of war and its effects on veterans, several clinicians have noted its applicability to CSA (Benedek 1985; Courtois 1988; Donaldson and Gardner 1985; Eth and Pynoos 1985; Finkelhor 1986; Gil 1988; Goodwin 1985; Lindberg and Distad 1985).

The essential feature of PTSD is '...the development of characteristic symptoms following a psychologically stressing event that is outside the range of usual human experience that would be distressing to almost anyone, and is usually experienced with intense fear, terror and helplessness' (APA 1994). Stressful events include rape or assault, major accidents or disasters, natural as well as acts of terrorism, and most recently CSA. To make a diagnosis of PTSD some of the following criteria must be present:

1. The experience of a traumatic event that would elicit symptoms of distress in most individuals such as a serious threat to one's own life or physical integrity, or that of an attachment figure.

2. A persistent re-experiencing of the traumatic event through:

    (a) recurrent and intrusive recollections

    (b) recurrent dreams of the trauma

    (c)   sudden feelings that the event is recurring including illusions, hallucinations, dissociation and flashbacks

    (d)   distress at exposure to traumas that symbolise or resemble the traumatic event.

3.   Persistent avoidance of stimuli associated with the trauma including numbing of responsiveness, as indicated by at least three of the following:

    (a)   avoidance of feelings or thoughts associated with the trauma

    (b)   avoidance of activities or situations that elicit recollections of the trauma

    (c)   psychogenic amnesia

    (d)   diminished interest in significant activities

    (e)   feelings of detachment or estrangement from others

    (f)   restricted range of affect (emotion) such as inability to experience feelings of love

    (g)   sense of foreshortened future.

4.   Persistent symptoms of increased arousal as indicated by at least two of the following:

    (a)   difficulty falling or staying asleep

    (b)   irritability or outbursts of anger

    (c)   difficulty concentrating

    (d)   hypervigilance

    (e)   exaggerated startle response

    (f)   physiologic reaction when exposed to events that symbolise or resemble aspects of the traumatic event.

Many of the diagnostic criteria in PTSD undoubtedly reflect some of the observed symptoms of CSA seen in children (see Chapter 7), such as flashbacks, lack of specific memories, dreams and nightmares, numbing and reduced emotion ('frozenness'), withdrawal, hypervigilance, aloneness, and being haunted by intrusive recollections of the trauma, but these criteria do not account for all the observed effects.

Horowitz (1997) in his 'completion tendency' theory proposes that failure to integrate traumatic experiences into existing schemas will make memories remain active and this will further interfere with normal functioning. This would account for nightmares, repetition, and numbing as a defence against trauma, but does not explain the common symptoms of anger, worthlessness and self-blame observed in children (Sanderson 1995).

In addition, not all children and adult survivors suffer from PTSD symptoms. Kilpatrick (1987) found that of 126 adult survivors of CSA 10 per cent had PTSD symptoms, with only 36 per cent having experienced PTSD in the past. This suggests that not all children or later adults suffer from PTSD, or the specified symptoms. Indeed, there are qualitative differences in observed symptomatology associated with CSA that cannot be explained by PTSD, in particular common phenomena such as shame, guilt, self-blame, self-destructive behaviours, sexual behaviours, revictimisation, or distorted beliefs about the self and others, and the fragmentation of the sense of self.

More importantly, given that not all children experience their CSA as traumatic at the time of onset, the criteria of 'helplessness in the face of intolerable danger, anxiety and instinctual arousal' has limited explanatory power when the CSA is not overtly accompanied by danger, threat or violence (Eth and Pynoos 1985). Some researchers have argued that in younger children and those who have been groomed over a number of years, CSA is a process which incorporates normal affectionate experiences that are slowly sexualised (Armstrong 1978; DeYoung 1987; Finkelhor 1979). This is so subtle and can occur over such a considerable period of time that the child may not necessarily experience the sexualised behaviour as trauma but as a 'normal' progression of affectionate behaviour engaged in by 'special' friends.

This suggests that much of the impact and experience of CSA cannot be seen entirely within the PTSD framework but must take into account the dynamics of the relationships which involve the betrayal of trust. Such betrayal and the meaning the child extracts from the experience may more accurately account for the commonly observed symptoms such as shame, guilt, self-blame and sexualised behaviours. Finkelhor (1986) argues that rather than a lack of integration of experience, children may tend to 'overintegrate' the CSA by applying learned behaviours indiscriminately and inappropriately. This would certainly account for the sexualised behaviour seen in children.

Janoff-Bulman (1992) suggests that PTSD occurs as a result of the shattering of assumptions when experiencing a traumatic event. In particular it shatters the assumption that the world is a safe place, which it clearly is not in the case of CSA. While the shattering of this illusion most certainly induces stress and anxiety, and explains some of the PTSD symptoms, it does not account for the range of behavioural symptoms, especially inappropriate sexual behaviour. These are much more likely to be acquired through learning or conditioning rather than the shattering of assumptions.

Limitations in the PTSD framework in relation to CSA have prompted some researchers to recommend that CSA should not be subsumed under PTSD but developed as a separate and distinct model that is more specific to the dynamics of sexual abuse (Briere and Runtz 1988a, 1988b; Finkelhor 1986; Summit 1983). One such alternative model has been proposed by Finkelhor and Browne (1985) which, in focusing on the dynamics of sexual trauma, is thought to account more comprehensively for the unique, yet commonly observed, symptoms seen in children and adult survivors.

## Traumagenic dynamics of the impact of child sexual abuse

This model presented by Finkelhor and Browne (1985) proposes that the best way to understand the impact of CSA is to examine the traumagenic dynamics inherent in CSA. Their model incorporates four crucial dynamics:

1. Traumatic sexualisation.

2. Stigmatisation.

3. Betrayal.

4. Powerlessness.

These four traumagenic dynamics account for the variety and diverse range of symptoms seen in CSA. Finkelhor and Browne (1985) argue that many of the symptoms seen in CSA are the result of overintegration of the trauma, which initially had a very high adaptive value but becomes maladaptive in adulthood, or where sexual abuse no longer occurs. It is a descriptive framework in which specific dynamics are thought to account for the activation of specific effects. As such it provides a more potent explanation of the impact of CSA than the PTSD model (see Table 6.1).

## 1. Traumatic sexualisation

This first dynamic explains how the child's sexual experience is shaped in inappropriate and dysfunctional ways. These are unique to CSA as they do not occur in other childhood traumas. They go some way to explaining learned sexual behaviours which re-enact the trauma, serve to obtain gratification or make sense of the experience. In CSA the child is rewarded for sexual behaviour inappropriate to its developmental level. The abuser exchanges attention and affection for sex, which the child may re-enact with others. In addition, sexual parts of the child are fetishised and accredited with distorted importance or meaning. The abuser also transmits misconceptions about sexual behaviour and sexual morality, which distorts the child's perceptions. The abuser is primarily conditioning the child by associating sexual activity with negative emotions, fear, confusion and unpleasant memories.

The psychological impact of traumatic sexualisation is an increased salience of sexual issues, confusion about sexual identity and sexual norms. The confusion of sex with love, care-giving and arousal sensations can lead to an aversion to any kind of intimacy, especially sexual intimacy. This results in behavioural signs and symptoms such as sexual preoccupations and compulsive sexual behaviours, precocious sexual activity, aggressive sexual behaviours, or promiscuity and prostitution in older children. In adult survivors these dynamics are thought to account for many sexual dysfunctions, flashbacks, difficulty in arousal, orgasm, and avoidance of, or phobic reactions to, sexual intimacy. Some adult survivors of CSA may also unconsciously sexualise their children, due to their own inappropriate sexual socialisation, making the child more vulnerable to sexual abuse.

## 2. Stigmatisation

This traumagenic dynamic focuses on the messages the abuser transmits to the child, distorting its perception. Often the abuser blames and denigrates the child, making it feel ashamed, bad, evil and worthless. Common ways of inducing such self-blame are 'You seduced me' or 'Look what you made me do', or labelling the child a 'bad girl', 'bad boy' or 'bitch'. This can be further reinforced through the covert, furtive and secretive aspects of the behaviour as something to be ashamed of. In pressurising the child to secrecy the child infers attitudes of shame about wrongdoing and the sexual behaviour. This can be further compounded if others have shocked or disgusted reactions to the disclosure, which is perceived by the child as further blame. This leads to the child being stereotyped as damaged goods.

The psychological impact of this is self-labelling such as 'seductive' or 'spoiled goods' (Herman 1992), leading to further profound shame and guilt, lowered self-esteem and a sense of differentness from others. This leads to a need to withdraw and hide or cover up the shame. This renders the child isolated and alienated from its peers and other family members. This withdrawal creates further anxieties, which may manifest in self-harming behaviours, including self-mutilation, drug dependency, delinquency, or in some cases suicide.

### 3. Betrayal

A major traumagenic impact of CSA is that the child's trust and vulnerability is manipulated by the abuser, leading to a deep sense of betrayal. This is particularly the case when the abuser is a trusted family member, friend or adult in whom the child has invested trust and on whom they depend for basic needs. The experience of betrayal is dependent on the closeness of the relationship to the abuser and whether the relationship initially started off as affectionate and seemingly nurturing, as is often the case in grooming. In essence CSA violates the child's expectation that others will provide care and protection. The child's well being is disregarded, as are its need for support, care, love and affection. According to Mollon (2000) its identity is being defined by the abuser as primarily a sexual being and the child's self-definition and sense of identity is annihilated by the projections imposed by the abuser.

The sense of betrayal is not just focused on the abuser, but may also include a sense of abandonment by other caretakers who fail to notice that the child is being sexually abused and thereby fail to protect the child. This is particularly evident in younger children who, due their cognitive stage of development, believe that adults, especially parents, are all knowing and all powerful and thus should be aware of what is happening to them and be able to ward off any danger. Betrayal can result in disenchantment in the child in losing a trusted figure, which can activate depression and grief.

Other common symptoms of betrayal observed in children are extreme dependency and clinginess, mistrust of adults, especially the same sex as the abuser, and impaired judgement in choosing other attachment figures. This can render the child vulnerable to further abuse. Alternatively the child may react in hostile and angry ways to avoid intimacy and closeness, as a protection from any future betrayals. This reinforces the child's sense of abandonment and alienation. If accompanied by aggressive behaviour the child may be labelled with a conduct or antisocial personality disorder, which results in further stigmatisation. This could lead the child into delinquent and criminal behaviour.

### 4. Powerlessness

The traumagenic dynamics of powerlessness consists of two components: (a) repeated overruling and frustration of desires and wishes, along with a reduced sense of efficacy, and (b) the threat of injury and annihilation, leading to disempowerment. Repeated invasion of the child's body against its wishes continues over time and the child becomes increasingly more vulnerable to other invasions, especially if the abuser uses force or trickery to engage the child in sexual acts. The child feels unable to protect itself or put a stop to the abuse and feels unprotected by others. This elicits repeated experiences of fear and helplessness, especially if the child feels unable to stop the abuse, or when others fail to recognise that the child is being sexually abused. According to Bentovim (2002), this fear and anxiety, along with the child's inability to control events, can lead to two opposing outcomes (see Figure 6.1).

The child either needs to find a way to control the abuse or resign itself to compliance. In the need to control, the child may identify with the abuser and attempt to triumph over its own powerlessness by exerting power over others. This compensates for the child's experience of powerlessness, resulting in the need to dominate and exert power and control over others, especially other children. This could take the form of bullying, abusive and aggressive behaviour, or in some cases sexually abusing other children. By doing this the child endeavours to triumph over trauma.

In resignation the child perceives itself to be a victim of others' actions. This leads to victim-type behaviour as the child lacks self-efficacy. Such a child will become overly compliant, turning anger and hostility towards the self. This can manifest in a sense of despair, hopelessness, depression, learning difficulties or self-destructive behaviours (Bentovim 2002).

The inability to control adverse events, accompanied by fear and anxiety, results in dissociation, nightmares, phobias, hypervigilance, somatic complaints, eating and sleeping disorders, and vulnerability to subsequent victimisation. It can also manifest itself in the child running away to avoid the sexual abuse. The child's inability to cope may manifest in not being able to concentrate at school, leading to problems that may include truanting. If the child identifies with the abuser and attempts to exert the power they were denied while being abused, they may start to dominate and control others through hostile and aggressive acts, including delinquency.

As can be seen in Table 6.1, Finkelhor and Browne's traumagenic model (1985) includes many of the observed symptoms subsumed under the PTSD model. However, it also offers a more comprehensive explanation of the impact of child sexual abuse, embracing a wider range of specific symptoms in children who are, or who have been, sexually abused. The model also proposes that the impact of CSA is related to the extent to which any one of the four dynamics are present and how they work in conjunction with each other. This allows for explanations of similar effects, which may nevertheless have different manifestations (Sanderson 1995). This has implications for treatment, which can be modified depending on whether the child shows victim-type behaviours or exerts power and control over others.

One crucial aspect of Finkelhor and Browne's model is that it conceptualises the impact of CSA as a process rather than simply as an event (Sanderson 1995). This allows different parts of the process to contribute to a different traumagenic dynamic, and for these to operate before, during and after the sexual activity. As such it takes into account pre-abuse experiences, which may increase risk and vulnerability to CSA, and the impact of post-abuse experiences such as disclosure.

The model also explains the differential impact of CSA on any one child, allowing for individual differences in terms of reactions to the sexual abuse, the meaning extracted by the child and how it copes with the trauma. For instance, a child who experienced a high degree of sexual traumatisation, especially if the body responded to the sexual contact, may have quite different reactions to and interpretations of the CSA than the child who experienced overwhelming powerlessness because the abuse was accompanied by physical violence and beatings (Sanderson 1995).

# Table 6.1 Traumagenic dynamics of the impact of child sexual abuse

## 1. Traumatic sexualisation

### Dynamics
- (a) Child rewarded for sexual behaviour inappropriate to developmental level
- (b) Abuser exchanges attention and affection for sex
- (c) Sexual parts of child are fetishised
- (d) Abuser transmits misconceptions about sexual behaviour and sexual morality
- (e) Conditioning of sexual activity with negative emotions and memories

### Psychological impact
- (a) Increased salience of sexual issues
- (b) Confusion about sexual identity
- (c) Confusion about sexual norms
- (d) Confusion of sex with love, care getting and arousal sensations
- (e) Aversion to sexual intimacy

### Behavioural manifestations
- (a) Sexual preoccupations and compulsive sexual behaviours
- (b) Precocious sexual activity
- (c) Aggressive sexual behaviours
- (d) Promiscuity
- (e) Prostitution
- (f) Sexual dysfunctions: flashbacks, difficulty in arousal, orgasm
- (g) Avoidance of, or phobic reactions to, sexual intimacy

## 2. Stigmatisation

### Dynamics
- (a) Abuser blames/denigrates victim
- (b) Abuser and others pressure child to secrecy
- (c) Child infers attitudes of shame about activities
- (d) Others have shocked reaction to disclosure
- (e) Others blame child for events
- (f) Victim is stereotyped as damaged goods

### Psychological impact
- (a) Guilt, shame
- (b) Lowered self-esteem
- (c) Sense of differentness from others

### Behavioural manifestations
- (a) Isolation
- (b) Drug or alcohol abuse
- (c) Criminal involvement
- (d) Self mutilation
- (e) Suicide

### 3. Betrayal

*Dynamics*

- (a) Trust and vulnerability manipulated
- (b) Violation of expectation that others will provide care and protection
- (c) Child's well-being disregarded
- (d) Lack of support and protection from parent(s)

*Psychological impact*

- (a) Grief, depression
- (b) Extreme dependency
- (c) Impaired ability to judge trustworthiness of others
- (d) Mistrust, particularly of men
- (e) Anger, hostility

*Behavioural manifestations*

- (a) Clinging
- (b) Vulnerability to subsequent abuse and exploitation
- (c) Allowing own children to be victimised
- (d) Isolation
- (e) Discomfort in intimate relationships
- (f) Marital problems
- (g) Aggressive behaviour
- (h) Delinquency

### 4. Powerlessness

*Dynamics*

- (a) Body territory invaded against child's wishes
- (b) Vulnerability to invasion continues over time
- (c) Abuser uses force or trickery to involve child
- (d) Child feels unable to protect self and halt abuse
- (e) Repeated experience of fear
- (f) Child unable to make others believe her

*Psychological impact*

- (a) Anxiety, fear
- (b) Lowered sense of efficacy
- (c) Perception of self as victim
- (d) Need to control
- (e) Identification with the aggressor

*Reproduced from Finkelhor and Browne (1985)*

Finkelhor and Browne (1985) have thus provided a highly workable model of the dynamics of the impact of CSA, which can explain the differential effects found in children. The model is not designed to be rigid or accepted uncritically. Rather it is intended to encourage rigorous empirical testing, which continues to produce new findings about the impact of CSA on children.

A more recent formulation for understanding the impact of child abuse has been proposed by Bentovim (2002). Bentovim endeavours to compare normative development to the development of children who have a history of abuse. While Bentovim's model was originally formulated to understand responses in children to any traumagenic contexts, his model does have some application to the understanding of the impact of CSA on children.

## Responses to traumagenic contexts

Bentovim (2002) argues that children who do not experience severe trauma in childhood are able to regulate their emotions, develop healthy attachments, and as a result of this are able to develop a sense of self. Such children are able to regulate, modulate, modify and have a sense of control over internal distress. In essence they are able to cope with normal stressful events. Through healthy attachment they are able to create a secure map of the self and significant others. This gives them confidence to separate from significant others, to explore their world, knowing that they are supported. This sense of self allows the child to have a positive view of themselves and be able to communicate their feelings and needs to others.

Children who have experienced severe trauma are not able to regulate their emotions in the same way. They form insecure attachments and do not have a secure sense of self. Bentovim (2002) proposes two distinct responses, either internalising responses or externalising responses. The child who internalises its responses to trauma has difficulty in the regulation of emotion and experiences dissociation, or blunting of emotions, leading to 'frozenness'. Intrusive thoughts and visualisations of the abuse, in which fragments of the abusive experience are recollected, haunt them.

Such children demonstrate insecure attachments that are fearful and disorganised, resulting in clinging behaviour. This reflects an absent vulnerable self, which is characterised by confusion of identity, guilt, self-blame, anxiety and sense of being a victim. They are often self-punitive and may engage in self-harming behaviours. The child who responds to trauma by internalising its experience describes accurately the child who is frozen, overly compliant and resigned to a victim identity.

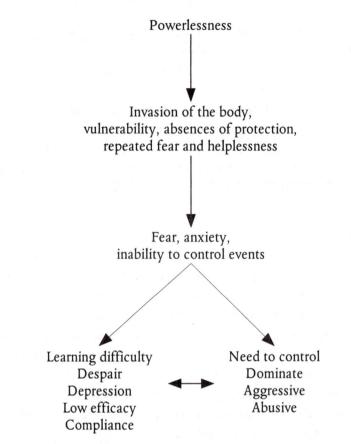

*Figure 6.1 Fear and anxiety, along with the child's inability to control events, lead to two distinct outcomes. Reproduced from Bentovim (2002).*

In contrast, children who respond to trauma with externalising responses demonstrate hyperarousal, explosive outbursts and relate to others in an intimidating or frightening style. They may have violent fantasies that eroticise anger and closeness, which they feel compelled to re-enact. Their attachments are also insecure in being indiscriminate, dismissive, disorganised and controlling. These children have a pervasive negative sense of self, which is seriously fragmented. They develop a false identity in which they identify with the abuser by adopting an aggressive style, which is blaming and punitive of others. This is often acted out in conduct disorders whereby the child may direct hostility and aggression at others, especially other children, including sexual aggression. This goes some way to explain the dynamics of those children who go on to sexually abuse other children.

Bentovim (2002) proposes that children who have been sexually abused tend to suffer from flashbacks and visualisations, which trigger abuse memories. This may prompt the child to re-enact their sexual abuse experience, often through inappropriate sexual activities. This can lead to dissociation and endeavours to delete these experiences from memory. Not surprisingly, these children tend to avoid people, places and things associated with the sexual abuse. They also suffer from hyperarousal, with powerful startle responses, are often irritable, distracted and have difficulties in sleeping, especially nightmares.

Both Finkelhor and Browne's (1985) model and Bentovim's (2002) formulation enable us to break down the various dynamics of CSA that give rise to the diverse range of signs and symptoms displayed by children as a result of sexual abuse. As the impact of CSA is not uniform it is crucial that parents and teachers have some knowledge about the various ways CSA can impact on children. Such knowledge permits a deeper understanding of the complex nature of the impact of CSA on children and the range of symptoms that are associated with CSA. These signs and symptoms will be discussed in the following chapter so that parents and teachers are aware of early warning signs to enable them to protect children from any further CSA.

## Chapter 7

# The Signs and Symptoms
# of Child Sexual Abuse

I remember trying to show my mother the sexual abuse but she never seemed to notice. I finally gave up when despite masturbating in front of her as a teenager she still took no notice.

Adult survivor of child sexual abuse

Looking back I can see all the signs [of CSA] were there, I just couldn't see them. If only I had known what he was trying to show me I could have stopped it sooner and he would still be alive.

Mother of 14-year-old victim of child
sexual abuse who committed suicide

Having looked at the impact of CSA on children, attention will now focus on how parents, teachers or others can tell if a child is being, or has been, sexually abused. Not all children are able to disclose their abuse due to fear of the consequences, and yet they may find a myriad of ways to communicate their fears and anxieties to other adults. These may be quite subtle and demand careful dissembling, or much more overt, and yet still be ignored.

As already seen, the impact of CSA can vary enormously between children, as can the range of symptoms. Although there are a lot of commonalties, there are also a lot of differences. The difficulty for parents, teachers and child protection workers is to know what signs and symptoms to look out for in order to act appropriately in protecting the child. Because there is such a diverse range of signs one must be careful not to take a 'shopping list' approach to manifestations of CSA, or assume that the presence of one symptom necessarily indicates that child has experienced CSA.

Parents and teachers must be careful not to base any concerns about a child being sexually abused on the presence of a single symptom. Many of the individual signs and symptoms can indicate other problems that the child might be experiencing. It is essential to look at the child and the constellation of a number of signs and symptoms, which may indicate CSA. This needs to be put into context in knowing the child, its family and social world, as well as any observed signs and symptoms.

To protect children adequately we need to guard against making judgements too quickly on whether they are being sexually abused, as misdiagnosis or premature intervention can cause the child and its family unnecessary traumatisation. Having said that, we must also be aware that children can go to some lengths to deny they are being abused, even when it comes to the attention of others. It is a delicate balance between being aware of the range of signs and symptoms, combined with sensitive observation, and attempts to communicate with the child to actually establish whether the child is being sexually abused or not.

Less direct communication may be seen in younger children below the age of five who are unable to verbalise their experience, especially if they have been groomed to believe that the sexual contact is a normal part of their social world and experience. Older children up to the age of 12 may also find it difficult to communicate their experiences of CSA directly, and seek indirect forms of communicating their distress. Although teenagers may have more sophisticated verbal abilities, they may find it equally hard to disclose CSA directly due to their embarrassment in feeling somehow implicated in the sexual abuse.

This chapter will first look at the effects of CSA, which give rise to a variety of signs and symptoms in children. While no individual symptom indicates CSA, changes in the child's behaviour in which a number of worrying signs are combined may give cause for concern. The observed effects of CSA can be grouped in the following categories:

1. Emotional effects.

2. Interpersonal effects.

3. Behavioural effects.

4.  Cognitive effects.

5.  Physical effects.

6.  Sexual effects.

Each of these categories will be discussed, along with a consideration of some of the signs or symptoms that the child might be displaying and what these represent. Parents and teachers need to be aware of these signs as children often *show* rather than *tell adults* that something is upsetting them. This is compounded in the case of CSA, either because the abuser has silenced the child with threats or because they are too terrified to tell or because they feel too embarrassed or guilty to disclose.

According to Stop It Now! UK and Ireland (2002) the most worrying things to watch out for are changes in behaviour, especially the following:

---

**What to watch out for in children**

- Acting out in an inappropriate sexual way with toys or objects
- Nightmares and sleeping problems
- Becoming withdrawn and clingy
- Personality changes, seeming insecure
- Regressing to younger behaviours, for example bedwetting
- Unaccountable fear of particular places or people
- Outbursts of anger
- Changes in eating habits
- Physical signs such as unexplained soreness or bruises around genitals, sexually transmitted diseases
- Becoming secretive
- Unaccounted for gifts or sums of money

---

While these are by far the most common signs associated with CSA, children are capable of showing parents and teachers a huge array of effects, each with a specific meaning. By exploring these, parents and teachers will be able to make more sense of what the child is trying to show through their communi-

...wers parents and teachers to take appropriate action to protect the child.

## Emotional effects

The impact of CSA can produce a range of emotional effects (see below). The most common one is shame. Shame serves a purpose in all cultures and ensures that individuals comply with social norms of behaviour. Generally children are taught that their private parts are something to be hidden and they are made to feel ashamed if they display, or play with, themselves in public. So when the child is coerced into sexual activity that involves these parts of the body, the child may feel ashamed of what it is doing. This sense of shame is also evoked due to the secrecy of the CSA and the furtiveness that may surround the sexual encounters. The child will sense that because it is secret there may be something shameful about the activity, despite the abuser's assurances to the contrary.

---

### Summary of the emotional signs of CSA

- Shame, humiliation, disgust, self-loathing, self-contempt, self-consciousness
- Guilt, embarrassment
- Fear
- Anxiety
- Confusion, bewilderment
- Powerlessness, helplessness
- Self-doubt, lack of confidence, lack of initiative
- Inferiority, worthlessness, inadequacy
- Anger, hostility
- 'Frozenness'

---

The child, whose body responds to the sexual contact with pleasure, sexual arousal, or orgasm, may feel doubly ashamed that its body responded, and in effect, betrayed it. This is particularly true for the older child who may know that CSA is wrong, and yet derives some pleasure from the sexual acts. Shame can be a potent factor in not disclosing the sexual abuse, as the child feels ashamed of its body, ashamed of itself, and ashamed of its feelings. This can lead to a fragmented sense of self, low self-esteem and extremely poor body image.

Shame is associated with a wide variety of emotions, which are triggered by the shaming experience. Most commonly shame evokes anxiety: anxiety about the self and survival, and anxiety about others. Associated with this are feelings of self-consciousness, helplessness, powerlessness, inferiority, worthlessness, self-loathing and self-contempt. It also elicits feelings of humiliation, disgust, bewilderment and confusion, especially in not knowing any better, as well as guilt and anger at the self for not being able to do anything about it. The child becomes doubtful and mistrustful of the self, and others, leading to an overwhelming lack of self-confidence.

A deep sense of inadequacy and lack of initiative accompany this lack confidence. The child feels so powerless internally, and externally, that it is unable to develop a sense of self-efficacy or competency. This is experienced as being useless, pathetic and stupid. The child feels unable to control either the external world or their chaotic internal world. This has a huge impact on their ability to regulate their emotions. They either feel nothing (as a result of dissociation) or they feel so overwhelmed by the intensity of their emotions that they fear internal combustion.

Thus their emotions are so polarised that they cannot regulate what they are feeling but instead they oscillate between these two extreme points. A by-product of being unable to regulate their emotions is the failure to self-soothe or comfort themselves. Their lack of trust in others as a result of CSA prevents them from seeking comfort and soothing from other adults. The child is too terrified to express their emotional turmoil or needs to others for fear of exposure or further abuse. This results in an emotional roller-coaster in which feelings cannot be expressed or contained.

Fear is another major symptom of CSA. Even if the child initially does not fear the abuse, the child will fear the secret being exposed and fear the consequences of that. The young child will fear parental reactions to finding out about the abuse and fear losing the 'special' relationship that they have with the abuser. In those cases where CSA is accompanied by violence, children will fear for their life if they do not comply, or reveal the secret.

Children under the age of five who are unable to verbalise their fear will display fearful reactions in a variety of ways, such as becoming fearful when their nappy is changed, or fearful in the presence of certain people (usually the abuser), in certain situations, alone at home with a certain babysitter, or going on access visits. In some cases the child may develop strong phobic reactions to things associated with the sexual abuse. Sometimes the fear is free floating in which the child is generally fearful of any situation or encounter with adults or older children. These children may develop obsessive/compulsive behaviours in order to establish a sense of control in response to a chaotic and out of control inner world.

The child may appear tense, nervous and anxious, reacting with high-level startle responses, constantly watchful of others, looking for reassurance and approval. The child will look vulnerable and display a high degree of dependency needs, general neediness, and a lack of autonomy. A common sign is 'frozenness' in which the child seems frozen in its watchfulness, lacking any spontaneity, and becoming an observer rather than a participant. Such children rarely show joy or liveliness. They appear haunted, and hollow, almost dead on the inside. In effect, they look traumatised.

The sexually abused may also experience a deep sense of hurt and anger. The child who internalises its responses to CSA will display signs of withdrawal, depression, sadness and self-blame. The externalising child will direct its hurt and anger outwards with displays of hostility, aggression and angry outbursts, and blame others. Whichever the way the child responds emotionally, the source is inner turmoil, shame, anxiety, fear and confusion.

## Interpersonal effects

The interpersonal effects of CSA in children focus on how they relate to others and the quality of their relationships (see boxed text below). The child who is deeply ashamed may avoid closeness in relationships because of their need to cover up, or conceal, their sense of shame. Their fear of exposure is so great that they may avoid intimacy with family members or friends for fear that the secret may 'slip out' inadvertently. The fear of this, and the accompanying sense of shame, are so great that the child will avoid closeness or intimacy to protect the secret. The child may withdraw so much to make it seem almost invisible. Chronic concealment and avoidance of closeness will result in the child not wishing to be held or cuddled, avoiding eye contact, trying to hide their face, and hiding their body under layers of clothes.

**Summary of the interpersonal signs of CSA**

- Fear of intimacy, avoidance of closeness/hugging/cuddling/contact with others
- Eroticisation of closeness, anger, hostility
- Lack of trust in self and others, wary
- Need to hide, conceal the self, shyness
- Lonely, isolated, alienated
- Reduced communication skills
- Inhibited, lack of spontaneity/initiative
- Role confusion – child/pseudo-adult
- Over-compliant, over-sensitive to others' needs and moods
- Self-sufficient
- Hostile, aggressive to others

The child just wants to merge into the background to avoid being in contact with others. They are inhibited about themselves, their identity and their bodies. The child's fear of being held or cuddled makes it hard for it to form any kind of attachment. It may appear to be chronically shy in social situations, especially with adults, in not drawing attention to itself, but also with other children. This results in the child feeling even lonelier, isolated and alienated from others. It may also avoid situations in which its body becomes a focus of attention, such as sports, swimming, or physical activities that involve undressing or changing in front of others.

The sexually abused child will lack many developmentally appropriate communication skills, and may show reduced smiling, reduced chatter, silence, reduced spontaneity, blunted curiosity, and lack of interest and exploration. The child will be mistrustful of others and appear extremely wary of any interaction with others. The child's lack of spontaneity and initiative is demonstrated in the passive acceptance of any adult direction, making it even more vulnerable to further sexual abuse.

Some children are ever-watchful or hypervigilant of others. In this watchfulness the child is constantly searching out and anticipating adults' responses. This is a self-protective strategy in which the child remains one step ahead in monitoring responses, and potential danger, in anticipation of what the adult might do next. It is a form of self-preparation for the child, arming or steeling itself for the next episode of sexual assault. If the child is fore-warned it might be able to avoid the assault through distraction techniques, or by 'psyching itself up' for the assault. Such children are in a constant state of 'readiness' and alertness, activating primitive fight/flight/freeze responses.

Child sexual abuse distorts the child's sense of identity and causes role confusion. On the one hand the child is encouraged to act in an adult sexual way, and yet it is still a child. A child who is being sexually abused and yet still treated as a child outside of the sexually abusive situation becomes confused about how it should relate to others, especially parents and other adults. These children display a 'pseudomaturity' in which they appear wise beyond their age, and take on quasi-adult roles. They may reverse adult/child roles by being protective of their parents or overprotective of other younger children, especially younger siblings. They almost become 'Little Mothers' or the 'man of the house'. They are oversensitive to others' needs and moods to the detri-ment of their own needs. This distracts from their own needs but also enables them to fulfil a need of being needed by, and by satisfying the needs of, others. These children appear very self-sufficient, which masks their own desperate neediness.

The sexually abused child is terrified of showing its vulnerability and needs in case these are further exploited. The abuser has betrayed the child's need for love and affection and the child cannot afford to show its vulnerabil-ity or neediness in case this leads to further sexual abuse. Such children also become over-compliant in being very 'helpful' to others, especially parents and teachers, in order to get external approval and proof that they are 'good', while internally feeling 'bad'.

The child who externalises its responses to CSA avoids closeness and intimacy with others through displays of hostility, explosive outbursts of anger and aggression. Not only is this a way of exerting power, dominance and control, it is also a way of remaining out of contact with others. This keeps the child safe in terms of not exposing the secret, and safe in never experienc-ing the sense of powerlessness they feel as a result of their sexual abuse. These children appear controlling, highly dismissive and punishing of others. All this is unconsciously designed to set up a barrier between the child and others and thereby avoid being in contact.

Being in contact triggers the child's vulnerability, neediness and sense of powerlessness. The child fears that its vulnerability will be exposed, or being overpowered, and needs to defend against it. In other words, the best form of defence becomes attack. An extremely potent effect of CSA is the eroticisation of anger and closeness. This prevents the child from being too close, as it fears any intimacy. Feelings of anger and hostility may also become eroticised especially if anger and aggression accompany the sexual abuse.

## Behavioural effects

Many children who have been sexually abused attempt to communicate their experiences through their behaviour. However, we must be careful not to assume that just because the child displays one of the following behavioural symptoms it has necessarily been sexually abused (see boxed text on p.234). A universal vehicle for communication in children is play. Play is a natural, creative way through which children gain meaning from their experiences and make sense of their world. Play is a way of adopting different roles and experiencing what it feels like to be a particular character. Play is also a way for the child to re-enact its own experience, gain understanding and obtain a sense of mastery. Play can also be a cathartic expression and release from inner turmoil, confusion and anxieties. Thus, play can reveal a lot about the inner world and experiences of the sexually abused child.

The child may re-enact its sexual abuse through role-play either with other children or with toys. When playing 'mummies and daddies' or 'doctors and nurses' the child might act out the sexual abuse. Scenes of the child being violated may be replayed, including sexual acts performed on the child, or ones the child had to perform on the abuser. In these games, the sexually abused child might direct other children as to how they should play these roles. In playing 'doctors and nurses' the child may focus its investigations on the child's genitalia, which reflects the abuser's preoccupation with the abused child's genitalia. The insertion of medication and objects into the vagina and anus as part of a medical procedure could represent what has actually happened to the child during CSA.

Much of this play is sexual in nature and is quite distinct from the mutual, consensual sexual exploration found in children who have not been sexually abused. Most children only engage in such sexual exploration sporadically and quite spontaneously. The sexually abused child will often want to bring sexual elements in role-play, and as such the play has a repetitive and obsessive quality to it. The sexually abused child is often overly serious in such play and does not display the sense of fun, delight and giggling that most children do when engaged in consensual sexual exploration. The sexual role-plays can seem rehearsed and premeditated, and under control of the child, who will be unwilling to deviate from the sequence of events. This indicates a need for repetition of the trauma to gain some sense of mastery over it.

When playing on its own, the child may act out CSA scenarios with its toys, such as dolls or teddies. In such play the child aims to become master or mistress of its own kingdom and may identify with the abuser in subjecting the toys to precisely the same violations that it has itself experienced. The child may also externalise its suppressed anger towards the toys, which it cannot do in real life against the abuser. It is useful to listen to the language that accompanies such re-enactments as they may reflect what the abuser has conveyed to the child, and how the child sees itself in relation to the abuser.

Along with play, children endeavour to communicate their inner and social world through drawing and painting. Young children often draw pictures of significant others in their world, which are usually simple stick figure-like drawings. These stick figures are often genderless and do not contain overt gender features, other than long hair or possibly a skirt shape. Rarely do these pictures include the hidden parts of the body, such as nipples, tummy buttons or the genitalia.

This is in contrast to the drawings of children who have been sexually abused. Their drawings often feature the sexual parts of the body in quite graphic detail. The child may draw overtly large penises or vagina-like shapes on adult figures. They may also include large breasts and nipples. The drawings may depict actual sexual activities, objects that are used during the sexual assault and other features that are present. Graphic detail of male genitalia is rarely, if ever, seen in drawings by children who have not been sexually abused.

Other children who have been abused may feel uncomfortable about including such graphic detail but may highlight certain features, such as extremely large hands or mouths that represent aspects and features of their abuse. Large red lips, or enormous hands, which are out of proportion to the actual figures, may symbolically represent features of their abuse such as inappropriate kissing, oral sex or fondling. One young girl who had been given sleeping tablets every time she was sexually assaulted repeatedly drew pictures in which tablets were featured, not really knowing why they were there. Other children may depict their sense of powerlessness and helplessness in the face of their abuser. Such drawings may contain monsters attacking children.

Children may also attempt to communicate their sexual experiences in their story-telling. These narratives may include their actual experiences of sexual abuse, or symbolic representations of being overwhelmed, threatened or chased by monsters. Although children have vivid imaginations, it is important to listen carefully and attentively to extract the meaning behind these stories and what the child is trying to communicate. Although stories featuring monsters are common fantasy tales that children make up, it is the quality of the story and what is being represented that may give a clue to whether the child is being sexually abused.

The use of language may also give clues and hints to the child's experiences. If the language contains very adult-like phrases and words, especially sexual ones, this may give some indication of an overly sophisticated knowledge about sexual behaviour and sexual activity. The child may be imitating the language used by the abuser without any real knowledge as to what it actually means. In trying to make sense of the language, the child may repeat and rehearse it in the hope of extracting some meaning.

The child's general recreational activities may also give a clue as to its internal and social world. Games that represent themes of destruction, extreme acts of violence, violation and annihilation may indicate the child's actual experiences. Punitive, cruel and sadistic acts against objects, toys, animals, household pets and other children may represent the child's experience of CSA. The fusion of anger and eroticism may also be re-enacted, representing the child's confusion of love, betrayal and exploitation present in CSA.

Children may also display behavioural or conduct disorders, in which they are prone to outbursts of anger or rage, frequently throwing tantrums. They are easily aroused, to the point of hyperarousal, have low impulse control, and a low frustration threshold. Such children seek constant stimulation and attention, and can be very demanding. They are generally aggressive and intimidating in their behaviour, both towards adults and other children. A more extreme symptom associated with CSA is the setting of fires as the following example shows.

## Timmy

Timmy, a small and frail six-year-old in foster care, did not really know why he was taken away from his mummy and daddy. He knew that they were sometimes horrible to him and made him do things that he didn't really like, but he couldn't really remember exactly what these were. The social workers kept asking him but he really wasn't sure. All he knew was that he felt 'yucky' when he had to do those things. Whenever he thought about what mummy and daddy made him do he would hide in his bedroom and play with matches. In fact he always felt better when he could set fire to things in his room, usually the quilt cover and sheets. He wasn't really sure why he did this but he knew it would make him feel better. He also wasn't sure why this would always have to be in his bedroom. All he knew is that he liked to see the flames lick into the air and that this made him feel good on the inside.

Younger children who have been sexually abused may appear to be inhibited in their curiosity, exploration and play. They have poor responses to novelty, appear tense and seem immobile or 'frozen', withdrawn and apathetic. In some cases they are irritable, with displays of excessive crying and difficulties in being pacified. There may also be problems around feeding and sleeping, which increases their irritability. Poor concentration makes them appear careless and seemingly accident-prone.

The sexually abused child may regress to an earlier stage of development. They may indulge in behaviour associated with a more infantile stage of development, in which they can express their needs for extra care and nurturing, or self-comfort. Common examples of regressive behaviour are thumb-sucking, wanting to be fed by a baby bottle, wearing nappies, or bedwetting. Bedwetting in children who have control over their bladders is often associated with children who are in emotional distress. Providing there is no medical reason for lack of bladder control, bedwetting usually indicates that the child is struggling with some difficult experiences. Similarly losing control of the bladder or bowels during the daytime, after potty training has been established, may indicate distress.

Obviously one must be careful to put this into perspective. Occasional accidents do occur in most children, and one needs to look at the frequency and regularity of loss of control, before assuming that the child is being sexually abused. This lack of control may reflect the lack of control that the child experiences in being subjected to sexual abuse. Soiling may also be a way of the child expressing its sense of being 'bad' and 'smelly' in the hope of avoiding further sexual assaults. This is also manifest in those children who do not wish to change their clothes or bathe. By making themselves 'smelly' and dirty they are trying to protect themselves from someone getting too close to them. It also serves to conceal their bodies of which they are ashamed.

Regressive behaviour is also a way for the child to 'pretend' to be a baby again and thereby avoid responsibilities associated with growing up, and what is imposed upon them through CSA. It is a way for the child to show its neediness for love, care, affection and protection. Such regressive behaviour is most often seen in younger children who are unable to verbalise their experiences. Such children become clingy, highly sensitive to admonishments of any kind, often cry at the slightest thing and become unusually demanding. In some ways they are testing to see if their parent(s) or carer(s) will be there for them to protect them from any future harm.

---

**Summary of the behavioural signs of CSA**

- Sexualised play
- Sexual themes in drawings, stories, games
- Regressive behaviour such as bedwetting, thumb-sucking, clinginess
- Conduct disorders, setting fires, tantrums
- Changes in sleeping and eating patterns
- Risky behaviours – running away, accident proneness
- Self-destructive behaviour – self-harm, suicide attempts
- Promiscuity
- Unexplained gifts and money

---

The sexually abused child may draw attention to their distress by changes in appetite behaviour, such as sleeping, stimulus-seeking or eating. Changes in sleeping patterns or changes in recreational activities may be signs of the child's distress. Changes in eating behaviours are characteristically either restricting the intake of food or comfort eating, which could lead to eating disorders. In restricting their food the child is attempting to exert control in an otherwise chaotic, and out of control, world. Also in starving itself the child may wish to physically disappear, to withdraw, from being the focus of any attention, in the hope of avoiding any further sexual abuse.

Alternatively the child may turn to comfort eating, partly to fill the emptiness they feel inside, or to put on weight and to make themselves as unattractive as possible. In a culture in which thinness is highly valued, the child believes that if it is overweight it will not be desired and thus avoids sexual abuse. A further illusory belief is that if the child is well upholstered it may be physically stronger to resist any sexual assault by fighting off the abuser. Sadly, losing or putting on weight does not necessarily protect the child from CSA. The dynamics of CSA are more about power than sexual attractiveness. For most paedophiles, the attractiveness of the child centres on its vulnerability and helplessness, rather than cultural stereotypes of attractiveness.

Some children develop bulimia, in which they overeat and then purge themselves. This constant cycle of overindulging in food and then making themselves sick by vomiting may symbolically represent their sexual abuse experience. Their sexuality is inappropriately aroused, over-stimulated and over-excited, which can include pleasurable sensations. However, because this sexual arousal is inappropriate, there is a need to punish themselves, which is represented by making themselves sick. This constant cycle of bingeing and purging has the desired effect of punishing the child for what it feels it is doing wrong in not being able to avoid, or escape, the sexual abuse.

Changes in eating behaviour, especially anorexia nervosa and to some degree bulimia nervosa, represent the sexually abused child endeavouring to gain some control in an out-of-control world. They are powerless in their abuse, and constantly controlled by the abuser's desires. They also feel out of control in being unable to disclose the abuse. The only area they feel they have any control over is what they put inside their body and what is eliminated. Such eating behaviours give the child the illusion of having a semblance of control in a chaotic life.

Other self-destructive behaviours can be seen, either overtly or well hidden. Examples of overt self-harm are hitting themselves, or banging their heads against walls and/or furniture. This is a way of releasing the internal emotional and psychological pain. Some children scratch themselves to the point of bleeding, picking at sores and scabs on the skin, preventing old wounds from healing, and risking further infection. Some children may use pumice stones, bleach, or other implements to scrub themselves red and raw. This is the child's attempt to undo the feeling of being 'dirty' and to feel 'clean'. Such children may also have frequent baths or develop obsessive-compulsive washing behaviours.

---

### Melanie

Her abuser was always telling Melanie that she was a 'very dirty little girl' for making him do the things he did to her. She didn't really understand what he meant, because really she didn't do anything. It was more about what he wanted to do, and made her do. She didn't really like his willie 'spitting' white stuff all over her because it made her feel all sticky and it didn't smell very nice. The first time it happened she thought that he had peed on her, which felt very dirty. All Melanie thought about when the abuser was doing things to her was that she was dirty and needed to wash herself. Yet however much she did, she never felt clean. She couldn't understand why, despite having three very hot baths every day, she still felt dirty. Even scrubbing herself with disinfectant and pumice stone made no difference to how she felt inside.

---

Some children may indulge in more extreme forms of self-mutilation, involving cutting themselves, especially in those areas of the body that have been the focus of the sexual abuse. In severe cases this may include the breasts, genitals and surrounding areas. Some sexually abused females regularly feel compelled to deliberately cut the inner and outer labia of the vagina with razor blades in the hope of obliterating the focus of their sexual abuse, while others cut the breasts and nipples.

Other forms of self-harm may be subtler. Some children have been known to self-medicate from a very young age by sneaking sips of alcohol from their parents' drinks cupboard. While they may not appear overtly drunk, they nevertheless are anaesthetising their internal pain. Older children may turn to swallowing painkillers, or medicines, while some go on to experiment with drugs. This can lead to lying and stealing, and other petty delinquency, in order to fund their drug taking.

Subtler forms of self-harm are characterised by the child putting itself at risk or in danger. The child may become accident-prone, or may deliberately court danger by walking out onto the road in front of traffic. These can be seen as pseudo-suicidal behaviours. By putting themselves into danger they may be seriously injured, or killed not at their own hands but through a serious or potentially fatal accident. In some cases, a slightly older child may attempt suicide as an alternative to the living death they believe themselves to be condemned to. A lot of sexually abused children do feel dead on the inside, in part due to the dissociation they have learned to practise, and so physical death seems to be a welcome alternative.

Sexually abused children may also engage in risky behaviours such as running away in the hope that they will escape any further sexual abuse. Sadly, running away puts them at risk from other sexually abusive adults who may give them shelter in return for sexual favours, thereby creating a further cycle of sexual abuse. This could lead to the child being forced into prostitution by their 'rescuer', who will then act as their pimp, selling their body to other paedophiles, either as part of a child sex ring or a child brothel. The child might rationalise this as a better alternative to CSA in that they are at least being paid for such sexual activity, as opposed to having it done to them with no financial reward. It addition, given that many sexually abused children place no value on themselves other than being desired sexually, and as a sexual object, they might as well market the only valued commodity they believe they have.

Such dynamics can be seen in older sexually abused children who may behave in a highly promiscuous manner, exchanging sexual activity for the love and attention they desperately crave. While these activities may be exclusively with peers, and appear to be consensual, the reasons behind such promiscuity can lie in a history of CSA. Sexually abused children learn to associate attention and affection with sexual behaviour and use their sexual knowledge to gain acceptance and affection from their peers. Often these children merely seek approval, acceptance and affection, as they did in the sexual abusive relationship, but know that they can only be permitted to have this if they perform certain sexual activities. Such promiscuity puts young adolescents at risk not only of sexually transmitted infections but also of pregnancy.

Bartering is a potent dynamic in the grooming process used by a paedophile who may reward the child for engaging in certain sexual activities, by offering money, clothes, or gifts in exchange for sexual contact. Typically, the abuser may give the child a mobile phone to be used exclusively to talk to the abuser. Unexplained gifts or money always necessitate careful questioning of the child to identify the source of such gifts. Money and gifts can be seen as part of the grooming process in which the abuser attempts to increase the sexual activity with the child on the promise of giving the child money or buying gifts. Sometimes the bartering is more subtle, as the following example shows.

---

### Zack

Zack had been sexually abused by his older brother from the age of 8 until 12. Zack was always quite clear that this was sexual abuse. When Zack was 12 he met an older man who offered him money to go to his hotel room with him. Zack agreed and was violently anally raped by the man. After the rape the man was very affectionate, holding, stroking and cuddling Zack, and paying him lots of attention. Zack loved this aspect of the encounter and felt that this, rather than the money, was his reward for letting the man rape him. This was the beginning of Zack's career as rent boy and male prostitute. Throughout Zack's 25-year career as a sex worker, it was the affection afterwards that was more of a driving force than the actual money he was paid.

In addition, the violence accompanying that first rape became fused with the love and affection received afterwards. This meant that Zack could only ever engage in extreme sado-masochistic sexual activity in which he had to be savagely beaten, whipped and raped prior to being embraced, at which point he was able to orgasm. When entering therapy Zack was adamant that his first experience of being a rent boy was not CSA because he had willingly entered into a bargain of trading violent sex for affection.

---

This case vignette clearly demonstrates the level of perceptual and cognitive distortion in which a violent act of rape is rationalised as being a consensual encounter because the child traded sex for affection. It also shows how violence is eroticised and becomes incorporated into learned sexual behaviour.

## Cognitive symptoms

As discussed in the previous chapter, the impact of sexual abuse on children results in a number of cognitive effects, not least poor concentration, poor attention, poor memory skills and limited understanding of the world (see boxed text on p.264). Psychologists use the term cognitive to describe such processes as perception, attention, and the storing, consolidation and retrieval of information. A number of other thinking processes are also crucial, such as how the child understands the world, how it extracts meaning, how it interprets experiences, planning and testing strategies of how to use information appropriately, decision-making and all the functions involved in learning from experience in an adaptive way. We have already seen how CSA and trauma can affect the child's ability to dissociate itself from its experiences, and how this affects the integration of self-identity and memory systems.

One effect of CSA is to distort the child's perception of the world. A seemingly loving relationship can turn into a sexually abusive nightmare. This leads to confusion about appropriate and inappropriate behaviours between adults and children. Sexually abused children are often made to feel guilty and somehow to blame for what is happening to them. This distorts their reality in that although they really are not doing anything, they blame themselves for what someone is doing to them, over which they have no power or control. It also distorts their perception about what is right and wrong, what feels good and what feels bad. Young children often have a belief that bad things only happen to bad people, a belief often reinforced in storybooks and films. A child at an early stage of cognitive development, who is not yet able to think abstractly, will believe that because something bad is happening to them they must therefore be bad.

Denial is a pervasive effect of CSA, not only in the child but also in abusers, other adults and society in general. Children who are horrified and terrified by CSA may deny that it is happening. Denying the reality of CSA to itself may be the only way the child can survive the abuse. Many abusers deny the reality of CSA by believing it to be an expression of love. Parents and adults may wish to deny CSA because it is just too terrifying and horrifying to believe that people can do such things to children. Society may also deny CSA because it does not really understand it or know how to deal with it. Fear of the consequences of disclosure can lead the child to deny CSA even if it is brought into the open, as in the following example.

---

### Alexandra

Alexandra's stepfather had been sexually abusing her from the age of seven. To cope with these nightly sexual assaults Alexandra tried to block out what was happening to her by thinking of nice things and wishing that the abuse would stop soon. When Alexandra went to her new secondary school another girl from her estate started to spread rumours about her and her stepfather having sex. Alexandra was horrified. She couldn't understand how this girl had found out about her stepfather and her. When Alexandra was called in to see the headmistress she was too embarrassed and too scared to tell the truth. She denied the rumours and assured the headmistress that her stepfather would never do anything as disgusting as that. Even though Alexandra had the opportunity to disclose the sexual abuse, her fear of the consequences of admitting the truth outweighed the opportunity to stop the CSA, a fact that always played on Alexandra's conscience.

---

It is important to know the cognitive stage of development the child is at in terms of understanding the meaning they extract from their experiences. A child who is not knowledgeable about the world, and thus relies on adults to guide and teach it appropriate behaviours, will believe what adults tell it. Thus a child below the age of five who has little or no knowledge of appropriate sexual behaviour, who is told that it is OK for adults and children to have sex, is likely to believe the adult. A child who is told 'Look what you made me do' or 'I can see you like me touching your penis' will believe the adult, even if this is in stark contrast to what they actually feel and experience. Such distortion of the child's perception and reality has enormous impact on the child in undermining its ability to trust its own experiences and judgements.

A further effect of distorted reality is that the child will withdraw from the reality of CSA into an inner world of confusion and turmoil. This withdrawal is necessary to protect itself, so that it can survive the experiences. Alternatively the child will enter a fantasy world in which it has the power and control that is markedly absent in the real world. The child may withdraw into daydreams, which impact on its ability to attend to what is going on in its surroundings. The child becomes preoccupied with its inner pain, making it impossible to focus or concentrate on the outside world.

This lack of concentration will be particularly evident at school. A child who is preoccupied with fear, terror, confusion, or anticipation of its next sexual assault will most probably not be able to attend to what it is supposed to be learning at school. Such children behave as though they are in a dream world and appear vacant in class, almost blunted in their responses. Their fear and terror of the reality of CSA make learning at school an irrelevance. In the child's life, knowing that Paris is the capital of France is just not on its list of priorities. Such a child will be worrying about the next sexual assault, how it will cope with the sexual abuse, and focus all its attention on surviving.

Such children may find it impossible to learn anything at school. Their difficulty in concentrating prevents them from taking the information in, storing it, learning and trying to remember it. Sexually abused children may therefore end up underachieving at school. Their poor educational progress is frequently misinterpreted as learning difficulties and, if ignored, may prevent the child from attaining any sense of academic achievement or ability.

Many of these children may well have the ability to be bright and enthusiastic students, who are not lacking in intelligence, yet they are not able to engage in lessons and apply themselves to their schoolwork. This underachievement furthers serves to reinforce an already poor self-image in which they believe themselves to be thick and stupid. This may prompt ridicule from teachers and peers and magnify their sense of isolation and alienation. This in turn feeds into feeling alone, helpless and useless, thereby increasing their vulnerability to further abuse.

In contrast, some children may overachieve at school. This may be because school is the only safe place for the child. Such children often arrive at school early, and are the last ones to leave, as school is seen as a respite from the CSA it experiences outside of that environment. The child may avoid going home if this is associated with being sexually abused. School also provides an opportunity for the child to distract itself from inner emotional turmoil by focusing all its energy on acquiring knowledge. This keeps the child safe from experiencing its emotional devastation and allows it to build up academic abilities that do not demand emotional energy.

Such children can often appear extremely bright, intelligent and wise beyond their years. They may become avid readers, constantly searching to quench their thirst for knowledge. Reading and learning become ways for the child to escape its terrifying reality and gain meaning in a consistently confusing world in which inexplicable things occur. Sexually abused children frequently develop cognitive skills such as planning, decision-making and developing avoidance strategies earlier than non-abused children do. This is due in part to the need to understand the incomprehensible but also to have the skills to anticipate and avoid sexual abuse.

The early development of such skills can lead to academically high achieving children going on to become very successful students who show great intellectual maturity but whose emotional maturity may be arrested at a much younger age of development. Retreating into books may prevent them from learning social skills in relation to peers, which may also keep them safe from becoming too close to others for fear of being exposed. Their relationship is with learning and knowledge, which does not let them down in the way that relationships with people can do.

Other cognitive symptoms associated with children who have been sexually abused include hypervigilance, in which the child is over-alert at all times in checking for any danger to itself. Some children deny their abuse as a way to survive it. This may lead them to minimise the sexual abuse, and the effect it is having on them. Other children may suffer from intrusive thoughts in which the sexual assault is repetitively replayed or have violent fantasises which they cannot control.

Depending on the cognitive developmental stage the child is at it can become 'stuck' in a particular way of thinking and understanding the abuse. Common cognitive distortions associated with CSA are: 'all or nothing' thinking, overgeneralisation, mislabelling, mental filtering, disqualifying the positive, jumping to conclusions, magnification or minimisation, emotional reasoning, 'should' statements, and personalisation.

In *all or nothing thinking* the child tends to see the world in extreme categorisation, either 'I am totally worthless' or 'Everybody else is brilliant'. Such thinking is characteristic of younger children who are not able to take into account the subtleties between these two extreme thoughts. While older children at a later stage of cognitive development are more able to tolerate ambivalence, the sexually abused child still tends to engage in such extreme thinking. In *overgeneralisation* the child generalises its experience to other situations. Examples of this would include 'I was abused by a man; therefore all men are sexual abusers'. This would account for a generalised fear of all men, and those children assume that all men want to be sexual with them. This can be seen in younger children who can only relate to adults of the same gender as the abuser in a sexual way.

*Mislabelling* is characterised by a child creating a totally negative self-image on the basis of one single fault, such as 'I didn't say no to the sexual abuse, or defend myself enough, therefore I am weak and pathetic, and it shows how useless I am'. Similarly, in *mental filtering* the child focuses exclusively on all the negative aspects of the self, thereby filtering out any good aspects of the self. This is linked to *disqualifying the positive*, in which the child finds it impossible to let in any positive experiences in other areas of its life, or discounts any positive abilities or attributes. An example of this would be the child negating its capacity to do well at school by saying to itself 'It is pure luck that I managed to get 10 out of 10, or the teacher must have felt sorry for me and gave me a high mark'.

In *jumping to conclusions*, or *arbitrary inference*, the child invariably draws a negative conclusion, which is not supported by the evidence. A common example of this is 'Everyone who knows me will blame me for the sexual abuse; they will not want to know me any more'. *Minimisation* or *magnification* can be extremely damaging to the child's self-esteem. In minimisation the child plays down the damaging effects of the sexual abuse as a way of protecting itself from acknowledging the real impact it has had. Such minimisation or denial enables the child to survive the experience, as the full impact may be too devastating to the sense of self. In magnification the child exaggerates its mistakes and deficiencies out of all proportion, which can lead to catastrophisation, such as 'I have been so damaged by the sexual abuse that I will never be able to lead a normal life, and I will always remain damaged'.

This type of thinking is related to *emotional reasoning*, which may be age-appropriate and certainly accurately reflects the child's experience. Emotional feelings are taken as absolute truths that can never change. A good example of this is when feelings of shame and guilt about the abuse are equated with feeling responsible for it. The child reasons that 'I was responsible for the abuse because I feel so bad about not having said no'.

Many sexually abused children hold unrealistic expectations of themselves, believing that they should always behave in accordance with these high expectations. Failure to live up to these expectations produces guilt, low self-esteem and anger. A common *should statement* is 'I should have said no or kicked the abuser where it hurts'. Such children are often perfectionists in trying to undo how bad they feel about themselves. Finally, in *personalisation*, or *misattribution*, the child assumes responsibility where there should be none.

A common example of this is the child taking on the full responsibility for the sexual abuse in such statements as 'I must have been responsible for the sexual abuse because I enjoyed it and my body responded to it'. Abusers who put this responsibility on to the child frequently reinforce this.

It is crucial when a child discloses CSA that adults provide the child with accurate and factual information to correct any inaccurate information fed to the child by the abuser. The child's beliefs and the meaning that it has extracted from the CSA need to be challenged and replaced by more accurate thoughts and understanding. A child is never responsible for sexual abuse, no matter how it behaves, and just because something bad has happened to the child, this does not make the child bad. Careful, sensitive and gentle listening to the child, helping it to gain a more accurate perception of the abuse, can go a long way to improving the child's self-esteem and allow it to let go of the burden of responsibility.

---

**Summary of the cognitive signs of CSA**

- Poor concentration, attention
- Dissociation
- Disruptions in memory
- Denial
- Withdrawal into fantasy
- Under/over achievement at school
- Hypervigilant
- Cognitive distortions

---

## Physical symptoms

One of the most difficult features of child sexual abuse is that very often it does not leave any physical signs or scars (see boxed text on p. 246). This is particularly the case when children have been groomed over a long period of time and there has been no penetration of the vagina or anus. This makes it extremely difficult to detect CSA purely through physical examination. If the sexual abuse is accompanied by violence and forced penetration there may be overt physical signs of CSA. If force and violence were used, the child may show bruising, and in some cases bleeding, especially in the thighs and genital area. Trauma to the breasts, buttocks, lower abdomen and thighs may also be present.

There may also be trauma in the oral, genital and rectal regions. If penetration took place the presence of semen may be detected in the genital and anal area. If no penetration has occurred, but the abuser has ejaculated on the child, there may be semen on the child's body, mouth or clothes. Forcing the child to bathe after the sexual assault, however, may obliterate these. There may be evidence of sexually transmitted diseases, including the risk of HIV infection. Some abusers who do not penetrate the child with a penis may cause visible damage through digital penetration, or inserting foreign objects into the genital, rectal or urethral openings.

Many abusers do not leave any visible signs of bruising, bleeding or trauma. Mutual masturbation or oral sex does not necessarily leave any physical signs. However, there may be physical symptoms that are associated with CSA. The child may have persistent and recurring itching, inflammation or infection in the oral, vaginal, rectal or urethral areas. If these cannot be explained medically then this might indicate sexual abuse. Unusual vaginal odours may also indicate sexual abuse. In older female children there is a risk of pregnancy. Often the child is too scared to tell who has impregnated her and it is too easy to always assume it is a boyfriend, or the result of consensual sexual activity.

More subtle physical signs are recurring psychosomatic illnesses, especially genital or rectal pain for which there is no medical explanation or actual infection. Some children get recurring sore throats, without actual infection, which could symbolise oral sexual abuse. Recurring tummy upsets, with no medical explanation, can represent the child's fear of damage from swallowing semen, or fear of pregnancy.

Other physical symptoms that could indicate some trauma or emotional distress in the child are a range of sleep disturbances, including fear of going to bed, insomnia, and recurring nightmares. Some children suffer from sleepwalking and night terrors, but these should not necessarily be associated with CSA, as there may neurological disturbances in sleep patterns. Eating disorders, poor hygiene and self-care may also indicate the child's emotional distress.

---

### Summary of the physical signs of CSA

- Bruises, bleeding
- Physical trauma in the oral/genital/rectal regions
- Physical trauma to breast/buttocks/thighs/lower abdomen
- Foreign bodies in the genital/rectal/urethral openings
- Itching/inflammation/infection of oral, genital, rectal areas
- Presence of semen
- Unusual odours from vaginal areas
- Sexually transmitted diseases
- Pregnancy
- Psychosomatic pains or illnesses
- Discomfort about body
- Sleep disturbances – nightmares, sleepwalking

---

## Sexual symptoms

The sexually abused child may try to communicate its sexual abuse experiences through unusual sexual behaviours (see boxed text on p.248). Children trying to come to terms with and understand CSA may engage in repetitive, persistent inappropriate sexual behaviours. These can be towards other children or be directed at other adults. Young children may genuinely believe that this is what adults want and like, as does their abuser, and are therefore compelled to behave in this way. The child believes that the only way to relate to other adults is to touch them in the sexual areas or to behave in a sexually seductive way. Such children will touch adults inappropriately or ask adults to touch them in the sexual areas. The child may rub itself against an adult, simulating sexual arousal and masturbation. They may also kiss adults other than the abuser in a sexual way. Such behaviours often represent what the child has been taught to do with the sexual abuser and, because they have been told that this is OK, they cannot understand why they are told off when behaving like this with other adults or children.

An overly sophisticated understanding of sexual behaviour, incorporating adult themes which fall outside developmentally appropriate knowledge, may also indicate that the child has experienced CSA. Compulsive masturbation, often publicly performed, may be a way of communicating the child's sexual abuse experience. Often this compulsive masturbation is not at all satisfying to the child. Some children become severely distressed after masturbation, writhing around on the floor in deep psychological and emotional pain. Repetitive and compulsive exhibitionism is another way that the child might try to communicate its abuse experiences.

In older children, early promiscuity may be a way for the child to re-enact the sexual abuse experiences. While the child might not be deliberately seeking out sexual contact with its peers, it believes that this is the only way to get attention and affection and is willing to offer her or himself sexually to satisfy such needs. This promiscuity can sometimes lead not only to pregnancy but also into prostitution, for the child who to some degree may already feel a prostitute aims to gain some control over the sexual abuse experience by at least getting paid for it. Many of the children in inner cities who are child prostitutes or rent boys have a history of child sexual abuse.

It can be seen that there are a number of signs and symptoms that are displayed by the sexually abused child. Some of these are a way for the child to draw attention to the sexual abuse and are a preferable way of communicating their inner turmoil than verbal disclosure. In some cases the symptoms are repetitive re-enactments of the sexual abuse that the child feels compelled to act out to gain meaning and mastery over the CSA. In other instances, the symptoms are learned behaviours that have been practised and rehearsed during the sexual abuse and become the only way the child knows how to relate to others.

What is clear is that the impact of CSA varies from child to child and that the signs and symptoms of CSA can vary enormously. One must guard against making premature assumptions that a child is being sexually abused in the presence of only one or two of the symptoms, as some may be associated with other problems or difficulties. It is crucial for adults to put the observed signs and symptoms into context and look at the constellation of indicators before assuming that the child is being sexually abused.

These signs and symptoms can only alert the adult to the child's pain and distress and are not fail-safe diagnostic criteria. The important thing is an awareness of which symptoms have been found to be related to CSA. Having acquired this knowledge and awareness of the myriad signs and symptoms, attention now needs to focus on how to interpret and understand these signs and symptoms in relation to the sexually abused child.

## Summary of the sexual signs of CSA

- Persistent inappropriate sexual behaviour with adults, children or toys
- Sexual themes in art, stories or play
- Overly sophisticated understanding of sexual behaviour
- Compulsive masturbation
- Exhibitionism
- Fear of sex
- Promiscuity
- Prostitution
- Menstrual problems
- Adolescent pregnancy

# Chapter 8

# Understanding the Sexually Abused Child

[One can] hear the 'offender within the child'. You may think you are talking to an eight-year-old child, but you might be talking to a 30-year-old in the child's head. It is in this process that we see the corruption of children.

Ray Wyre (1996)

We couldn't understand at first why he hadn't told us. Now we know how confused he was. He felt that it was his fault even though he hadn't wanted it to happen.

Parents of a teenage boy
who was sexually abused by two friends

The impact of child sexual abuse (CSA) is not uniform and can vary from child to child. An example of this is the case of three daughters, all of whom were regularly sexually abused by their father. One daughter minimised the CSA to the point that she allowed the father to be in frequent contact with her own children, while another emigrated to the other side of the world, intending never to return and to stay out of contact. The third daughter was determined not to let her father get away with the CSA he had committed over 20 years; she intended to amass sufficient evidence against him so that he could be prosecuted and imprisoned.

This example clearly demonstrates that responses to CSA, and later outcome, are quite diverse. Some children and later adults show very few negative effects, whereas others seem to have a lifelong history of mental health and psychiatric problems. A further question is why some children who have been sexually abused go on to sexually abuse others. As yet psychological research is unable to answer these questions fully, or account fully for the diverse range of responses. However, there are a number of factors that are currently thought to have some explanatory power.

In trying to understand the sexually abused child we need to be aware of these factors so that we can accurately interpret the child's behaviour. It is crucial when we have concerns about a child being sexually abused that we get the best help possible for the child to enable it to come through its experience as unscathed as possible. Sadly this is often not the case as the financial resources are so limited that children, or indeed their parents, may not be supported through disclosure and the aftermath of CSA. Therapeutic input is often expensive, time-consuming and under-resourced and, as such, not easily available to these most vulnerable children.

This is at best foolhardy and at worst a further abuse of the child. Given the current evidence that shows one in eight children who have been sexually abused go on to sexually abuse as older children and later adults, it seems imperative that children who have been sexually abused get appropriate help in order to prevent the further abuse of children. The pyramidal nature of CSA indicates that many paedophiles abuse up to 200 children before being caught (Long and McLachlan 2002). This means that each paedophile could potentially be creating 25 future paedophiles, each of whom could go on to abuse up to 200 children.

These figures may be only the tip of the iceberg, as many paedophiles and sexual abusers are never caught so we have no way of assessing accurately the number of children who are being abused. And what of those children who do not go on to abuse? They may be more prone to drug and alcohol dependency, mental health and psychiatric problems, with a huge financial impact on already over-stretched health services.

This chapter will endeavour to provide a deeper understanding of the sexually abused child, especially in relation to how the child understands and interprets CSA. It will explore how the child makes sense of the world at different stages in its cognitive development. How the child makes sense of CSA enables adults to understand why children find it difficult to disclose, and why some children go on to sexually abuse other children. To understand this, the impact of shame will be discussed as a way of explaining the difference between those children who internalise and those who externalise their response to CSA. I will argue that the externalising child may be more easily identified as having problems, although not always recognised as linked to CSA. If such a link exists, early therapeutic intervention can prevent a pattern of future CSA.

## How children make sense of their world

The developing child is thought to go through a number of cognitive stages of development, which facilitate an increasingly deeper understanding of its world. Piaget and Inhelder (1973) argued that children go through four major stages of cognitive development in which their thinking processes become increasingly more adult-like:

1. The sensorimotor stage, 0–2 years.

2. The pre-operational stage, 2–7 years.

3. The concrete operational stage, 7–11.

4. The formal operational stage, 11–15.

In the *sensorimotor stage* the child is mainly focused on sensory and motor experiences, with only the beginning of language and thought developing. The child is dependent on the physical representation of things and relies on the guidance of adults to identify and name objects. Such a young child is reliant on adults communicating and defining experiences. During the *pre-operational stage* the child begins to use language, and while thought processes are increasingly more sophisticated, the child is not able to conceptualise or reason with adult logic. Thus children at this stage tend to generalise, e.g. 'All men are daddies', 'All four legged animals with a tail are dogs'.

The child is egocentric in that it can only use its own experience as a frame of reference in understanding its experiences. Therefore, a common interpretation is 'If I feel bad then I must be bad'. The child also has no real concept of time, which is an abstract measure, and will find it difficult to accurately recount events in the past. A child may say 'last week' when recalling something that happened six months ago. This can be a problem when giving evidence, or being questioned in court about CSA. These inaccuracies, due to the lack of cognitive ability for abstract thinking, have often been misinterpreted as lying, and thereby undermine the child's testimony.

This is a major factor in the low prosecution rates of paedophiles. Of the few cases (10%) of CSA that actually come to court, only about 5 per cent result in a prosecution. It is crucial that children's testimony is not undermined due to a lack of understanding of the child's cognitive capacity. Paedophiles know that children are not seen as credible witnesses and that they are malleable in how they make sense of the world, and they play on this by deliberately distorting their reality. It is shocking that this should be reinforced in a criminal justice system that undermines the child's credibility as a witness through a blatant lack of understanding of the child's cognitive abilities. If children are asked questions, which take into account their stage of cognitive development and how they make sense of the world, they inevitably provide accurate answers. For example, instead of phrasing questions within an abstract concept of time (weeks, months, years), questions should be relevant to the child's existing knowledge and understanding such as, 'Was it before or after your birthday/Christmas/the summer holidays?' to enable the child to provide more evidentially correct answers.

During the *concrete operational stage* the child's thinking becomes more adult-like but is still not capable of sophisticated abstract thought or consistent use of adult logic. As the use of adult logic is inconsistent, problem solving can at times still be quite random. The final stage of *formal operations* is characterised by increasingly systematic and organised thinking, including formal logic and abstract thought. Despite the sequence of these stages, Piaget did not believe that all children reach this last stage.

Children who are sexually abused during any one of these stages will extract meaning and understanding dependent on which stage of development they are at. The child in the *sensorimotor stage* is driven by its sensory experience and whether it feels pleasure or not. It does not yet have the knowledge or experience to differentiate between what is appropriate or not. To understand its sensory responses the child relies on its parent(s) or caregiver(s) for guidance to give the sensory experience a name. A simple example is that if the child smiles when eating something that tastes nice, the parent(s) will say 'That is nice/yummy/good'.

Naming sensory stimuli and responses facilitates the child's understanding and interpretation of its experiences, and what feels 'good' and what feels 'bad'. This can become distorted if the child is told the opposite of what it actually feels. A child who falls over and hurts itself and cries, yet is told 'Don't be so silly, it is just a scratch, it doesn't hurt', will become confused between its actual perception and feeling and how it *should* be named or experienced.

The child in the *pre-operational stage* is still using its own frame of reference in making sense of the world and relying on guidance from adults to extract meaning and interpretation about its world. During this stage children are still naïve and lacking in knowledge and need to rely on adults for their information about the world. They are heavily influenced by what adults tell them about the world in order to make sense of it. Due to their dependency needs, children at this age are extremely trusting of adults and see no reason to question their interpretations and answers to questions. It is through adults that children gain access to knowledge about the world. This is reinforced by children being instructed to defer to the adults' knowledge.

In most cases adults ensure that they provide accurate knowledge and interpretations to the child to facilitate its growing understanding of the world. Child sexual abusers, however, have a vested interest in distorting the child's reality and interpretations so that they can control the child and rationalise to themselves that CSA is OK and not doing the child any harm. Thus, when the child sexual abuser tells the young child that it is OK to have sex with adults, and that this is normal behaviour, the child is inclined to believe him or her even if it is contrary to its own perception.

The child in the *concrete operational stage* will begin to have some understanding of appropriate and inappropriate behaviour, and may begin to question its experience in terms of gaining understanding. However, its reasoning still lacks adult logic and is subject to many random errors. The child still does not have enough knowledge or experience of the world to make fully informed choices and decisions. The child is still dependent on adults or older children for guidance. Its thinking and reasoning still lack the sophistication of adult thought in not being able to take all aspects and permutations of an experience into account. Children during this stage still tend to make simplistic interpretations such as, 'As I didn't stop the abuse, I must have wanted it, and so it is my fault'.

The child in the concrete operational stage is not yet able to tolerate or fully understand the concept that parent(s) or adults, who are mostly perceived as caring and loving, are also harmful perpetrators (Stern and Newland 1994). The child's lack of understanding and dependency on adults prevent it from seeing the adult as harmful as it is totally reliant on adults for its survival. To ensure its survival the child cannot afford to see the adult as 'bad', or monstrous. To retain the image of the adult as loving and caring the child has to block out the negative aspects of the adult. One way of doing this is to blame itself as being 'bad', or monstrous. In this the child becomes the perpetrator and the adult the victim. This is most evident in the grooming process where love, affection and caring are fused with abuse and sexual violation, and abuse within the family.

In the final *formal operational stage* most, although not all, children begin to develop formal logic and the capacity for abstract reasoning that most resembles adult thinking. It is at this stage, if the child has been abused over a number of years and has normalised its experiences, that it may begin to question the appropriateness of CSA. Alternatively, a child who is first abused during this stage, who knows it is inappropriate and yet feels powerless to stop it, can develop negative thoughts about itself in relation to not having tried hard enough to stop the abuse.

The cognitive stage at which the abuse starts, and the number of developmental stages it straddles, can have a specific impact on the child's thoughts and interpretations around the CSA, and how it makes sense of it. Most children, for instance, will extract a different meaning about a one-off sexual assault from that of persistent CSA, which goes on for years, or a different meaning about a single sexual assault by someone not known to the child from that of being sexually assaulted by someone they know and trust. Children who are severely traumatised by CSA may be prevented from going through the appropriate cognitive developmental stages and become 'stuck' in a particular way of thinking and understanding the abuse.

Abusers capitalise on children's unformed knowledge and understanding of the world by distorting the child's perceptions. They alter reality by what they say, which leads to further distortions in the child's responses (see Table 8.1).

As can be seen, how the child makes sense of the CSA has a huge influence on how the child perceives itself and its experiences, which accounts for differences seen between children.

There a number of other factors that influence the impact of CSA on an individual child. To some degree the child's general health and constitutional factors, as well as personality, must be considered. Children vary enormously in their responses to experiences generally. Some toddlers who fall become highly aroused with strong reactions to the pain, whereas others just get up and carry on. While this is undoubtedly influenced by genetic, constitutional and personality factors, responses can be influenced by environmental factors, not least parental reactions.

| Table 8.1 Common examples of paedophiles' manipulation of children | |
|---|---|
| *Paedophile says* | *Child interprets* |
| 'Look what you made me do' | 'I did do that, it is my fault' |
| 'You like this, you're smiling' | 'I must like it because I didn't cry' |
| 'Here's some money' | 'I'm being paid' |
| 'You took the money' | 'I'm a prostitute' |
| 'You did it for free' | 'I must like it' |
| 'You're too pretty' | 'I attract it' |
| 'You could have said no' | 'I didn't say no, therefore I must have wanted it' |
| 'You came back' | 'I must want it' |
| 'You began the game' | 'So I did. It must be my fault' |
| 'You didn't tell' | 'It can't be that wrong' |
| 'I'm sorry' | 'That's OK' |

When understanding the impact of CSA on children, these factors need to be taken into account, along with environmental influences. Consideration also needs to be given to the pre-abuse experiences of the child in terms of attachment and quality of relationships. The more securely attached the child is, with a good quality of relationship in which it can communicate well with parent(s) or carer(s) who are responsive to the child, the more likely it is that the child can work through the betrayal of trust by the abuser.

The securely attached child is able to permit itself to be comforted and reassured, safe in the knowledge that the parent(s) is there for them and is willing to let the child express itself without judging or punishing the child. The insecurely attached child may not trust its parents(s) or carer(s) to listen or hear its communication and respond appropriately. Such children fear communicating their emotional distress as they are unable to predict the parental response, or fear that the parent will blame and punish the child, by making it feel responsible for the CSA.

Other factors surround disclosure and the post-abuse responses. Children who receive positive responses to disclosure, such as being believed or reassured that it is not their fault, and who are able to express themselves freely, will have more chance of coming to terms with the abuse than those who experience negative responses to the disclosure. In addition, post-abuse responses are crucial. These are often dependent on how the child's parent(s) deal with CSA. If they are devastated or blame themselves, they may subtly communicate this to the child, who may feel responsible for the havoc it has created in making the disclosure.

Some families are torn apart by revelations of CSA, and split up as a result of disclosure. Each parent may blame the other parent for not noticing, especially if the abuser is a friend or relative from one side of the family. The parent who is linked to the abuser may blame himself or herself for allowing the abuser access to the child. Alternatively the parent may blame the child for destroying the friendship or relationship. The other parent may blame their partner for introducing or allowing the abuser to be alone with the child. In such cases the intensity of emotion can be so palpable and loaded with anger, blame, and hurt that the parental relationship breaks down. This will feed into the child's fear of disclosure, reinforcing a sense of blame and responsibility, with the child wishing he or she had never said anything.

Some parents are so devastated about discovering that their child has been sexually abused that they are unable to be emotionally available to the child. They may unconsciously blame the child, and not be emotionally there for them. CSA takes away a sense of safety and trust in the world and this can have such an impact on the parent(s) that they feel tainted by the CSA and unable to trust in the world again. They may become so concerned about their own reactions and responses that they are unable to understand and be there for the child. The child may experience this as being blamed, and feel further rejection and abandonment. This contributes to an already low self-esteem and over-inflated sense of responsibility, which the child takes into adulthood.

One must remember that many paedophiles do not just groom the child but also groom the parent(s) and other adults in order to build up trust so that they can gain access to the child. Thus the parent(s) and other trusting adults have also been betrayed and abused by the abuser. This awareness of being manipulated and duped sits uncomfortably with the parent(s). It is crucial to recognise how much power and control the abuser had not only over the child, but also over the parents. While many parent(s) may use this as a way of understanding how the child must have felt, some feel deeply ashamed and violated, and are unable to be there for the child. This can lead to a huge distance between the parents and the child with each suffering in silence with no support.

---

### Keith

Keith had always idolised his father. To him he was a hero who was universally liked by everyone and had a certain status in the community as a 'really great guy'. One day when Keith was 15, his older brother told him that his father had been sexually abusing him from the age six. Keith refused to believe this. Not his father, he couldn't possibly do such a thing. Keith continued to disbelieve his brother until years later when a nephew and niece both disclosed that they were being abused by their grandfather. Keith could no longer deny the reality. Yet this caused a huge split in the family among the siblings and whether to tell the mother. Keith believed his mother would be as furious and angry with his father as he was, only to discover that she had actually witnessed her husband sexually abusing her grandson but refused to believe what was in front of her eyes. Needless to say Keith's whole world crashed down, as he was now unable to trust his own perceptions or relationship with his mother or father.

---

Equally children who are not believed and punished for the disclosure may feel ridiculed and abandoned. This is especially so if the abuser is a close friend or relative, or indeed a partner. It can be hard to believe that someone so close to the family can have sexually abused the child. Some parents would rather disbelieve the child than confront the reality of seeing a trusted person as a paedophile. The example above illustrates this well.

When a child is not believed, especially when there have been witnesses to the CSA yet it is being denied, the child feels further betrayed and abused, producing even more shame and guilt. The child not only feels more helpless and powerless, but also realises that it is totally alone and cannot rely on anyone else to help. Any anger that may be present can become internalised and turned against the self, resulting in self-harming and destructive behaviour.

## Understanding children's resistance to disclosure

A lot of parents and teachers cannot fully understand why children do not disclose CSA. Parents often believe that they have a good close relationship with their child in which the child can talk about anything. While this in essence may be true, what parents and teachers do not take into account is the power the child sexual abuser has over the child in silencing it. While this can be achieved through threats of violence and/or death, or by implicating the child in criminal activities, most frequently it is through manipulation of the child's reality and emotions.

The most obvious reason why children find it difficult to disclose is that they are forced to keep the secret under threat of violence or death. Some sexual abusers threaten to hurt the child physically, or threaten to kill the child. The threats may be made against the child or a close family member, such as mummy or daddy, or a younger sibling. To reinforce this threat the abuser may harm or kill a pet, or animal, to prove that he or she is capable of that. Such threats render the child 'speechless' in that they are too terrified to talk about what is happening for fear of the consequences.

As already discussed younger children do not necessarily see CSA as abuse due to their age and lack of knowledge. Young children look to adults to make sense of the world and if they are told that sexual activity between adults and children is normal they will believe this and normalise the CSA. In addition, very young children are not able to verbalise their experiences, therefore reducing the risk of disclosure. These are all factors that many paedophiles capitalise on by deliberately targeting younger children.

Many children are unable to disclose because of the subtlety of the grooming process. Initially, the child may not be aware of any ulterior motives as the abuser's behaviour is primarily non-sexual and, as such, is not offending against the child. This puts the child in a dilemma as to what is there to tell. By the time sexual activity starts the child may be so invested in the abuser that it submits to the CSA to make him or her happy. The child has been seduced into an illusion of love, equality and mutuality in which the child is complicit in the sexual behaviour. Therefore for the child to tell would be to reveal the child's own part in the CSA. Child sexual abusers distort the child reality to such a degree that the child believes that it seduced the adult and that the child is the abuser, while the adult is the victim. This makes it hard to disclose.

**Reasons that children may find it hard to disclose**

- Threats
- Younger children see CSA as normal and do not label it as abuse, cannot tell
- The grooming process is so subtle the child may not be aware of ulterior motive
- Investment of trust in the friendship
- In early stages of grooming no actual offence is committed so what can the child tell?
- Distortion of reality – abuser manipulates child's reality so the child feels like the abuser, and the abuser is the victim; the 'offender within the child'
- Secrets – abuser manipulates the child into keeping innocuous secrets prior to the sexual secrets, joint secrets
- Fear of punishment
- Fear of not being believed
- Corruption of child – make child an offender – gets the child to commit offences such as alcohol, drugs, recruiting other children, sexually abusing other children, child pornography – producer and distributor; invalidates testimony, disqualified from giving evidence
- Child's confusion – shame, guilt, embarrassment

Child sexual abusers encourage the child to keep a number of other 'secrets' which are innocuous. If the child exposes the sexual secret then the other secret things may also come out. The child may well fear being punished for these as much as the sexual activity. If the sexual abuser has also befriended and groomed the parent(s), or he or she is a close family member, the child will fear not being believed. It is crucial for parent(s) and teachers to remember that most paedophiles are 'nice' people who are charming and respected members in the community. If it is hard for parents to believe that someone they knew would behave in such a way with a child, it is not surprising that the child fears not being believed, and blames itself for having seduced the adult.

Child sexual abuse is in essence a corruption of the child – not just sexually but in terms of its distortion of reality. A further corruption is when the abuser seduces and coerces the child into engaging in criminal activities, be it the illicit use of cigarettes, alcohol or drugs, or in recruiting other children to sexually abuse. The child is no longer a victim but also a criminal, which further reduces the risk of disclosure. One area where this is of particular concern is in the paedophile encouraging the child to take sexual photographs of itself and sending them via the Internet or mobile phone. This technically makes the child both a producer and distributor of child pornography. The paedophile may use this as leverage in ensuring the child's silence.

Paedophiles consistently remind the child of the illicit activities they have engaged in to date and how this will undermine their disclosure and any evidence they may provide. This is especially the case in older children, who fear that they will be prosecuted for their part in whatever criminal activity is engaged in. This fear is in part supported by the criminal justice system undermining the child's testimony in court as being contaminated and corrupt. This in turn reduces the chances of getting a conviction. In combination the child will feel even more trapped in a cycle and pattern of CSA which it feels it cannot escape.

What is clear is that the majority of sexually abused children feel confused about CSA and have a number of very potent and powerful feelings which they are unable to express. These strong feelings, which are confusing and at times overpowering, may prevent the child from disclosing CSA because the child just does not know where to start and what to say. One of the most powerful feelings underlying much of CSA is shame. Shame is so insidious in CSA that it is worth looking at in more depth, especially its relationship to those children who go on to sexually abuse other children.

## Child sexual abuse and shame

The presence of shame and guilt almost invariably accompany CSA and both have a huge impact on the child's self-esteem and how it interprets the sexual abuse. The experience of shame is also a factor in whether the child internalises its experience and how it may externalise it. One way to gain a deeper understanding of the sexually abused child is to look at its experience of abuse within the context of shame.

Shame and guilt are often used synonymously by people. In fact children and adult survivors tend to use the term guilt rather than shame in statements: 'I feel really guilty' rather than 'I feel ashamed'. Yet when exploring their experiences more deeply their deep sense of shame emerges. Many children and indeed adults are not clear that there are a number of significant distinctions between shame and guilt. It is useful to look at these before exploring the shame in relation to CSA.

## Guilt

Guilt is usually associated with a specific action, or omission, which transgresses acceptable forms of behaviour and is deserving of punishment. This is in stark contrast to shame, which is characterised by a general failing of character. Guilt instils a sense of tension, remorse or regret, which motivates reparative action such as atonement, which is payable by the appropriate display of a guilty conscience in an amount sufficient to assuage the justified anger the offence gave rise to. In contrast to shame, guilt does not require the reformation of an entire person but merely a change in actions that are within the voluntary control of the wrongdoer. Guilt also allows for more constructive, less hostile conflict resolution by the wrongdoer, by apologising and asking for forgiveness. Shame is less amenable to such easy conflict-resolution, peaceful forms of communication.

## Shame

Shame is more diffuse than guilt and overwhelmingly self-focused. It is characterised by self-negative evaluation of some specific behaviour (or lack of behaviours) when an internalised standard has been violated. In shame the entire self feels exposed, inferior and degraded, which is much more powerful and intense than guilt. Shame is characterised by preoccupation with others' opinion: beliefs about the self, what the self ought to be and the ideal self. Shame often requires an entire transformation of character, including physical transformation such as skin colour, body type, age, and state of health. Shame is also the internalisation of the social judgements of others, leading to self-loathing, self-contempt, self-disgust, and self-hatred.

Finkelhor has already pointed out the relationship between shame and stigmatisation (Finkelhor 1984; Finkelhor and Browne 1985). Stigmatisation is defined by the emotional experience of shame and a self-blaming attributional style. In stigmatisation the perpetrator and others blame the victim and, when this is accompanied by the need for secrecy, shame can arise.

This is especially the case in events that happen to children *without their control or desire.*

More importantly, confusion around excitation and pleasure can lead to shame when the body deceives/betrays the child by responding with pleasure to sexual excitation to what cognitively is confusing or uncertain. The fusion of affection, love and sexual abuse leads to attributions about the self, which can lead to shame. This can lead to feelings of deservedness and responsibility such as, 'I deserve to be (ab)used'; 'I am responsible for the abuse'. Internal, stable and global attributions for negative events predispose the child to develop feelings and thoughts about the self. These can occur during the abusive experience and subsequent to the abuse such as, 'This happened to me because I am a bad person'.

The child begins to denigrate itself, express a desire to hide or to 'become invisible' and to avoid exposure, leading to chronic concealment. Examples of self-denigration include: 'I am stupid, awful, a bad person, a blob'. As adults, shame ensures that CSA continues to be kept secret. For many children, CSA is experienced as an attack on, or loss of, social attractiveness, and a failure in role expectation. This is further enhanced if the social environment promotes the denigration of the self and humiliation.

According to Mollon (2002) CSA is an extreme form of psychic devastation, or projective identification, in which the abuser is in touch with the weaker, needier, younger, immature, dependent, helpless part, the part that is derided and feared. By having sex with a child who is weak, needy, young, immature, dependent and helpless, the abuser connects to areas of the self that are abhorred, held in contempt, loathed, and feared by the abuser. This is so terrifying to the abuser that the child is forced to play these parts, especially the neediness, dependency and helplessness. For the abuser, having sex with a child is a mode of communication, a form of autoerotic narcissism, in which the abuser is having sex with him/herself (Mollon 2002). It is also about total power and control over another – the child.

Child sexual abuse is also an act of cruel subjugation and submission, a sadistic act of humiliation. The abuser symbolically humiliates those parts of him/herself that s/he hates through the agency of the child. Sex to the abuser is an instrument of domination, a transformation of extreme aggression directed at the abuser him/herself but through a child. The more stereotypically childlike and innocent the child, the more valuable (appealing) it is to the abuser. If the child is not helpless, needy, weak, dependent and submissive the child loses its value and function in terms of the abuser's desire and arousal.

This may account for the finding that increasingly younger children are featured in child pornographic images. As children in Western culture become more sexualised at an early age by the media, and through fashion, paedophiles may turn to younger children to fulfil their fantasy of 'purity' and 'innocence'. Also as older children become more knowledgeable and 'streetwise' about sexuality, the power of manipulation and grooming is reduced. Younger children may be more pliable and more easily manipulated and less likely to disclose, reducing the paedophile's risk of exposure.

### Childhood responses to shame

To cope with chronic feelings of shame, the child is likely to develop a false self as it adapts to the abuser's acceptance, and acceptance by others. This leads to the inhibition of honest communication to enable the child to conceal CSA and accompanying shame. The child conceals its feelings of weakness, neediness, vulnerability, inadequacy and dependency by developing a façade of strength and confidence. This can be seen as a form of *compensatory grandiosity* or arrogance. The child pretends to be invulnerable and believes itself to be omnipotent by oppressing the emotionally needy part of the self. This is a form of an internal turning against the self, which can lead to a fragmentation of self and lack of core identity.

The child experiences a sense of helplessness and feels like an object in the entanglement with the abuser. This produces a repudiation of intimacy. The child's reality is totally distorted by the abuser in its understanding of what is appropriate and what is not, how it should behave in relation to others and what it can and cannot do. Beliefs about the self and what it means to be a child are also distorted. As such the abuser is exerting total power and control over the child, from which the child feels it cannot escape.

## The focus of shame

The child may focus its shame on any one, or a combination of the following:

- The body – this can lead to eating disorders, or the wish to disfigure through self-mutilation.

- The body in action – performance in sport, dance, physical exercise, conversation and sexual activity.

- Achievement failure – the child's constant striving to reach certain standards.

- Relationships – loss of attractiveness, both physical and social.

- Feelings – a range of confused feelings of anxiety, contempt, excitement, anger, envy, needing others, dependency, crying, expressing pain, vulnerability, saying 'I love you'.

- Group shame – the child feels stigmatised by others.

## Negative feelings associated with shame

There are a large number of negative feelings associated with shame which further inhibit the child from being itself or disclosing the sexual abuse. The most common are anxiety, including self-consciousness, helplessness, inferiority, and interpersonal anxiety. Confusion is prominent, not least for not knowing better. The child will also feel anger at the self, at the abuser and others for not recognising the CSA. This is compounded by those children who feel ashamed of feeling anger. Humiliation is a strong component in CSA, as is disgust, especially disgust at the self, the abuser, the sexual acts, the child's body and its responses to the sexual abuse. The indignity of CSA leads to an overwhelming self-focus, especially in feelings of worthlessness, incompetence and contempt for self. Fear and hostility are accompanied by sadness, along with feelings of vulnerability and dependency. The combination of excitement and pleasure and feeling aroused give rise to a sense of betrayal by the body, or body deception, leading to an even deeper sense of shame. In CSA the child internalises the 'shame-less' act of the abuser and feels itself to be an object of observation, judged by the abuser as being merely a sexual object in which through *projective annihilation* (Mollon 2002) the child becomes only what the abuser wants the child to be.

*Behaviours associated with shame*

Shame elicits a range of behaviours, many of which can be seen in children who have been sexually abused. Shame leads to a dilemma in which the child wishes to express its inner world but also needs to suppress it. The child needs to cover up its shame for fear of further shame. Strategies employed to ensure that the CSA and associated shame remain hidden include:

- Avoidance – in actions, feelings, thoughts, behaviours, withdrawal.
- Concealment – cover up physically and psychologically, use of alcohol, drugs.
- Readiness or heightened attentiveness.
- Compensation – psychological strategies such as pride, grandiosity, narcissism and 'shamelessness'.
- Aggression.

In avoidance the child has to hide its shame, which results in chronic concealment or the need to be invisible. This is frequently expressed in shyness, withdrawal, avoidance and secrecy. The more withdrawn and concealed the child is, the less likely their shame will be exposed, which reduces the risk of revealing CSA. The child will avoid eye contact, hide their face or body and actions. They hide their face by covering it up with the hair and their bodies by wearing baggy clothes that conceal their body shape. In covering up the shame to themselves, some children resort to the use of alcohol or drugs to nullify their experience of shame and CSA. Children who have been sexually abused and suffer from shame often display a heightened level of attentiveness, or readiness, in which they are hypervigilant to others' attentions. This is a form of protection so that the child knows and pre-empts any further attacks on the self.

A form of concealment seen in shame is compensation, in which the child is conscientious in covering up the shame by adopting opposite feelings, thoughts and behaviours. The most common examples of compensation in shame are pride and grandiosity. The child who feels inadequate and useless becomes a perfectionist. The child who feels worthless will adopt the pretence of being proud, self-confident and arrogant. Accompanying this is a sense of narcissism in which the child is only able to see the world through its own eyes and will seek satisfaction in whatever way it can. This often manifests in 'shameless' acts of behaviour, especially hostility and aggression, in which the child feels no empathy for its victims. In many respects this is the profile of the child as bully. By externalising its feelings of anger, the sexually abused child becomes aggressive, and in identifying with the aggressor, it is no longer the victim but becomes the abuser. In many respects, the child triumphs over the sexual abuse by no longer being the victim. It is this type of child who is most likely to go on and sexually abuse other children.

## Understanding children who go on to sexually abuse

Research shows that some children who have experienced CSA go on to sexually abuse other children. Current data show that adolescents and teenagers commit approximately 30 per cent of CSA. This is quite an alarming statistic, which is of huge concern to child protection workers and professionals. Skuse (2003) and Salter *et al.* (2003) found that approximately one in eight children who have been sexually abused go on to sexually abuse. While it is still unclear precisely why some children go on to sexually abuse, while others do not appear to, some factors have been associated with an increased risk of becoming an abuser. One such factor is whether the child internalises its responses to CSA or externalises them.

### The internalising child

As seen in Chapter 6, the impact of CSA varies from child to child with some children internalising the sexual abuse experiences while others externalise them. The internalising child tends to turn its feelings of pain, hurt and anger against the self. This is not surprising, as the child feels helpless and unable to control what is happening to it. In being powerless to do anything about the sexual abuse, the child begins to accept and resign itself to its fate. Such children become withdrawn, and absent. This is a form of self-protection that turns into resignation.

The internalising child denigrates itself, becomes compliant and submissive. This child is often passive in its anger, which it turns inward. This leads to a need and desire to hurt the self. This is seen in self-destructive behaviours, including eating disorders, alcohol or drug abuse and a range of self-mutilatory behaviours. The conflict in shame between expressing and suppressing becomes so great that the child will seek to hide and conceal its shame to the point of invisibility. A good example of this can be seen in the following case vignette.

## Kim

Kim's older brother was the apple of his mother's eye and could do no wrong. He was frequently left in loco parentis when mum went out in the evening to her little bar job. In her absence Kim's brother turned from a sweet angelic brother to a monster who terrorised his siblings through physical force and violence. As Kim got older, his brother started to single him out from the other siblings to sexually assault him. This became a nightly activity whenever mother was working. Kim was too terrified to disclose anything for fear of his brother's violence. Kim withdrew into silence. He was obedient, helpful and always ready to please. He never got angry and was extremely biddable. In many ways he was a model child.

What his mother did not know was that Kim felt so deeply ashamed that he had to hide himself away and withdraw from his peers and all social activities. Kim became studious, wishing to be at home in his room with his computer working at his studies. While in his room, especially after the sexual assaults, Kim would get out a razor blade and start to cut his penis and scrotum. This went on undetected for some time until one evening Kim's mother went into his room to check on something, when she saw that Kim had passed out in a pool of blood. The hospital managed to save Kim's life and suggested he be hospitalised to undergo psychiatric treatment. This was when Kim's mother first discovered the extent of the sexual abuse that had been going on for a number of years and how it had impacted on Kim.

This example shows how the internalising child, because of its withdrawal and compliance, may never come to the attention of parents, teachers or other professionals. Yet these children are very vulnerable and may not be offered any kind of help or therapeutic input. They may subsequently represent the large number of adults with severe psychiatric disorders who become dependent on health services. Clinical evidence suggests that female children are more likely to internalise CSA, in part due to differential socialisation between males and females, and more likely to represent adult mental health users. Although this has certainly been the case historically, it seems that more adolescent females do externalise their CSA experiences and go on to sexually abuse younger children, especially in their capacity as babysitters.

It is crucial that the internalising child's symptoms are understood and not ignored. It is quite understandable that parents with 'easy' children, who appear to have no problems, are polite and helpful, may fail to recognise any hidden signs of CSA. These children become very adept at hiding their shame. This does not mean to say that they do not feel it. It is essential that changes in behaviour are explored and understood and, if appropriate, linked to any trauma such as CSA that the child may be experiencing. It is only then that appropriate therapeutic input can be provided so as to circumvent a lifelong pattern of mental health problems or prevent the abuse of other children.

### The externalising child

In contrast, the externalising child is rarely ignored and often comes to the attention of parent(s), teachers and other professionals. However, the behaviour that brings the child to the attention of adults is not always necessarily linked to a history of CSA. The externalising child is often angry, hostile, aggressive and has low impulse control. The child may also have conduct problems or behave in a physically threatening way to other children. The externalising child may be covering up a sense of shame related to CSA by becoming the aggressor and bully, rather than the victim. The hostile behaviours are a way of avoiding being in contact with others, thereby reducing the risk of disclosure.

The externalising child may be seen as having a number of problems but these are not necessarily identified as being related to CSA. Many adults and professionals will focus on aspects of the child's behaviour and relate them to a number of factors, but do not always consider that CSA and shame may be at the root of the behaviour. This means that the child's experience is ignored and it is not provided with the appropriate therapeutic input. This can result in the child continuing to behave in inappropriate ways towards other children, including sexually. In the absence of such therapeutic intervention, the likelihood of a lifelong pattern of sexual offending against children is increased, as can be seen in the following example.

# Cindy

Cindy, although small for her age, had always been extremely feisty. From a young age she would regularly hold her own, even among slightly older children. Cindy would use verbal abuse and emotional blackmail to manipulate girls with threats of violence. She would pull their hair, pinch and bite them. Cindy was equally hostile and aggressive towards boys and other adults. She would not tolerate being restrained or reprimanded and would fight anyone who attempted to curb her. Cindy was assessed by an educational psychologist, who diagnosed conduct disorder linked to her sense of inadequacy due to her dyslexia. Although Cindy was statemented and given extra input for her dyslexia, other emotional issues were not explored sufficiently.

Although Cindy was not liked among her peers, she nevertheless managed to get them to do what she wanted. And what Cindy wanted more than anything was to explore other girls sexually. Cindy had always wanted to play 'doctors and nurses' as long as she could remember. She liked to force open another girl's legs, investigate the genitals and push things inside the opening. Initially these were just sweets and small objects but as she got older they included hairbrush handles, bottles and other objects. Sometimes her friends got bored with this game, which drove Cindy to such frustration that she would force the other children to submit under threat of physical violence. As Cindy grew older, she continued to play this game with younger children who knew no better and seemed to enjoy it as long as she was not too violent. However, the games always ended up being violent, as Cindy wanted to insert larger and larger objects.

When Cindy was 15 one of the little girls she had been babysitting told her parents what Cindy had been doing to her. When Cindy was investigated by child protection officers and social services it emerged that Cindy had been sexually abused from a very young age by a man and a woman who were close friends of the family. Cindy had never been able to disclose the CSA to her parents because they were best of friends with her abusers. She feared that she would not be believed and punished for telling such 'dirty, filthy lies'. Her sexually abusing other children was a way for Cindy to escape her sense of helplessness and vulnerability by making herself into the abuser and other children her victims.

## Risk factors associated with victims of CSA going on to sexually abuse

- The relationship between the offender and child: the closer the relationships, or if a primary carer, the greater the risk
- Age of child when it came under the influence of the abuser, not just when the actual sexual abuse starts but when grooming process begins
- Distorted thought processes and beliefs transferred on to child
- The abuser's fantasises, both sexual and non-sexual, transmitted to the child
- Length of time abuser spent with child – days, weeks, months, years
- Whether abuser was seduction or anger-motivated
- The psychological, emotional, physical and social controls used to overcome victim's resistance
- Abuser's pattern of behaviour
- Emotional needs of child attached to the abuse, whether they were met and anchored in the abuse
- Motivation of the offender – sex, anger, power, control, fear
- Changes of mood during offending cycle – loving to aggressive to loving
- Strategies employed by victim to survive
- Age of child in relation to developing sexual fantasises, how abuse affected fantasy life
- Behaviours adopted by the child to regain power over their life, negotiation, bargaining, and semblance of control or power on any level
- Involvement of other children – did victim have to recruit or abuse other children?
- Did victim act out abuse experience on other children or siblings?
- Type of abuse, range, frequency
- Relationship with non-abusing carers, unmet needs, to what extent these needs were satisfied by the abuser
- Presence of bizarre elements in the sexual abuse
- What extent bizarre elements were used to control the child

Thus it can be seen that while externalising children may come to the attention of adults and professionals, they may not link the behaviour to CSA. This has huge implications for those children who are sexually abused and who may go on to abuse. Researchers have also highlighted a number of other significant factors that are associated with victims of CSA going on to sexually abuse other children (Wyre 2002).

It can be seen from the risk factors below that the closer the relationship between the child and abuser, the younger the child, and the greater the influence the abuser had over the child, the more likely he or she will distort the child's reality in normalising CSA. This can increase the likelihood that such a child might go on to sexually abuse in adolescence or adulthood. In addition, the more controlled the child felt by the abuser, the type of sexual activity, and the strategies employed both by the abuser and the child all play a significant role. Children who were encouraged to recruit other children or to engage in sexual activity with children are also much more at risk of later sexual offending against children.

While these factors have been associated with the likelihood to go on to sexually abuse children, it is not clear to what degree each contributes to a cycle of sexual abuse. It is imperative that researchers identify which factors are the most likely to increase the risk and how this may be minimised. To engage in such research professionals need to identify victims of CSA as early as possible and provide appropriate therapeutic input. In addition, appropriate intervention with adolescents who sexually abuse children will enable professionals to gain a better understanding of why some children go on to sexually abuse others.

Such knowledge is essential for parents and teachers to further their understanding of CSA and not only detect it but get appropriate help for children as soon as possible. It is only when equipped with such knowledge and awareness that parents can feel empowered to protect children. Accurate knowledge about how CSA impacts on children and how to really understand the sexually abused child is the only way that parents and teachers can adequately protect children. How this is translated into practical help and advice is the subject of the following chapter.

## Chapter 9

# Protecting Children from Child Sexual Abuse in the Community

The best way to keep your family safe is to educate yourself about child sexual abuse. The earlier we can see what is happening, the earlier we can do something to stop the abuse.

*Mother of sexually abusing adolescent*

I can see there was a lot of secrecy in our son's life that we thought was normal, but now we know what he was hiding. If someone had told us that it was OK to talk to him about these things, or showed us how to do it, maybe this wouldn't have happened.

*Mother of sexually abusing adolescent*

If one is to believe the number of people who download child pornography from the Internet, the sexual interest in children is widespread. While not all users of Internet child pornography necessarily go on to sexually abuse children in reality, there is no doubt that some do. This indicates that children are vulnerable to sexual contact with adults. Awareness of how child sexual abusers target and befriend children through the grooming process empowers parents, teachers and other adults to more adequately protect children from child sexual abuse (CSA).

It is imperative that to protect children parents and teachers need to have access to accurate informed knowledge that separates out fact from fiction about the nature of CSA. It is not helpful to frighten parents and children about the dangers of CSA, or to fuel myths that distort reality. Arguably if parental fears are unduly heightened, these fears will be transmitted to their children, making them equally scared. This renders children prisoners in their own homes in being too frightened to go out in to the community. Ultimately this makes children suspicious, which prevents them from learning crucial social skills and how to live safely in their community. These skills are necessary to develop into healthy adults who embrace life rather than fear it.

Children should not be restricted in acquiring appropriate skills that will enable them to function in their community. It is unhealthy for children to feel restricted in their movements by frightening them to such a degree that they become reclusive. Rather than make children fearful and suspicious it is crucial that we equip them with sufficient, age-appropriate knowledge to be aware and cautious of potential dangers. This is part of the learning process that enables children to develop a sense of autonomy and independence, which prepares them for necessary adult skills.

The hysteria that at times surrounds CSA in 'naming and shaming' of paedophiles merely lulls all of us into a false sense of security. As already stated, although there are currently 21,413 sex offenders on the Sex Offenders' Register, this does not represent the full extent of child sexual abusers. In many respects CSA is a 'phantom offence' (Wyre 2000) in that only 10 per cent of CSA comes to the attention of the criminal justice system, and only 5 per cent results in a conviction. Given these low detection and conviction rates, estimates suggest that the actual number of child sexual abusers is closer to 250,000. This clearly shows that there are many child sexual abusers who do not come to the attention of the criminal justice system, who are still 'unknown'. Just focusing on the paedophiles known to the authorities focuses attention away from the unknown child sexual abusers who continue to target and groom children.

While there may be a value in the controlled access to names on the Sex Offenders' Register to certain members of the community, there are also a number of dangers. Concentrating on the 'known' diverts attention away from the as yet 'unknown'. In addition, there is the danger of vigilantism. Strong public reaction to paedophiles, and what they do to children, while perfectly understandable, nevertheless does not justify the hunting down, hounding and attacking of them. This merely serves to drive them further underground so that they again become 'unknown' to the police and community. Furthermore, there is evidence that such stigmatisation and accompanying fears of being tracked down increase the anxiety levels in the paedophile, which may prompt him or her to sexually abuse a child to relieve the stress that they are under.

What is much more empowering for parents and children is to have access to accurate knowledge of how paedophiles operate in the community, what strategies they use, how they can be detected and how to equip children with appropriate knowledge. This chapter aims to inform parents and teachers of what to be aware of in relation to CSA and most importantly how to convey this knowledge to children without instilling fear and panic in them so that they are able to feel safe in their community. Guidelines and helpful tips will be given on how to communicate the dangers of CSA to children in a calm and balanced way to get the information across most effectively. It will also provide useful information about how to protect children from grooming on the Internet, along with guidance on what to do if parents or teachers suspect, or know, that a child is being sexually abused.

## The grooming of parents

Although much consideration has been given to how paedophiles target and groom children, less attention has been directed at how the parents are groomed in order for the paedophile to get access to their children. It is clear from statistical data that it is no longer sufficient to warn our children about 'stranger danger' as the majority of CSA (87%) is perpetrated by someone 'known' to the child. Often the parents and teachers also know them. As described in Chapter 4 child sexual abusers are most often members of the local community, not necessarily strangers.

They can be members of the child's immediate or extended family, they may be neighbours, acquaintances, respected authority figures in the child's life such as teachers, or a worker at school, sports or music coaches, leaders of a youth group, a worker in a caring profession, or otherwise involved in local children's activities. Paedophiles are often attracted to places, professions and activities that allow them easy access to children. In being around children, and engaged in a variety of activities with them, they give the impression of being 'known' to the child.

One must be careful though in the use of the phrase 'known to the child'. It is extremely difficult to define 'known' and what this actually means. Does it mean familiar in the sense that they are recognised and identifiable by the child, or does it mean that the child 'knows' them because they occasionally see them on the street, participate in non-sexual activities with them, or socialise with them because they are 'known' to the family or friends.

The issue of 'knowing' someone is quite complex in that it begs the question how well do we really 'know' anyone in terms of his or her character, personality, motivation or sexual predilections. People rarely discuss their sexual proclivities and these often remain 'unknown'. Sexual interest is usually inferred about someone based on their general attitudes and behaviours, and is subject to interpretation. This means that people frequently make assumptions about other people's sexual interests, which are based on how 'normal' and likeable someone appears. This is particularly the case with child sexual abusers who invariably portray themselves as 'nice', normal people. And in many respects on the surface they are. They can be charming and pleasant, good fun and good company, who enjoy all the normal things that the average person does. They are rarely suspicious or odd looking, and do not always appear to be overly friendly or physically close towards children.

This is part of the deception and power that child sexual abusers wield. By being 'nice' they are accepted not only by adults but also by children. By looking and behaving normally they are included in activities with families and children without raising any doubts or suspicions. They need to be nice people to be accepted by adults and children so that they do not stand out in a crowd and can get access to children. Many paedophiles work extremely hard at creating such an image by demonstrating good social skills and appropriate non-sexual behaviour around children. To divert suspicion they may make extremely negative statements about child sexual abusers, claiming to be passionately for the protection of children from such monsters.

Many paedophiles know that in order to get close to children they need to be accepted by the parents and other adults in that child's life. To do this they present a façade, or mask, that is appealing to parent(s) and which engenders trust. Such paedophiles are highly manipulative and subtle in their deception of the parent(s) of children in masquerading as normal and nice. They know they need to infiltrate the family and gain the parent(s)' trust before they can get access to the children. If the parent(s) trust the abuser it is much more likely that the child will. Being a 'pied piper' type figure also reduces the risk of disclosure once sexual activity is engaged in. Many paedophiles are arch masters at hiding their real motivation in befriending the parents of children, never letting their mask slip. To succeed in grooming the child they need first to succeed in grooming the parents. Only nice people not monsters can achieve this. Thus they are often very good at making friends, appearing warm, friendly and very approachable.

By the time the first sexual abusive activity occurs, both the parents and the child are well and truly 'hooked' into the abuser's deception, without any idea of his or her intention to sexually abuse the child. The trust and friendship is now so embedded that should they find out that anything untoward is going on, many parent(s) react with absolute shock, surprise or disbelief. Even in the presence of incontrovertible evidence they still find it hard to believe and cannot understand how they got there. They may be wracked with guilt for not realising that they have been duped and deceived all along.

Thus, parents are just as vulnerable to being groomed and manipulated by child sexual abusers with little awareness of what is happening. So how can parents know that someone they know and trust does not have ulterior motives, or intentions to sexually abuse their child? There are no simple answers or solutions to this, other than an awareness of how they interact with their child, especially when no other adults are around, and to have an open dialogue with their children about the time they spend with this special friend.

It is not healthy to be overly suspicious of all adults that the child comes into contact with, but it helps to have an open mind about ulterior motives, no matter how nice they are. It is also important for parents to question their own feelings around an individual who spends a lot of time with their child. An open dialogue between the parent(s) and child about their respective feelings around the person and what sort of activities they engage in when they are together also helps to monitor the quality of the relationship.

While such awareness can go some way to protect the child while in the abuser's presence, the level of deception can be so subtle and clever that it is often hard to see any ulterior motive or sexual intention. Thus, there are no guarantees that parents and other adults can see through the fact that they may be being groomed. It is for that reason that an open dialogue with children should be encouraged in which the child feels able to discuss everything with their parents. This includes any minor and major transgressions they may have engaged in.

A useful example is for the child to know that they need not have secrets from their parents. It may help to differentiate between secrets and surprises.

While secrets can be nice, such as not telling mummy what her birthday present is, secrets can also be a way of not telling adults about bad things. In contrast, surprise may be a better word to use as it includes such things as mummy's birthday present. Child sexual abusers are known to use phrases such as 'our special secret' to encourage the child not to tell or disclose CSA.

---

### Clues suggesting that someone has a sexual interest in children

- The language many child sexual abusers use about children may give some clues – paedophiles often refer to the 'innocence' or 'purity' of children

- They may be unusually knowledgeable about all the latest interests and crazes that children have, often more knowledgeable than parents about the latest language and phrases used by children, the latest fashions, games, films, music and videos

- They may show abnormally high levels of patience to play games with the children that most adults and parents would not have. How many adults have the time or inclination to play computer games for hours on end, or watch an endless round of children's videos or movies?

- Regularly offer to babysit children for free or take children on overnight outings

- Treat a particular child as a favourite, making them feel 'special' compared with others in the family, single out a particular child

- Buy children expensive gifts or give them money for no apparent reason

- Prefer the company of children to that of adults and spend all their spare time with children rather than spending time with people of their own age

- If they are invited to the abuser's house the parent may notice that the décor is quite child-oriented, with lots of children's games, activities, videos and toys around

- Paedophiles attempt to manipulate exclusive time with children by encouraging other adults to go off and enjoy themselves. They can come across as happy to sacrifice their own adult fun for the sake of the child's. They insist on time alone with the child without any interruptions.

## The grooming of children

Some paedophiles do not necessarily groom the parents but target a specific child who may be 'known' to them without really knowing the parents of family. By taking a strong interest in the child, its activities and concerns, the abuser gains the child's trust to open up about his/her life at home, school and relationships. In doing so the abuser is able to find out if there are any difficulties in the family and to check how good the relationship between the child and the parent(s) actually is. If there are difficulties and the child is not very close to the parents, this will make the paedophile's job easier.

Finding out the child's unmet needs at home, or any inner void, will help the paedophile to know what to focus on in providing whatever is not being met by the parents. This may be extra special attention, encouragement, building self-esteem, giving the child confidence to excel in some area, or providing emotional support and understanding. The paedophile might act as a confidante to the child by encouraging it to share and express all its worries, fears and concerns, making the child feel heard and understood. This is designed to create a bond between the child and the abuser in which the child builds up trust and comes to rely and depend on the abuser for emotional understanding, support and attention.

Paedophiles rarely pick children at random. They can be skilled at identifying children who may be vulnerable to their approach. They are likely to target a child who looks friendless and who is not likely to challenge or resist their approach. Such children are less likely to confront the child sexual abuser or to make a fuss when approached. In fact they may initially appreciate being singled out for special attention. Such children are less likely to resist when the relationship is sexualised and less likely to disclose because of the investment they have made in the friendship. By the time any sexual activity occurs the child will have invested so much trust in the paedophile that they might comply with the sexual activity because they do not want to lose the friendship. Child sexual abusers are very clever in using emotional blackmail with the child. They might say things like, 'If you really cared for me you would let me touch you sexually' or 'I really care about you, and you care about me. This [sexual activity] would make me feel really happy and complete'.

**Children most at risk**

- Looks vulnerable
- Is timid
- Looks young for their age
- Is too trusting
- Seeks love or affection
- Is lonely or bereaved
- Lacks confidence
- Is being bullied
- Is disabled or unable to communicate well
- Is in care or away from home
- May already be a victim of abuse
- Is eager to succeed in activities such as sport, school or other interests, which may allow him/her to be manipulated by a potential abuser

The paedophile may emphasise their own loneliness or isolation and make the child feel sorry for them. And because the abuser has been so kind and emotionally supportive of the child throughout the grooming process the child feels obliged to give something back to show how much they value the friendship. They want to make the abuser happy as this ensures that the friendship, which up till that point has had such huge value for the child, continues. The child may know it is wrong to engage in such sexual activity but compromises itself for the sake of the friendship. Such arch manipulation by the abuser ensures the child's compliance and submission to the sexual activity and minimises disclosure as the child is made to feel complicit in the abuse.

This compliance further fuels the child sexual abuser's distortions in believing that the child fully agreed and consented to the sexual activity and wanted it. The net effect is that the child believes that he/she has invited the abuse. Even though many children tolerate the sexual contact this does not mean that they want it or enjoy it. The paedophile transforms this into a belief that the child enjoys the sexual abuse and that it is not doing them any harm. Many paedophiles work on the principle that because the child does not say no or resist the sexual advance this indicates the child's interest and desire.

They refuse to see that the level of manipulation and distortion of the child's reality is what prevents the child from saying no and resisting.

Some paedophiles will use other forms of persuasion. Abusers distort the child's reality by telling the child that what is happening is not wrong and is a way of showing each other love and affection. A young and naïve child will find this plausible, especially if the abuser uses child pornography to reinforce the verbal message. Another way to get the child to collude in the sexual contact is to offer the child presents such as money, sweets, video games, CDs or DVDs. Some abusers play on this in offering the child long desired treats that the parents either refuse, or cannot afford to buy, such as a mobile phone. A further coercion could be the promise of special trips, days out to theme parks or holidays.

In some cases the abuser will offer illicit privileges such as staying up late, or illicit gifts such as cigarettes, alcohol or drugs. What the child does not realise is that because these are illicit and have to be kept secret from the parents, the abuser is preparing the child to keep the CSA secret. If the child discloses the sexual abuse the parents may also find out about other illicit and secret things they have engaged in. Alcohol and drugs may also be a way of disinhibiting the child as a prelude to sexual activity so the child is not fully aware of what is happening to them.

Another way for the paedophile to coerce the child is to play upon the child's natural fear, embarrassment or guilt. The child's sense of guilt or shame about the sexual contact and fear of the parents finding out serves to further silence the child. This is reinforced by the paedophile in telling the child that it will get into trouble and be punished, or that he or she will not be believed.

Some child sexual abusers use threats of violence to force the child to agree to the sexual contact. These include violence to the child, or threats of violence to someone else close to the child such as members of the family, or to the child's pet. It is not unknown in familial sexual abuse for the abuser to threaten to hurt or sexually assault a younger sibling. Often the child enters into what it thinks is a bargain by agreeing to the sexual abuse as a way of protecting a brother or sister, often to find out later that the abuser reneges on the bargain. In those instances where the abuser hurts or kills the child's pet he or she gives a clear demonstration of the power he or she can wield and also reinforces the child's fear that they can just as easily be hurt or killed.

In the case of paedophiles who sexually abuse a large number of children, or who are part of a paedophile ring, they may force the child to recruit other children into the abuser's clutches. Children may be less suspicious and more trusting of an older child, thus making it easier for them to be recruited. The older children may also be coerced, or forced, to exert peer pressure on the younger children to comply, keep silent and so ensure that the secret is kept safe. In some cases these older children will be forced to sexually abuse other, younger children. The guilt associated with this may be so enormous that it prevents the child from breaking the silence.

Corrupting the child is also seen in cases where the paedophile encourages a child to take sexual photographs of itself, which the child then sends via the Internet to the paedophile. In doing this the child unwittingly commits a criminal offence in becoming both a producer and distributor of child pornography. This implicates the child in sexually offending, making it feel complicit in the CSA, further ensuring its silence. Should such a case come to court the child's testimony will be undermined, given that it has committed a criminal offence.

---

### Clues to watch out for in the grooming of children

- Someone who pays an unusual amount of attention to your child
- Someone who gives the child gifts, toys and money
- Someone who favours the child and extends privileges to it, making it feel 'special'
- Someone who frequently offers to take the child on trips, outings and holidays
- Someone who seeks every opportunity to be alone with your child
- Someone who tries to exclude other adults from taking part in the child's activities
- Someone who tries to exclude other children, siblings and peers from taking part in the child's activities
- Someone who isolates the child from others

282 / THE SEDUCTION OF CHILDREN

## How to keep children safe

In order to keep children safe and to protect them it is important that parents and teachers build upon their knowledge of the child and provide a warm, open and trusting relationship with the child to communicate effectively. To ensure the child's safety a number of factors need to be considered. First, parents and teachers need to take great care when entrusting a child into the care of another adult, no matter how well 'known' they are, especially if this includes unsupervised contact. Second, parents and teachers need to provide the child with guidance about how to be safe in the community and to be aware of potential dangers. Third, it is important to provide the right environment in which the child can talk about any concerns or doubts they might have.

---

### Entrusting children to other adults

- Be aware of and alert to any signs of behaviour that you feel uncomfortable about
- If you have doubts, listen to them and carry out careful checks
- Do not leave your child with anyone you have reservations about
- Do not allow unsupervised contact without making careful checks first
- Find out as much as possible about babysitters and those who look after children
- Do not use unregistered child minders or foster parents
- Always ask crèches, nurseries, schools and other children's activities groups what checks and procedures they have in place for protecting and dealing with abuse
- Make unannounced checks and visits
- Talk to the child about the time spent with the person, what they did, whether the child enjoyed it, whether the child felt uncomfortable about anything at any point

---

## Talking to children about potential dangers and safety

When talking to children about potential dangers it is crucial to do so in a calm, controlled and non-threatening way. Frightening the child is counterproductive and will not get the message across effectively. If the child is afraid it will not be able to hear the message as it is dealing with its fears and anxieties. Adults should be calm and collected and firm in getting their message across. This is sometimes difficult in such an emotive subject such as CSA. The parents may feel uncomfortable about talking about such issues, and this discomfort will be transmitted to the child non-verbally. This can serve to make the child uncomfortable and switch off to ward off the anxieties and fears it senses in the parent.

If parents can apply principles from other child safety messages and apply these in the same way to CSA the child will feel much more reassured and able to take the message on board. A good example of this is teaching child road safety. Parents are able to teach even very young children about the need to stop, look and listen before crossing the road without displaying high degrees of discomfort. Parents and adults need to access the same calm, controlled way of conveying safety messages about other dangers in the community. It may be helpful for parents to view what they are trying to convey as simple safety messages rather than focusing on the 'sexual' components underlying the message.

Simple messages such as never going out alone, never going into anyone's house no matter how well known, or accepting presents or invites without checking with mummy or daddy first, can be introduced from a very young age. And if constantly reinforced will become automatic behaviour, like 'the green cross code'. Parents can further reinforce these messages if necessary when incidents occur in the local community, or national news. These are opportunities to discuss the incident with the child and to check the child's knowledge and understanding. This can be supported by role-plays of what the child would do in such a situation, including a designated 'safety' place where there is always someone who cares.

Parents need to use age-appropriate language, containing sufficient information to put the message across. Children have different concepts of 'danger' and 'strangers' at different stages of development and these differ from an adult's concept. It is important to be aware of the child's level of understanding so as not to confuse the child. When explaining what is meant by danger the parent can say to a young child that something is dangerous that hurts the child, using a familiar example of when the child last hurt itself, reminding it how much that hurt, and that such pain can be experienced again in the presence of danger.

Parents also need to discuss what is meant by 'stranger' and how to differentiate between a familiar person, such as a neighbour or acquaintance whom they know by sight but do not spend time with, and someone whom they regularly visit and spend time with.

While parents may encourage children to be polite to neighbours in saying 'hello' or 'good morning', this does not mean that the child should accept invitations to go off alone with the neighbour or indeed visit the neighbour in their home. Children should be firmly instructed always to check with the parent or a designated, trusted adult before going anywhere, or accepting anything from anybody, no matter how familiar or well known they are. This can easily be implemented as a basic ground rule, like many other ground rules that parents have.

An example could be saying to a young child that 'Some adults are very nice to children in offering them sweets or invitations to visit but you must always check with mummy or daddy before accepting them'. This conveys the message that they should never accept anything from another adult without checking this first. It is essential to know what the child is most susceptible to. For some this may be the offer of sweets, toys, or playing computer games, while for the child who loves animals it may be an invitation to see kittens or puppies.

Having identified what the child is most susceptible to, it can help to role-play scenarios of how the child can say, 'No, I need to check with my mummy or daddy first' to see where the child's resistance can be broken. Such role-plays reinforce the message and enable the child to find ways of not being persuaded. Also role-play allows the child to practise how it should behave, which makes it easier for the child to integrate the message as part of its behaviour. Practising such scenarios enables the child to incorporate it into its daily life.

Children also need to be provided with accurate information about the dangers of grooming and how someone can pretend to be nice yet have an ulterior motive. When discussing grooming the parent must use age-appropriate analogies to ensure that the child understands what is meant. This does not mean going into graphic details about what child sexual abusers do, as the child will not necessarily understand these. A message such as, 'Many adults are nice to children in front of adults, but may not be so nice when they are on their own with children' can help the child understand why it needs to be cautious in accepting invitations without checking with the parents first. It is not necessary to go into detail in terms of the ways in which such adults may be horrible, but simply to convey that the child must be cautious in investing their trust.

Everyday experiences familiar to the child can be used to reinforce the message that someone can pretend to be nice and kind most of the time and sometimes also be mean to the child. A real life example of someone who has been rude or horrible to the child and how much that upset them is an effective way of getting the point across. Another good example is when a child whom they are friends with behaves in a mean and horrible way to them it makes it clear that someone can be nice a lot of the time and yet at other times can be mean.

While it is important to many parents to instil politeness to others in their children, it is helpful to let the child know that in certain situations they have the parents' full permission to protect themselves, even if this means being impolite to an adult. Children need to know they have a right to feel safe in the community and in the presence of adults. Therefore if children feel unsafe, threatened, scared, uncomfortable or confused they have a right to say 'No' and to get out of that situation as quickly as possible. In those instances it is more important to get out of the situation than it is to be polite. Along with that, the child needs to know it will not get into trouble for either its lapse of politeness or for telling the parents what happened.

This is vital as the child might blame itself for getting into the situation in the first place. The child might feel that it has disobeyed the parent by accepting an invitation or the offer of sweets and that it will get into trouble for that. It is essential that the child knows that when they are in such a threatening situation, they will not be blamed or punished for how they got there, but that it is the person who put them into that situation in the first place who is in the wrong. This will help the child to know that it is OK to tell parents what has happened rather than keeping the secret for fear of being punished for their part in it.

It is also important to tell children that if they feel threatened or uncomfortable about being approached by someone in a public place they are allowed to make a fuss. By shouting, screaming or even being rude to the adult the child is more likely to draw attention from other adults who can help the child get out of a potentially dangerous scenario. The abuser needs to avoid drawing attention to him or herself and is likely to abandon the approach as a result of other adults noticing the child's distress. This is why paedophiles tend to target timid children who are afraid to say no or challenge an adult for fear of being punished. In practising with the child how it can best draw attention to such a scenario, the child can rehearse how it can protect itself in situations of danger or threat. The child needs to know that there will always be someone there to help him or her and that it has a right to feel safe.

This is particularly pertinent because paedophiles use many strategies to persuade the child that they are safe and can be trusted. A classic example is when the abuser poses as someone known to the parents and who claims to have been sent by them to collect the child or give the child a lift home. In making such an approach the abuser can seem highly plausible, especially if they have access to information that indicates that they really do know the parents. It is important to discuss with the child the likelihood of such a scenario being genuine. Ideally the parent should designate a trusted adult who would be called upon in an emergency to collect the child, and that the child is not to go off with anyone other than that designated person.

In an emergency when the designated person cannot be contacted, the child must go back into the safety of the building or centre where it is to be collected from and talk to a responsible adult about its fears. This is better than waiting around outside, putting the child at risk from someone else offering the child a lift. In terms of pretending to be friends of the parents, it is essential that the child knows who the parent(s) consider to be trusted friends and who they would actually entrust their child to. This would not necessarily include plausible work colleagues or vague acquaintances. It may also help to have a code word or a specific question, such as the mother's maiden name or a grandparent's name, to ask as a way of screening the genuineness of the approach.

A further safety measure is to stress to the child that they should never go out alone but should always ensure that they go out with a friend when they go out to places or to play outside. Whichever friend they go out with they should stay together until they are back in the safety of their home. This applies even when there is a falling out between friends and one of the children decides to go off on their own. It is crucial to instil the importance of remaining together, to avoid splitting up, and to be in sight and hearing of each other.

This guidance is equally important for teenagers, who may have been drinking, taking drugs, or become romantically involved with another peer. To leave someone who has had too much to drink on their own is to put them at risk. If they are concerned about a friend in such a condition it is appropriate to seek the help and advice of parent(s), or a responsible adult, rather than leave the friend to their own devices. It is important to stress that the teenager will not get into trouble for drinking, as it is more important that they are safe.

It is crucial that parents are able to talk about safety measures and potential dangers openly rather than shrouding them in secrecy. Secrecy can create fear and embarrassment in the child, making it reluctant to talk about such safety issues. In addition, given that secrecy is such a potent factor in the sexual abuse of children, it is essential that parents themselves avoid any secrecy to enable the child to be open and honest. If parents feel comfortable in talking about certain issues, children will take their lead, which allows them to talk more openly about their experiences.

An example of such openness about sexual issues is to teach even quite young children that their bodies are their own and that no-one has the right to touch them or treat them in a way that makes them feel scared, uncomfortable or confused. If something like that does occur they must feel they can tell their parent(s) without getting into trouble. Such a message can be reinforced in everyday situations that, while innocent, may nevertheless be uncomfortable for the child such as a relative who, upon meeting or saying goodbye, embraces or kisses the child. The child may feel embarrassed by this or uncomfortable, yet is told by the parent that it is being rude or impolite to not submit to the embrace. Such admonishment teaches the child that it has no right over its own body or personal space and must submit itself to adults' touching, hugging and kissing. Even though this is entirely innocent, it is important to listen to how and why it makes the child uncomfortable or embarrassed, and to give the child permission to say no. A gentle word with the relative may be well placed in asking them to desist from such physical contact, and not put the child into such an uncomfortable situation in the future, rather than telling the child it is rude or bad for not wanting to be hugged or kissed.

Encouraging the child to see its body as its own, over which it has a right to decide who can touch it, enables the child to protect itself from unwanted physical attention. This is crucial, especially if it involves the genital areas. The child needs to know that it has a right to say 'No' to another adult or child touching it without feeling bad for saying 'No'. In addition the child needs to feel reassured to not fear punishment for not complying with others' requests to touch the child inappropriately. Even very young children can be taught to differentiate between 'good' and 'bad' touch. If children are taught about appropriate and inappropriate touching from a young age, they are less likely to be seduced by 'misinformation' provided by paedophiles. They will be more able to challenge such requests and feel more comfortable telling parent(s) or trusted adults about such touching.

Along with this the parents also need to convey to the child that it is unlawful for older children or adults to touch children's genitals, and that if they do the child is *never* to blame and will not get punished, no matter what the other person has told the child. While the child is under 16 no one has the right to touch him or her sexually and it is the person who does so who is at fault, and will be punished, not the child. The parent(s) need to convey this message in a neutral, matter of fact way in which there is no doubt at all in terms of who is at fault and where responsibility, blame and punishment lies.

This clear message is also of value to the adolescent or teenager who may believe themselves to be a willing participant in sexual activity with an older person. No matter how much the adolescent child might want this, it is nevertheless unlawful, and the older person, as the adult, must know better and should not pressurise the child to engage in what is an illicit activity. It is the older person who should know better, and if they genuinely cared for the child then they would not coerce them into something that is not acceptable or lawful. If they do love and care for the child then they will be prepared to wait until the child is above the age of consent.

Many of these safety messages, while warning of the dangers of CSA, do not necessarily focus on sexual abuse. The messages convey general attitudes about the right of a child to feel safe, to say 'No' to someone or something that makes them feel uncomfortable, and not fear punishment. Many parents fear talking to children about CSA because they believe they have to talk to them primarily about the sexual issues involved. In reality, this is only a small part of the safety messages, which are designed to emphasise safety rather than graphic discussions about sexual abuse. Talking to children about safety equips them with accurate information, rather than misinformation, and gives them confidence to be assertive in relation to others who make them feel uncomfortable.

Talking to the child clearly demonstrates an openness of communication, which in turn enables the child to feel confident in talking to parent(s) about a wide variety of things they experience, without feeling embarrassed or afraid of punishment. This is what protects children. Depriving children of knowledge and shrouding dangers of CSA in secrecy fails to protect them and makes the paedophile's seduction that much easier. In the words of one convicted paedophile, 'Parents are partly to blame if they don't tell their children about [sexual matters] – I used it to my advantage by teaching the child myself'.

### Safety messages

Remember, although parents always need to be aware that there may be paedophiles operating in the local community, it is important to keep a sense of perspective. The vast majority of people do not sexually abuse children, so be cautious about frightening or worrying children unduly. By talking to children and providing them with accurate information, both parents and children will feel more secure in being protected from CSA. Equally, it will enable children to benefit from developing safe friendships with adults without fear of being abused.

Parents and teachers need to be aware that they can teach their children about the dangers of CSA and grooming in a variety of ways without having to go into graphic sexual detail. While all these messages do not guarantee that the child will never be at risk, it does ensure that the child or teenager has access to knowledge and information that may minimise the risks. In line with the National Centre for Missing and Exploited Children the messages on the follwing page need to be emphasised.

There is little point in enforcing such safety messages in children if they are not supported by a warm, open relationship with them in which they know that they are able to discuss any worries, fears or concerns that they may have. This includes secrets that others, especially adults, have asked them to keep. It is important for children to know that they will not be in trouble if they talk about their concerns. Make sure that the child feels listened to and heard.

**Messages to emphasise**

- Always check first with parents or a trusted adult before going anywhere or getting into a car with anyone, even someone I know

- Always check first with parents or a trusted adult before accepting anything from anyone, even from someone I know

- Always take a friend whenever I go out and never go out alone to play or go to places unaccompanied

- Always make sure that the child knows its name, address, telephone number and the parents' names

- It is OK to say NO if someone tries to touch them or treat them in a way that makes them feel scared, uncomfortable or confused and to get out of that situation as quickly as possible

- Always tell a parent or a trusted adult if they are feeling scared, uncomfortable or confused

- Remember it is OK to say NO and there is always someone to help and they have a right to be safe

- Encourage the child to believe in themselves to be strong, smart and have a right to be safe

## Knowing the signs and symptoms of CSA

The signs of CSA can manifest in emotional, behavioural, cognitive or physical symptoms. The child may also test reactions to CSA by giving hints and clues about the abuse, or it may disclose it. Initial clues that the child may be suffering from CSA revolve around changes in the child's behaviour. However, it is important to recognise that no one single sign or change in behaviour necessarily indicates CSA. It is the constellation of signs and symptoms within the context of the child's environment that needs to be considered (see Chapter 6).

### Summary of some of the main warning signs of CSA in children

- Acting out in an inappropriate sexual way with toys, objects, children, adults or pets
- Use of sexually explicit language and knowledge previously not seen
- Increased aggressive behaviour, outbursts of anger
- Nightmares or sleep problems
- Personality changes
- Regressing to younger behaviours such as bedwetting
- Increased insecure behaviours such as clinginess
- Changes in eating habits
- Unaccountable fear of particular places or people, or refusal to continue with usual social activities
- Refusal to attend school or lack of concentration (often linked to doing badly at school)
- Becoming withdrawn or depressed
- Recurring physical complaints with no supporting medical evidence
- Physical signs such as unexplained soreness or bruises around genitals, sexually transmitted diseases
- Becoming secretive
- Having new exclusive relationships with adults or other children
- Accumulated gifts or money that cannot be accounted for

## Protecting children from being groomed through the Internet

It is crucial that parents are aware of the dangers of grooming on the Internet (see Chapter 4) in order to protect children. Parents need to familiarise themselves with computer technology and the Internet in order to monitor Internet access. In the same way that parents discuss other dangers with their child, it is important to discuss the dangers of the Internet. Websites such as ChatDanger (see Appendix 1 at the end of this book) give helpful advice to parents about how to talk to their children about the dangers of the Internet and what they can do to protect their children.

**What parents need to know and do to protect their children from CSA**

- Always know where your children are
- Always know who they are with and agree a time when they should return
- Always ensure that your children know where you are at all times, and where you can be contacted
- Make time for your children
- Build up an open good trusting relationship with your children
- Always listen carefully to their fears and concerns and let them know they should not be worried about telling you anything
- Be alert about anyone who is paying an unusual amount of attention to your children
- Be alert about anyone who buys your children's affection by buying them sweets, giving them money or expensive gifts, videos or computer games
- Be cautious about anyone who has unsupervised contact with your children
- Find out as much as possible about anyone who is looking after them
- Talk to your children about 'appropriate' touching, 'good' and 'bad' touch
- Do not be too embarrassed to talk to your children about the dangers of CSA and grooming
- Help your children to understand what is unacceptable behaviour between adults and children
- Encourage your children to tell you if anyone, including a relative or friend, is behaving in a way that worries them
- Teach your children to feel confident to refuse to do anything that they feel is wrong or frightens them
- Explain to your children the difference between 'good' and 'bad' secrets. Tell them, for example, that it is OK to have a secret about a surprise birthday party, but not about anything that makes them feel unhappy or uncomfortable
- Know the range of behaviours of adults or older children that give cause for concern
- Know the signs and symptoms of CSA

Most children who have access to computers tend to use them much more than their parents. Many of them are also more knowledgeable about the Internet than their parents are. Yet in order to keep the child safe from Internet dangers it may help if parents become more knowledgeable. There are a number of websites designed for parents to enhance their knowledge about computers and Internet use (see Appendix 1 at the end of this book).

Parents need to take an interest in children's Internet use and what they are doing online. If parents are not sure how the Internet works, it helps to ask the child to show them. Many children are delighted to demonstrate their knowledge, especially if it outstrips that of their parents. Showing an interest in what your child encounters on the Internet will massively reduce the potential for some other person to show an interest, for all the wrong reasons, in what your child is doing.

In an ideal world it is best to have the computer in a family room where a number of people have access to it and are aware of what the child is doing, rather than in the child's bedroom. If the child has exclusive use of the computer and it is located in the child's bedroom, it is essential that parents pop their head around the door at frequent intervals to check on the child and what it is doing. This is not spying on the child but a way of taking care of them and protecting them. Surfing the Internet from the comfort and safety of home gives a false sense of security to both parents and children as they are apparently safe at home, inside the house.

It is also useful for parents to set up rules for going online. These could include the time of day and length of time the child is allowed online, and the appropriate areas and sites they can visit. It is appropriate to specify which sites are not to be accessed without parental permission. While no-one is suggesting that parents should censor Internet use, parents must be clear and knowledgeable about how and when technology is used to harm children. ChatDanger list seven key steps that parent(s) should take. These are now described.

### 1. TAKE TIME TO LEARN HOW THE INTERNET WORKS

Keep the computer in a family room, not locked away in a bedroom, spend time surfing together with children and learn from them how the Internet works.

## 2. DISCUSS THE SAFETY ISSUES OF INTERNET CHAT ROOMS WITH YOUR CHILDREN

Discuss the potential dangers of the Internet with children in a caring and sensitive way that enables them to see the dangers for themselves. Most children will respond more positively if they are encouraged to be smart or 'cool' on the Internet rather than being given a list of 'Thou shalt not'. Encourage children to visit sites such as ChatDanger and go through the chat tips together.

### 3. MAKE SURE YOUR CHILDREN KNOW NEVER TO REVEAL PERSONAL DETAILS ABOUT THEMSELVES IN A CHAT ROOM

Remind the child that everyone he or she meets in chat rooms is a stranger, and remains a stranger even though the child might consider them to be a friend. Children should never reveal any personal details about themselves, school or family, address, telephone number, or password. They should never give out their mobile number or their e-mail address. Such information can give someone direct access to the child, without the child or parent knowing anything about who is contacting them. Even something as harmless as when and where their next football or hockey match is being held, or their favourite pizza restaurant, could give someone direct access as all of these could be a clue to the child's identity. The same principle should apply to advice about meeting a stranger in the street. As the child does not know that person they should not reveal personal details. People children meet in chat rooms are as 'unknown' and 'strange' to them as a stranger in the street. Due to the anonymity of the Internet people can masquerade and pretend to be anyone they want to. Similarly, children should never give out credit card details without the parent's permission and never send photographs or pictures of themselves.

### 4. NEVER ALLOW YOUR CHILDREN TO MEET ANYONE THEY HAVE CONTACTED IN A CHAT ROOM WITHOUT GOING WITH THEM

Do not allow children to meet anyone they have contacted via the Internet without going with them. Always go along too, and meet in a public place where there are lots of people around. Children and teenagers should NEVER arrange to meet anyone they have encountered online without a responsible adult being present. Be especially careful about children using chat rooms unsupervised, especially those that are not moderated. Parents are the best people to know whether their child is mature enough to use an unmoderated chat room. Make sure the child knows the dangers and sticks to the agreed safety rules.

### 5. STICK TO THE POSITIVE

Take an interest in the way children use the Internet and encourage them to visit sites that reflect their interests. Just as with good TV programmes take the time to find the best and most useful websites and chat rooms for you and your family (see Appendix 1 at the end of this book). Childnet has produced a special directory called Launchsite, which includes 50 excellent online projects that are safe for children.

### 6. CONSIDER USING FILTERING SOFTWARE

Parents can buy software that can help block sites they may not wish their children to be exposed to, such as sexually explicit material, hate and violence sites, alcohol and gambling. Software can also help parents monitor the time the child spends on the computer and material they have been viewing as well as block outgoing and incoming information. Remember that such software is no substitute for good parental involvement and is not 100 per cent effective.

### 7. KNOW WHO TO REPORT TO

If your child tells you that they are being harassed by someone they think is an adult in a chat room who wants to meet them offline, you should discuss this fully with your child and contact your local police immediately. Sometimes it is very difficult for a child to talk about inappropriate online or offline contact. Professional organisations have specialist child welfare staff (see Appendix 1 at the end of this book) or try ChildLine 0800 1111 or NSPCC Child Protection Helpline 0800 800 5000.

To emphasize such messages, British Telecom in association with Chilren's Charities Coalition on Internet Safety, launched a new initiative in February 2004 in the form of an Internet Green X Code (BT 2004). This consists of the slogan STOP THINK STAY SAFE! The code encourages children to STOP before giving out any personal details, to THINK and question everything as things aren't always what they seem, and to STAY SAFE! by talking and spreading the word. This simple catchy code will hopefully enable children to avoid dangerous situations by staying alert (BT 2004).

A further consideration for parents and teachers is to advise children against opening links to other sites they might encounter in a chat room as these sites may be pornographic. Similarly they should not open e-mails from anyone they do not know, as they may contain pornographic or upsetting images, or viruses that could harm the computer. If parents and teachers do come across child pornography, harmful or illegal material on the Internet they should report it to the Internet Watch Foundation. This is an industry-funded body, which seeks to have illegal material removed from the Internet and refers it to the police. The Internet Watch Foundation telephone hotline is 08456 008844, or it can be reported online at www.iwf.org.uk/hotline/report.htm. Alternatively, contact the police Child Pornography Information Line on Freephone 0808 100 0040. Pornography, including child pornography, is easy to find on the Internet, even by accident. Encourage children to tell you if they find something online that disturbs them while reassuring them that they will not be punished as a result.

*Chat room safety*

Chat rooms are a great way for children to keep in touch with friends and to meet people with common interests such as music, football or television programmes. Chat rooms are incredibly popular and there are hundreds and thousands of them. They are essentially harmless and a lot of fun. But the child needs to be reminded that there are risks attached to chat rooms because they can never tell who anyone is, and so there is a risk that paedophiles or child sexual abusers can trawl them looking for children. Children have to be reminded that because of the anonymity of meeting people online, adults may pose as teenagers or children in order to strike up a friendship and eventually try to meet the child.

It is important to emphasise that the child should never enter a private chat room but to stay in public areas, which are much safer as the chat room is open to all to read. Going into a private chat room is the equivalent of stepping out of a party full of people into a private room and having a separate conversation with a stranger. This is extremely dangerous, as no-one else can read what is being written, and it is a classic way for paedophiles to get a child on their own. The paedophile invites the child into a private, one-to-one conversation that enables them to start grooming the child and building up a relationship.

If the child is being pestered by someone they do not like in a chat room they should leave the chat room immediately, and activate the facility to block messages from that person. Some chat rooms also let you report abusive behaviour by clicking on an appropriate link. Chat rooms are not the only places where children can make contact with people. They can also make contact online in places called newsgroups, communities, groups or clubs and by using instant messaging. Whether they are contacting people through these places, or through chat rooms, the safety rules remain the same: no personal details and no meeting up with anyone unless they are accompanied by a responsible adult.

In order to address these issues the Internet Crime Forum have provided the following online safety messages from the ChatWise, StreetWise programme they developed to protect children. All children should be equipped with these safety messages.

---

### Online safety rules for children

1.   Don't give out personal details, photographs or any other information that could be used to identify you, such as information about your family, where you live or the school you go to.

2.   Don't take other people at face value – they may not be what they seem.

3.   Never arrange to meet someone you have only ever previously met on the Internet without first telling your parents, getting their permission and taking a responsible adult with you. The first meeting should always be in a public place.

4.   Always stay in the public areas of chat where there are other people around.

5.   Do not open an attachment or downloaded file unless you know and trust the person who has sent it.

6.   Never respond directly to anything you find disturbing – save or print it, log off, and tell an adult.

In a similar vein, Childnet International has provided five safety rules that children need to remember when using the Internet, referred to as SMART rules (see below).

---

### SMART rules

#### SAFE
Staying safe involves being careful and not giving out your name, address, mobile phone, school name or password to people online.

#### MEETING
Someone you meet in cyberspace can be dangerous. Only do so with your parents'/carers' permission and then when they are present.

#### ACCEPTING
Accepting e-mails or opening files from people you don't really know or trust can get you into trouble as they may contain viruses or nasty messages, or access personal details about you.

#### REMEMBER
Someone online may be lying and not be whom he or she say they are. If you feel uncomfortable when chatting or messaging, end the conversation.

#### TELL
Tell your parent or carer if someone or something makes you feel uncomfortable or worried.

---

It is crucial that parents do not over-react to children using the Internet, as it has enormous advantages as a medium to access information and encourage the acquisition of knowledge. But there are some danger signs to look out for that may indicate that the child is using the Internet inappropriately.

Only the parent can decide what is an excessive amount of time but if being online dominates and is prioritised above other social activities it could be considered to be excessive. If the child spends all its time online in preference to meeting and being with friends or family, this may indicate a problem. This has to be balanced with the knowledge that most teenagers love chatting endlessly either via the telephone or online so this may be relatively normal. It may help to moderate Internet access to specific times to encourage the child to engage in other social activities.

Remember that if parents over-react, the child might clam up and withdraw even further, or might simply start using the Internet elsewhere. In such cases it is even harder to monitor the child's Internet activity. The focus should be on clear, firm and non-threatening safety messages in which the child can feel confident about protecting him or herself. Parents also need to be aware of new technology, which allows for Internet use through mobile phones. The new 3G mobile phones include Internet facilities as well as digital cameras, both of which can be used and manipulated by paedophiles to target children for sexual grooming.

---

**Danger signs of inappropriate Internet use**

- Child spending an excessive amount of time online
- Child behaving secretively while online, trying to minimise screen, trying to hide what they are doing
- Decrease in other social activities
- Reduction in social interaction with friends, peers and family
- Talk of a 'boyfriend' or 'girlfriend' they may have met online

---

## The role of teachers in protecting children from CSA

On average, teachers spend more time with children than any other adults, in some cases including parents. This puts them in a unique position to get to know children and to monitor changes in behaviour. Providing they have accurate knowledge about CSA, teachers can be pivotal in identifying children who may be suffering and provide a safe environment in which the child can disclose. In addition, schools and teachers can play a central role in teaching children about the dangers of CSA and how they can best protect themselves.

Schools and teachers can take a lead in educating children about CSA by providing structured classes and teaching similar to the green cross code. Because children view parents and teachers as their main source of advice in many areas, it is imperative that there should be some synergy between home and school in reinforcing safety messages. These should include not only general safety messages about the dangers of CSA and grooming but also the dangers of the Internet.

School programmes could include practising and rehearsing basic safety messages as well as role-plays of potentially dangerous scenarios, with advice for children about how to avoid them and what to do if they feel they are in danger. These can be incorporated with existing programmes, such as those provided by Kidscape and other charities, which teach children about bullying. These can be reinforced by police officers in the same way that they give general talks to children about road safety or drugs.

What is crucial is that whatever structured programmes are offered to children they reflect accurate knowledge about CSA and no longer focus on 'stranger danger' but include current knowledge that 87 per cent of CSA is perpetrated by someone known to the child and 30 per cent of CSA is perpetrated by adolescents. Providing children are given such accurate information it is possible to empower them to be fully aware of the dangers of CSA and how best to protect themselves.

It is also crucially important that all teachers are adequately trained in an understanding of CSA, not just in terms of the complex issues involved but also the impact CSA has on the child. It is only if teachers have adequate understanding of the sexually abused child that they can hope to identify those children at risk or those who are being abused. In addition, such knowledge empowers teachers to identify those children who may be sexually offending. Early identification of adolescent sexual abusers not only protects other children, but also allows for appropriate interventions to be made in getting help for victims of CSA.

While most schools appoint specific teachers to deal with issues of CSA and any concerns that individual teachers may have, it is vital that all teachers receive adequate training in identifying CSA. Individual teachers are most likely to know the child well and be the first to notice changes in behaviour. Teachers are a valuable source of information about children and should be included in the effective protection of children from CSA. Leaving it to designated 'specialist' teachers or other professionals may undermine the capacity for all teachers to spot early warning signs and to monitor children who are at risk of CSA. It is also crucial that the designated teachers who have a responsibility in managing cases of CSA have regular access to new information and knowledge about issues around CSA so that effective and appropriate interventions can be implemented.

Having explored the many ways in which parents and teachers can protect children from CSA, it is necessary to conclude by giving useful information on what to do if they suspect that a child is being sexually abused or if a child discloses CSA.

## What to do if you suspect that a child has been abused or is likely to be abused

You may wish to talk through any initial feelings of shock, embarrassment or anger with a trusted relative or friend. However, in order to protect the child and other children, further action will be needed. Teachers will have clear procedures within each individual school that need to be observed and implemented. The NSPCC recommend that parents and other adults can:

- Phone the free 24-hour NSPCC Child Protection Helpline (0800 800 5000) to talk through the options, which include seeking help for your own child and reporting the abuser
- Report their concerns directly to local professional services such as their health visitor, doctor, local police Child Protection Officer or social services department.

Parents and other adults must not seek to confront the abuser by breaking the law themselves or taking the law into their own hands in attacking, assaulting or harrassing the suspected abuser, or his/her property (e.g. vigilantism).

## What to do if a child discloses CSA

If a child discloses CSA:

- Listen to the child
- Although upset by what the child has disclosed, do not react in a way that may add to the child's distress
- The child needs to know that he/she is not to blame and is believed
- Allow the child the opportunity to talk about what has happened but do not put any pressure on him/her to do so

- Tell the child that he/she is right to talk to you. Don't tell him/her off if the abuse occurred because he/she disobeyed basic ground rules such as walking in a place that is out of bounds
- Report any concerns directly to local professional services such as the health visitor, doctor, local police Child Protection Officer or social services department.

It is evident that parents and teachers can provide effective safety messages for children about how to be safe in the community and when using the Internet. This is a good starting point but arguably needs to be supported by wider community-based prevention and protection frameworks. The next chapter will consider what the community at large can do to minimise and prevent the sexual abuse of children.

## Chapter 10

# *The Prevention*
# *of Child Sexual Abuse*

The bottom line is that these people are not monsters sent from another planet. They come out of our communities and we have to find ways of working with them in the community while at the same time keeping the community safe.

Reverend Hugh Kirkegaard

If we are to protect children we have to take on responsibility for the perpetrator as well as the victims.

David Wilson, Professor of Criminal Justice

The prevention of child sexual abuse (CSA) is not just the responsibility of parents, teachers, child protection workers and the police. It is a responsibility that all adults in the community need to share. Leaving the protection of children to only those who have children, or who are designated as being responsible for them, puts them at risk and makes the child sexual abuser's job much easier. To prevent CSA and to protect children effectively requires the involvement of all adults. As such it is something that society at large needs to address to ensure children's safety. While many parents have great fear and loathing for paedophiles, to protect children effectively we need to understand what motivates paedophiles. Given that paedophiles are a product of society means that society needs to take on responsibility for both perpetrators as well as victims of CSA.

To ensure the prevention of sexual offending against children, CSA needs to become a priority for all members of society. Children have a right to be safe in their community and to be protected by that community. This can be achieved by providing accurate information about the issues around CSA and separating fact from fiction. Only such awareness enables adults to dispel myths and stereotypes that serve to distort the reality of CSA. Access to accurate information serves to provide adults with knowledge that enables them to protect children effectively, rather than lull them into a false sense of security. We also need to know what drives child sexual abusers and the strategies they use to sexually abuse to better understand them and to adequately protect children.

It seems that the taboo is not CSA and that it happens, but talking about it. Sexually abused children invariably cannot talk about their abuse experiences. Parents and adults find it equally hard to talk about it. Everyone agrees that CSA is terrible but we are still afraid to talk about the issues in a calm and balanced way. If adults find it hard to talk about CSA, it is hardly surprising that children will find it difficult too. Awareness of CSA and healthy public dialogue can empower parents and teachers to address the issues within the home, school and community. Not talking about CSA does not make it go away but colludes with the abuser's need to silence.

Such a public dialogue is dependent on informed knowledge, which in turn needs to be supported by a change of attitude by the Government, criminal justice system and the media, as well as local communities. It is only with such knowledge that attitudes and beliefs about CSA can change to the extent that society no longer tolerates CSA and can fully protect children. Global changes in attitudes and beliefs are also necessary in order to control child pornography. This would allow consensus across nations around issues of sexual consent, making it much harder for children to be sexually exploited.

To prevent CSA, outdated attitudes and misconceptions need to be challenged and replaced with more accurate knowledge. Only such changes will enable society and the public to move from *reaction* to *prevention*. The first step in this process is to talk about CSA, and no longer allow it to remain a 'phantom offence' (Wyre 2000), swept under the carpet. Society can no longer collude with abusers in denying the reality of CSA. To end such collusion requires a national public health and education campaign, along with changes in the criminal justice system, including treatment and rehabilitation. The media plays a hugely influential role in the formation and maintenance of attitudes and beliefs, and as such should be encouraged to avoid sensational-ism and regulate the sexualisation of children. When this is combined with harnessing schools and the community in taking responsibility then we can really progress from vigilantism, to protection, to prevention of CSA. Only this will provide a clear message that our society will no longer tolerate the sexual abuse of children.

This chapter explores what can be done to prevent CSA. It argues that what is desperately needed is a forum in which to talk about CSA, along with a national public health and education campaign appropriately supported by the media. Access to accurate knowledge and understanding of CSA empowers parents and teachers, which in turn empowers children to prevent CSA. Such a campaign needs to run parallel to changes in the criminal justice system and treatment of paedophiles. It is only when these are combined with community initiatives that we can truly protect children from CSA and move towards the prevention of sexual offending against children.

## Public health and education campaign

In order to separate fact from fiction, and to dispel myths and stereotypical beliefs about CSA, it is essential that accurate information be provided not just to children, parents and teachers, but to all adults. It is crucial that clear messages are provided in order to address the issues in CSA adequately and move from reaction to prevention. The emphasis should be on informing not preaching. It is evident from what has been covered in this book that we need to rethink radically our approach to managing CSA. We should not just rely on professionals to take on that role but for the whole community to take responsibility for providing strategies that make us and our children more self-aware and safe, rather than providing a security blanket or comfort zone that merely makes us feel better.

An effective national public health and education campaign requires ade-quately funded, cross-government strategy, involving the Department of Health and not just the criminal justice system and child protection agencies. Such a campaign needs to explain the real risks posed by child sexual abusers and the need for local treatment services that can be supported by the commu-nity. It is crucial to acknowledge that most of what is known about CSA is derived from only 10 per cent of cases. That is to say that as only one in ten cases of CSA gets reported so our knowledge is based on that one case and very little is known about the other nine. Not only are these cases not reported, often they fail to get a conviction. The outcome is that resources are targeted only at those 10 per cent of cases known to us rather than the 90 per cent as yet unknown.

Many child protection professionals believe that sexual offending against children in this country is virtually out of control with 'abysmally low' conviction rates (Wyre 2000). It is clear that most cases of CSA do not get to court, and of those that do, the majority fail with only a 5 per cent conviction rate. This is especially the case with the sexual abuse of children under the age of five. The perpetrators are virtually immune from prosecution because of the difficulties of obtaining evidence from such young children, a factor that many child sexual abusers know and capitalise on.

A public health and education campaign aimed not just at children or professionals but at parents and all adults is the only way to ensure a preventative philosophy that can promote attitude change. To date the emphasis has been on providing a sticking plaster rather than focusing on the causes of CSA. Donald Findlater, former manager of the Lucy Faithfull Foundation's Wolvercote Clinic, proposes that CSA should be considered like any other public health issue, such as smoking, drinking and drug abuse.

Findlater uses the analogy of attitudes to drink–driving a decade ago, when it was still considered socially acceptable, and the health service focused all its effort and resources into rectifying the human damage. As a result of massive public health campaigns against drink–driving, attitudes have changed dramatically, with drink–driving now seen as totally unacceptable and a concomitant reduction in human damage. Thus investment in health education can promote radical changes in attitudes and beliefs, which in turn facilitate the prevention of CSA. This would reduce the cost to the health service and criminal justice system in terms of treatment of victims and perpetrators.

Such public health education needs to be supported by the media in minimising the sensationalist reporting of CSA issues, including ill-thought campaigns such as naming and shaming of paedophiles. Tragically, and yet ironically, naming and shaming merely drives child sexual abusers underground to remain even more hidden. Sensationalist coverage of high profile cases only serves to perpetuate myths and misconceptions such as 'stranger danger' when all the evidence shows that 87 per cent of CSA is perpetrated by a person known to the child. Much more stringent regulations and guidelines are needed to ensure more accurate reporting so that the majority of children suffering CSA are really protected and not just the minority who have been identified.

---

### Public health education messages

- Child sexual abusers are 'nice people' not monsters. In the words of Ray Wyre: 'Monsters don't get close to children, nice men do, that's why children like them'
- Paedophiles groom adults in order to gain access to children
- Around 87 per cent of child sexual abuse occurs within the family or by people known to the family and the child, such as a parent, neighbour, family friend, doctor, teacher
- The abduction and sexually motivated murder of children by strangers is committed by a minority of predatory paedophiles. Approximately five to eight children are abducted and murdered each year, a figure that has remained static for the last 30 years
- Only one in nine cases of CSA is reported – the other nine are not
- Only 10 per cent of CSA cases get to court
- The conviction rate for child sexual abusers is extremely low at around 5 per cent
- Most CSA is not a one-off event but persistent and systematically perpetrated over a number of years
- One in six children are sexually abused in their lifetime
- Child sexual abuse occurs across all age groups from babies to teenagers
- One-third of CSA is perpetrated by teenagers and adolescents
- Twenty to twenty-five per cent of CSA is perpetrated by females
- Naming and shaming, or hounding paedophiles merely drives them underground, making it harder to police them and increasing the threat they pose
- Many paedophiles can be taught to manage and alter their abusing behaviour

Tink Palmer from children's charity Barnardo's argues that 'adults have a duty to keep children safe from harm, but this is only possible if they have sufficient information to assess when a child is really at risk'. Thus it is essential that the public are properly informed about the realities of CSA, and any public health and education campaign needs to include the information listed on the previous page.

### Stop It Now! Campaign

A pre-emptive campaign designed to prevent rather than react to CSA is Stop It Now! UK and Ireland. Based on a successful campaign started in Vermont, USA, in 1995 by Fran Henry, herself a survivor, it aims to dispel the taboo of paedophilia and increase awareness that child sexual abusers can be treated. Rather than placing the onus of reporting onto the child it is placed on the would-be abuser to seek help before offending. Children should not carry the primary burden and responsibility of stopping the cycle of abuse. Adults need to shoulder that responsibility to enable adequate prevention measures. Thus Stop It Now! UK and Ireland aims to reach out to abusers and would-be abusers, provide public education as a medium for social change and conduct research to advance prevention.

---

**Aims of the Stop It Now! Campaign**

- Provide an early warning system
- Raise awareness of child sexual abusers
- Helpline to encourage adults who are worried and uneasy about their sexual inclinations to seek help
- Encourage others to seek professional advice
- Challenge abuser to stop abuse
- Encourage would-be abusers to seek treatment
- Work with families and friends about how to confront child sexual abusers
- Build a social climate that says we will no longer tolerate the sexual abuse of children

---

To date the Government has funded two local Stop It Now! initiatives, which provide an educative role as well as a helpline to those who are sexually aroused by children and fear that they might act on this. The primary aim is to prevent CSA happening in the first place or at least stop it as early as possible. It endeavours to access perpetrators before an offence is actually committed, or those who are worried by their sexual inclination but do not know where to go for help. It provides a confidential freephone helpline to give support and guidance and help in seeking treatment (Freephone Helpline 0808 1000 900 or e-mail: help@stopitnow.org.uk).

While the climate of public fear and loathing that surrounds CSA makes it less likely that child sexual abusers will come forward, it is hoped that adults who are aroused and have sexual fantasies about children but have not yet committed an offence will come forward. It also aims to help in cases where an offence has occurred but is not yet reported, and provide help and support to those abusers who wish to stop abusing. Stop It Now! UK and Ireland also offers support to family members who suspect their child of being sexually abused.

The helpline is the first port of call for any would-be abuser. Thereafter they will be referred on to appropriate treatment providers once the nature of the problem has been established. While the helpline cannot offer treatment, it uses a traffic light warning system of red, green and yellow to evaluate the severity of the behaviour reported. Although the helpline provides anonymity and confidentiality to the caller, they do, however, reserve the right to call appropriate agencies if a child is deemed at risk.

Stop It Now! UK and Ireland emphasises that the majority of CSA takes place in families or by those known to the child and aims to make families safer places to be. It also provides information in jargon-free language for parents and the public as follows:

- Information on early warning signs
- Help for adults to identify signs of sexual abuse and aberrant behaviour
- Information on typical and atypical sexual behaviour in children
- Self-protection programmes for children such as 'good touch, and bad touch'.

Stop It now! UK and Ireland is supported by an alliance of various children's charities – Barnardo's, ChildLine, NCH, NSPCC – and other charities such as the Lucy Faithfull Foundation and the National Organisation for the Treatment of Abusers (NOTA). It is also supported by the police, the probation service and representatives of government and statutory agencies. The Government, through the Home Office and the Department of Health, has provided Stop It Now! UK and Ireland with a start-up fund of £100,000. It remains to be seen how successful this campaign is, both in terms of increased awareness and the number of callers seeking help via the helpline. Early signs are encouraging. During the first pilot year in Surrey and Derbyshire Stop It Now! UK and Ireland have already received over 700 calls, including one man who has called three times because of his concern about being sexually aroused by his children's friends. The helpline number is Freephone 0808 1000 900 and the website address is www.stopitnow.org.uk.

While these are encouraging responses to the need for better education and prevention of CSA they need to be extended to a national campaign with adequate financial support. It is hoped that this is something that will be seriously considered by the Government as a vital strategy in the protection of children and the prevention of CSA.

## The media

It is essential that the media collaborate with any national public health education campaign by supporting the messages and disseminating appropriate information. The media has a powerful influence on the formation and perpetuation of attitudes and beliefs. The media also has the capacity to distort facts and manipulate public opinion by exploiting public fears and fuelling prejudice. It is imperative that the media refrains from colluding with the exploitation of public perception, something that child sexual abusers all too readily do in the sexual exploitation of children. Such collusion reflects the manipulation and deception seen in the grooming process and ultimately implicates the media in the sexual abuse of children. An example of such collective collusion is the perpetuation of the myth of 'stranger danger' seen in the tabloid press. If the media wishes to avoid becoming complicit in the sexual abuse of children, it needs to end such highly irresponsible reporting, along with the sexualisation of children through the media.

Sensationalising a minority of high profile cases of child abduction and murder is counterproductive and only serves to create 'deviancy amplification and moral panic' (Silverman and Wilson 2002). Ironically this can actually impede the protection of the majority of children by narrowing the focus of attention on the minority that come to light. While these high profile cases are tragic and need to be reported, they nevertheless rarely reflect the reality of CSA. They are mostly perpetrated by predatory paedophiles, many of whom are strangers and not known to the child. As previously stated, the majority of CSA occurs in the home or by someone familiar to the child. Children are at no greater risk in 2003 of being abducted and killed by a stranger than they were 30 years ago. But they are unacceptably vulnerable to CSA and exploitation by adults known to them and whom they should be able to trust.

Focusing on the few cases that attract such huge media attention merely serves to lull the public into a false sense of security that CSA is perpetrated by strangers who abduct and murder children. It does not inform them of the daily, systematic and persistent CSA that can go on over a number of years in their own neighbourhood. Sensationalism merely fuels moral panic and creates hysteria, such as the naming and shaming campaign provided by some tabloid newspapers. It is ironic that those tabloids that have fuelled the most panic are the ones that provide the biggest contradictions in combining moral outrage with the salacious coverage of the sexual behaviour of celebrities. This smacks not only of hypocrisy but also of inconsistency in providing mixed messages that only further confuse the complexity of CSA.

Such tabloid newspapers, along with the rest of the media, need to take responsibility for their reporting and realise that rather than providing helpful information to the public they are colluding with the myths that play into the majority of perpetrators' hands. By diverting attention away from the reality of CSA, paedophiles remain protected, allowing them to continue to abuse children rather than keep them safe. Demonising paedophiles only makes the problem of CSA more intractable. Encouraging the hounding and persecution of paedophiles forces them underground, making it harder to police them. In their isolation, where they only mix with other paedophiles, they feel marginalised and see themselves as victims. In this frame of mind they have little to lose by reoffending. This means they become an even greater threat.

Public misconceptions about paedophiles undermine the efforts to reduce the threat they pose. Paedophiles are 'nice men not monsters' and as Baroness

Howarth, adviser to ChildLine, says, 'The idea of the monster is very unreal. They are much like everybody else except they abuse children – which is what is monstrous about it'. This would suggest that our efforts should be focused not just on child sexual abusers as monsters, but on how to prevent the monstrous acts of CSA. Calls for draconian punishments of identified child sexual abusers ignore the majority of as yet undetected sexual abuse of children.

Proper governmental funding of projects and programmes can go some way to help understand and manage paedophiles in altering their abusing behaviour. Accurate reporting that reinforces clear public health messages provided by the Government and the Department of Health is the only sure way to protect children effectively and prevent CSA.

The media also need to look at their role in the sexualisation of children. Increasingly younger children are targeted as consumers of adult products such as fashion, cosmetics, music and entertainment. This has led to children not only dressing in adult sexualised ways but also behaving as mini-adults in their imitation of artists from the world of music and entertainment. This is especially true in the case of children's fashion with major outlets like Argos marketing and selling adult underwear, such as thongs and bras, to prepubescent children. The cosmetic industry has also had an impact with girls as young as six or seven having regular beauty routines involving full adult-like make-up, manicures and pedicures.

The music and entertainment industry also sexualises children in exposing them to explicit sexual behaviour in music videos. They present pop idols such as S Club Juniors, Britney Spears and Christina Aguilera, who consistently show images of sexualised behaviour that children are likely to imitate without knowing the consequences of such behaviour. Films and videos, as well as books and teenage magazines, further reinforce such sexualisation, which increasingly includes sexually explicit material of an adult nature, rather than reflecting age-appropriate knowledge and understanding.

The media need to avoid self-indulgent polemic, which condemns rather than explains CSA, and move away from the belief that 'nothing works' in terms of treatment to focus on 'what can work'. In doing so they can be influential in directing collective energies to the heart of the problem, which is the protection of children and the prevention of CSA rather than naming and shaming and community notification. Accurate reporting of projects such as Stop It Now, treatment programmes such as SOTP, and rehabilitation initiatives such as Circles of Support and Accountability, which have been demonstrated to effect change, is crucial.

## Criminal justice system

The Government and criminal justice system need to address the real issues of CSA by implementing appropriate reforms. Such reforms need to be clearly thought out and not represent a vehicle to gain the electorate's vote. Changes in legislation should not be based upon reflex reactions to gain political votes and kudos, which inevitably tumble either in terms of the logistics of implementation or the lack of funding to enforce it. This merely provides a short-term comfort zone in which the public's fears are temporarily assuaged because the Government is seen to be doing something. Real changes are needed, which are committed to the protection of all children, not just the few who come to the attention of the criminal justice system. Criminal justice policies should no longer consist of comforting sound bites but be based on careful analysis.

While some of the issues are addressed in the new Sexual Offences Bill, which is due to become law on 1 May 2004, many are not. There is a need for change along a number of dimensions, not just new legislation. These need to focus around sentencing of those persistent paedophiles who have no desire to change and will always remain a risk, and different patterns of sexual offending and the impact these have on children. Issues around the registration of sex offenders, treatment programmes and rehabilitation also need to be addressed. Most important is greater provision of specialist training in CSA for all criminal justice professionals, including training in new technology and its use by paedophiles in accessing and distributing child pornography.

The new Sexual Offences Bill, while addressing a number of issues such as grooming on the Internet, may not be sufficient to protect children adequately. One of the major problems in the new 'anti-grooming' legislation is how this will actually be implemented in terms of prosecution. It may become a legal nightmare in terms of defining 'intent' and at which point this can be judged to exist. How evidence will be gathered to monitor 'grooming' is a further concern. If this legislation is to benefit children it needs to be supported by adequate resourcing and funding to ensure optimal implementation.

Discrepancies in sentencing also need to be addressed. Many professionals and parents believe that the sentencing for sexual offences against children has been extraordinarily lenient and inconsistent, with too much discretion given to judges. While the new Bill aims to tighten up the sentencing for certain types of offences it is debatable how well the criminal justice system will be able to cope. Custodial sentencing is phenomenally costly and there are not enough prisons to house the many people who have a sexual interest in children. It will be virtually impossible, for instance, to prosecute all 7300 names being investigated by Operation Ore. Currently there are insufficient resources to investigate offenders, let alone prosecute or sentence. Such financial considerations play a crucial role in deciding how best to deal with paedophiles.

A related problem is one of treatment. Custodial sentences do not deter paedophiles from sexually offending against children. Treatment can enable up to two-thirds of paedophiles to manage their sexual desires sufficiently to stop reoffending. However while the SOTP is available in 27 prisons, it is not compulsory for all child sex offenders but is dependent on prisoners 'volunteering'. Current figures show that just over one-sixth of sex offenders actually receive treatment while in prison, which is well below government targets. Treatment outside of custodial sentencing is even less well resourced with hardly any provision for treatment in the community. This puts children at further risk.

One possible solution, proposed by some child protection professionals, would be to introduce categories of CSA in terms of offending and harm that could be implemented along similar principles to illegal drug offences. Thus a structure similar to class A, B and C drugs could be considered in relation to offending sexual abuse behaviour. This would need clarification and considerable evaluation in terms of assessing harm to the child, which may be relative to each individual case.

It may be also pertinent to differentiate between patterns of abuse and the effects these have on children. Persistent sexual offenders need to be looked at differently in terms of sentencing and treatment. This is crucial as many paedophiles commit up to 150 offences against children, involving a large number of children prior to being caught and prosecuted. Such systematic and persistent CSA needs particular consideration by the criminal justice system, which tends to focus only on specific instances, dates and times for the offence that is being prosecuted. Future changes in the criminal justice system should take into consideration the sexual abuse patterns in CSA and how they impact on the child. Further consideration needs to be given to the different patterns, to the effects of organised and multiple abuse in contrast to individual abuse, and how this is dealt with in terms of sentencing and treatment.

Sexual abuse within the family also needs to be considered. Recommendations have been made to move away from the term incest to familial sexual abuse, to include not just blood relatives but anyone within the family structure in a position of responsibility or authority who abuses a child under 18. Parallel recommendations are to be made for adoptive parents and 'serial boyfriends'. The sexual abuse of a child in the family compared with outside the family is a double betrayal as families are supposed to be safe places not hothouses for abuse and sexual exploitation. The impact of the trauma and long-term effects may be different for individual members of the family, including those siblings who are not sexually abused.

There has been much controversy surrounding the Sex Offenders' Register (SOR) in part due to the number of anomalies that need to be adjusted for. The Sex Offenders' Register was implemented as a result of the Sexual Offenders Act in 1997. This means those sex offenders convicted before 1997 are not included. This is to say that the Register is not retrospective. Only those sex offenders convicted or cautioned after 1997 appear on the SOR. It follows that those sex offenders who have not been reported, caught or prosecuted are not registered.

Currently it is difficult to establish how many of the 21,413 people on the Sex Offenders Register are paedophiles as there is no national database of paedophiles on the register, although this is due to be rectified with the implementation of VISOR in the summer of 2004. The absence of such a database makes accessing information on paedophiles laborious and time- consuming.

Many child protection professionals will welcome a national UK database, along with an EU-wide register of paedophiles which can be easily accessed by all the EU member states. This is crucial given the increased movement of individuals across the EU. Such a register is essential with regard to the sexual trafficking of children and the increase in employment mobility, especially for those seeking employment in which they have access to children. While an EU paedophile register might be difficult to establish and manage, due to different attitudes and laws around age of consent and CSA within each member state, it is a necessary measure to ensure the protection of children both in the UK and across the EU.

Many child protection professionals believe that the monitoring of perpetrators on the SOR is shockingly under-resourced, which means that offenders have to be classified as very high, high, medium and low risk. Usually statutory agencies are only able to monitor very high-risk offenders and not others due to lack of resources. While initially all sex offenders are seen weekly, this rapidly reduces to monthly after a relatively short period of time. Thus there is limited contact, with no real support or adequate supervision. This makes it much easier for paedophiles to abscond and to sexually abuse children.

Further consideration needs to be given to community notification and the controlled public access to information about convicted sex offenders, not least do-it-yourself justice. Until the public can be trusted not to engage in vigilantism, in which they persecute and hound paedophiles, forcing them from their homes and absconding supervision arrangements, there is little to be gained by forcing them underground. They merely pose a bigger threat and remain hidden. There are number of considerations and potential dangers associated with implementing so called 'Sarah's law'. Evaluation of the success of the USA equivalent, called Megan's law, showed that before the law was first implemented in Washington in 1995 reoffending rates were 22 per cent. According to the NSPCC this only reduced to 19 per cent in 1996, which, while a slight drop, was not deemed to be statistically significant.

Further research is required before informed decisions about community notification can be made. We need to know what impact vigilantism actually has, how increased harassment drives paedophiles underground, and what extra threat this poses to children. We also need to assess whether adults or children do actually change their behaviour as a result of community notification and how this can help the community. Until this is clarified with appropriate evidence it is difficult to assess the real value or danger of community notification.

Most importantly community notification presupposes the false belief that paedophiles are rendered harmless by fear of exposure. Clearly the majority are not. If anything, fear of exposure and harassment only create extra pressure, which may promote the very thing the public fear, reoffending. It is understandable that the community wants access to knowledge, but it is of the wrong kind. Knowing what the minority 10 per cent of convicted paedophiles look like or where they live does not protect children from the 90 per cent of child sexual abusers who have not been convicted and continue to commit sexual offences against children. The public is so distracted in focusing on the few that they unwittingly allow the sexual abuse of many. This false sense of security is highly dangerous in that it fails to protect the very children who need the most protection.

Changes in treatment provision for both victims and perpetrators also need to be made. Locking them up in prison does very little, if anything, to encourage reform or rehabilitation. The pent-up stress of being in prison may easily explode upon release, prompting the commission of an offence that the paedophile has been merely fantasising about and masturbating to while in prison. Paedophiles are just as isolated in prison as they are in the community, being segregated from the rest of the prisoners for their own safety. This isolates and marginalises them, and by being thrown together with other child sex offenders may well fuel fantasies and increased knowledge about how to sexually offend against children and avoid getting caught. It also serves to fuel distorted beliefs about CSA when the paedophile is among their peers, seeing themselves as misunderstood and the victims of society's ignorance. This makes it more likely that they will reoffend.

Beliefs about treatment of child sexual abusers have changed dramatically over the last 30 years, moving from 'nothing works' to looking at 'what works' and those interventions that 'do work'. The primary form of treatment in prison is the Sex Offenders' Treatment Programme (SOTP), first introduced in 1991 as a reaction to the 'nothing works' philosophy historically held (Martinson 1974) and the awareness that 'some things do work', proposed by later researchers such as McGuire and Priestley (1985). The things that are most frequently believed to work are changes in beliefs around sexual offending against children, and the management of fantasies and impulses to sexually abuse. It is thought that such management can reduce reoffending by between 10 and 30 per cent.

Although SOTP is quite effective in the short term, it is less so in the long term. The type of treatment provided by SOTP, which essentially focuses on behaviour modification in managing sexual desires and not acting on them, may require ongoing therapeutic input to reinforce newly learned behaviours. This is virtually never available to paedophiles once released back in to the community. This seems a false economy as, given the vilification of paedophiles in the community and the lack of support, other than supervision by the probation service, it increases rather than lowers the risk of reoffending. The stress of being demonised, the isolation and lack of adequate and sustained support may all contribute to reoffending after a period of time.

Many people believe that providing treatment for sex offenders diverts precious resources away from adequate treatment for victims, both children and parents. The victims, their families and parents also need help and treatment intervention to come to terms with CSA. The majority of victims do not receive help, support or treatment for the trauma of CSA. It is thought that in the absence of adequate support and help many victims of CSA are unable to heal from their experiences. They often end up suffering from later mental health problems such as depression, alcohol and drug dependency, necessitating psychiatric care. This in turn means that they become over-represented in adult mental health care, consuming an enormous amount of health expenditure to undo the long-term effects of CSA. Further expenditure is also required in those cases where victims of CSA turn to criminal activities, including sexual offending against children, requiring custodial sentences.

It may be much more cost-effective for already stretched health and prison budgets if appropriate treatment and support for victims is provided when the victim is still a child to minimise the risks of later mental health problems, or the risk of becoming part of the criminal justice system. It is a false economy to rely on children to 'get over' CSA just because the sexual abuser has been prosecuted and sentenced without acknowledging their need for appropriate help and support to grow into healthy adults. In the words of Donald Findlater, Director of the now closed Wolvercote Clinic: 'The treatment of sex offenders has phenomenal health implications. Mental hospitals are full of people sexually abused as children. If the Wolvercote had stayed open, I'm sure within a year we'd have saved the health service millions.'

Given the difficulties faced by paedophiles in the community makes the rehabilitation of child sexual abusers a priority. There are insufficient projects that focus on treatment and support of child sexual abusers when released from prison. An already over-stretched probation service and police force cannot always provide adequate supervision. In the absence of properly funded professional agencies, it is necessary to explore alternative methods, including community-based projects that can facilitate the rehabilitation of child sexual abusers, such as the Circles of Support and Accountability.

Plans to fit released paedophiles with electronic tags in order to keep track of them more adequately is not the answer. These are desperate measures, which attempt to solve what appears to be an unsolvable problem in an under-resourced and over-stretched criminal justice system. The silicone chip used in the electronic tag aims to monitor physiological arousal, such as heart rate and blood pressure. These are thought to increase prior to an imminent sexual offence against a child, thus alerting the relevant agencies to the possibility of a sexual attack. However, such physiological arousal can be increased for other reasons, not just an imminent sexual assault, which could lead to a lot of false alarms that take up valuable resources. Also paedophiles could surgically remove the tag, or train themselves to lower physiological arousal through biofeedback.

Most importantly, if the paedophile does not believe that they are doing anything wrong and are not nervous prior to an assault, the chip would not register physiological changes. Even if the arousal does register an imminent attack it will only indicate the whereabouts of the abuser and not necessarily prevent the assault. Such electronic tracking is insufficient to prevent CSA and only has a value in keeping tabs on known paedophiles. They do not help prevent sexual assaults against children by sexual abusers who are 'unknown' to the criminal justice system. This, like the Sex Offenders' Register and community notification, merely lulls parents and teachers into a false sense of security and does nothing to rehabilitate paedophiles.

### Training for all criminal justice professionals

There is a desperate need to ensure that all professionals involved in the criminal justice system receive adequate training about CSA. This includes lawyers, barristers and judges so that they have a depth of understanding of the complex issues in CSA, such as patterns of abusing, differences between familial sexual abuse and abuse outside the family, the impact of organised and multiple abuse, as well as the psychological and emotional effects of CSA on the child and later adult survivors. It is not until these are adequately understood and taken into consideration that the range of professionals within the criminal justice system can make appropriate decisions and implement legislative changes that really do protect the child and foster the prevention of CSA.

## Treatment as prevention

It is clear that treatment is a crucial component in the prevention of CSA. Historically there have been a number of specialist, residential clinics such as the Gracewell Clinic in Birmingham and the now closed Wolvercote Clinic, Epsom, which have provided treatment for both convicted and non-convicted sex offenders, including child sexual abusers. Unfortunately these have suffered from lack of financial and community support. Invariably they have been closed down because local residents are reluctant to have such clinics in their community for fear of the risk posed to their children by sex offenders. This has reduced effective treatment of sex offenders after leaving prison and this increases the chances of reoffending.

Such clinics have also been involved in the risk assessment of sex offenders referred by the civil courts and social services. They have carried out an important service in providing knowledge about and understanding of child sexual abusers. The work that they have done over the years has not only protected numerous children from being sexually abused but has also provided a knowledge base about sexual offending patterns that has enabled us to understand the motivations of child sexual abusers and the strategies they use to target and groom children. It is invaluable information that underpins the implementation of effective prevention programmes. It is a tragedy that such clinics are not properly funded and maintained.

While the Government has pledged to reopen the Wolvercote Clinic at another site, what is crucial is the need to provide more secure residential facilities for the treatment of sex offenders. These need not be designed just as an alternative to prison, but as the place to make appropriate risk assessments and provide follow-up treatment when paedophiles are released into the community. Such secure residential units could provide an alternative to imprisonment.

Children who have been sexually abused also need adequate treatment programmes. This is especially so for victims of CSA who go on to sexually abuse other children. Currently it is thought that up to one-third of sexual abuse is committed by under-18s. Around 500 teenagers are convicted of sex offences each year yet there are very few projects that deal with young abusers. Experience shows that it is vital to identify potential child sexual abusers as early as possible before they get locked into a cycle of sexual offending against children. Therapeutic intervention for the victims of CSA can minimise the risk and prevent the further sexual abuse of children.

It is crucial to help victims of CSA before they reach their teens prior to the activation of the fantasy-sexual arousal cycle. If not treated, such fantasies can begin to incorporate sexually abusive images, which could result in the attack or abduction of younger children, then subjecting them to sadistic acts of sexual abuse, not unlike that which they themselves experienced in childhood. There is a desperate need for the provision of more treatment projects for young sexual offenders to provide appropriate therapeutic interventions. These have considerable potential in helping those victims of CSA who are at risk of sexual offending against other children. The earlier therapeutic intervention is provided, the less likely it is that the child will go on to a lifelong career of sexual offending. This is a powerful and potent way to prevent future CSA.

Research at the Institute of Child Health and Great Ormond Street Hospital shows that one in eight boys who have been sexually abused go on to sexually abuse other children (Salter *et al.* 2003; Skuse 2003). It is crucial that children receive early intervention to circumvent a lifelong pattern of CSA. Victims of child sexual abuse have often experienced appalling traumas in their childhoods where no-one has been there to help or protect them. To deprive them of appropriate treatment is to fail them yet further and at a significant cost in the future.

There is also a huge cost in that sexually abused children who do not receive treatment may end up in the prison population. The Office for National Statistics for the year 2000 shows that one-third of young people aged between 16 and 20 in custody had been sexually abused before imprisonment (Wheaton 2003).

Special provision needs to be made for children who have been sexually abused in the family. Taking them into care, without giving them access to treatment programmes, is not a satisfactory option. By being removed from the family the child feels it is being punished for the sexual abuse. Being deprived of its family, non-abusing parent and siblings can make such children feel isolated and alienated and vulnerable to further sexual abuse, especially while in care.

The Government needs to consider radical alternatives in the case of familial abuse in which the sexual abuser is removed from the family and the remaining family is given support to deal with the aftermath of the abuse. Some states in the USA have implemented such projects in which the sexual abuser is forced to leave the family home, not given a custodial sentence and goes into a residential treatment centre. This allows them to remain in employment where they are responsible for the continuing financial support of the family. This reduces cost to the state in terms of welfare benefits and the cost of custodial care.

The aim of treatment is to maintain the abuser's financial responsibility to the family and take responsibility for their offences in engaging in treatment. Ideally, after treatment and careful risk assessment serious consideration is given to reuniting the family. This is dependent on the response to treatment, the level of risk and whether the family wishes to be reunited. Throughout this process the child victim and the family are given support to repair the havoc and damage caused as a result of the CSA.

## Rehabilitation and prevention

The rehabilitation of child sexual abusers is dependent on the provision of continuing treatment and support after release. This is only possible with a multi-agency approach. To rely primarily on supervision by an already over-stretched police and probation service, or merely placing sex offenders on the SOR, is insufficient. The Government has set up 42 Multi-Agency Public Protection Arrangements (MAPPA) for each police force in England and Wales. These monitor the 21,413 registered sex offenders across the country as well as monitoring 27,477 violent sex offenders who are not eligible for registration. This is an enormous task that is extremely difficult to implement. This means that the supervision of those on the SOR can only be minimal, or focus on those considered to be a high risk.

The MAPPA place a duty on the police and the national probation service to assess and manage risks posed by offenders in every community in England and Wales. This is achieved in partnership with other agencies, including the prison service, the health services and local authority housing and social services. MAPPA can recommend increased police monitoring, special steps to protect victims and the use of closely supervised accommodation. They also have the power, when appropriate, to disclose information to a range of people in local communities, including schools and employers.

It is clear that the Government is endeavouring to minimise and manage the risks posed by paedophiles, although these can never be eliminated totally. It is for this reason that there needs to be an increase in appropriate treatment provision for paedophiles, which is both a follow-up to treatment received in prison and which is ongoing to maintain non-offending behaviour.

To prevent CSA it is necessary to provide preventative treatment for those individuals who have sexual fantasies about children but have not yet acted upon them, or who have recently started offending and have not yet been identified by the authorities. Such prevention may stop would-be child sexual abusers acting on their fantasies and circumvent a lifelong pattern of sexually offending against children. This is what Stop It Now! UK and Ireland aims to do. It is crucial to learn from these pilot initiatives so that they can be implemented nationwide and benefit all potential child sexual abusers.

It is evident that we need to rethink radically our approach to managing CSA within communities, not just leave it to skilled professionals. As David Wilson (2002) suggests, 'If we are to protect children we have to take on responsibility for the perpetrators as well as the victims'.

## Community initiatives and prevention

Risk management starts at home and in the community. If we leave the responsibility for paedophiles primarily to professionals, community fears can become magnified in terms of whether these professionals can actually be trusted. This can induce panic and fear reactions, which amplify the problem. The community needs a balanced approach, which is not vindictive but develops strengths to deal with the problems rather than distancing or avoiding them. Evidently the problem does not go away by hounding a few hundred known paedophiles.

Paedophiles come from the community and are therefore a part of the community. The community has a responsibility to them. Isolating, excluding and persecuting them prevents us from understanding what drives them and how they manipulate and exploit children. The focus needs to be on reform not revenge.

*Circles of Support and Accountability*

One way in which the community can help to protect children is by support-ing schemes that aim to help child sexual abusers to be integrated back into the community. One such scheme, Circles of Support and Accountability, is modelled on a Canadian initiative set up by the religious Society of Friends, the Quakers. The aim of the scheme is to befriend paedophiles released from prison and to help them reintegrate in the community. It is based on the prin-ciple of restorative justice, in which the harm done needs to be acknowledged, along with the prevention of further victimisation. The two principles of support and accountability are reflected in the five C's of the circle:

1. Circles – rather than one-to-one relationships.

2. Consensus – non-custodial or authoritarian.

3. Covenant – emphasising responsibility and accountability.

4. Celebration – celebrating important milestones.

5. Community – focus is on being community-based rather than institutional.

Indications of the success of these schemes come from the Canadian experi-ence of 33 such projects, which demonstrate that less than half of those paedophiles befriended reoffend within the high-risk time of the first two years after release. These promising indications have prompted the Govern-ment to fund three such projects in the UK in conjunction with the Society of Friends, Thames Valley Police and Ox-Bucks Probation Service. The Home Office is currently considering funding further pilots. Helen Drewery, secre-tary of the Quaker Crime and Community Justice Committee in the UK, maintains that 'This way we help the man develop a normal lifestyle which is the opposite of living as an introvert when fantasises can too easily grow. We help him to see he can make friends and have a different life style'. This reduces the risk to the community, risk to victims and risk to the sexual offender.

Essentially the Circles of Support and Accountability is a befriending programme in which the child sexual abuser is the 'core member' of a Circle of four to six people who will work together with him. A covenant is drawn up by all the members of the Circle, including the core member, which details what happens if the covenant is broken. The core member has to state his commitment to no longer sexually offend against children. In return the other members of the Circle offer friendship, daily telephone contact and regular weekly meetings. Telephone contact can be on a 24-hour basis during crises, and support can continue for as long as necessary, in some cases years, although the members may change throughout that time.

The members provide regular sustained support, while also helping with finding employment and housing. In addition they offer support and help in dealing with the police, probation service, the media and angry community activists. Members will also go out shopping, on walks or visits, and involve the core member in regular social encounters such as playing sports, having coffee or going out for meals or to parties. Members also ensure that the core member attends appointments and meetings. In essence the Circle of Support provides friendship and a sense of belongingness that many child sexual abusers have never had. This minimises their isolation, loneliness and stigmatisation, allowing them to integrate into and become a valued member of the community.

Circle members do not judge the core member but provide a sense that people do care and that they are not isolated or excluded. In their support they transmit the message that paedophiles are not programmed to offend but that they have choices in their behaviour. Most importantly, the members are in close, intimate contact with abusers, and as such are able to see early warning signs or any worrying changes in behaviour or routine that may be cause for concern. In being in 24-hour contact they provide a level of support that most professionals, such as the probation service, counsellors or therapists cannot do, lessening the likelihood of reoffending. Common warning signs Circle members may notice include:

- starting to drink
- missing an appointment
- stopping shaving or bathing
- using inappropriate language
- showing signs of withdrawal
- showing signs of depression and stress.

If Circle members are sufficiently concerned they can, in consultation with the rest of the Circle and the core member, contact the police to ensure appropriate measures are taken. Evidence from the Canadian project shows that while some agreements have been broken, there is a reduction in reoffending in some instances as high as 60 per cent. While there are risks attached to such befriending programmes, they nevertheless go some way to offering support. The risk of reoffending against children can never be entirely eradicated, whatever intervention programmes are implemented. Arguably the risks increase in the absence of support when paedophiles are stigmatised, harassed and hounded. The Circle of Support can make a valuable contribution to some paedophiles in genuinely reintegrating them back into the community.

While the Circles of Support essentially act as advocates by mediating conflicts between the community and the core members and offering support through crises and difficulties, they nevertheless also confront and challenge paedophiles' attitudes and behaviour, especially if these are offence-specific. Being held accountable and responsible for their offending behaviour, along with support in the community, is arguably a potent mixture which really attempts to rehabilitate and reintegrate the child sexual abuser back into the community. By being in active participation with the offender, Circles of Support replaces punishment-led attitudes while focusing on deterrence and prevention.

The sense of belongingness also has an impact on making choices about reoffending, as many of the abusers do not wish to disappoint the Circle members, or let them down. Circle members begin to feel like a caring, supportive family and act as role models in how to deal with people and how to manage problems and difficulties. This engenders social responsibility and accountability for the actions of the core member, which serves to make the community safer in minimising sexual offending against children.

In focusing on befriending and the building of normal, healthy relationships, the Circle allows the child sexual abuser to function more adequately in the community, something they have probably never been able to do before. In the words of the reverend Hugh Kirkegaard, 'The bottom line is that these people are not monsters sent from another planet. They come out of our communities and we have to find ways of working with them in the community while at the same time keeping the community safe.'

Circles of Support and Accountability initiatives are very different from the SOTP treatment offered in prison. They are not based on cognitive behavioural modification or deviancy control and are not run by professionals. They rely on volunteers from the community who make the child sexual abuser feel wanted, showing them that there are people prepared to work with them, care for them and stand by them even if they mess up. They are like a supportive family, advocating inclusiveness not exclusion. By alleviating the pressure of stigmatisation and isolation, stress is reduced, which enables paedophiles to make informed choices rather than returning to familiar patterns of offending behaviour.

Such inclusion enables the offender to become a valued and contributing member of the community rather than someone who is labelled and can only ever be the label they have been given. Such initiatives as Circles of Support need to be assessed, evaluated and considered seriously if we are to protect children in the community. Pragmatically we will never be able to lock up all paedophiles, even if we were able to detect them, afford to investigate and prosecute them. There are not enough prisons and insufficient resources to build more.

In addition, it seems impossible to treat all child sexual abusers, judging by the widespread use of child pornography. There are barely sufficient resources to investigate, let alone prosecute and convict the 7300 names passed on to Operation Ore. Thus we can no longer rely on sentencing and custodial treatment of child sexual abusers. If we do, we will fail to protect children in the interim while we wait in the hope that someone else will take care of the problem. It is much better to access resources that are available and implement them now than waiting for a miracle to happen so that at least some children will be protected. Thus community-based initiatives may be a much more realistic and viable way to protect children and prevent further CSA.

Prevention programmes such as Stop It Now! UK and Ireland also go a long way to prevent would-be child sexual abusers acting on their fantasies. It is through such initiatives that aim to provide appropriate help and support that we really can prevent CSA, rather than through pure punishment and custodial sentencing. To really prevent CSA there has to be a multi-faceted approach, which includes the uniting of professionals and the community to provide the best methods of deterrence to minimise the risk of sexual offending against children.

*Neighbourhood Watch*

Further consideration should be given to introducing the protection of children into Neighbourhood Watch schemes. Such schemes could include a greater awareness for the public of the potential dangers to children out alone who look vulnerable or at risk. It would involve keeping a watch on children to ensure that they are safe and monitoring adults who consistently seek out child-oriented activities and play areas. Noticing a series of unsupervised children frequenting the homes of certain individuals in the neighbourhood may be cause for concern. Such concerns should be passed on to, and discussed with, the local police who will make appropriate decisions around any necessary investigation.

Being aware of children's safety in the community serves to unite the neighbourhood, with all adults taking responsibility for protecting children rather than leaving this primarily to parents, the police or children themselves. Only when CSA becomes a joint responsibility can children be adequately protected and exercise their right to be safe in their community.

*Schools*

Teachers in schools and nurseries also have a crucial role to play. Teachers often have more contact with children on a daily basis than any other adults, including parents. They are at the forefront of noticing changes in behaviour in children and implementing adequate child protection procedures. While most schools have these and usually designate one member of staff with the responsibility, it is crucial that all teachers are trained to understand the issues of CSA and how to spot early warning signs.

Teachers also need to be aware of colleagues' behaviours in relation to children. They need to be aware of some of the signs that may indicate an unhealthy interest in children such as:

- paying specific children extra special attention
- awarding privileges to specific children
- scheduling private tuition time with specific children
- colleagues who try to manipulate exclusive time with children
- colleagues who try to exclude children from other peers and adults

- colleagues who try to arrange exclusive outings, trips and overnight stays with specific children without informing the rest of the staff.

While the majority of teachers are committed adults who have children's best interests at heart and who ensure their safety and protection, it is known that some teachers do have an unhealthy sexual interest in children. It is crucial that all teachers ensure good child protection practices and are aware of those who do not do so that they can protect children appropriately.

Schools can also protect children by implementing child protection programmes such as 'safe touch and bad touch', which enable children to speak out, especially if the abuse occurs within the family. When supported by appropriate sex education programmes, children can learn to differentiate between appropriate and inappropriate behaviours between adults and children. This prevents them from normalising their experiences and thus ensuring their silence. In having an open dialogue about CSA, children will be empowered to talk and discuss their experiences without feeling embarrassed or guilty. Schools should be safe places, which can foster such debate and a resource to help children share their experiences.

Schools must ensure that they can provide a safe environment in which children are valued and allowed to talk about their experiences without being stigmatised. They must provide the right forum for children to draw accurate conclusions about their experiences to empower them to seek appropriate help and support.

To develop adequate protection and prevention takes time, resources and effort. To develop such a climate necessitates changing people's attitudes around CSA to make the sexual abuse of children unacceptable. This can only be achieved by providing access to accurate information and knowledge about CSA to all adults who will empower the children to speak out and end the silence. Members of the public need to be encouraged to move from demands for retribution and revenge, as seen in vigilantism, to responsible risk management and proper effective prevention, in which all children can feel safe.

It is only when we fully engage in the prevention of CSA that we will achieve our aim of creating a society that no longer tolerates the sexual abuse of children. Only this will allow children to grow up in a non-threatening environment in which they can enjoy the freedom of childhood and learn the necessary skills to develop into healthy adults and responsible members of the community. Locking children up in their homes, restricting their movements and terrifying them about the dangers of CSA renders children helpless and suspicious.

The best way to protect children is to know and understand CSA. Parents and teachers need to educate themselves so that they can talk to children in a calm and balanced way. Although we fear and loathe the horror of CSA, not talking about it gives child sexual abusers the power to abuse. By keeping our children and ourselves naïve about sexuality and CSA allows the child sexual abuser to 'educate' the child. To empower children to speak out we need to support them by listening to them and ensuring that their voices are heard. Ignoring their voices silences them and renders them speechless, much as the child sexual abuser does to his victim.

Parents, teachers, adults and children need to be empowered through accurate knowledge and understanding of CSA to fully protect children. It is only with such empowerment that attitudes and beliefs can change. CSA will no longer be tolerated and children will be free from the tyranny and fear of child sexual abuse. This is the only way to stop the fear of CSA from dictating and restricting children's development and behaviour. Children have a right to live in a world in which they are no longer vulnerable to sexual abuse and sexual exploitation, a world in which they can trust rather than fear.

# Useful Websites

## Child safety organisations

**www.childline.org.uk**
ChildLine is the UK's free 24-hour helpline for children and young people in trouble or danger.

**www.childrenspartnership.org**
Children's Partnership.

**www.consumer.gov.uk/consumer_web/safety.htm**
The Consumer Gateway: produces a wide range of free child safety literature.

**www.crin.org**
Child Rights Information Network (CRIN).

**www.ecpat.net**
End Child Prostitution and Trafficking (ECPAT).

**www.interpol.com**
The International Police Organisation (Interpol).

**www.kidscape.org.uk**
Kidscape is the registered charity committed to keeping children safe from harm or abuse. Kidscape focuses upon preventative policies/tactics to use before any abuse takes place. Kidscape has practical, easy-to-use material for children, parents, social workers, police and community workers. Kidscape works to keep children safe.

**www.missingkids.co.uk**
United Kingdom Missing Children website.

**www.missingkids.com**
The (American) National Center for Missing and Exploited Children's online resource for information on missing children and child sexual exploitation.

**www.missingpersons.org**
A UK charity dedicated to helping missing persons and supporting their families.

**www.nchafc.org.uk**
NCH Action for Children (UK).

**www.nsbf.org/safe-smart/full-report.htm**
National School Boards for Education - safe and smart.

**www.nspcc.org.uk**
NSPCC Helpline, Kids Zone Homepage, NSPCC home page.

**www.safe-and-sound.org.uk**
Child safety and first aid courses from safe-and-sound.org.uk.

**www.savethechildren.org.uk**
Save the Children.

**www.stopitnow.org.uk**
Information about what to look out for in children who are being abused, or who abuse. Also runs a helpline for potential and actual child sexual abusers.

**www.stopitnow.com**
American website providing similar information and advice for parents and help for potential paedophiles to the UK and Ireland website.

**www.the-childrens-society.org.uk**
Children's Society.

**www.unchr.ch/html/menu2/6/crc.html**
UN Committee on rights of the child.

**www.unesco.org/webworld/highlights/innocence_010799.html**
United Nations Educational, Scientific and Cultural Organisation (UNESCO).

**www.unicef.org**
United Nations Children's Fund (UNICEF).


## Internet safety organizations and information

**www.bbc.co.uk/webwise**
BBC Webwise site

**www.bt.com/education/funstuff**
BT's Internet Green X Code and activities to help children to learn about Internet safety.

**www.chatdanger.com**
Childnet International sponsored website giving advice to parents and children on teenage safety on the Internet, and giving advice on teenage safety in chat rooms.

**www.childnet-int.org**
Childnet is a non-profit organisation working around the world to help make the Internet a great place for children. This site gives details of the various projects they are running in the four key areas of Access, Awareness, Protection and Policy.

**www.cyberangels.com**
Internet child safety organisation that addresses pornography, hate sites, paedophiles and violence.

**www.disney.co.uk/DisneyOnline/Safesurfing/main.html**
Disney Safe Surfing.

**www.getnetwise.org**
GETNETWISE.

**www.icra.org**
Internet Content Rating Association (ICRA).

**www.safety.ngfl.gov.uk**
Provides advice and information in relation to all aspects of Internet safety for parents. Includes the Highway Code, the Safe and Sound Challenge and research on the road and vehicle safety.

**www.iwf.org.uk/safe**
The Internet Watch Foundation's guide to safe use of the Internet. This will help you find the best advice on the net about its dangers for young users and how to avoid them.

**www.kidsmart.org.uk**
Simple tips you need to know about staying safe online, a great directory of positive sites on the Internet, and a teachers' area with worksheets, posters and fun classroom activities.

**www.media-awareness.ca**
Media Awareness Network (Canada).

**www.pagi.org.sg**
Parents Advisory Group on the Internet (PAGI).

**www.parentsonline.gov.uk/safety**
Guidelines and information for parents on Internet safety. Also provides parents with information on Internet terminology.

**www.pin.org.uk/safety/safetyset.htm**
Parents Information Network. There are lots of sets of 'Internet Safety Rules' available from all sorts of organisations, but the most effective way to protect your family is probably to develop your own code together. That will be something your children are far more likely to remember.

**www.safekids.com**
Tips, advice and suggestions to make your family's online experience fun and productive.

**www.stiftung.bertelsmann.de/intercontent**
The Bertelsmann Foundation.

**www.wiseuptothenet.co.uk**
In March 2001 the Task Force on Child Protection on the Internet was established by the Home Office. It is a unique partnership of Government, industry, police and charitable organisations, working together to tackle the danger posed to children by online paedophiles. This website provides information to help parents advise their children on chatting safely online. As part of the campaign a booklet has been produced that provides additional tips and advice which can be downloaded from the site.

**www.yahooligan.com/parents**
The goal is to provide you with the information you need to make informed decisions about your family's web use.

## Protective software

**www.childrensinternet.com**
Parents can test drive browsers for children of all ages and check out the features that are included when you subscribe to the service.

**www.cyberpatrol.com**
Protect your children from inappropriate material.

**www.email-connection.com/KWFINAL.html**
Animated browser that sets up an exclusive Internet neighbourhood of pre-approved sites. The software takes care of blocking the rest.

**www.heynetwork.com**
Creates a closed community where friends and family can safely communicate, explore and make purchases. Is in English, French and Spanish.

**www.internet-safari.com**
Animated, secure browser with a jungle theme. Designed to filter sites and make the web safe to explore.

**www.netmom.com**
Net Mom.

**www.netnanny.com/home.html**
Content filtering. Blocking and monitoring software for children and organizations.

**www.safesurf.com**
Internet filtering solution.

**www.solidoak.com**
CYBERsitter allows parents to override blocked sites, add their own sites to block and specify allowable times to access the Internet, and maintains a detailed log of all Internet activity and violations.

## Sites for children

**www.education-world.com**
Browser geared towards educational purposes and curriculum with weekly features.

**www.green-park.co.uk**
A safety website for children aged four to nine years.

**www.kiddonet.com**
Browser and play place for children.

**www.surfmonkey.com**
The Surf Monkey Kids Browser provides children with pre-screened, child-friendly websites and monitored chat rooms, etc. It has a kid-safe directory with information, links and entertainment.

**www.yahooligans.com**
Provides a child-safe directory in tune with the school curriculum as well as updated features such as news, sports and joke pages.

## Hotlines

*England*

**www.iwf.org.uk**

*USA*

**www.cybertipline.com**

*Ireland*

**www.hotline.ie**

*International hotlines*

**www.inhope.org**

# Glossary of Internet Terms

## Address

An address is how you find places on the Internet. Typically it begins www (world wide web) and then has the name of the company or institution concerned. For example, the education section of the Houses of Parliament is at http://www.explore.parliament.uk/. The things that look like full stops are pronounced 'dot'. A website address is different from an e-mail address, which is used to contact an individual. E-mail addresses contain the @ symbol (pronounced 'at'). The e-mail address for Parliament's Education Unit is edunit@parliament.uk. A fictional example for an individual might be joebloggs@parliament.uk. If you were to read this aloud it would sound like: 'Joe Bloggs at Parliament dot UK'.

## Attachment

An attachment is a file that can be sent with (attached to) an e-mail or other message on the Internet. It may contain text, pictures, photographs, graphics, sound or video.

## Browser or web browser

A piece of software, i.e. computer instructions or computer program, which lets you explore (browse) the Internet. The best-known are Internet Explorer and Netscape Navigator. One will come pre-installed in your computer.

## Chat room

A place on the Internet where people communicate by typing messages (or by speaking using a microphone and headsets). The text is displayed almost instantly in the computer screens of everyone else in the chat room, wherever they are in the world. Someone a teenager meets in a chat room might become one of their 'friends' even though they have never met in the real world.

## Click

Pressing one of the buttons on a computer mouse to execute a command. For example, you might 'click on' a small picture in order to enlarge it, or – on a financial site – click on the word 'Savings'.

## Cyberspace and Cybercafes

Cyberspace is another way of referring to the Internet. Cybercafes (or Internet cafes) contain rows of computers and offer public access to the Internet for a fee. They may or may not serve food and drink.

## Download

To transfer information from the Internet to your computer. More often than not it will be free. For example, you can 'download' a picture you might want to print out, or 'download' software that allows you to chat. You can even 'download' a piece of music.

## E-mail (electronic mail)

Messages sent electronically (over the Internet) from one computer to another, to an e-mail address.

## Favourites

An icon on the Internet's browser that allows you to add to a folder web addresses that you use often or don't want to forget. This could be used to save the addresses of approved chat rooms, which you could agree with your child.

## Filter

A means of blocking certain types of material from your computer. For example, with the right software, you can filter out sites that contain violence, sex, hate or racist material.

## Hardware/software

Hardware is the equipment, such as computer monitor (or screen), keyboard and mouse. Software is the computer program or instructions that allow you to use it. For example, word processing software lets you type documents or letters. Some software packages come pre-installed in your computer and are free to use. Other, more advanced, packages can be bought. Still others (e.g. those that allow people to chat) can be downloaded, free of charge, over the Internet.

## Headsets

Many computers are supplied with the facility to transmit sound, with the necessary software and hardware, and headsets and a microphone. These can be used to talk in real time (just like the telephone) to another computer-user anywhere in the world. Potentially a boon, and a way to save money on phone bills, they could expose your child to unwelcome and/or unsuitable conversations when they don't know the other user.

## Icon

A small picture, often self-explanatory, which performs a function when you click on it. For example, if you click on the icon of a printer, the printer will print the page you are looking at.

## ICQ (I seek you)

An Internet program you download (from www.icq.com) that tells you which of your friends are online and lets you contact them. Among other things, the program lets users chat, send messages and files, exchange web addresses, and play games.

## Instant Messaging or IM

You can Instant Message a friend on the Internet in much the same way as you can send a text (written) message to their mobile phone. Both parties must agree to receive messages from each other to use the service, and it is an easy and useful way of keeping in touch with friends. It works much like a chat room, where you exchange typed messages more or less instantly. But other people can be invited in to take part. Person B might say to person A: can person C join in? You don't know who person C is…so there is a theoretical opportunity for abuse. Unlike chat rooms, Instant Messaging is more closely associated with a network of friends. So if strangers are invited in, it could be easy for them to find out things about your child and his or her friends – for example, that they meet in McDonalds every Saturday at 7pm, or even where they live. If a stranger is present, the safety rules should apply.

## Internet

A global network of computers that connects people and information. Also known as the 'net'.

## IRC (Internet Relay Chat)

Another form of online chat. You need to download a program to use it. See www.mirc.com/ for more information. As with any kind of chat, the same safety rules apply.

## ISP (Internet Service Provider)

Though you need a Browser to let you explore the Internet, you need an ISP to connect you to it in the first place. ISPs are commercial companies that have different ways of charging for their services. Some well-known examples are AOL, BT, Demon, Freeserve, and MSN.

## Modem

A hardware device that lets computers communicate with each other over telephone lines. It may be located outside or inside the computer.

## Mouse

A small device that is attached to the computer by a cord. Moving and clicking on the mouse lets you navigate around the computer screen. Laptop or portable computers don't have an external mouse; the functions are incorporated into a ball or pad on the keyboard instead.

## Newsgroups and similar services

Discussion groups. Unlike chat rooms, they are not 'live'. Participants post (i.e. write) messages for others to read, just like a notice board. Newsgroups are devoted to specialist subjects from sport to celebrities. In addition to newsgroups, clubs and communities allow people to exchange information on topics of interest. All of these are potentially open to abuse, e.g. through people posting illegal material such as child pornography.

## Online/Offline
Being 'online' is being connected to the Internet. 'Offline' is often used as another term for real world.

## Profile
Some chat rooms let you complete a personal profile which can be made available to other chat room users. Children and teenagers should never include any information in a profile that could identify them.

## Spam
Like 'junk mail', spam is e-mail you don't want and haven't asked for. It can be sexually explicit, which is another reason your children shouldn't give out their e-mail address when they are online.

## URL
Another term for an Internet address. (It stands for Uniform Resource Locator but no-one calls it that.)

## Web (World Wide Web)
The enormous collection of sites that has been put on the Internet by companies, organisations and individuals. Sometimes used to mean the Internet, but strictly speaking, only one area of it. Newsgroups and Internet Relay Chat, for instance, are Internet services, not web services. You and your children, however, will be able to access both.

## Webcams
Webcam (short for web cameras) are special video cameras that can be linked to the Internet. Just like ordinary cameras, you point them at something – say a view of a beach – and the image appears, more or less live, on your computer screen. It's a fantastic way of seeing another place or person. But they could be used illegally, or unpleasantly, to send or receive naked or pornographic pictures of individuals.

## Whispering and private chat rooms
Whispering is a way of sending a private message to an individual in a chat room. This is like having a private conversation with a stranger and, in general, as in the real world, it is safer to stay in the public area of the chat room where there is some safety in numbers. Private chat rooms, which can be set up from within a public chat room, are a bit like a splinter group going off to another room at a party.

# References

Abel, G.G., Becker, J.V., Mittleman, M., Cunningham-Rathner, M.S., Rouleau, J.L. and Murphy, W.D. (1987) 'Self-reported sex crimes on non-incarcerated paraphiliacs.' *Journal of Interpersonal Violence 2*, 1, 3–25.

Anderson, S.C., Bach, C.M. and Griffith, S. (1981) 'Psychosocial sequale of interfamilial victims of sexual abuse.' *Child Abuse and Neglect 5*, 407–411.

Anderson, C.L. and Alexander, P.C. (1996) 'The relationship between attachment and dissociation in adult survivors of incest.' *Psychiatry 59*, 240–254.

Anderson, A.K. and Phelps, E.A. (2000) 'Perceiving emotion: there's more than meets the eye.' *Biology 10*, 15, 551–554.

APA (1994) *Diagnostic and Statistical Manual of Mental Disorders* (4th edn). Washington DC: American Psychiatric Association.

Araji, S.K. (1997) *Sexually Aggressive Children: Coming to Understand Them.* Thousand Oaks, CA: Sage Publications.

Armstrong, L. (1978) *Kiss Daddy Goodnight.* New York: Hawthorn.

Aylwin, A.S., Celland, S.R., Kirkby, L., Reddon, J.R., Studer, L.H. and Johnston, J. (2000) 'Sexual offence severity and victim gender preference: a comparison of adolescent and adult sex offenders.' *International Journal of Law and Psychiatry 23*, 2, 113–124.

Bagley, C. and Ramsay, J. (1986) 'Sexual abuse in childhood: psychosocial outcomes and implications for social work practice.' *Journal of Social Work and Human Sexuality 4*, 33–47.

Benedek, E.P. (1985) 'Children and psychic trauma.' In S. Eth and R.S. Pynoos (eds) *Post Traumatic Stress Disorder in Children.* Washington, DC: American Psychiatric Press.

Benn, H. (2003) Quoted in the *Independent*, 30 January, London.

Bentovim, A. (2002) 'Dissociative Identity Disorder: a developmental perspective.' In V. Sinason (ed) *Attachment, Trauma and Multiplicity: Working with Dissociative Identity Disorder.* London: Brunner Routledge.

Black, J.A. and Debelle, G.D. (1995) 'Female genital mutilation in Britain.' *British Medical Journal 310*, 17 June 1995, 1590–1592.

Blunkett, D. (2002) *Protecting the Public: Strengthening Protection Against Sexual Offenders and Reforming the Law on Sexual Offences.* Sexual Offences Bill White Paper. London: Home Office.

Bremner, J.D. (1999) 'Does stress damage the brain?' *Biological Psychiatry 45*, 797–805.

Bremner, J.D. (2002) *Does Stress Damage the Brain?* New York: Norton.

Briere, J. and Runtz, M. (1988a) 'Post sexual abuse trauma.' In G. Wyatt and G. Powell (eds) *Lasting Effects of Child Sexual Abuse.* London: Sage.

Briere, J. and Runtz, M. (1988b) 'Symptomatology associated with childhood sexual victimisation in non-clinical samples.' *Child Abuse and Neglect 12*, 51–59.

British Telecom (2004) *The Internet Green X Code.* London: BT.

Burgess, A.W., Hartman, C.R. and Clements, P.T. (1995) 'Biology of memory and childhood trauma.' *Journal of Psychosocial Nursing and Mental Health Services 33*, 3, 16–26.

ChildLine (2003) *Annual Report.* London: ChildLine.

Conn, J.H. and Kanner, L. (1940) 'Spontaneous erections in early childhood.' *Journal of Paediatrics 16*, 337–340.

Conrad, S.R. and Wincze, J.P. (1976) 'Orgasmic reconditioning: a controlled study of its effects upon the sexual arousal and behaviour of adult male homosexuals.' *Behaviour Therapy 7*, 155–166.

Courtois, C.A. (1988) *Healing the Incest Wound: Adult Survivors in Therapy.* New York: Norton.

CSEC (Commercial Sexual Exploitation of Children) (2001) World Congress Against Commercial Sexual Exploitation of Children, Japan, 17–20 December.

deMause, L. (1976) *The History of Childhood: Evolution and Parent–Child Relating as a Factor in History.* London: Souvenir Press.

deMause, L. (1991) 'The universality of incest.' *Journal of Psychohistory 19*, Fall, 2.

deMause, L. (1993) Paper presented at the British Psychoanalytic Society, London.

deMause, L. (1998) 'The history of child abuse.' *Journal of Psychohistory*, Winter, 25, 3.

deMause, L. (2002) *The Emotional Life of Nations.* London: Karnac Books.

Department of Health (2003) Safeguarding Children: What to Do If You Are Worried a Child is Being Abused. Childrens's Services Guidance. London: Department of Health.

DeYoung, M. (1987) 'Disclosing sexual abuse: the impact of developmental variables.' Child Welfare LXV, 3, 217–223.

Donaldson, N.A and Gardner, R. (1985) 'Diagnosis and treatment of traumatic stress around women after childhood incest.' In C.R. Figley (ed) Trauma and in its Wake: The Study and Treatment of Post Traumatic Stress Disorder. New York: Brunner Mazel.

Durkin, K.F. and Bryant, C.D. (1999) 'Propagandising pederasty: a thematic analysis of the on-line expulcatory accounts of unrepentant paedophiles.' Deviant Behaviour 5, 1, 41–62.

ECPAT (End Child Prostitution in Asian Tourism) (2004) Online database: .

Eldridge, H. (1998) The Therapist Guide for Maintaining Change: Relapse Prevention for Adult Male Perpetrators of Child Sexual Abuse. London: Sage.

Eldridge, H. (2000) 'Patterns of sex offenders and strategies for effective assessment and intervention.' In C. Itzin (ed) Home Truths about Child Sexual Abuse. London: Routledge.

Elliott, M. (ed) (1993) Female Sexual Abuse of Children: The Ultimate Taboo. Essex: Longman.

Elliott, M. (1994) 'What survivors tell us – an overview.' In M. Elliott (ed) Female Sexual Abuse of Children. New York: Guilford, pp.5–13.

Eth, S. and Pynoos, R.S. (eds) (1985) Post Traumatic Stress Disorder in Children. Washington, DC: American Psychiatric Press.

Faller, K.C. (1984) 'Is the child victim of sexual abuse telling the truth?' Child Abuse and Neglect 8, 473–481.

Faller, K.C. (1987) 'Women who sexually abuse children.' Violence and Victims 2, 263–76.

Farid, H. (2003) 'A picture tells a thousand lies.' New Scientist 179, 2411, 38.

Findlater, D. (2002) Quoted in J. Silverman and D. Wilson (eds) Innocence Betrayed: Paedophilia, the Media and Society. London: Polity Press.

Finkelhor, D. (1979) Sexually Victimised Children. New York: Free Press.

Finkelhor, D. (ed) (1984) Child Sexual Abuse: New Theory and Research. New York: Free Press.

Finkelhor, D. (1986) A Sourcebook on Child Sexual Abuse. Beverly Hills, CA: Sage.

Finkelhor, D. (1994) 'The international epidemiology of child abuse.' Child Abuse and Neglect: The International Journal 18, 409–17.

Finkelhor, D. and Browne, A. (1985) 'The traumatic impact of child sexual abuse: a conceptualisation.' American Journal of Orthopsychiatry 55, 530–541.

Finkelhor, D. and Russell, D. (1984) 'Women and perpetrators: review of the evidence.' In D. Finkelhor (ed) Child Sexual Abuse: New Theory and Research. New York: Free Press, pp.171–87.

Fonagy, P. (2002) 'Multiple voices versus meta cognition: an attachment theory perspective.' In V. Sinason (ed) Attachment, Trauma and Multiplicity: Working with Dissociative Identity Disorder. London: Brunner Routledge.

Ford, D. (2004) Home Office, e-mail communication, 20 January.

Forrest, K.A. (2001) 'Toward an aetiology of dissociative identity disorder: a neurodevelopmental approach'. Journal of Trauma and Dissociation2, 2, 5–25.

Fraser, G.A. (ed) (1997) The Dilemma of Ritual Abuse. Washington, DC: American Psychiatric Press.

Friedrich, W.A. (1987) 'Behaviour problems in sexually abused children.' Journal of Interpersonal Violence 2, 381–390.

Friedrich, W.N., Beilke, R.L. and Urquiza, A.Y. (1986) 'Behaviour problems in sexually abused young children.' Journal of Paediatric Psychology 11, 47–57.

Fromuth, M.E. (1985) 'The relationship of child sexual abuse with later psychological and sexual adjustment in a sample of college women.' Child Abuse and Neglect 10, 5–15.

Gil, E. (1988) Treatment of Adult Survivors of Childhood Abuse. Walnut Creek, CA: Launch Press.

Glaser, D. (2000) 'Child abuse and neglect and the brain.' Journal of Child Psychology and Psychiatry 41, 1, 97–116.

Glasser, M., Kolvin, I., Campbell, D., Glasser, A., Leitch, I. and Farrelly, S. (2001) 'Cycle of child sexual abuse: links between being a victim and becoming a perpetrator.' British Journal of Psychiatry 179, 482–494.

Goldman, R. and Goldman, J. (1982) Children's Sexual Thinking. London: Routledge and Kegan Paul.

Goodwin, J. (1985) 'Post traumatic symptoms in incest victims.' In S. Eth and R.S. Pynoos (eds) Post Traumatic Stress Disorder in Children. Washington, DC: American Psychiatric Press.

Groth, A.N. and Birnbaum, H.J. (1978) 'Adult sexual orientation and attraction to underage persons.' Archives of Sexual Behaviour 7, 3, 175–181.

Groth, A.N, Hobson, W.F. and Gary, T.S. (1982) 'The child molester: clinical observations.' In J. Conte and D.A. Shre (eds) Social Work and Child Sexual Abuse. New York: Howarth.

Healy, M. (1997) 'Child pornography: an international perspective.' Prepared as a working document for the World Congress Against Commercial Sexual Exploit- ation of Children. Retrieved from the World Wide Web: http://www.usis.usemb.se/children/csec/ 215e.htm.

Herman, J.L. (1992) *Trauma and Recovery.* New York: Basic Books.

Home Office (2003) *Multi-Agency Public Protection Arrangements: 2nd Annual Reports on the 42 Police and Probation Areas in England and Wales.* London: Home Office.

Horowitz, M.J. (1997) *Stress Response Syndromes: PTSD, Grief, and Adjustment Disorders* (3rd edn). Northvale, NJ: Aronson.

Hosken, F. (1993) *The Hosken Report: Genital and Sexual Mutilation of Females* (4th rev edn). Lexington, MA: Womens International Network News.

Itzin, C. (2002) 'Incest, "paedophilia", pornography and prostitution: conceptualising the connections.' In C. Itzin (ed) *Home Truths About Child Sexual Abuse: Influencing Policy and Practice. A Reader.* London: Routledge.

Janoff-Bulman, R. (1992) *Shattered Assumptions: Towards a New Psychology of Trauma.* New York: Free Press.

Jones, T. (2003) 'Child abuse or computer crime? The proactive approach.' In A. MacVean and P. Spindler (eds) *Policing Paedophiles on the Internet.* Bristol: The John Grieve Centre for Policing and Community Safety.

Kanner, L. (1939) 'Infantile sexuality'. *Journal of Paediatrics 4,* 583–608.

Kilpatrick, A.C. (1987) 'Childhood sexual experiences: problems and issues in studying long range effects.' *Journal of Sex Research 23,* 2, 173–196.

Kinsey, A.C., Pomeroy, W.B. and Martin, C.E. (1948) *Sexual Behaviour in the Human Male.* Philadelphia: Saunders.

Kinsey, A.C., Pomeroy, W.B. and Martin, C.E. (1953) *Sexual Behaviour in the Female.* Philadelphia: Saunders.

Kleeman, J.M. (1975) 'Genital self-stimulation in infant and toddler girls.' In I. Marcus and J. Francis (eds) *Masturbation from Infancy to Senescence.* New York: International University Press.

Kluft, R. (1984) 'Multiple personality in childhood.' *Psychiatric Clinics of North America 7,* 1.

Krystal, J.H. (1988) *Integration and Self Healing: Affect-Trauma-Alexithymia.* Hillsdale, NJ: Analytic Press.

Krystal, J.H., Bennett, A., Bremner, J.D., Southwick, S.M. and Charney, D.S. (1995) 'Toward a cognitive neuroscience of dissociation and altered memory functions in post traumatic stress disorder.' In M.J. Friedman, D.S. Charney and A.Y. Deutch (eds) *Neurobiological and Clinical Consequences of Stress: From Normal Adaptation to Post Traumatic Stress Disorder.* New York: Lippincott-Raven.

Krystal, J.H., Bremner, J.D., Southwick, S.M. and Charney, D.S. (1998) 'The emerging neurobiology of dissociation: implications for treatment of post traumatic stress disorder.' In J.D. Bremner and C.R. Marmar (eds) *Trauma, Memory and Dissociation.* Washington, DC: American Psychiatric Press.

Landis, J.T. (1956) 'Experiences of 500 children with adult sexual deviation.' *Psychiatric Quarterly Supplement 30,* 1, 91–109.

Langfeldt, T. (1981a) 'Childhood masturbation: individual social organisation.' In L.L. Constantine and F.M. Martinson (eds) *Children and Sex: New Findings, New Perspectives.* Boston: Little, Brown.

Langfeldt, T. (1981b) 'Processes in sexual development.' In L.L. Constantine and F.M. Martinson (eds) *Children and Sex: New Findings, New Perspectives.* Boston: Little, Brown.

Langmade, C.J. (1988) 'The impact of pre and post-pubertal onset in incest experience in adult women as measured by sex anxiety, sex guilt, sexual satisfaction and sexual behaviour. Dissertation.' *Abstracts International 44,* 917.

Laws, D.R. and Marshall, W.L. (1990) 'A conditioning theory of the aetiology and maintenance of deviant sexual preferences and behaviour.' In W.L. Marshall, D.R. Laws and H.E. Barbaree (eds) *Handbook of Sexual Assault: Issues, Theories and Treatment of the Offender.* New York: Plenum Press, pp.209–229.

Laws, D.R. and Marshall, W.L. (1991) 'Masturbatory reconditioning with sexual deviates: an evaluative review.' *Advances in Behaviour Research and Therapy 13,* 13–25.

LeDoux, J.E. (1994) 'Emotion, memory and the brain.' *Scientific American,* June.

LeDoux, J.E. (1998) *The Emotional Brain: The Mysterious Underpinnings of Emotional Life.* New York: Simon and Schuster.

Lightfoot, S. and Evans, I.M. (2002) 'Risk factors for a New Zealand sample of sexually abusive children and adolescents.' *Child Abuse and Neglect: The International Journal 24,* 1185–1198.

Lindberg, F.H. and Distad, L.J. (1985) 'Post traumatic stress disorder in women who experienced childhood incest.' *Child Abuse and Neglect 9,* 329–334.

Long, B. and McLachlan, B. (2002) *The Hunt for Britain's Paedophiles.* London: Hodder and Stoughton.

MacFarlane, K., Waterman, J., Conerly, S., Damon, L., Durfee, M. and Long, S. (1986) *Sexual Abuse of Children: Evaluation and Treatment.* London: Holt, Rinehart and Winston.

MacKay, J. (ed) (2000) *The Penguin Atlas of Human Sexual Behaviour: Sexuality and Sexual Practices Around the World.* Australia: Penguin Books.

MacVean, A. (2003) 'Understanding sexual predators on the Internet: towards a greater knowledge.' In A. MacVean and P. Spindler (eds) *Policing Paedophiles on the Internet*. Bristol: The John Grieve Centre for Policing and Community Safety.

Marshall, W.L., Barbaree, H.E. and Fernandez, Y. (1999) *Cognitive Behavioural Treatment of Sexual Offenders*. Chichester: Wiley.

Martinson, F.M. (1981) 'Eroticism in infancy and childhood.' In L.L. Constantine and F.M. Martinson (eds) *Children and Sex: New Findings, New Perspectives*. Boston: Little, Brown.

Martinson, F.M. (1994) *The Sexual Life of Children*. Westport, CT: Bergin and Garvey.

Martinson, R. (1974) 'What works? Questions and answers about prison reform.' *Public Interest 35*, 22–54.

Matthews, J.K. (1993) 'Working with female sexual offenders.' In M. Elliot (ed) *Female Sexual Abuse of Children*. Essex: Longman.

Matthews, J.K., Matthews, R. and Speltz, R. (1991) 'Female sexual offenders: a typology.' In M.Q. Patton (ed) *Family Sexual Abuse: Frontline Research and Evaluation*. Newbury Park, CA: Sage Publications, pp.199–219.

McConaghy, N. (1975) 'Aversive and positive conditioning treatments of homosexuality.' *Behaviour, Research and Therapy 13*, 309–319.

McGuire, J. (ed) (2000) *What Works: Reducing Reoffending. Guidelines from Research and Practice*. Chichester: Wiley.

McGuire, J. and Priestley, P. (1985) *Offending Behaviour: Skills and Strategies for Going Straight*. London: Batsford.

Meiselman, K.C. (1978) *Incest: A Psychological Study of Causes and Effects with Treatment Recommendations*. San Francisco: Jossey-Bass.

Mollon, P. (2000) 'Is human nature intrinsically evil?' In U. McCluskey and C. Hooper (eds) *Psychodynamic Perspectives on Abuse: The Cost of Fear*. London: Jessica Kingsley Publishers, p.75.

Mollon, P. (2002) 'Dark dimensions of multiple personality.' In V Sinason (ed) *Attachment, Trauma and Multiplicity: Working with Dissociative Identity Disorder*. London: Brunner-Routledge.

Murphy, W.D. (1990) 'Assessment and modification of cognitive distortions in sex offenders.' In W.L. Marshall, D.R. Laws and H.E. Barbaree (eds) *Handbook of Sexual Assault: Issues, Theories and Treatment of the Offender*. New York: Plenum Press.

NCH (2004) *Child Abuse, Child Pornography and the Internet*. London: NCH (John Carr).

NCIS (National Criminal Intelligence Service) (2002) *National Criminal Intelligence Service UK Threat Assessment*. London: NCIS.

Nemeroff, C.B. (1999) 'The persistent neurobiological consequences of early untoward life event: treatment implications.' Lecture presented at the 152nd Annual Meeting of the American Psychiatric Association. Reviewed in D. Lott, 'Childhood trauma, CRF hypersecretion and depression.' *Psychiatric Times 16*, 10.

NSPCC (National Society for the Prevention of Cruelty to Children) (2003) *Annual Report*. London: NSPCC.

O2 (2004) *UK Mobile Operators Announce Joint Code of Practice for New Forms of Content*. O2 press release, 19 January.

O'Connell, R. (1998) 'Paedophiles networking on the internet'. In Arnaldo, C. (ed) (2001) *Child Abuse on the Internet*. Paris: UNESCO/Berghahn.

O'Connell, R. (2002) cited in Batty, D. 'Charities urge leniency for youth pornographers.' *The Guardian*, 25 April.

O'Connell, R. (2003a) *A Typology of Child Cyber Sexploitation and On-line Grooming Practices*. Preston: Cyberspace Research Unit, University of Central Lancashire.

O'Connell, R. (2003b) *From Fixed to Mobile: The Morphing of Paedophile Activity on the Internet*. Preston: Cyberspace Research Unit, University of Central Lancashire.

O'Connell, R. (2003c) cited in Hill, A. 'Paedophiles set picture phone trap.' *The Observer, 29 June*.

O'Connell, R. (2003d) cited in Silverman, J. 'Paedophiles: who are they?' *The Independent, 19 January*.

Oxford University Press (1993) *Shorter Oxford English Dictionary*. Oxford: Oxford University Press.

Pedowatch (2004) Online information: www.pedowatch.com.

Perry, B.D. (2000) 'Traumatised children. How childhood trauma influences brain development.' *Journal of the California Alliance for the Mentally Ill 11*, 1, 48–51.

Perry, B.D. (2002) 'Childhood experience and the expression of genetic potential. What childhood neglect tells us about nature and nurture.' *Brain and Mind 3*, 79–100.

Peters, S.D. (1984) *The Relationship Between Childhood Sexual Victimisation and Adult Depression Among Afro-American and White Women*. Unpublished doctoral dissertation, University of California.

Phelen, P.(1995) 'Incest and its meaning: the perspectives of fathers and daughters.' *Child Abuse and Neglect: The International Journal 19*, 7–24.

Piaget, J. (1952) *The Origins of Intelligence in Children*. Madison, CT: International Universities Press.

Piaget, J. and Inhelder, B. (1973) *Memory and Intelligence*. New York: Basic Books.

Pollack, S.D. and Sinha, P. (2002) 'Effects of early experience on children's recognition of facial displays of emotion.' *Developmental Psychology 38*, 784–791,

Prentky, R., Knight, R. and Lee, A. (1997) *Child Sexual Molestation: Research Issue.* Washington: US Department of Justice.

Print, B. and Morrison, T. (2000) 'Treating adolescents who sexually abuse others.' In Itzin, C. (ed) *Home Truths about Child Sexual Abuse: Influencing Policy and Practice. A Reader.* London: Routledge.

Protectkids (2004) Online information: www.protectkids.com.

Putnam, F.W. (1985) 'Dissociation as a response to extreme trauma.' In R.P. Kluft (ed) *Childhood Antecedents of Multiple Personality.* Washington, DC: American Psychiatric Press.

Reynolds, J. (2002) Quoted in J. Silverman and D. Wilson (eds) *Innocence Betrayed: Paedophilia, the Media and Society.* London: Polity Press.

Russell, D. (1984) *Sexual Exploitation: Rape, Child Sexual Abuse and Sexual Harassment.* Beverly Hills, CA: Sage.

Russell, D.E.H. (1986) *The Secret Trauma: Incest in the Lives of Girls and Women.* New York: Basic Books Inc.

Salter, A.C. (2003) *Predators. Paedophiles, Rapists and other Sex Offenders: Who they are, how they operate and how we can protect ourselves and our children.* New York: Basic Books.

Sandberg, G.G. and Marlatt, G.A. (1989) 'Relapse fantasies.' In D.R. Laws (ed) *Relapse Prevention with Sex Offenders.* New York: Guilford Press.

Sanderson, C. (1995) *Counselling Adult Survivors of Child Sexual Abuse* (2nd edn). London: Jessica Kingsley Publishers.

Sapolsky, R. (1996) 'Why stress is bad for your brain.' *Science 273,* 749–750.

Saradjian, J. (1996) *Women Who Sexually Abuse Children: From Research to Clinical Practice.* Chichester: Wiley.

Schore, A.N. (2002) 'Dysregulation of the right brain: a fundamental mechanism of traumatic attachment and the psychopathogenesis of post traumatic stress disorder.' *Australian and New Zealand Journal of Psychiatry 36,* 9–30.

Seto, M.C., Maric, A. and Barbaree, H.E. (2001) 'The role of pornography in the etiology of sexual aggression.' *Aggression and Violent Behaviour 6,* 35–53.

Saradjian, J. (1996) *Women Who Sexually Abuse Children.* London: Wiley.

Saradjin, J. (1996) *Women Who Sexually Abuse Children: From Research to Clinical Practice.* Chichester: Wiley.

Schore, A.N. (2002) 'Dysregulation of the right brain: a fundamental mechanism of traumatic attachment and the psychopathogenesis of post traumatic stress disorder.' *Australian and New Zealand Journal of Psychiatry 36,* 9–30.

Seto, M.C., Maric, A. and Barbaree, H.E. (2001) 'The role of pornography in the etiology of sexual aggression.' *Aggression and Violent Behaviour 6,* 35–53.

Shaw, J.A., Lewis, J.E., Loeb, A., Rosado, J. and Rodriguez, R.A. (2000) 'Child on child sexual abuse: psychological perspectives.' *Child Abuse and Neglect: The International Journal 24,* 12, 1591–1600.

Silverman, J. and Wilson, D. (2002) *Innocence Betrayed: Paedophilia, the Media and Society.* London: Polity Press.

Skuse, D. (2003) Quoted in *The Guardian,* 7 February, London.

Spindler, P. (2003) 'Combating child abuse on the Internet: a law enforcement strategy.' In A. MacVean and P. Spindler (eds) *Policing Paedophiles on the Internet.* Bristol: The John Grieve Centre for Policing and Community Safety.

Stern, M. and Newland, L.M. (1994) 'Working with children: providing a framework for the role of counselling psychologists.' *The Counselling Psychologist 22,* 3, 402–425.

Stop It Now! UK and Ireland (2002a) *Child's Play? Preventing Abuse Among Children and Young People.* Stop It Now! UK and Ireland. www.stopitnow.org.uk.

Stop It Now! UK and Ireland (2002b) *What We Need to Know to Protect Children.* Stop It Now! UK and Ireland. www.stopitnow.org.uk.

Sullivan, J. (2002) 'The spiral of sexual abuse: a conceptual framework for understanding child sexual abuse.' *NOTA News,* April.

Sullivan, J. and Beech, A. (2003) 'Are collectors of child abuse images a risk to children?' In A. MacVean and P. Spindler (eds) *Policing Paedophiles on the Internet.* Bristol: The John Grieve Centre for Policing and Community Safety.

Sullivan, J. and Beech, A. (2004) *Assessing Internet Sex Offenders.* In M.C. Calder (ed) *Child Sexual Abuse and the Internet.* Lyme Regis, Dorset: Russell House Publishing.

Summit, R.C. (1983) 'The child sexual abuse accommodation syndrome.' *Child Abuse and Neglect 7,* 177–193.

Taylor, M. (1999) 'The nature and dimensions of child pornography on the Internet.' Paper presented at the US/EU International Conference, *Combating Child Pornography on the Internet,* Vienna, Austria, 29 September to 1 October, www.stop-childpornog.at/.

Taylor, M., Holland, G. and Quale, E. (2001a) 'Typology of paedophile picture collections.' *The Police Journal 74,* 2, 97–107.

Taylor, M., Quayle, E. and Holland, G. (2001b) 'Child pornography, the internet and offending.' *ISUMA, The Canadian Journal of Policy Research 2*, Summer, 94–100.

Teicher, M.H. (2002) 'Scars that won't heal: the neurobiology of child abuse.' *Scientific American*, March.

Teicher, M.H., Andersen, S.L., Polcari, A., Anderson, C.M. and Navalta, C.P. (2002) 'Developmental neurobiology of childhood stress and trauma.' *Psychiatric Clinics of North America 25*, 2, 397–426.

Terr, L.C. (1991) 'Child traumas: an outline and overview.' *American Journal of Psychiatry 148*, 1, 10–20.

Terr, L.C. (1994) *Unchained Memories*. London: HarperCollins.

Toubia, N. (1994) 'Female genital mutilation and the responsibility of reproductive health professionals.' *International Journal of Gynecology and Obstetrics 46*, 127–135.

Toubia, N. (1996) *Female Genital Mutilation: A Call for Global Action*. New York: Women's Ink.

Tsai, M. and Wagner, N.N. (1978) 'Therapy groups for women sexually molested as children.' *Archives of Sexual Behaviour 7*, 5, 417–427.

Tufts New England Medical Center (1984) *Sexually Exploited Children: Final Report for the Office of Juvenile Justice and Delinquency Prevention*. Washington, DC: US Report of Justice.

UNICEF (United Nations Children's Fund) (2004) *Child Prostitution Statistics*. www.unicef.org.

Urquiza, A.J and Beilke, M. (1988) *The Effects of Childhood Sexual Abuse in an Adult Male Population*. Unpublished doctoral dissertation, University of Washington.

van der Kolk, B. (1994) 'The body keeps the score: memory and the evolving psychobiology of post traumatic stress disorder.' *Harvard Review of Psychiatry 1*, 253–265.

Vizard, E. (2000) *Characteristics of a British Sample of Sexually Abusive Children*. Keynote presentation to BASPCAN (British Association for the Study and Prevention of Child Abuse and Neglect) National Congress, University of York, September.

Vizard, E., Monck, E. and Misch, P. (1995) 'Child and adolescent sex abuse perpetrators: a review of the research literature.' *Journal of Child Psychology and Psychiatry 36*, 5, 731–756.

Ward, T., Fon, C., Hudson, S.M. and McCormack, J. (1998) 'Classification of cognition in sex offending. A descriptive model.' *Journal of Interpersonal Violence 13*, 129–155.

Ward, T. and Hudson, S.M. (2000) 'A self-regulation model of relapse prevention.' In D.R. Laws, S.M. Marshall and T. Ward (eds) *Remaking Relapse Prevention with Sex Offenders: A Sourcebook*. London: Sage.

Ward, T., Keenan, T. and Hudson, S.M. (2000) 'Understanding cognitive, affective and intimacy deficits in sexual offenders: a developmental perspective.' *Aggression and Violent Behaviour 5*, 1, 41–62.

Wheaton, J. (2003) 'Mothers of the victims tell their story.' In A. MacVean and P. Spindler (eds) *Policing Paedophiles on the Internet*. Bristol: The John Grieve Centre for Policing and Community Safety.

Williams, L. (1992) 'Adult memories of childhood abuse: preliminary findings from a longtitudinal study.' *The APSAC Advisor*, Summer, 19–20.

Williams L.M. and Finkelhor, D. (1990) 'The characteristics of incestuous fathers: a review of recent studies.' In W.L. Marshall, D.R. Laws and H.E. Barbaree (eds) *Handbook of Sexual Assault: Issues, Theories and Treatment of the Offender*. New York: Plenum.

Wilson, D. (1999) 'Delusions of innocence.' In E. Cullen and T. Newell (eds) *Murderers and Life Imprisonment*. Winchester: Waterside Press.

Wilson, D. (2003) 'Missing the real danger to children.' *The Guardian*, 22 August.

Wolf, S.C. (1984) 'A multifactor model of deviant sexuality.' Paper at Third International Conference on Victimology, Lisbon, Portugal, November 1984.

World Health Organisation (1996) *Female Genital Mutilation: Information Kit. Women's Health. Family and Reproductive Health*. Geneva: World Health Organisation.

World Health Organisation (1999) *Female Genital Mutilation: A Joint WHO/UNICEF/UNFPA Statement*. Geneva: World Health Organisation.

Wyre, R. (1987) *Working with Sex Offenders*. Oxford: Perry Publications.

Wyre, R. (1996) 'The mind of the paedophile.' In P. Bibby (ed) *Organised Abuse: The Current Debate*. Basingstoke: Arena.

Wyre, R. (2000) 'Paedophile characteristics and patterns of behaviour: developing and using a typology.' In C. Itzin (ed) *Home Truths About Child Sexual Abuse: Influencing Policy and Practice. A Reader*. London: Routledge.

Wyre, R. (2002) Quoted in J. Silverman and D. Wilson (eds) *Innocence Betrayed: Paedophilia, the Media and Society*. London: Polity Press.

Wyre, R. (2003) Presentation at MOSAC Conference (Mothers of Sexually Abused Children), 25 September, London.

# Subject Index

CSA refers to child sexual abuse.

*see also* detection; disclosure

pornography
- and consent issues 21
- early exposure and CSA development 85, 115
- incidence of concurrent CSA offending 140–1, 143–5
- prevalence 40, 129, 149
- as 'reinforcer' in cycle of arousal 85–6
- use in grooming 175–6, 181, 183
- and viewer culpability 54, 133
- *see also* Internet pornography

post traumatic stress disorder (PTSD) 209–12

powerlessness 215–16, 218, 219, 220, 226

pre-school children
- fear responses 226–7
- and female sexual abusers 18–19
- grooming techniques 178–80
- impact of CSA on cognitive development 251–4
- incidence of abuse 21–2
- and paedophile preferences 27, 104, 106–7, 110, 137, 169, 195, 263
- sexual development 59–67, 68
- startle reflexes 227

predatory paedophiles 99, 156

prevention methods 12–13, 303–30
- Circles of Support and Accountability 324–7
- community notification 316–17, 322–3
- counselling for CSA victims 321
- credit card reporting systems 152–3
- custodial sentences and reoffending 123, 124–7, 314, 317
- databases and registers 19, 50, 315–16, 322–3
- educating children 26–7, 55–7, 98, 188–90, 328–9
- effectiveness 25–6, 123, 125, 316
- electronic tagging 319
- Internet policing activities 147–8, 149–53, 154–6
- national and local campaigns 12, 155, 305–10, 316
- public health education programmes 12, 155, 305–10, 307
- Sexual Offences Bill and grooming 44, 129, 148, 153–4, 165–6, 313
- treatment programmes prior to offending 123–4, 308–10, 320–2
- *see also* child protection strategies; treatment of CSA

prison *see* custodial sentences

probation services 125, 315–16, 322–3

*see also* befriending programmes (CSA offenders); community supervision

promiscuity 237

prosecution and conviction rates 19, 251–2, 306, 307

prostitution
- as consequence of abuse 237, 247
- international prevalence 38, 40, 41

protection of children *see* child protection strategies

Protectkids (2004) 129, 156

'provocation' 22, 27
- *see also* child sexuality

psychological impact *see* impact of CSA

psychological mechanisms 84–6, 86–92, 96–7, 121, 142–5
- in adolescent offenders 121, 122
- justification processes 94, 96–7, 142–5
- motivational factors 92–6, 131–5, 140–1, 262–3

psychosis, women abusers 111–12

PTSD *see* post traumatic stress disorder

public health education programmes 12, 155, 305–10
- key messages 307

punishment *see* custodial sentences; vigilantism

questioning child victims 251–4

reflexive responses, infants 63

registers *see* databases and registers

regressed paedophiles 106–7, 195

regressive behaviours in child victims 224, 233–4

rehabilitation programmes 124–7, 322–7
- accessing help 309
- community befriending schemes 324–7
- specialist clinics 320

relationships
- abuser–victim 82, 99, 105–6, 109–10, 193, 201, 214–15
- closeness and severity of impact 201
- difficulties in later life 213
- friendship problems 227–30, 263
- *see also* families and CSA; incest

reoffending 123, 124–7, 314, 317

reporting procedures 301–2

reporting rates 307

research, on child sexuality 57–8

residential treatment programmes 320

role-play 230–1

running away 237

sadistic sexual activities 201, 238
- and Internet pornography 135, 137

Sadowski, Luke 147–8

safety awareness 272–4, 282, 289
- entrusting children to other adults 283
- key child protection strategies 292
- teaching children safety rules 289, 290
- *see also* child protection strategies

Sarah's Law 316

schools *see* education and schooling

secrecy 174, 176–7, 227–30, 259–60

self-blame 20, 176–80, 205, 213–14, 225–6, 243–4, 262
- *see also* guilt; shame

self-denigration 214, 226, 243, 262–3

self-exploration 62–3

self-harming behaviours 214, 219, 235–7, 266–8

self-identity, distortions following CSA 191, 214, 263

self-mutilation 236, 267

sex education 26–7, 55–7, 287–9
- as pretext to CSA 184

The Sex Offenders' Register 19, 50, 315–16
- avoiding detection 172
- and Internet pornography 115–16

Sex Offenders' Treatment Programme (SOTP) 124–7, 314, 317
- effectiveness 125, 317

sexual activities 42, 43–4, 44–5, 103–6, 177, 178
- cyber-rape 156–7, 161–2
- and physical violence 200–1, 238
- sadistic behaviours 135, 137, 201, 238
- type and severity of impact 200
- use of games 175, 178–9, 179, 185
- *see also* cyber-rape; grooming; Internet pornography

sexual arousal
- in children 20, 63–4, 262
- in paedophiles 85–6, 87–92, 94, 95

sexual intimacy in later life 213

Sexual Offences Bill 165–6, 313
- and Internet grooming 44, 129, 148, 153–4

'sexual tourists' 53

sexualised play, as consequence of abuse 230–1

sexuality
- defined 59
- *see also* child sexuality

shame 225–6, 260–6

sibling abuse 38–9, 42, 118, 267

signs and symptoms 222–48, 260–6
- behavioural signs 42, 43, 44, 76–80, 230–8, 265–6
- categories 223–4

# Author Index